KV-466-128

Table of Contents

Foucher, Michel and Hamilton, Daniel, eds. *France, America and the World: A New Era in Franco-American Relations?* (Washington, D.C.: Center for Transatlantic Relations and Fondation Robert Schuman, 2009).

Center for Transatlantic Relations
The Paul H. Nitze School of Advanced International Studies
The Johns Hopkins University
1717 Massachusetts Ave., NW, Suite 525
Washington, D.C. 20036
Tel. (202) 663-5880
Fax (202) 663-5879
Email: transatlantic@jhu.edu
http://transatlantic.sais-jhu.edu

Fondation Robert Schuman
29, bd Raspail
F-75007 Paris
Tel. +33(0)1.53.63.83.00
Fax +33(0)1.53.63.83.01
Email: info@robert-schuman.eu
http://www.robert-schuman.org

ISBN: 978-0-9801871-9-9

Sommaire

Acknowledgements

In this book French and American experts examine key issues facing France and the United States and offer recommendations for joint or complementary actions that could also revitalize the bilateral relationship.

The Franco-American Strategic Group, whose work was undertaken from summer 2008 to spring 2009, with two seminars held in Paris and in Washington, was inspired by a desire to enhance bilateral relations and Euro-American partnership. It comprises ten French and American authors and two co-directors with experience in government, academic and the think tank world. They share operational views on the following themes: France and the U.S. in the face of major strategic challenges; approaches to the Middle East and the Mediterranean; engagement with African nations; strategic options with regard to Russia; and the responsibilities incumbent on the U.S., France and Europe in addressing global economic challenges. The group offers the reader tools for renewed, effective Franco-American cooperation.

The Franco-American Strategic Group was sponsored by the Robert Schuman Foundation and the Center for Transatlantic Relations at the Paul H. Nitze School of Advanced International Studies. We are grateful to Jean-Dominique Giuliani and Pascale Joannin, the Chairman and Director General, respectively, of the Robert Schuman Foundation, for their support of our work and their own substantive contributions to the discussion. We are grateful to a number of senior officials and other experts who joined our deliberations, in particular Jean-David Levitte, special adviser for Foreign Policy to President Sarkozy; Pierre Vimont, French Ambassador to the United States; Jean François-Poncet, former French Minister of Foreign Affairs, Member of the French Senate; and Jim Hoagland, editorialist at the *Washington Post*. We also wish to thank Mathilde Durand and her colleagues at the Foundation, as well as Gretchen Losee and Katrien Maes of the Center, for their assistance in this effort. We express appreciation to Esther Brimmer, who initiated this project while still at CTR before joining the U.S. Department of State. All authors express their personal views and not those of their institutions.

Daniel Hamilton and Michel Foucher
Co-directors of the Franco-American Strategic Group

Introduction

A New Era in Franco-American Relations?

Daniel Hamilton and Michel Foucher

France is America's oldest ally. Yet the relationship has always had its share of frictions, and even reached what was perhaps an historic low in connection with the Bush Administration's invasion of Iraq in 2003. A desire to get the relationship back on track was certainly one reason why the French public and French opinion leaders followed the 2008 U.S. election campaign so closely. But it was clearly not the only reason. France, like most of Europe, was initially intrigued, and then genuinely excited, by the prospect of Barack Obama as the next U.S. President. In fact, if the French could have voted in America's election, they would have voted overwhelmingly for Barack Obama.

No sooner had Obama sealed his victory, however, than pundits began looking for potential points of convergence and friction between the incoming administration and *le Vieux Continent.* Critics quickly argued that regardless of who would become President, the transatlantic partnership had objectively lost its traditional importance, that the values and interests of Europeans and Americans seemed to have diverged, and that many transatlantic institutions were of little relevance to 21st century challenges. Others argued that the President-elect had no deep personal connection to Europe, and so would be more inclined to look to other partners to help address America's problems.

Even before assuming office, President Obama acted to allay such suspicions. The President named a national security team with strong orientations to Europe, including Vice President Biden and Secretary of State Clinton, as well as national security advisor Jim Jones, former Supreme Allied Commander Europe, who speaks fluent French and grew up partially in France. Immediately upon assuming office, executive orders were issued to close the Guantanomo Bay detention facility, a source of considerable Franco-American and European-American acrimony. Consultations were then initiated across the Atlantic on ways to tackle the global economic crisis, devise a new strategy on Afghanistan, and consider new approaches to the Middle East. The President's trips to France in April and June 2009 underscored the interest on both sides of the Atlantic in relaunching a more effective partnership.

These opening signals, while potentially positive for a reinvigorated Franco-American relationship, beg more fundamental questions. How will the Obama administration approach the staggering range of domestic and international challenges facing it, and how might it consider working with France and Europe? Are France and its European partners willing and able to engage the United States in an ambitious new partnership, given their preoccupation with European construction and serious challenges at home? The United States and France will be obliged to reexamine how best to advance common interests where they exist, while containing the consequences of diverging priorities when they inevitably arise. Our authors have examined five key areas that are likely to be significant tests of a reinvigorated Franco-American relationship.

It's Still the Economy, Stupid

Few issues are likely to shape European-American relations in general, and Franco-American relations in particular, over the next few years as the global economic crisis. This epochal event has erased any doubt about how interconnected the transatlantic economy has become. The deeper and more prolonged the Great Recession, the greater the risks of inward, insular policies on both sides of the Atlantic. Our common challenge is to show our citizens and millions around the world that it is possible to reap globalization's benefits while making its costs bearable to those most directly affected, without succumbing to protectionist temptations. This requires more than large dollops of fiscal and monetary stimuli. Bolder thinking and action are needed. The financial crash and related recession, in fact, offer France and America both necessity and opportunity to reposition their economies, their bilateral relationship, and ultimately the West itself to deal with 21st century economic challenges.

One of the most important ways France and America can tackle global economic challenges and to seize the benefits of an open world economy is for each to get its act together at home—to reposition itself as an open, resilient economy fit for globalization. In general, France needs to balance its strong social welfare provisions by endowing its economy with greater suppleness and adaptability, and the U.S. needs to balance its vaunted flexibility with a stronger social safety net to give Americans the reassurance and support they need to compete in an open global economy. The common challenge for leaders in each country is to show their citizens that it is possible to reap globalization's benefits while making its costs bearable to those most directly affected.

A second level economic task for both partners is to capitalize on the profound and growing stake each has in the other's economic success. Bilateral economic ties between France and the U.S. are dramatic testament to the deep integration that characterizes transatlantic commercial relations, and strong evidence that the economic interests and future prosperity of the U.S. and France have never been as interdependent and intertwined as they are today. Two million French and American workers owe their jobs to healthy Franco-American economic ties.

Third, much of the U.S. economic agenda with France must be conducted with the European Union. Transatlantic markets are among the most open in the world, yet various non-tariff barriers prevent the emergence of a more prosperous transatlantic marketplace. Given the immense size of the transatlantic market, even small changes to align domestic regulations could generate far bigger economic payoffs than further transatlantic tariff reductions.

Fourth, to paraphrase an old Chinese adage (borrowed prominently by President Obama's chief of staff Rahm Emanuel), "a crisis is a terrible thing to waste." Economic recessions are invitations for change, for new ideas. The present economic climate is ripe for change, and is thus an ideal time for the U.S., France and other European partners to work jointly on such large scale initiatives as energy security, sustainable economic development and global climate change. Innovation in these areas could generate new long-term avenues of growth and prosperity. Europe and North America are better positioned than most other economies to break the link between the generation of wealth and the consumption of resources. Breaking this link is an historic challenge—but also an opportunity to move toward entirely different patterns of consumption and competitiveness. Transatlantic cooperation and innovation could lead the way.

Jean-François Jamet echoes these views, but offers some additional considerations. The core of the crisis is the social challenge created by unemployment and the general economic downturn. France is well equipped for these challenges in the short-run due to its existing welfare programs, but will face difficulties over the long-term with the inflexibility of its labor market. The U.S., on the other hand, will be more capable of facilitating labor movement, but is not equipped to provide its citizens with an adequate social safety net to endure the crisis. Both need to invest in better education and training—the United States should improve its primary and secondary education, while Europe must invest more in higher education and improve the governance of its universities.

Jamet is also concerned about the levels of debt generated by the Obama Administration's ambitious stimulus spending—a good example of continuing Franco-American differences over management of the economy. Jamet worries about an inflationary spiral and in global imbalances, which could prolong the crisis. He suggests that one of the greatest challenges is the hoarding of capital in China, and proposes two solutions to the problem: decreasing debt in the U.S. and encouraging Chinese consumption through the creation of a more robust social welfare system.

Jamet argues that Euro-Atlantic cooperation will be essential to tackling the world economy's current challenges. He suggests that the close cooperation between the European and American central banks be extended to encompass the structure and prudential framework for the credit derivatives market; supervision of banks and insurers active at the international level; the appropriateness of accounting norms, balance-sheet transparency, and the regulation of bonuses; as well as an obligation for banks to set aside more reserves each year to guard against liquidity and insolvency risks. In the sphere of the environment and energy, Jamet underscores the necessity for the U.S. and EU to find an accord at the Copenhagen summit on climate change in December 2009; share best practices; define common standards; and adopt a common strategy to develop clean technologies. He recommends that the United States and Europe abandon their numeric targets and subsidies for biofuels, given that the current technology increases the prices of foodstuffs, is costly and relatively ineffective.

In terms of improving global economic governance, Jamet not only recommends closer coordination, he urges the EU to adopt common representation at the World Bank and the IMF, as it already has at the WTO. At the same time, the IMF's role should be reviewed; it should focus on the certification of national accounts, the prevention of financial crises, the granting of aid to states subject to currency crises, and on carrying out macroeconomic studies. It should cease its structural-adjustment programs and its non-emergency loans, which should be a competency reserved for the World Bank. Finally, in addition to committing to conclude the Doha round, the United States and the EU should jointly examine the possibility of using multilateral accords open to all signatories and permitting those that wish to pursue trade integration.

Strategic Questions

Bruno Tertrais lays out upcoming strategic challenges: Russia and China, Afghanistan (where Washington did not receive the military commitment it had expected from the Europeans), Iran (where the new American approach deserves concerted dialogue with European capitals so that efforts can be mutually reinforcing), the anti-missile defense system (in which a pragmatic attitude and no longer an ideological one on the part of the U.S. is an EU interest), the future of nuclear arms (which calls for in-depth, discrete dialogue between Washington, London and Paris). Tertrais believes that there is good potential for Franco-American cooperation on strategic issues, looming challenges include the danger of disagreement in the handling of the Afghan crisis and the problem of nuclear disarmament.

Among the key strategic questions France and America face together is the future of NATO. For many Americans, NATO's solidarity and effectiveness will be decided in the caldron of Afghanistan, where the Obama Administration is doubling the size of the American military contingent. Leo Michel cautions, however, that the injection of more U.S. forces is likely to reinforce perceptions in parts of Europe that Afghanistan is an "American war" and strengthen calls for a drawdown of European participation. He acknowledges that NATO as an institution might survive an ambiguous outcome in Afghanistan, but he questions how effectively it would function in an atmosphere of mutual allied recrimination.

Michel also notes that Russia's behavior in Georgia and elsewhere in the former Soviet space has refocused attention on NATO's collective defense role, particularly among eastern and northern Europeans. But he asserts that NATO's "unipolar moment" has passed. Today's Russia, he argues, does not represent the type of existential threat posed by Soviet Union. More broadly, many Europeans no longer view the most pressing threats to their security, or the tools needed to address them, as predominantly military. And opinion polls suggest that Europeans are less confident than a decade ago that U.S. interests, strategy, and policies closely match their own.

NATO's relationship with the European Union (EU) also poses a strategic challenge. The EU has made incremental progress in developing its European Security and Defense Policy (ESDP). But European defense budgets remain relatively low, and some ESDP military operations are proving more difficult and expensive than anticipated. Increasingly, many EU members look toward their civilian capabilities—including police mentors and experts in justice, corrections, customs, and public administration—as key tools to be deployed in crisis prevention or crisis management operations. Indeed, from Michel's perspective, one of the anticipated benefits of President Nicolas Sarkozy's more positive approach to NATO's relations with the EU, as well as his stated intention to boost French participation in NATO structures, would be to improve implementation of the "comprehensive approach" in Afghanistan, Kosovo, and future crisis management and stabilization efforts where both organizations are involved.

Michel argues that the long-term objective of a close relationship between NATO and the EU should not be to diminish the decision-making autonomy of either organization; or to attempt to define a formal division of labor; or to encourage one organization to systematically inject itself into missions conducted by the other. Rather, it should be to ensure transparency, avoid contradictions in their respective approaches and, more positively, to benefit from synergies.

Increasingly, however, Euro-Atlantic security cooperation cannot be limited to NATO or the NATO-EU relationship. Globalization has blurred the dividing lines between "external" and "internal" (or "homeland") security. Fortunately, an important and growing bilateral U.S.-EU relationship already exists in areas such as counterterrorism, transportation security, non-proliferation and combating transnational crime.

As the EU increasingly serves as the Europeans' venue for strategic discussions and decision-making on these and other interrelated security issues—for example, policy toward Iran—Michel notes that the United States will want to ensure that its views are taken into account before EU policies are set in stone.

Michel concludes that overall, Washington and Paris will continue to share important interests in strengthening transatlantic defense and security ties encompassing NATO, the NATO-EU relationship, and bilateral cooperation. In terms of operations, the French and American militaries cooperate today—most importantly, in Afghanistan and Kosovo—and no doubt will cooperate in the future in diverse missions, theaters, and frameworks inside and outside Europe. Moreover, French defense and national security policies and capabilities influence, directly or indirectly, those of other key U.S. allies and partners. Overall U.S. interests would be well-served by a more capable, responsive, and cooperative French defense and national security structure that encourages other Europeans, through deeds as well as rhetoric, to increase their military capabilities and make them available for NATO as well as EU missions.

In all such endeavors, the tone of U.S.-French relations will be of vital importance. Many Americans refer to U.S. "leadership" of the Alliance, thinking this concept is essentially an accurate reflection of objective facts—in particular, the real disparities in military capabilities between the United States and our Allies. But for many in France—and no doubt elsewhere in Europe, too—the notion of "American leadership" has come to be understood, at best, as an outdated Cold War notion or, worse, an irritating expression of dominance by an imperfect *hyperpuissance*. In Michel's view, Washington might best achieve its long-term goals with fewer rhetorical invocations of its "leadership" role and more of what it has often (but not always) done so well: acting resolutely—always in a spirit of true partnership—as a catalyst, builder, and ultimate defender of a democratic and prosperous transatlantic community. This would oblige Americans, from time to time, to leave more space and accord more confidence to their European allies. At the same time, Paris would need to be realistic about its vision of European defense and to continue, within the Alliance and in its bilateral relations with Washington, to work for pragmatic and "win-win" solutions, even if these are not always the most politically flashy.

The Middle East and the Mediterranean

Turning to regional security challenges, Ian Lesser notes that the Gaza crisis underscored the importance of developments in the Middle East and the Mediterranean for the new Obama administration, and for Europe. But he also suggests that the American capacity for engagement and the dynamics of partnership, from Morocco to the Gulf and beyond, may change substantially over the next few years. The new regional agenda is likely to see growing interaction between Washington and Paris, with new incentives for closer policy coordination. He believes there will be opportunity for more explicit cooperation on "Mediterranean" strategy—a longstanding French interest, but a relatively underdeveloped aspect of U.S. foreign policy.

Lesser suggests that the sharp change in American foreign policy style signaled by the Obama Administration, together with a more imaginative approach to French and European interests on the periphery of Europe, could create favorable conditions for closer cooperation. His short list of shared strategic priorities includes stability in Gaza and prompt reinvigoration of peace process diplomacy, with fewer U.S. reservations about European engagement; working together to promote regional diplomacy in support of U.S. disengagement from Iraq, including strategies to hedge against chaos and separatism; addressing together the challenge of a nuclear Iran, possibly including a sustained strategy of containment if Tehran opts for a prolonged near-nuclear posture; development of a more explicit bilateral approaches to the Mediterranean; and more productive Franco-American discussions of Turkey's growing importance.

According to Jean-Pierre Filiu, Obama's actions thus far have pleased France. Obama has spoken words the French have waited to hear from an American President—a willingness to engage with the Muslim world, and an end to the rhetorical "war on terror." Obama has also started to do what France was expecting from him: pursuing a two state solution for Israel and Palestine and closing the Guantanamo Bay detention facility. He believes that the Obama administration has renewed Washington's commitment to finding a sustainable solution to the conflict in the Middle East via the establishment of a Palestinian state. France can only encourage the U.S. desire to return to an authentic peace process and its readiness for renewed, ambitious dialogue, notably in its contribution to direct negotiations between Israel and

Syria and continuous efforts to support inter-Lebanese political dialogue. Filiu views the main problem in the Middle East to be the weakness of national parties, which allows al-Qaeda to assert control over a
number of nations. He believes that the U.S. and France need to cooperate in order to diffuse these terror networks, especially in monitoring jihadist websites and the growth of an electronic global terror network. Both Paris and Washington also have to confront the spread of
global jihadist networks across the Mediterranean region. The U.S.
seems ready to recommit to finding a joint solution and understands
that due to history and geography, what happens on the southern and
eastern shores of the Mediterranean affects European security.

Africa Rising

Nathalie Delapalme believes that France and the U.S. have similar
interests in Africa, since both want to halt the danger posed by failed
states and to exploit the economic potential of the region. Africa is currently undergoing deep changes with its integration into the global
economy. The population has doubled, there is a growing middle class,
and people are moving to the cities. These changes hold economic
potential, but also pose significant health risks pertaining to inadequate sanitation, limited resources, lawlessness, disease, and drug trafficking. In order to combat these challenges, while helping Africa to
develop its national resources and modernize its economies, Delapalme
recommends the prioritization of Africa policy in the EU. In addition,
Europe and the U.S. need to create a stronger link between security
and development and reform the global development structure to
enhance the effectiveness of foreign aid.

France and the U.S. should agree that they have common interests
and advantages in this major strategic arena, because of the dangers,
the stakes and potential held by the African continent, together with
emerging competition by China, India and the Gulf on this continent,
which lies on Europe's doorstep. Africa harbors every single type of
danger inherent to the modern world in terms of security, health, and
the environment. But it also offers great potential for world growth.
France enjoys a unique experience in terms of commitment to development aid and in crisis management in spite of questions raised by public opinion and the emergence of formidable competitors. Paris points
specifically to the interaction between development and conflict settle-

ment and underscores the importance of enhancing African regional organizations. The election of President Obama, she notes, sent a message of hope to which Africans are prepared to lend an ear. A joint Franco-American agenda should include accelerated crisis settlement efforts, in particular by building Africa's own capabilities; an economic approach based on the reality of African interests and growth rather than on compassion; efforts to encourage progress in governance and respect for human rights; and concerted efforts to bring African players into the international system.

As the U.S. and France debate what directions they should take toward Africa, Gwendolyn Mikell suggests that they need to be guided by an understanding of the complex local and global realities that Africa now faces. The Africa policies of the Obama Administration will need to be sensitive to the social contexts in different African countries, as well as how people perceive policies as impacting their lives. Therefore, Africa policies must depart from past practices by not being security-driven, but by also recognizing and utilizing effectively the other two legs of the three-legged stool mentioned by Secretary of State Hillary Clinton—diplomacy and development.

Mikell suggests that instead of an exclusive focus on anti-terrorism or AFRICOM, there needs to be greater concern with how to engage the needs, aspirations, and initiative of African publics and civil society, and to strengthen democratic institutions that help offset and prevent crises. As the U.S. and France continue commitments made to development, they need to consider how to expand the fight against HIV/AIDS and other diseases so that they assist in rebuilding health systems within African countries, giving Africans the capacity to attack these problems from the ground up. Given the predominantly moderate nature of African Islam throughout the continent, what are needed are development approaches that reinforce this moderate stance, rather than derail it. The Obama administration should be supportive of collaborative initiatives focused on how to prevent the exploitation of African state vulnerabilities through strategic partnerships with African states and regional organizations, as well as with the U.N. This will involve breaking old unilateralist behavioral molds so that multilateral initiatives are more in sync with African needs and developments on the ground.

A "Reset" with Russia?

Celeste Wallander notes that President Obama faces the challenge of high expectations and deep concerns for U.S.-Russia relations. By the end of the Bush Administration relations between the two countries had dipped to their worst point since the end of the Cold War. The United States and Russia have many mutual interests, and Russia has the potential to become a constructive stakeholder in the international system. But Russia's recent choices are threatening the potential for security and prosperity based upon cooperation and international rule of law. Wallander suggests that a new American strategy to pursue our security, political, and economic interests with Russia should be based on four key components: establish the terms for security in Eurasia by reaffirming the independence and sovereignty of all the post-Soviet states; anchor Russia in Europe in close coordination with France and other European allies; develop a common transatlantic approach to the politics of energy in Eurasia; and launch effective bilateral and multilateral arms control negotiations.

These goals, she suggests, have to be achieved in a manner consistent with our values, at a time when values/interests priorities are a complicating issue in transatlantic relations. Integrating Russia and the other countries of the former Soviet Union into a peaceful, prosperous and rules-based community of nations remains an American strategic interest. Russia still has the potential to emerge as an important partner and a contributor to solving some urgent global and regional challenges. The U.S. has a strong interest in signing a commercial nuclear agreement with Russia and in seeing Russia as a member of the World Trade Organization (WTO) and the OECD. But to enjoy the benefits of membership, Russia must accept in full the terms and responsibilities. Closer cooperation between NATO and a democratic Russia, including membership, should remain a long-term strategic goal.

Wallander also makes the point that the U.S. should not preclude the potential for Russia to choose to reengage with the international community responsibly and credibly. This is Russia's choice to make, she notes, but it America's responsibility to continue to make possible. Neo-containment is not the right strategy. Although the challenge is much greater than it appeared two decades ago, the right strategy is a recommitment to meaningful and effective Russian integration. And only a transatlantic approach can make such a strategy effective.

Maxime Lefebvre believes that since 1989 Russia and the West have not succeeded in building a strong partnership, and that Russian-Western relations have been particularly tense since 2003/2004. He points to key moments in the deterioration of the relationship, including the U.S. mission in Iraq, NATO enlargement, the proposition to place missile shields in Poland and the Czech Republic, the recent conflict in Georgia, and the 2008 energy crisis. He argues that despite the return of an authoritarian Russia, the EU needs to maintain its strategic partnership, while finding more innovative solutions to engage with Wider Europe aside from the policy of EU enlargement, which he believes is not currently a viable option. Lefebvre believes that the EU and the U.S. needs to cooperate with Russia by integrating Russia into European security structures and economic structures such as the WTO. The opening of dialogue by the Obama Administration on subjects of common interest (disarmament, non-proliferation, Iran and Afghanistan) augurs well. Maybe the Russians will use this renewal in dialogue with Washington to try and change the balance of power on the continent with the EU, whose power of attraction in the eyes of eastern Europe is growing, in an attempt to win a "sphere of influence."

Lefebvre acknowledges, however, that Russia policy remains an element of discord between Europeans, due to varying economic interests, history and geography. The French position is to consider these as part of a vast geographical context, naturally including North America, stretching from Vancouver to Vladivostok. The new American approach offers Europeans a chance to redefine a lucid strategy for commitment. Both Wallander and Lefebvre agreed that a weak and crumbling Russia would be more dangerous than the status quo. It is in the best interests of the transatlantic community to engage with Russia, rather than to isolate it.

Conclusion

In sum, our authors highlight many opportunities for renewed partnership and suggest specific areas worthy of joint or complementary action. Yet they also point to differences in approach between our two countries, some rooted in geography and history, some in outlook and perspective. Differences are apparent in some specific ways each country has sought to deal with the global financial crisis and proposals for future global governance; regarding the urgency and level of effort that is likely to be required in Afghanistan and its surrounding region; over the appropriate tools and institutional mechanisms needed to extend stability to wider Europe and engage Turkey as a strategic partner; and on the scope and pace of new initiatives in arms control and disarmament. Yet new synergies of effort seem available in terms of tackling climate change and sustainable growth; addressing Africa's rise; confronting challenges to peace and development in the Middle East and Mediterranean; developing a new strategic concept for NATO and forging a truly "strategic" partnership with the EU; and engaging Moscow in new patterns of cooperation while holding firm to core principles and reassuring allies in the process. Above all, there is an opportunity to move the Franco-American and European-American partnership beyond its traditional focus on the challenges of European stability toward a more global perspective. Whether Americans will have the patience to engage their European partners on this basis, and whether France and Europe will demonstrate the will to act coherently together in this type of partnership—those are the open questions likely to test future relations.

Part One:

Economic Perspectives

Chapter One

France and the United States: Confronting Global Economic Challenges

Jean-François Jamet

Summary

A crisis that is economic, financial, and even social; energy, environmental, and food risks; an increase in inequality and the lure of protectionism—the challenges with which the world economy is confronted are numerous and simultaneous. Given the scope of these challenges, the transatlantic link is extremely valuable and deserves a strong political push. To meet both current and future challenges, the American and European administrations must define shared objectives and common actions, of which we give here several examples. They can also promote the stability of the world economy, the competitiveness of their own economies, and their citizens' support for international openness. France, traditionally wary of both globalization and the United States, can play an important role in this rapprochement and can make itself a force for the promotion of a better-regulated globalization.

Introduction

The world economy is in crisis. The shock is even more severe given that the world has recently enjoyed strong growth (4 percent between 2001 and 2007), stimulated by the development of international trade and the emergence of the BRICs (Brazil, Russia, India, and China). The economy is today destabilized by several major phenomena. The real estate crisis and the securitization of debt were the causes of the most serious financial crisis in the United States since 1929, which rapidly spread to Europe. The economic crisis that followed is everywhere the cause of a wave of business failures and a serious rise in unemploy-

**Figure 1   Stock Market Movements 2000–2009
(Base 100 = January 2000)**

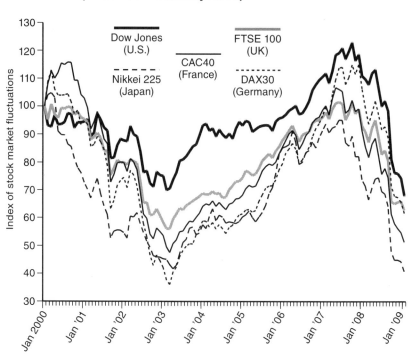

Source: Eurostat and the Robert Schuman Foundation, ©FRS.

ment. World trade has shrunk. The prices of raw materials have generally increased, leading in 2007-2008 to a food crisis and an oil shock.
Pressure on natural resources has grown, and inequality remains very
high both on a global scale and within countries. These upheavals have
consequently led economic actors to feel increasingly uneasy about
globalization and increasingly uncertain about the future.

In this context, the United States, France, and developed countries
in general are looking for both short- and long-term solutions. In order
for these solutions to be effective, it is essential that they be coordinated—a withdrawal of these economies into isolation would plunge
the global economy into a prolonged stagnation. While France has
implemented some of the internal structural reforms necessary to
improve its competitiveness, its economic policy is also linked to its

partners in the euro zone and in the European Union. European cooperation is particularly necessary to assist the weakest member states. It is also at this level that one must think about the transatlantic economic relationship. The trade and, above all, the financial links between the planet's two major economies are in fact very strong. In a world that is regionalizing at the same time as it globalizes, it is important to develop the transatlantic market, since the size of the domestic market is an essential asset for global competition. Transatlantic cooperation should also permit the development of common responses to the current economic challenges.

Common Challenges

The Worldwide Spread of the Financial Crisis

Since July 2007, the global economy has experienced a financial crisis, the cost of which has been estimated by the IMF at $4 trillion. This crisis was in the first instance the result of the bursting of the real estate bubble in the United States. Its effects spread to the rest of the financial system due to a sharp loss in the value of risky mortgage debt (subprimes), and their associated derivative products. The subprime crisis then weakened banks, precipitated a fall in stock market indices (Figure 1) and depressed the real economy in the United States and in Europe through several transmission channels, notably through the integration of financial markets[1]. In 2009, GDP is projected to shrink by 3 percent in France and by 2.8 percent in the United States.

Banks have become highly reluctant to lend, not only to individuals and to businesses, but also to each other. This situation, in which the banks hold dubious debts and face a liquidity crisis, has plunged financial markets into uncertainty regarding the extent of the losses. Because of this, many credit institutions and banks have gone bankrupt, or they have been rescued only due to public intervention or their purchase by other, less-affected banks or by sovereign funds. Furthermore, nonfinancial companies were in turn affected by the credit crunch. Business failures and unemployment are rising rapidly—in 2010, the latter is expected to reach 10.1 percent in the United States (compared to 4.6

---

[1] For an analysis of the financial crisis, see *Crise financière: analyses et propositions*, special edition of the Revue d'économie financière et de risques, June 2008.

Figure 2   Real GDP Growth Rates (in Percent) in 2007, 2008 and 2009: international Comparisons

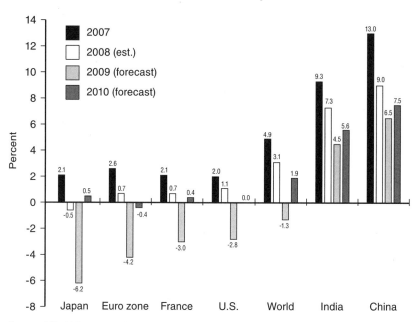

Source: World Bank and OECD.

percent in 2007) and 10.3 percent in France (as against 7.3 percent in 2008). In this extremely troubled context, world trade is forecast to shrink by 13.2 percent in 2009, amplifying the crisis. The world is now in a global recession; world GDP is predicted to decline by 1.3 percent in 2009 (Figure 2) despite the continuance of relatively high growth in emerging countries.[2]

While the Fed and the ECB have coordinated their interventions and expanded their tools of intervention in order to allow the credit markets to keep functioning, the European and American responses to the crisis differed at first. In the United States, the Fed lowered its rates spectacularly (Figure 3), while the Treasury and the American Congress orchestrated first a budgetary stimulus in January 2008 and then,

---

[2] If the financial crisis spread further to these countries (for example, through a slowdown in trade flows or through the financial sphere), that would plunge the world economy into an even more serious crisis, particularly given that some rich countries are net importers of capital (Chinese savings, for example, being largely invested in the United States).

Figure 3   ECB, Fed, and Bank of England Monetary Policies: Overnight Interest Rates (2007–2008)

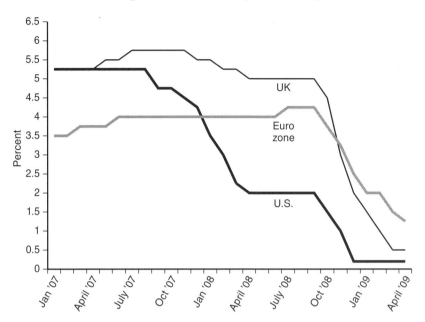

Source: European Central Bank, Bank of England, Federal Reserve.

in September, reached an agreement on the Paulson Plan, which aimed to recover several hundred billion dollars in assets linked to subprimes. Finally, newly elected President Barack Obama announced in January 2009 a stimulus plan worth $775 billion. The American deficit will thus surpass 10 percent in 2009 and 2010, bringing the public debt to 87 percent of GDP in 2009 and 97 percent in 2010. The United States thus made the choice to substitute public debt for private in order to avoid economic collapse and a prolonged depression. This effort is made possible by investors' preference for government securities (seen as less risky) and by the low interest rates which these bonds offer. However, the risk is that this situation will change when the economy rebounds, with the possibility of a bond crash and an increase in the interest rates paid on the public debt. Given that fact, it is essential that the stimulus measures be reversible, and it is necessary to carefully prepare the exit from the crisis. In particular, great quantities of liquidity have been put into circulation and might feed strong inflation once the rebound gets underway. Now, it is important to note that over the past fifteen years inflation has generally taken the form of a financial and real estate bubble. It will thus be very important to vigilantly limit the money supply during the rebound to avoid generating a bubble that could lead to a new catastrophe within a few years.

In the euro zone, inflation has for some time prevented the ECB from lowering its rates to the same degree as the Fed (Figure 3). Rescue plans for the banking system were adopted by member states along the lines of the British model, in some cases going as far as nationalization of troubled institutions. Cooperation was more difficult with regard to stimulus plans; the appropriateness of a stimulus plan was examined at the national level, according to the situation and the constraints particular to each state. The Commission did in fact propose in December 2009 that the European states as a group adopt a budgetary stimulus plan worth 1.3 percent of their GDP,[3] but the amount of resources mobilized and the nature of the plans vary considerably from one state to another (Figure 4). This is explained in part by differences in the countries' margin for maneuver: thus, countries like Italy and Hungary do not have much ability to act because of their already excessively high levels of public debt, and the deterioration of Ireland's public finances due to the considerable weight of the recession constrains that country from a strict policy.

The Return of Scarcity

If globalization allows the prices of some products to fall by increasing production capacities and reducing costs, the same is not true of those products for which supply is intrinsically limited, in particular natural resources. World growth has thus contributed to a spectacular increase in the prices of energy and food.

The price of oil rose from $20 per barrel in January 2002 to $146 in July 2008, before returning to $38 at the end of 2008 (Figure 4). This rise was exacerbated by underinvestment in production and refining capacity as well as by political instability in several producing countries. The price increase has negative consequences for growth in

---

[3] Communication of the Commission to the European Council, *Un plan européen pour la relance économique*, November 26, 2008—COM(2008) 800.

Figure 4   Budgetary Stimulus Plans (Funds Committed in Form of Lower Taxes or Extra Spending for 2008–2010, Percent of 2008 GDP)

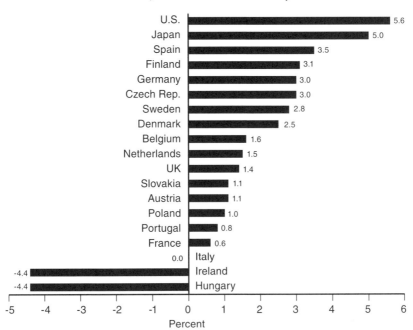

Source: OECD.

importing countries,[4] but it also has other implications—for example, the growing importance of "pipeline geopolitics," which increases energy insecurity.

The price of food, too, rose by 95 percent between 2001 and 2008 (Figure 4). There are several causes: rapid consumption growth in emerging countries, the rise in the price of oil (which affects production costs), bad harvests linked to unfavorable climactic conditions (droughts, floods), the development of biofuels, which tends to index the prices of certain agricultural raw materials to energy[5], and even

---

[4] See for example Jean-Francois Jamet, « L'impact de la hausse des prix du pétrole sur la croissance de la zone euro », *Questions d'Europe—Policy Papers de la Fondation Robert Schuman*, January 2008. http://www.robert-schuman.org/question_europe.php?num=qe-85.

[5] See Juan Delgado and Indhira Santos, "The New Food Equation: Do EU policies add up?" *Bruegel Policy Brief*, July 2008 (http://www.bruegel.org/8105). The research conducted to date does not conclusively assign the blame to speculation.

**Figure 5   World Oil and Food Prices 2001–2009
(Base 2001 = 100)**

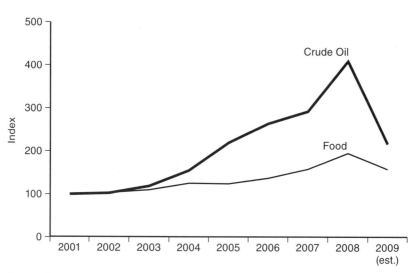

Source: FMI, Department of Energy and author's calculations.

Notes: Crude Oil (petroleum), Simple average of three spot prices (APSP); Dated Brent, West Texas Intermediate, and the Dubai Fateh. Commodity Food Price Index includes Cereal, Vegetable Oils, Meat, Seafood, Sugar, Bananas, and Oranges Price Indices.

local difficulties particular to certain poor countries (insufficient storage capacity and poor infrastructure quality).

Finally, pressure on natural resources poses multiple environmental problems: global warming, which increases the frequency of extreme climactic events, the exhaustion of water resources and fish stocks, multiple types of pollution, and the loss of biodiversity. The list is long and the economic and human cost potentially considerable.

The pressure on resources will continue to grow in the coming years. With a global population that will grow from 6.5 billion in 2005 to 8.3 billion in 2030, the world's primary energy needs, for example, will grow by 55 percent.[6] Furthermore, the temptation for producing countries to form cartels is strong. Russia, for example, is openly in

---

[6] *La France dans quinze ans : tendances et ruptures, opportunités et risques*, report of the Conseil d'Analyse Economique, April 2008. http://www.strategie.gouv.fr/IMG/pdf/CAE_Prospective2025-avril__3.pdf.

Table 1   Share of World GDP, Growth, and Living Standards: International Comparisons (Percent)

	Share of world GDP (PPP), 2008	Share of world GDP (PPP), 1997	Share of world GDP (current prices), 2008	Avg. annual growth rate, 2001–2007	GDP per capita, 2008 (euros-€), PPP
France	3.1	3.7	4.8	1.7	25,765
Euro zone	15.8	18.6	22.6	1.8	25,479
EU 27	22.3	25.5	30.9	2.3	23,233
U.S.	20.9	23.2	23.1	2.4	35,363
Japan	6.4	8.5	7.8	1.6	25,944
China	11.4	6.4	6.8	10.1	4,469
India	4.8	3.4	2.0	7.3	2,096
Brazil	2.8	3.1	2.7	3.3	7,744
Russia	3.2	2.7	2.9	6.6	12,153
World	100.0	100.0	100.0	4.0	N/A

Source: FMI and author's calculations.

favor of the creation of a cartel for wheat and has already laid the foundations for a natural gas cartel.

The New Face of the World Economy... and Its Persistent Imbalances

World growth is now driven by the BRICs (Figure 5). In 10 years, their share of world GDP has grown from 15.6 percent to 22.2 percent (in PPP), while their share of international trade in goods and services is up from 5.8 percent to 11.5 percent. While the BRICs have brought an unprecedented number of workers into the world economy, they are also major markets, with 2.8 billion people. Moreover, they are political powers that must now be taken into account in the governance of the global economy. The transformation of the G7 into the G20 and the commitment taken in April 2009 to increase the decision-making weight of emerging countries in the IMF and the World Bank go in this direction.

The world economy is also marked by important imbalances. The Asian countries are structurally net capital exporters, while the United States is a net importer as a result of its twin deficits (trade deficit and public deficit). This situation corresponds to the fact that the United States saves less than is necessary to finance its debts. The difference is made up by foreign, particularly Asian, saving, which allowed the United States to enjoy particularly low interest rates in the 1990s and 2000s and to finance both an economy founded on easy access to credit and increasingly high debt loads. In a floating exchange-rate regime, this should have resulted in a depreciation of the dollar against Asian currencies, which in turn would have allowed a rebalancing of capital flows and the American trade balance[7]. However, this did not happen because certain Asian countries, particularly China, wish to preserve their export-led growth and refuse to see their currencies revalued. They maintain a fixed or semi-fixed exchange rate with respect to the dollar by using their central banks' foreign-currency reserves (which are very significant, given these countries' trade surpluses.) The current crisis highlights the need for a rebalancing, which can take different forms: an increase in American saving (which has begun, with a recessionary effect on consumption), the revaluation of Asian currencies (unlikely), a reduction in the saving rate in Asia (in favor of consumption), or the monetization of American debt (financing of the debt by the Fed's issuance of dollars, with the consequence of an increase in inflation, which will reduce the real value of American debt). Each of these paths is difficult and implies a sharing of the costs among the Asian countries and the United States. But the longer the adjustment is delayed, the greater the risk, as the decline in consumption in the United States already shows.

The other persistent imbalances in the world economy are those of inequality and poverty. Despite rapid growth in emerging countries, inequality has remained stable at the global level[8] due to an increase in within-country inequality. Between the early 1980s and the middle of the 2000s, the highest percentile's share of national income has gone

---

[7] See Olivier Blanchard, Francesco Giavazzi, and Filipa Sa, "The U.S. Current Account and the Dollar", Brookings Papers on Economic Activity, 2005, 1-66.

[8] See Branco Milanovic, "An Even Higher Global Inequality than Previously Thought: A Note on Global Inequality Calculations Using the 2005 ICP Results", *World Bank Policy Research Working Paper Series*, 2007 (http://papers.ssrn.com/sol3/papers.cfm?abstract_id=1081970). In 2002, the Gini coefficient for world income inequality was 0.7, which is higher than for any country taken individually.

from 10 percent to 20.9 percent in the United States and from 7.6 percent to 9 percent in France.[9] In effect, there exist winners and losers from globalization and from technological change within each country, as a result of the international allocation of labor toward the most productive sectors and locations. Moreover, the figures are reminders that the fight against poverty in the world is far from being won—in 2005, 1.4 billion people made do with less than $1.25 a day.[10]

In the Face of Crises, the Temptation of a Retreat into Protectionism

The current crises and the adjustments arising from globalization reinforce the lure of protectionism. This is demonstrated in the context of the food crisis by the imposition of export taxes and bans on the export of certain food commodities. It has also resulted in the blockage of the Doha round, as a deal could not be found between the United States and India with regard to the safeguard clause, which authorizes developing countries' imposition of special agricultural customs duties in the event of an overly large rise in imports or an excessive fall in prices.

In developed countries, the difficulties of certain industries (for example, the automobile industry in the United States and the textile industry in Europe), as well as fear of offshoring and of foreign sovereign funds, have led to a resurgence of protectionist talk. In Europe, voices are raised in favor of using the community preference against what is portrayed as social, environmental, and fiscal dumping by emerging countries. In the United States, the Obama administration has inserted a "Buy American" clause in its stimulus plan in order to aid the steel industry. In both the United States and Europe, many manufacturing sectors wish to see quotas imposed on imports coming from China.

While the difficulties facing workers in declining industries cannot be ignored and the anti-dumping fight is justified, it is important to remember that protectionism is dangerous. It would have the consequence of reinforcing tensions in world markets, with the risk of starting a tariff war and aggravating the crisis, as was the case in the 1930s.

---

[9] Jean Pisani-Ferry. "Progressive Governance and Globalisation: the Agenda Revesited", *Bruegel Policy Contribution*, April 2008. http://www.bruegel.org/6715.

[10] Source: World Bank.

It is already a given that world trade will fall in 2009 for the first time in more than 25 years. Since Europe is now the main player in the globalization of trade in goods and services, it would thus be the first loser from a sharper contraction in international trade.[11]

Reform, Despite the Crisis—Perspectives for the French Economy

Unsatisfactory Performance

While France remains the second largest economy in the EU and the fifth largest in the world, its recent economic performance has been relatively disappointing (Figure 3). In terms of growth, employment, productivity improvements and exports, France is situated below the European average. In addition, France has a number of urgent social problems, such as urban ghettoization in the suburbs and a high level of school failure, with 15 percent of students leaving the educational system without a diploma.

The recent performance of foreign trade has raised worries about the competitiveness of the French economy. Although France enjoyed a current account surplus of 3.5 percent of GDP in 1999, it now has a deficit of more than 1 percent of GDP. French businesses have in effect lost market share in a large number of their areas of specialization. This loss of competitiveness contrasts with the remarkable performance of Germany, the world's leading exporter, which has increased its market share. Part of the explanation lies in the geography of French exports, which in recent years have been insufficiently oriented toward the rapidly growing countries of Central and Eastern Europe and Asia, as well as in different macroeconomic strategies in France and Germany.[12]

---

[11] See Jean-Francois Jamet, "La préférence communautaire ou les illusions du protectionnisme européen," *Questions d'Europe—Policy Papers de la Fondation Robert Schuman*, January 2008. http://www.robert-schuman.org/question_europe.php?num=qe-64.

[12] Germany has chosen to base its growth on exports, by reducing labor costs at the risk of reducing domestic consumption. In contrast, growth in France is driven by consumption. Today Germany is at once the leading customer of and the leading supplier to France (accounting for 19 percent of imports and 15 percent of exports in 2007). It thus seems that the consumption slowdown in Germany has hurt French exports, while the good performance of consumption in France has favored German exports. In fact, between 2000 and 2007, French imports of products from Germany increased by 50 percent while exports to Germany rose only by 25 percent.

A Strong Distrust of Globalization

The French prove to be particularly suspicious of globalization. In 2008, 66 percent of them judged globalization to be a threat to French employment and companies, compared to just 25 percent who viewed it primarily as an opportunity for companies through the opening of markets. This is far more than for the EU 27 as a whole, in which 43 percent of those surveyed saw globalization largely as a threat, compared to 39 percent who viewed it as an opportunity.[13] According to a survey by the German Marshall Fund,[14] a majority of those questioned in France are in favor of maintaining trade barriers in order to protect domestic firms even if that could potentially lead to slower growth. The French also manifest a particularly strong desire for protection against economic risks and the fear of offshoring. While offshoring represented only 5.8 percent of all job losses in firms of more than 100 workers between 2002 and 2007,[15] these losses are traumatizing and are associated with the decline of industrial employment in France (down 8.2 percent from 2000 to 2006). In addition, the current crisis is accelerating the closure of industrial facilities in Europe. Going forward, it is unlikely that manufacturing jobs thus lost will be recovered once the crisis is over. New production capacity will be installed near the most dynamic markets—that is to say, in emerging countries.

French Policy Toward the Economic Crisis

While distrust of globalization leads to economic nationalism and politicizes the closure of industrial facilities, it also creates the desire to make the French economy more competitive through structural reforms aiming to increase competition in the goods market, improve the functioning of the labor market and higher education, and even to reform the tax system and the public service. These reforms were undertaken by the current government, which announced its intention to pursue them in spite of the crisis. In the context of slowing growth, the government chose to commit to a 26 billion euro stimulus plan, which notably includes 10.5 billion euros in public investment, support for business, and aid for the automobile sector. Notwithstanding, 10

---

[13] European Commission, *Eurobarometer Standard 69*, 2008.

[14] German Marshall Fund of the United States, *Perspectives on trade and poverty reduction, a survey of public opinion*, 2007.

[15] Source: European Restructuring Monitor.

Table 2   France's Economic Performance

	France	Rank within EU 27	Average of EU 27	Average of euro zone	United States	Japan
Growth and standard of living						
Share of world GDP (current prices), 2008	4.8%	2	30.9%	22.6%	23.1%	7.8%
Average annual growth rate, 2001–2007	1.7%	23	2.3%	1.8%	2.4%	1.6%
Growth rate, 2008	0.7%	19	1.0%	0.9%	1.2%	-0.3%
GDP per capita, 2008 (in euros at PPP)	25,765	11	23,233	25,479	35,363	25,944
Employment						
Unemployment rate, end-2009 (forecast)	9.8%	24	8.7%	9.3%	9.1%	4.9%
Employment rate, 2007	64.6%	17	65.4%	65.7%	71.7%	70.6%
Youth (15–24 years) employment rate, 2007	31.5%	16	37.2%	38.0%	53.1%	41.4%
Seniors (55–64 years) employment rate, 2007	38.4%	19	45.1%	43.6%	41.4%	66.1%
Change in industrial employment, 2000–2006	-8.2%	18	-5.4%	-2.2%	-15.8%	nd
Public finances						
Public deficit, 2009 (forecast, percent of GDP)	-5.4%	24	-4.4%	-4.0%	-10.2%	-6.8%
Public debt, 2008 (percent of GDP)	63.9%	22	58.7%	66.1%	65.5%	196.3%
Competitiveness						
Average annual productivity growth rate, 2000–2007	1.0%	22	1.8%	1.1%	1.5%	1.8%

	France	Rank within EU 27	Average of EU 27	Average of euro zone	United States	Japan
Average annual export growth rate, 2000–2007	7.7%	23	11.6%	11.1%	5.8%	5.8%
Share of world merchandise exports, 2007	4.0%	2	16.5%*	N/A	8.4%	5.1%
Ranking for competitiveness of the economic environment (World Economic Forum), out of 131 countries, 2008	16	8	nd	nd	1	9
Knowledge economy						
Total R&D spending (percent of GDP), 2006	2.1%	6	1.8%	1.9%	2.6%	3.3%
Business R&D spending (percent of GDP), 2006	1.1%	7	0.9%	nd	1.7%	2.5%
Number of patents granted by the European Patent Office and the United States Patent and Trademark Office, 2007 (per million residents)	114.2	8	97.6	123.7	302.9	343.0
Annual spending on higher education, 2005 (thousand euros, PPP)	9.3	9	8.3	8.8	21.0	10.3
Enrollment rate in higher education, 2006	56.2%	17	nd	nd	81.8%	57.3%
Inequality and poverty						
Income inequality— Gini coefficient (0 = perfect equality, 100 = perfect inequality), 2006	27	9	32.0	nd	47	24.9
Poverty rate after social transfers (poverty threshold = 60 percent of median income), percent, 2006	13%	8	16%	16%	24	nd

*excluding intra-community trade.

Source: Eurostat, IMF, WTO, World Bank, EPO, OECD, Groningen Growth and Development Center, and author's calculations.

billion euros in projected funds from the French stimulus plan consist of an accelerated payment of money owed by the state to SMEs and therefore do not really represent additional funds. The OECD thus estimates that the French stimulus plan for the period 2008-2010 will reach just 0.6 percent of GDP. To date the government has refused to finance consumption stimulus measures, deeming investment to be the priority. It has focused its attention on a call for morality in executive compensation, on an enhanced payment for partial unemployment, and on the implementation of an "active solidarity payment" meant to ensure a decent standard of living for the most underprivileged without going so far as to discourage them from returning to work. Taking into account the risk of a major increase in unemployment, it would be desirable to reach agreement with large firms—along the lines of the Air France model—with regard to job preservation in exchange for increased intra-firm professional mobility and temporary efforts at salary moderation. It would also be helpful to implement a special effort to retrain the jobless, which would benefit the unemployed themselves and also the country's competitiveness.

Medium-term Priorities for French Economic Policy

The presidential election of 2007, the government's later decisions, and the economic slowdown have all encouraged an intense economic debate over the course of the last two years. It is possible to extract the main positions:

- Restore the means to conduct a countercyclical budget policy, which will require a cleanup of the public finances in the medium term. Since 1981, the public deficit has never fallen below 1.5 percent of GDP. Over the same period, the public debt has gone from 22 percent to 65 percent of GDP. It will likely reach 75 percent in 2009 and 80 percent in 2010. When growth returns, it will thus be necessary to make deficit reduction a priority, in order to be able to stimulate the economy during a crisis period—this ability is cruelly lacking today. To get to this point, a code of budgetary responsibility could be put in place with procedures leading to a more countercyclical management of the public finances. In addition, the current efforts to reduce public spending at the national level should be accompanied by similar efforts at the level of subnational units, for which staff levels and expenses have increased rapidly in recent years. One possibility is to reduce the number of administrative ranks in order to limit duplications and produce economies of scale.

- Pursue the reform of the pension system, which constitutes an implicit public debt and which will require financing by 2020. In particular, it would be helpful to simplify the system by making it more transparent and by following the Swedish model of a points-based pension.[16]

- Increase both the employment rate and productivity. This supply-side policy would encourage work in underemployed populations (the young, women, and seniors) by reducing arrangements that discourage work (for example, the job-search exemptions for seniors) and by facilitating the return to work (for example, by making childcare easier for single mothers). Job readiness and higher productivity also presuppose greater investment in higher education and training; the functionality of these areas should also be reviewed, in order to improve educational quality and the system's success at imparting professional qualifications. In France, spending on higher education represents just 1.1 percent of GDP, compared to 2.3 percent in the United States.

- Reduce entry barriers to regulated, free, and artisanal professions in order to encourage the development of jobs in services.

- Encourage the development of SMEs. France has a deficit in mid-sized businesses (between 50 and 500 workers) and small corporations (between 500 and 3000 workers), which are nonetheless those that grow most quickly and create the most jobs. It is necessary, then, to limit the effects of the regulatory threshold, to encourage the spread of information technology, and to facilitate intergenerational transmission as well as access to financing and consulting services. The Conseil d'Analyse Economique (CAE) has also proposed the imposi-

---

[16] On this point, see Antoine Bozio and Thomas Piketty, *Retraites : pour un système de comptes individuels de cotisations. Propositions pour une refonte générale des régimes de retraites en France*, April 2008, http://www.jourdan.ens.fr/piketty/fichiers/public/BozioPiketty2008.pdf.

tion of a lower corporate tax rate (18 percent, for example) for the first million euros of taxable profit.

• Limit urban segregation. In order to encourage the integration of poor suburbs, an important effort is necessary to develop local businesses, public and private transportation, and microcredit, and to improve social housing.[17] It is also essential to facilitate access to educational and job-training programs for youths who go to school in the suburbs, for example by encouraging job training in rotation.

The European Horizon

For France as for other European countries, globalization is first and foremost Europeanization. Not only does the EU account for two-thirds of French foreign trade, but decisions are made at the European level in several essential fields: monetary policy, trade negotiations, agriculture, competition, and the internal market. In addition, the majority of technical norms related to industrial security, the environment, and consumer protection are now defined within the framework of community directives or regulations.

In this context, it is possible and necessary to improve the economic governance of the European Union.[18] This concerns the coordination of economic policy, financial regulation,[19] the allocation of agricultural aide within the framework of the CAP,[20] and even the implementation of the Lisbon Strategy.[21] In the shorter term, with the risk of currency crises in several countries that are not members of the euro zone (Hungary, Latvia, Romania, etc.), the European Union must guarantee economic solidarity among its members. This implies in particular an

[17] On this subject, see Eric Maurin, *Le ghetto français. Enquête sur le séparatisme social*, La République des Idées/Le Seuil, 2004.

[18] See Jean-François Jamet, "La gouvernance économique de l'Union européenne : controverses et pistes de réformes," *Questions d'Europe—Policy Papers de la Fondation Robert Schuman*, July 2007. http://www.robert-schuman.org/question_europe.php?num=qe-67.

[19] See Jean-François Jamet, "Quelle peut être la réponse européenne face à la crise financière ?" in *Crise financière : analyses et propositions*, Revue d'économie financière, 2008.

[20] See Nicolas-Jean Bréhon, "L'agriculture européenne à l'heure des choix : pourquoi croire à la PAC?" *Notes de la Fondation Robert Schuman*, no. 44, November 2008.

[21] See Yves Bertoncini, Vanessa Wisnia Weill, "La stratégie de Lisbonne : une voie européenne dans la mondialisation," *Notes de la Fondation Robert Schuman*, no. 41, September 2007.

Figure 6   Movement of the Euro Against Major Currencies 1999–2008 (Base 100 = January 1999; Feb. 2000 for the Yuan)

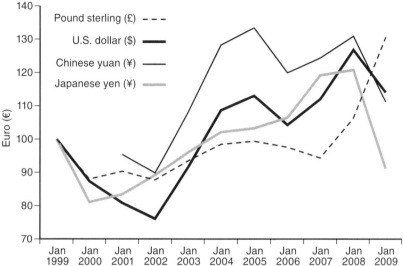

Source: Eurostat and the Robert Schuman Foundation, ©FRS.

assurance that the ECB will provide loans to the central banks of countries exposed to currency crises, but also tight coordination with the IMF, the establishment of a European guarantee fund, and even an increase in the amount of structural funds. Finally, to promote the freeing up of credit and the recapitalization of big companies, the ECB could create a special line of credit for the purchase of Treasury bills.

Another particularly controversial subject on the agenda is the exchange-rate policy for the euro.[22] Since its creation, the euro's volatility has been very high (Table 2). This is extremely harmful to exporting businesses, in particular industrial companies, for whom the movement of costs becomes unpredictable. In addition, the euro appreciated strongly between 2002 and 2008 against the major currencies.

---

[22] On this point, see the report of the Conseil d'Analyse Economique, cowritten by Michel Didier, Agnès Bénassy-Quéré, Gilles Bransbourg, and Alain Henriot, *La politique de change de l'euro*, 2008.

Therefore, it would be desirable for the Eurogroup to define its positions with regard to exchange rate policy, as the community treaties give it the ability to do after prior consultation with the ECB. It would be particularly useful if, in periods of low inflation, the ECB would take the exchange rate target into account in its interest-rate policy in order to avoid an excessive appreciation of the euro. This will be even more necessary when exiting the crisis, given the risks of inflation in the United States. Furthermore, action is necessary to reduce the euro's overvaluation against the Chinese currency. Without going so far as to demand the Chinese authorities let the yuan float, it would be helpful to propose that China peg its exchange rate to a basket of currencies instead of just to the dollar. This would allow a gradual transition toward a more flexible system without calling into question the dollar's status as a reserve currency in the short term.

Issues in the Transatlantic Partnership

The Transatlantic Economy, Heart of Globalization

The United States and the European Union represented in 2008 54 percent of world GDP (43.2 percent at purchasing power parity), 26.6 percent of world trade in manufactured goods, and 46.7 percent of world trade in services.[23] They are also by far the principal sources and recipients of foreign direct investment—they are the source of 70 percent of the world stock of FDI and the destination for 60 percent.

The transatlantic economy is also very integrated,[24] with very low customs tariffs (about 3 percent on average). In 2007, the United States absorbed 23 percent of the European Union's exports of goods and services, while the EU was the destination for 21.5 percent of American merchandise exports. Notwithstanding, this share is in decline in favor of Asian countries. The integration of the transatlantic economy is even more visible in the level of cross-investment. In 2007, the EU represented 75 percent of the FDI stock received by the United States, while 46 percent of the FDI stock in the EU came from the United States.

---

[23] Not counting intra-community trade.

[24] For more details, consult Daniel S. Hamilton and Joseph P. Quinlan, *The Transatlantic Economy 2009*, Center for Transatlantic Relations, JHU-SAIS, 2009.

Thus, it is important to note that globalization in intangibles is above all a synonym of Americanization for the EU member states. In sectors such as cinema, software, audiovisual materials, book publishing, and even pharmaceuticals, the large majority of imports come from the United States.[25] This sometimes leads Europeans to experience the commercial relationship with the United States as a relationship of direct competition—not just economic, but cultural. On the other hand, in the United States European competition in certain fields (aeronautics, defense, agriculture, and steel, for example) is unacceptable. It is in the interest of both the EU and the United States to learn how to discuss these issues openly, accepting cultural differences and examining how to respect them while also promoting the interests of each. This would allow for limits on the technical regulations that govern trade and for the allocation of public markets in such a way that they do not become an undeclared instrument of protectionism between the two sides of the Atlantic.

The Transatlantic Market, a Foundation for International Competitiveness

Given the emergence of the BRICs, whose large markets permit companies based there to achieve substantial economies of scale, it is essential that the United States and the EU take advantage of their large internal markets, for reasons of competitiveness and attractiveness to investment. Beyond the necessary pursuit of the implementation of the single market in Europe, it is in the interest of both the United States and Europe to develop a transatlantic free-trade zone, which would benefit both consumers (lower prices, common technological standards) and companies (a larger market). The main barriers are not customs barriers but regulatory ones.

At the initiative of Angela Merkel, an agenda was defined in 2007 to reduce non-tariff barriers within the framework of the Transatlantic Economic Council, which was established for this purpose. The goal is to put all subjects on the table, including services, financial markets, telecoms, energy, public markets, and even cosmetics and electrical

---

[25] See Daniel Cohen and Thierry Verdier, *La mondialisation immatérielle*, Report of the Conseil d'analyse économique, August 2008. http://www.cae.gouv.fr/rapports/dl/076.pdf.

products.[26] Furthermore, the TEC should be the place for a dialogue among industries on questions of standards, innovation, and patents in sectors such as energy, nanotechnologies, biofuels, health, and even electronics. As was concluded at the informal EU-United States summit held in Prague on April 5, 2009, the arrival of a new administration in the United States is an opportunity to reinforce the economic relationship between the EU and the United States, in particular by supporting the work of the TEC. Nonetheless, taking into account the change in administration at the EU level, it will be important that the new Commission provide another strong push for the TEC at the end of 2009.

A Common Agenda to Combat the Current Challenges

To deal with the world economy's current challenges, cooperation between Europe and the United States is not just useful, but necessary. In several areas, there should be a goal of deepened consultation in order to develop common positions or actions:

- This is already the case in the context of the financial crisis. The European and American central banks have, for example, worked in close cooperation to coordinate their interventions with the aim of calming tensions in the interbank credit market. The G20 in April 2009 also agreed to move forward on increasing the IMF's resources by $500 billion, increasing by $250 billion the guarantees for the financing of world trade, and also formalizing its commitments in terms of regulation (tax havens, ratings agencies, and hedge funds) and financial supervision (with the extended mandates given to the Council of Financial Stability). Furthermore, it is essential that this effort be pursued in many directions: the structure and prudential framework for the credit derivatives market (in particular for CDSs[27]), supervision of banks and insurers active at the international level, the appropriateness of accounting norms,

---

[26] See for example "Transatlantic integration—delivery time is now", *Current issues—Deutsche Bank Research*, June 2008. http://www.dbresearch.com/PROD/DBR_INTERNET_EN-PROD/PROD0000000000225962.PDF.

[27] On this point, see Julien Cantegreil, Romain Rancière, and Aaron Tornell, "Future régulation financière : deux règles simples", *Telos-eu.com*, April 6, 2009.

balance-sheet transparency, the regulation of bonuses,[28] and even the obligation imposed on banks to set aside more reserves each year to guard against liquidity and insolvency risks.

- In the sphere of the environment and energy, cooperation between the United States and the European Union is indispensable. On the environmental front, the United States and Europe have to date had a disagreement over which strategy to adopt (the definition of numeric targets, the participation of emerging and developing countries). However, it is essential to find an accord at the Copenhagen summit on climate change in December 2009. Within the framework of the energy-climate package adopted in December 2008, Europe has set itself the goal of reducing its greenhouse gas emissions by 20 percent and bringing renewable energy's share of EU energy consumption to 20 percent by 2020. For its part, the new American administration has already announced its desire to set greenhouse gas emissions reduction targets and to put in place a cap-and-trade system (market for emissions quotas), which in the future could be linked to the European system that already exists. Beyond this rapprochement on the climate question, concrete cooperation between the United States and Europe on environmental matters is absolutely necessary. This includes the sharing of best practices, the definition of common standards, the identification of opportunities for each in the area of clean technologies, which will probably be the basis of the next industrial revolution, and the adoption of a common strategy to develop these technologies. In energy matters, it is in the common interest of the United States and Europe to reduce their dependence on oil and natural gas. To do that, it would be helpful to work together and to provide significant support to long-term research efforts in recycling, the use of hydrogen, 3rd- and 4th-generation hydrocarbons, emissions capture, and 4th-generation nuclear energy. Furthermore, the United States can benefit from European expertise in the area of wind and solar energy (both areas in which Germany is the leader) as well as nuclear energy (in which France is the world

---

[28] For all these subjects, refer to "Reconstruire la finance pour relancer l'économie", *Amicus Curiae*, Institut Montaigne, March 2009 (http://www.institutmontaigne.org/ac-crise-3045. html).

leader). Finally, the United States and Europe should abandon
their numeric targets and subsidies for biofuels, given that the
current technology increases the prices of foodstuffs, is costly,
and is not the most effective way to reduce CO_2 emissions in
either Europe or the United States.

- In response to international competition and inequalities, the
United States and Europe must invest in education and training. In fact, economic studies show that inequality depends in
large part on the imbalance between the economy's demand
for qualified labor and the supply of qualified labor produced
by the education and training system.[29] In the area of training,
the United States and Europe have a common challenge: to
develop training that is adapted to labor market needs and is
capable of helping to retrain workers in declining sectors and
the unemployed. With regard to the educational system, it
would be useful to share best practices, as one party's strengths
often correspond to the other's weaknesses. The United States
should thus improve its primary and secondary education,
while Europe must invest more in higher education and improve the governance of its universities.[30] On the European
side, for example, it is possible to learn from the American experience of bringing together universities and companies (for
the financing of universities, research, and apprenticeships), to
review the organization of the first years at university in order
to improve the employability of those who leave the university
at this stage, and to encourage the mobility of European students, by for example creating a standardized European test
for master's admissions.

- Improve global economic governance. The United States and
Europe can contribute in decisive fashion to an improvement
in world economic governance. From this perspective, the creation of the G20 and the commitment taken during the London summit to give greater decision-making weight to emerging countries in IMF and World Bank decisions were significant

---

[29] Claudia Goldin and Lawrence E. Katz, *The Race between Education and Technology*, Belknap Press, 2008.

[30] See the recommendations of Philippe Aghion, Mathias Dewatripont, Caroline Hoxby, Andreu Mas-Colell and André Sapir, "Higher aspirations: An agenda for reforming European universities", *Bruegel Blueprint Series*, 2008.

advances. These should be used to the fullest to better deal with the global economy's problems, in particular trade and monetary imbalances, and to improve financial supervision. For its part, the EU could adopt common representation at the World Bank and the IMF,[31] as it already has at the WTO. At the same time, the IMF's role should be reviewed; it should focus on the certification of national accounts, the prevention of financial crises, the granting of aid to states subject to currency crises, and on carrying out macroeconomic studies. At the same time, it should cease its structural-adjustment programs and its non-emergency loans, which should be a competency reserved for the World Bank. This would make the IMF more independent of political pressures and enable it to recenter its mission. In parallel fashion, it is essential to subject the World Bank to regular outside audits and to develop the traceability of its aid and loans, in order to increase its transparency and effectiveness. For its part, the WFO should be given sufficient institutional and financial means to be able to respond in adequate manner to food crises without having to request the necessary funds during an emergency. Finally, even if trade negotiations are blocked, the WTO remains indispensable, in particular to avoid backsliding. As well as committing in a concrete way to concluding the Doha round, it would be helpful for the United States and the EU to jointly examine the possibility of using multilateral accords open to all signatories and permitting those that wish to pursue trade integration.[32]

Conclusion

An economic and financial crisis, the return of scarcity, rising inequality, and the risk of protectionism—the challenges confronting the world economy are numerous and simultaneous. Given the size of these challenges, the transatlantic link is extremely valuable and deserves strong political support. To meet current and future chal-

---

[31] See Emile-Robert Perrin, "La représentation de l'Union européenne dans les institutions financières internationales : Vers une chaise unique ?" *Questions d'Europe—Policy Papers de la Fondation Robert Schuman*, February 2006. http://www.robert-schuman.eu/question_europe.php?num=qe-20.

[32] See Simon J. Evenett, "Getting over those Doha blues," *Vox*, August 2008 (http://www.voxeu.org/index.php?q=node/1503).

lenges, the next American and European administrations should define shared objectives and common actions, of which we have given examples. The partners can also promote the stability of the world economy, their competitiveness, and their citizens' support of international openness. France, which is traditionally wary of globalization and of the United States, can play an important role in this rapprochement and make itself a force for the promotion of a better-regulated globalization.

Chapter Two

"A Crisis is a Terrible Thing to Waste": Franco-American Leadership for a New Economic Agenda

Daniel S. Hamilton

The global financial crisis and related recession, together with political changes in both the U.S. and Europe, offer France and America both necessity and opportunity to reposition their economies, their bilateral relationship, and ultimately the West itself to deal with 21st century economic challenges.

In this context France and the United States face four interlocking tasks. First, each country is faced with daunting economic challenges at home. The task for each is to invest the resources and political capital needed to reform its own economy, without being seduced by protectionist temptations. Second, each needs to understand better its respective stake in strong Franco-American economic links, and to do what is possible to strengthen those ties even further. Third, much of the U.S. economic agenda with France must be conducted with the European Union. It is imperative that the U.S. and the EU work together to strengthen transatlantic economic ties. Fourth, strong bilateral and U.S.-EU ties can ensure that the U.S. and France work together and with other key partners to address global economic challenges.

The Setting

Few issues are likely to shape Franco-American relations over the next years as the global economic crisis. Although the U.S. was the epicenter of the global financial crisis, French and European banks were only too happy to join the sub-prime rush that has shaken the global economy. In fact, the financial crisis should put to rest any doubt about how interconnected the global economy has become over the past few decades. At the crisis began, the prevalent feeling in France and Europe was that America's financial problems, triggered by the U.S. subprime meltdown, were just that—America's problems. There was much talk of global decoupling—the capacity of Europe and the emerging markets to go their merry way despite a weakened United States. Such was the level of confidence in Europe that the European Central bank opted to raise interest rates in early summer 2008, a signal that growth in the eurozone was adequate and that the real challenge was inflation, not growth.

This all changed in the early fall of 2008 when Europe, including France, found itself in the throes of a financial crisis and an economic recession courtesy of the financial tsunami whipped up by the United States. Such are the ties of globalization and the depth of transatlantic ties that a problem in the U.S. quickly translates into a problem for Europe and France. Globalization cuts both ways—in good times, it bestows multiple benefits on nations that are open and receptive to cross-border flows of capital, goods, ideas and people. In bad times, there is no place to hide.

In the end, many banks in Europe, including France, were all too willing to embrace the risky lending practices of their American counterparts, bulking up on risky debt instruments while relying on short-term loans, rather than deposits, to finance their activities. This, along with lax regulations, a growing appetite for risk, the proliferation and securitization of new investment instruments, and cheap and copious amounts of credit have engulfed Europe in the global credit crisis. While authorities in France and elsewhere have moved quickly to shore up their respective banking sectors, the damage to the real economy has been done. The U.S., France and the eurozone are in a deep recession.

It is no wonder, then, that French and Americans are gloomy about globalization. Yet both France and the United States have been two of globalization's great winners. A variety of forces — rapid technological diffusion, greater trade opportunities, lower barriers to investment, policy reforms at home — have generated greater flows of goods and services, people, capital and ideas within France and America and between both countries and the rest of the world. On the whole, these forces have fostered large gains for each country: robust growth in exports and imports; strong outflows and inflows of investment; greater technological diffusion; net portfolio inflows; net inflows of labor; more jobs and higher GDP growth.[1]

These gains have not been evenly shared, however, and do not directly benefit every worker, firm, and community. There have been winners and losers. Globalization's gains are widespread, but often they may seem abstract or diffuse. Globalization's pains, on the other hand, can be tangible and traumatic, and can have an outsized impact on particular companies or communities. Globalization is not the only source of economic change and disruption in the U.S. or France, but like other sources it can inflict real costs on particular members of society.[2]

On both sides of the Atlantic, publics and opinion leaders alike understand that their prosperity is tied to an open, vibrant global economy, yet most believe that globalization's gains and pains have not been fairly shared within society. Many are anxious about the pace of global economic change. They worry that a job gained abroad means a job lost at home, that their hard-won prosperity could simply slip away. They are concerned that the future winners of globalization could live in Mumbai or Shanghai rather than in Toledo or Toulouse.

These concerns are real, widespread, and legitimate. They are exacerbated, in turn, by problems made at home.

The challenge on both sides of the Atlantic is to manage the crisis intelligently without succumbing to protectionist pressures.

Task I: Building Open, Resilient Domestic Economies

One of the most important ways France and America can tackle global economic challenges and to seize the benefits of an open world economy is for each to get its respective act together at home—to reposition itself as an open, resilient economy fit for globalization. Each is challenged to adopt a bold program for domestic revival that favors investment in the future over consumption for the moment; that

---

[1] See Daniel S. Hamilton and Joseph P. Quinlan, *France and Globalization* (Washington, D.C.: Center for Transatlantic Relations, 2008), available in English at http://transatlantic.sais-jhu.edu/Publications/FRANCE_AND_GLOBALIZATION.pdf and in French at http://transatlantic.sais-jhu.edu/Publications/France_face_a_la_mondialisation.pdf.

[2] For an analysis of globalization's impact on Europe, see Daniel S. Hamilton and Joseph P. Quinlan, *Globalization and Europe* (Washington, D.C.: Center for Transatlantic Relations, 2008).

helps citizens to prepare for and weather change, rather than protect them from it; and equips those who are disproportionately affected by globalization to participate and share in its benefits.

In some ways, such an agenda evokes Western responses to the collapse of globalization's first era in depression and war in the first half of the last century. Following those monumental disasters, Western countries reopened their economies, but also constructed social safety nets at home that helped those hurt by the churn of international integration and continuous economic change. They combined openness with security. Each side of the Atlantic struck a somewhat different balance, with Americans on the whole favoring more openness and the French favoring greater security. Both versions are under new pressure today. In general, France needs to balance its strong social welfare provisions by endowing its economy with greater suppleness and adaptability, and the U.S. needs to balance its vaunted flexibility with a stronger social safety net to give Americans the reassurance and support they need to compete in an open global economy. The common challenge for Paris and Washington is to show their citizens and millions around the world that it is possible to reap globalization's benefits while making its costs bearable to those most directly affected.

America's Challenge

The U.S. needs to strengthen its threadbare social safety net. Americans are struggling against a rising tide of economic insecurity that engulfs them from all sides.[3] Successive U.S. administrations have addressed this insecurity in piecemeal, patchwork fashion. Yet such efforts have failed to offer Americans the support they need to cope with rapid economic change.

The recession has brought the economic struggles Americans face into sharp relief. Over the last generation, 95 percent of wage earners have seen their wages decline, after adjustment for inflation, according to a study published by the National Bureau of Economic Research in 2007. 47 million citizens lack health insurance, nearly 1 in 6 Ameri-

---

[3] I am indebted to Bruce Stokes for his succinct analyses of this challenge. See for example Bruce Stokes, "Balance of Payments: Homeland Insecurity," *Congress Daily*, February 28, 2008. See also Gene Sperling, "A Powell Doctrine for the Economy and a Grand Bargain," *Roll Call*, November 20, 2008.

cans. Fear of losing one's healthcare coverage is the principal concern people express when they face unemployment. Moreover, when people lose their jobs, they have only a one-in-three chance of qualifying for unemployment insurance.

As Americans have struggled to maintain their standard of living in the face of these challenges, they have borrowed more and more money. The ratio of household debt to disposable income, which between the mid-1960s and the mid-1980s was fairly stable at a little over 60 percent, has reached 130 percent.

In addition, the U.S. government estimates that Americans entering the labor force today are likely to have 12-15 different jobs in their lifetimes, about double the number of job expectancy of their parent's generation.

Despite this tremendous flux, Americans find themselves with an economic safety net that is weak and ragged. The U.S. is the only major industrial country not to provide universal health care. Unemployment insurance replaces only about 30 percent of the lost income of low-wage jobless workers in the United States. By comparison, the average low wage unemployed worker in other industrial countries gets benefits totaling 55 percent of their lost income. And Washington spends a fraction of what most European countries spend on retraining.

These are serious challenges, but hardly desperate ones. Washington may be broke, but America is not poor. The U.S. remains the world's foremost economic power. But Americans are paying a high price for evading hard choices. Our crisis is essentially political, not economic.

Instead of succumbing to pressures to shield Americans from an open economy—which would be both an economic and a political disaster—the U.S. must act to help Americans cope with rapid economic change by forging a new, comprehensive, three-pronged social compact: universal health care, universal unemployment insurance and universal retraining. A social safety net built on those three pillars will provide Americans with the reassurance they need to go forward in an increasingly uncertain world.

France's challenge

France is conflicted when it comes to globalization. On the one hand, France has been one of globalization's greatest beneficiaries, and stands primed to benefit even more. On the other hand, polls consistently confirm that the French population is deeply skeptical, even fearful, of globalization. France's main globalization challenge seems to be to align popular impressions with the realities behind France's integration into the global economy, while capitalizing on French strengths and helping those adversely affected by globalization.

French consumers, workers and companies have all prospered from globalization. Tens of thousands of French jobs are created and preserved annually thanks to U.S., European or Asian investments. 1 in 7 French employees works for a foreign-owned company, compared with 1 in 10 in Britain and 1 in 20 in the United States. France is a major beneficiary of foreign direct investment, receiving $481 billion between 1997 and 2006. It is also an important location for significant R&D investments by foreign companies, primarily from Europe and the United States. Almost half of the top 40 companies listed on the Paris stock exchange are owned by foreign investors. France ranks relatively high as a global innovation leader. Moreover, it can approach globalization from a strong base: France's productivity is high, its demographics are healthy, its infrastructure is well-developed and its public services are strong.

France is potentially well positioned to take of advantage of the globalization of services; in 2006 it accounted for 4.1 percent of global services exports. The country's basic economic prospects are sound; in recent years output has grown and public finances have improved. Unemployment, while still inordinately high, has fallen. France compares well with most countries in terms of attracting global talent. It registers positive net inflows of professional and technical workers and benefits from strong knowledge flows. Moreover, on balance France appears to be a net beneficiary of on- and offshoring. Between 2003 and 2006 the proportion of French job losses attributed to offshoring was minimal. According to the OECD, in 2005 offshoring accounted for only 3.4 percent of total French job losses. The bulk of these jobs went to other EU nations, not to other continents.

France enjoys a high average educational level, which should help the workforce to be relatively adaptable by international standards, and a large proportion of younger workers has tertiary qualifications. Regional labor mobility is also relatively high in France in comparison with other EU partners.

Despite these benefits, polls repeatedly show the French people alarmed about the impact of globalization on practically every aspect of French life. A widespread feeling of pessimism and insecurity threatens to subvert France's ability to gain further from globalization. Such fears are not entirely unfounded. France has slipped from 15th to the 18th most competitive nation in the world on the Global Competitive Index, and is 23rd on the Networked Readiness Index. Over the past quarter of a century, France has slipped from 8th to 19th in national rankings of gross domestic product per head. In 1991 French GDP per capita was 83 percent that of the United States. Today it is 71 percent. The difference corresponds almost exactly to the gap between these two economies in terms of the per capita number of hours worked. French is second only to Norway in the OECD in terms of hourly productivity rates, but the French enter the workforce later than in most other countries, they then work fewer hours and retire earlier. Moreover, unemployment has remained above 8 percent for a quarter century. Youth unemployment is particularly high at 22 percent. Only 41 percent of the adult population works, one of the lowest labor participation rates in the world. The French public's instinctive belief that it is slipping behind a number of other nations is objectively true.

France is benefiting from many aspects of globalization. But the pace of change elsewhere can be staggering and demoralizing as France confronts its own challenges. There is a widespread perception among the French public that a lack of purchasing power is constraining growth. But the country's growth difficulties are not due to low consumer demand but to rigidities that impede supply and impair export performance. The need to reform rigid labor market institutions and practices requires France to adopt strategies that support workers and promote work opportunities, rather than protect particular jobs. Labor markets must become more flexible through abolition of the legal limit on working hours in favor of individual company negotiations with their workforce. The aging population will soon have a real impact on labor force developments and public finances, although France continues to register relatively strong birth rates and an increase in population, in contrast to many other EU partners.

France remains a highly competitive country, but its uneven export performance is further testimony to deep-seated domestic rigidities. French companies are benefiting from a shift in export patterns to developing countries, but have not yet tapped the full potential of this shift. Measures to strengthen the export capacity of small- and medium-sized companies could bolster overall export performance. The services sector is an important strength of the French export economy that has yet to be exploited fully. As France moves ever closer to a knowledge-based service economy, it must keep and embellish its competitive strengths in high-tech goods and services or suffer a decline in economic welfare. Yet France appears to lack many key microregions or technology clusters that can drive innovation and growth, and is inadequately mobilizing its R&D resources.

Recent reforms introduced by the French government are intended to address these rigidities and stimulate economic growth — but they have been gradual and uneven, and the rest of the world is not standing still.

Today, President Sarkozy calls on France to "play the game of globalization"—and France plays the game of globalization relatively well, despite popular impressions to the contrary, and despite the current economic turmoil sparked by the Great Depression. France has gained considerably from the expansion of global trade, investment and capital, but has benefited unevenly from flows of people and ideas. France has great core strengths and the wherewithal to capitalize from globalization. But change is proving difficult for a society used to looking to the state to provide jobs, redistribute incomes, protect against unwanted imports, promote prestigious industrial sectors, and project national grandeur.

As so often in the past, the debate in France is likely to be the key to the debate in Europe. An open, globally engaged France can both shape and benefit considerably from globalization; a closed, sullen and inward France could lose a great deal. Given both the depth of concern and the potential for great gain, it is important for France to find a new consensus on globalization—a task rendered more difficult by the global financial crisis and attendant recession.

Task II: Promoting Bilateral Economic Ties

A second level economic task for both partners is to realize the profound and growing stake each has in the other's economic success. Economics is not necessarily zero-sum. In a growing economy, your success can also be mine. Bilateral economic ties between France and the U.S. are dramatic testament to the deep integration that characterizes transatlantic commercial relations, and strong evidence that the economic interests and future prosperity of the United States and France have never been as interdependent and intertwined as they are today.

In fact, despite the media's (misguided) tendency to equate trade with commerce, and notwithstanding all the excitement surrounding emerging markets, one of the defining features of the global economic landscape over the past decade has been the increasing integration and cohesion of the transatlantic economy in general, and U.S.-France ties in particular.

U.S.-France commercial interests are bound together by foreign investment—the deepest form of economic integration—as opposed to trade—a well known yet rather shallow form of integration. The primacy of foreign direct investment in driving U.S.-French commerce is reflected in the robust infrastructure that links the United States and France. This commercial infrastructure has been under construction for over a half-century, but remains largely invisible to publics and opinion leaders on both sides of the ocean. The following indices offer a clearer picture of the deep integrating force that makes the U.S.-French commercial link among the strongest in the world.

Gross Product of Foreign Affiliates

Figure 1 charts the sizable total output of U.S. foreign affiliates in France (almost $55 billion in 2007) and of French affiliates in the United States (more than $60 billion). Each figure is equal to or greater than the GDP of many nations.

Overseas Assets of Foreign Affiliates

America's overseas commercial presence, as measured by foreign assets of U.S. companies, is substantial, totaling nearly $10 trillion in 2005. The bulk of these assets, or 62 percent, are located in Europe,

Figure 1   U.S.-French Linkages:* Gross Product of Affiliates

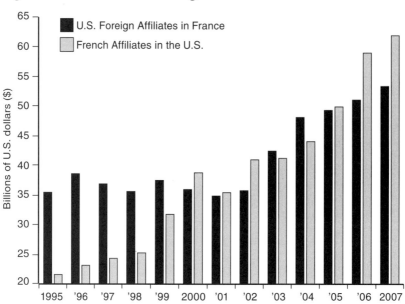

Source: Bureau of Economic Analysis.

*Data for majority-owned foreign affiliates.

Notes: Data for U.S. foreign affiliates in France 2006 and 2007 are Center for Transatlantic Relations' estimates. Data for French affiliates in the U.S. 2007 are Center for Transatlantic Relations' estimates.

with the largest shares in the United Kingdom, the Netherlands, and Germany. While lagging the others, U.S. assets in France alone, totaling almost $300 billion, were greater than total U.S. assets in South America in 2005, as well as many other developing regions, including Africa, the Middle East, Eastern Europe and OPEC.

Total French assets in the U.S.—over $800 billion—are among the largest of all foreign investors in the United States. Only the United Kingdom, Switzerland, Germany and the Netherlands have a larger asset base in the U.S. than France. It is interesting to note that French assets in the U.S. are almost 3 times larger than U.S. assets in France, a factor related to the surge in French FDI in the United States over the past decade. Figure 2 charts the assets of U.S. and French affiliates in each other's country.

Figure 2   U.S.-French Linkages:* Assets of Affiliates

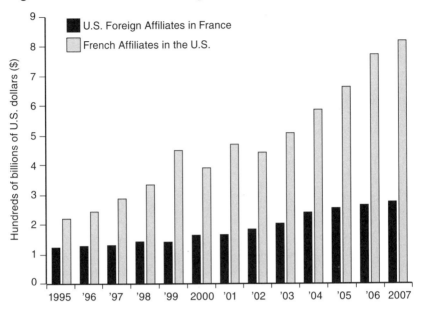

Source: Bureau of Economic Analysis.

*Data for majority-owned foreign affiliates.

Notes: Data for U.S. foreign affiliates in France 2006 and 2007 are Center for Transatlantic Relations' estimates. Data for French affiliates in the U.S. 2007 are Center for Transatlantic Relations' estimates.

Affiliate Employment

Thousands of workers in the United States and France are employed by foreign affiliates from each nation. Indeed, about half a million American workers were employed directly by French affiliates in 2007—among the largest numbers of workers employed by foreign investors in the U.S. Tens of thousands of additional American jobs are tied to U.S. exports to France, although these are harder to quantify. Only British and German firms employed more American workers in 2007.

U.S. affiliates in France employ even more people in France—roughly 585,000 French workers in 2007. U.S. affiliates in France employ early 20 percent more people than U.S. affiliates in China. Figures 3 and 4 chart these employment effects, which are understated, since these numbers do not include French jobs created by French exports to the

Figure 3   U.S.-French Linkages:*
Affiliate Employment

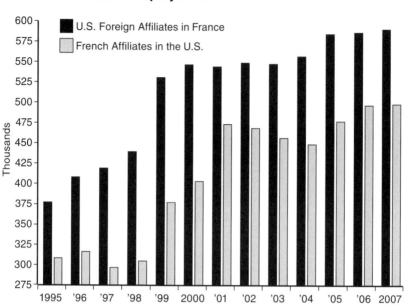

Source: Bureau of Economic Analysis.

*Data for majority-owned foreign affiliates.

Notes: Data for U.S. foreign affiliates in France 2006 and 2007 are Center for Transatlantic Relations' estimates. Data for French affiliates in the U.S. 2007 are Center for Transatlantic Relations' estimates.

United States, and do not account for indirect employment effects of nonequity arrangements such as strategic alliances, joint ventures and other deals. In short, it is likely that at least 2 million French and Americans owe their livelihoods to close bilateral economic ties.

Research and Development of Affiliates

While R&D expenditures remain biased towards the home country, foreign affiliate R&D has become more prominent over the past decade as firms seek to share the costs of development, spread the risks and tap into the intellectual talent of other nations. Alliances, cross-licensing of intellectual property, and mergers and acquisitions—these and

Figure 4   U.S.-French Linkages:*
Affiliate Manufacturing Employment

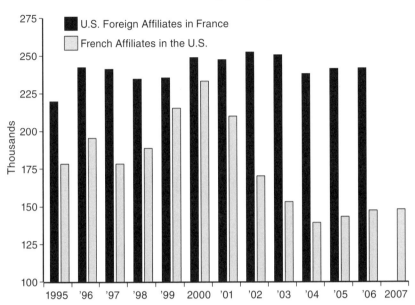

Source: Bureau of Economic Analysis.

*Data for majority-owned foreign affiliates.

Notes: Data for U.S. foreign affiliates in France 2006 and 2007 are Center for Transatlantic Relations' estimates. Data for French affiliates in the U.S. 2007 are Center for Transatlantic Relations' estimates.

other forms of cooperation have become staples of the U.S.-French partnership, and are reflected in Figure 5.

Accordingly, U.S. affiliates invested close to $1.5 billion in R&D in France, a reflection of France's skilled, innovative workforce and corporate America's penchant for leveraging skilled assets any place in the world. Conversely, America's highly skilled labor force, entrepreneurial culture and first-class universities have been key drivers attracting R&D capital from French firms. Indeed, in 2007, French affiliates in the United States invested $3.5 billion in R&D capital in the United States. Corporate France's R&D activity in the U.S. has been critical to continued French economic vitality and profitability. R&D expenditures of French affiliates in the U.S. account for 15 percent of total French R&D expenditures.

Figure 5   U.S.-French Linkages:*
R&D Expenditures of Affiliates

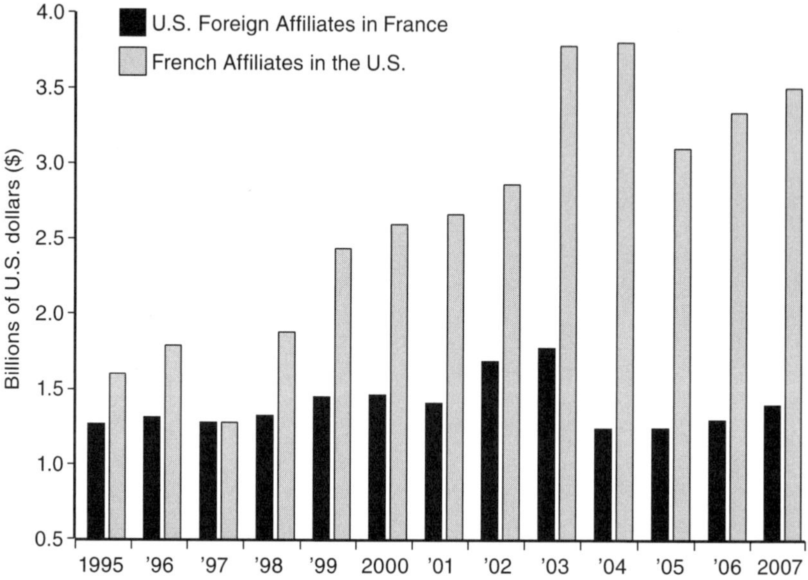

Source: Bureau of Economic Analysis.

*Data for majority-owned foreign affiliates.

Notes: Data for U.S. foreign affiliates in France 2006 and 2007 are Center for Transatlantic Relations' estimates. Data for French affiliates in the U.S. 2007 are Center for Transatlantic Relations' estimates.

Intra-firm Trade of Foreign Affiliates

Foreign affiliate sales are the primary means by which goods and services are delivered across the Atlantic. Trade is secondary, although the two modes of delivery should not be viewed independently of each other. They are more complements than substitutes, since foreign investment and affiliate sales increasingly drive trade flows. Indeed, a substantial share of U.S.-French trade is considered intra-firm trade or related party trade, which is cross border trade that stays within the ambit of the company. It's Michelin of France sending parts and components to Michelin in the U.S., for instance. Reflecting the tight linkages between French parent companies and their U.S. affiliates, roughly 49 percent of U.S. imports from France and 34 percent of U.S. exports to France consisted of related party trade in 2006.

The strong role of related-party trade partially explains why currency fluctuations have less of an impact on transatlantic economic ties than Economics 101 might suggest. While a strong euro, in theory at least, would be associated with a decline in French competitiveness in the United States, the fact that many French multinationals produce, market and distribute goods on both sides of the ocean gives firms a high degree of immunity to a dramatic shift in exchange rates. Under this structure, trade flows are driven more by demand in the host nation. The stronger the demand in the U.S., the better are sales of French affiliates, which in turn generate more demand (a.k.a imports) from the parent company in France for parts and components irrespective of exchange rate movements. Related-party trade key to understanding the profound and growing stake French and Americans have in the economic success of the other, and why they share a mutual interest in reviving domestic growth on each side of the Atlantic.

Foreign Affiliate Sales

Foreign affiliate sales are the primary means by which U.S. and French firms delivery goods and services to each other's respective markets. In 2007, for instance, U.S. foreign affiliate sales in France totaled more than $210 billion, well in excess of U.S. exports to France the same year. Similarly, French foreign affiliate sales in the United States totaled roughly $193 billion in 2007, far above U.S. imports from France. In other words, foreign affiliate sales tell one story of U.S.-French ties, while trade tells another.

Trade alone is a very misleading benchmark of international economic ties, and yet the media and many opinion leaders make this mistake continuously. If one simply looks at U.S. trade flows, for instance, France would rank well behind other nations like China, Canada, Mexico and the United Kingdom. From this vantage point, it's not hard to make the case that many emerging markets like China and Mexico are more important to U.S. commercial interests than France, or that rapidly developing economies have become more important to France than the United States. The story changes dramatically, however, when one considers foreign affiliates sales. Based on the later, the U.S. ranks as the single most important market in the world to France, and France ranks as one of the most important markets in the world to the United States. Figure 6 demonstrates how these sales have increased in recent years.

Figure 6   U.S.-French Linkages:* Affiliate Sales

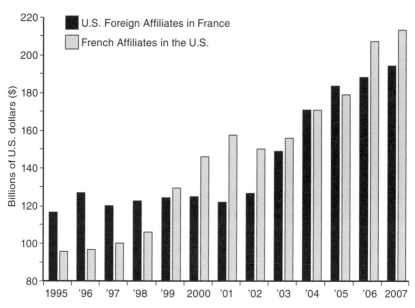

Source: Bureau of Economic Analysis.

*Data for majority-owned foreign affiliates.

Notes: Data for U.S. foreign affiliates in France 2006 and 2007 are Center for Transatlantic Relations' estimates. Data for French affiliates in the U.S. 2007 are Center for Transatlantic Relations' estimates.

Foreign Affiliate Income

In terms of profits, Europe easily remains the most important region in the world for corporate America, accounting for half of U.S. global affiliate earnings in 2006 and for 55 percent of the global total over the balance of this decade. In 2007 U.S. affiliates in France earned more than $6 billion and French affiliates in the U.S. posted earnings of roughly $11.5 billion. For many companies, strong demand in the partner country can help to offset sluggish growth at home—another tie that binds.

Time to Seize the Opportunity to Deepen U.S.-French Ties

These indices convey a more complete picture of international economic flows than simple tallies of export and imports. Foreign direct

Figure 7   U.S.-French Linkages:* Affiliate Income

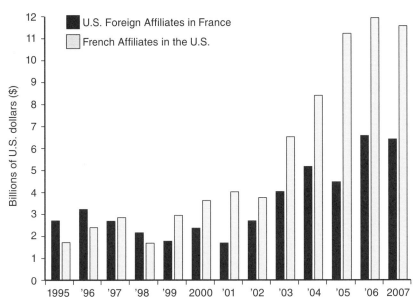

Source: Bureau of Economic Analysis.
*Data for majority-owned foreign affiliates.

investment represents the economic backbone of the U.S.-French partnership, with other variables like overseas assets, affiliate employment and sales, related party trade, services and others derived from the level and depth of investment linkages. U.S. and French commercial linkages are among the deepest in the world, with both parties benefiting greatly from over a half century of strong investment and trade ties.

This mutual interest in each other's prosperity is another reason why domestic reforms are so essential. Without French policies designed to address labor rigidities and tax reform, U.S. multinationals might increasingly look elsewhere when it comes to investing in France. How Paris handles its related challenges of immigration and integration, promotes innovation, pursues environmental standards and reacts to its shifting demographics will also affect future U.S. investment flows.

In the United States, diverging regulations and technical standards, Sarbanes-Oxley-type legislation, temptations towards state aid to industry and overzealous security measures such as 100 percent cargo screening could act to halt or slow the pace of French and European investment in the United States.

On both sides of the Atlantic, the potential for greater integration of various service activities is huge. Services are the "sleeping giant" of the transatlantic economy—an economic force which, if awakened and unleashed, could offer tremendous opportunities for consumers, workers and companies in France and America. Yet regulations are uneven, and non-tariff barriers in both nations and within the EU have prevented U.S.-French service activities from growing and becoming fully integrated. Given France's membership in the European Union, aligning standards and clearing away commercial hurdles often requires action between the U.S. and the EU—a third level economic challenge for Paris and Washington.

Task III: Advancing U.S.-EU Economic Relations

Franco-American economic ties are in many ways a microcosm of the broader U.S.-European commercial relationship. Europeans and Americans have become so intertwined that we are literally in each other's business—we own each other. These linkages underpin a $3.75 trillion economy that provides up to 14 million jobs on both sides of the Atlantic.[4] No commercial artery in the world is as large as the one binding together North America and Europe. No two regions of the global economy are as economically fused as the two parties straddling the Atlantic, making the transatlantic economy the largest and wealthiest in the world.

Transatlantic markets are among the most open in the world and are deeply integrated through dense flows of investment, affiliate sales and related-party trade. Yet various barriers persist that prevent the emergence of a free transatlantic marketplace. These include traditional tariff barriers, as well non-tariff barriers and regulations that restrict foreign ownership of domestic resources, assign monopoly status to government enterprises, pose significant regulatory hurdles for

---

[4] See Daniel S. Hamilton and Joseph P. Quinlan, *The Transatlantic Economy 2009: Annual Survey of Jobs, Trade and Investment between the United States and Europe* (Washington, D.C.: Center for Transatlantic Relations, 2009).

prospective foreign investors or discriminate between domestic and foreign bidders.[5]

Transatlantic tariff barriers are generally low, averaging between 3 and 4 percent of annual transatlantic trade. Tariff levels in the European Union, however, are more widely dispersed than those in the U.S., and tariffs in both the EU and the U.S. are higher on specific products in sensitive sectors, such as textiles, wearing apparel and leather products, or as a result of preferential trade agreements.[6]

Because transatlantic tariffs are generally quite low and European and U.S. industries are so deeply intertwined with each other, non-tariff barriers are more important impediments to a free transatlantic marketplace. Remaining non-tariff barriers consist largely of domestic regulations, including safety norms, different health, environmental or engineering standards, rules of origin or labeling requirements. Such measures are due in part to different societal preferences and priorities, but also to a significant degree to a lack of coordination or adequate information exchange between regulators and legislators on each side of the Atlantic, who are subject to different legal mandates or engage in different oversight procedures.

These barriers to transatlantic integration tend to be concentrated in certain sectors of the economy. In general, barriers in manufacturing tend to be low, while barriers in services and agriculture tend to be relatively high. Since agriculture comprises a relatively small and services a relatively high percentage of overall transatlantic economic output and employment, gains from liberalization in services relative to agriculture would be quite high.

---

[5] For an assessment of these barriers for certain industries, see Daniel S. Hamilton and Joseph P. Quinlan, eds., *Deep Integration: The Changing Geography of the Transatlantic Economy* (Washington/Brussels: Center for Transatlantic Relations/Centre for European Policy Studies, 2005). See also the contributions to the 2004-2005 U.S.-EU Stakeholder Dialogue (available at http://www.ustr.gov/World_Regions/Europe_Mediterranean/ Transatlantic_Dialogue/Section_Index.html); see also OECD, *The Benefits of Liberalising Product Markets and Reducing Barriers to International Trade and Investment: The Case of The United States and the European Union*, Economics Department Working Paper 432, Paris, June 2005, pp. 7-10.

[6] Transatlantic Business Dialogue, "Report to the 2005 U.S.-EU Summit: A Framework for Deepening Transatlantic Trade and Investment," April 2005 (http://128.121.145.19/ tabd/media/TABD2005SummitReportFINAL051.pdf); and OECD, ibid.

In Europe, the OECD reports that sectoral barriers to FDI appear highest in transport services, telecommunications and particularly electricity. In the U.S. FDI restrictions on transport services and telecommunications are higher than in the average EU country.[7]

Potential Benefits of Further Transatlantic Liberalization

In June 2005, an OECD report estimated that a package of structural reforms in the EU and the U.S. that included reduction of competition-restraining regulations, tariff barriers and FDI restrictions could lead to permanent gains in GDP per capita on both sides of the Atlantic of up to 3 to 3.5 percent, and cause additional benefits to other OECD countries of up to 1.5 percent of GDP per capita. Over the course of an average 40-year working life of an individual, the OECD estimates that the cumulated addition to earnings would equal between one-half and more than a full year's worth of earnings.

Moreover, the implied reforms are relatively narrow and exclude labor market, financial market, agricultural or tax reforms, any of which could also strengthen transatlantic economic integration and performance. Thus the OECD study is thus conservative in its conclusions.[8]

The OECD study suggested that such output gains would require ambitious reforms in key sectors. Competition-restraining regulations in most EU15 countries would have to be reduced considerably in domestic air, rail and road transportation, electricity and gas, and telecommunications. The United States would have to focus reforms on electricity and rail transportation. The greatest reduction of restrictions on foreign direct investment in the United States would need to come in transportation services, while in the European Union it would need to be most extensive in electricity generation. Reductions in tariff levels in the European Union would have to be concentrated on agricultural products; in the United States, tariff reductions would imply relatively more adjustment to rates of protection on textiles, apparel and other manufactured goods.[9]

---

[7] OECD, op. cit., p. 19.

[8] OECD, op. cit., pp. 5-7.

[9] OECD, op. cit.

In short, given the size and the deep inter-linkages between the U.S. and European economies, the removal of remaining tariff and non-tariff barriers, coupled with enhanced economic and regulatory cooperation between the U.S. and the EU, could be the catalyst for a significant boost in economic growth, employment, investment and innovation across the transatlantic marketplace, could further enhance the attractiveness of the transatlantic economy in a globalizing world, and could enable the U.S. and the EU to act as pathfinders for regulatory policy cooperation and market opening beyond the transatlantic economy.

The Transatlantic Economic Council and its Critics

Efforts to liberalize transatlantic markets by focusing on domestic barriers began with the 1995 New Transatlantic Agenda, and have been continued with varying degrees of enthusiasm by the U.S. and EU. The newest incarnation was the creation of the Transatlantic Economic Council (TEC) in 2007. The goal of the TEC is to improve U.S.-EU regulatory cooperation and if possible remove barriers to the free flow of goods, services, technology and ideas across the Atlantic.

As soon as the TEC was launched, critics sharpened their knives. Most confused the initiative with the old and largely discarded idea of a U.S.-EU Transatlantic Free Trade Area (TAFTA), which they argued would be so big it would destroy the multilateral trading system. Such criticism, however, falsely characterizes the initiative or misses the point. The initiative is not about trade—and thus it does not compete with the Doha round or other trade initiatives—because trade really isn't the problem across the Atlantic. Transatlantic trade tiffs steal the headlines, but overall, transatlantic trade barriers are very low. Since the transatlantic economy is driven by investment more than trade, the most important transatlantic economic obstacles are not "at the border" trade barriers but "behind the border" domestic barriers to the free flow of capital, goods and services.

Moreover, given the immense size of the transatlantic market, even small changes in aligning domestic regulations on both sides of the Atlantic could generate far bigger economic payoffs than further tariff reductions.

The key now is to engage two important constituencies—legislators and regulators. Deep transatlantic integration can mean that domestic non-tariff measures can become transatlantic non-tariff barriers. Most of this is not willful; domestic regulatory agencies are simply not designed to take into account the deeply—but unevenly—integrated nature of the transatlantic marketplace. Regulatory authorities, of course, have the duty to ensure that specific products are suitable for use in their jurisdiction. Given deep integration, however, greater consistency and coordination among EU and U.S. risk assessment and regulatory review procedures can benefit companies, consumers and the broader public.

The TEC promises to break new ground in this regard by enabling regular communication and exchange of information on a variety of health, safety, environmental, consumer protection and security standards, examining different approaches to risk assessment. A key premise of such efforts could be recognition of the essential 'equivalence' of testing and regulatory procedures, which are rigorous on both sides of the Atlantic. Rather than seeking to harmonize all standards—an impossible task that is likely to create more rather than less bureaucracy—each side could agree to mutual recognition of their respective standards, much as the member states of the European Community agreed to achieve between themselves in the 1980s.

The test is now whether the Transatlantic Economic Council will be able to deliver on its potential. The results thus far have been disappointing, and remain rooted in Franco-American differences. Yet at this time of economic crisis, a *relance* of the TEC, with a focus on transatlantic regulatory cooperation, coupled with more strategic U.S.-EU discussions on using transatlantic leadership to emerge from the economic crisis, could open up new economic opportunities.

Those who worry that an ambitious transatlantic economic initiative could threaten the multilateral system should consider that the opposite may be true. Europeans and Americans certainly share an interest in extending prosperity through multilateral trade liberalization. But even a successful Doha agreement on global trade will not address such pressing "deep integration" issues affecting the European and American economies as competition policies, corporate governance, more-effective regulatory cooperation, taxes and other issues. Nor will it address cutting edge issues raised by European and American scientists and entrepreneurs, who are pushing the frontiers of human discovery in such fields as genetics or nanobiotechnology, where there are neither global rules nor transatlantic mechanisms to sort out the complex legal, ethical and commercial tradeoffs posed by such innovation. There are no patented 'European' or 'American' answers to these challenges. In fact, for most of these issues, neither side has even sorted out the appropriate questions, much less the answers.

Transatlantic markets are the laboratory of globalization. Given deep transatlantic integration, Europeans and Americans face issues that neither yet faces with others. That is why the "multilateral versus transatlantic" dichotomy is a false choice. The United States and EU should advance on both fronts simultaneously: push multilateral liberalization through Doha and other channels and press transatlantic initiatives in services, financial markets, telecommunications, energy, innovation policies and other areas not yet covered by multilateral agreements.

Over the next two decades, the prospect of a shift in the global economic balance is very real. But a number of 'big emerging markets' do not necessarily share some of the core legal principles or basic mechanisms that underpin open international commerce. Instead of spending significant political capital on transatlantic disputes over bananas, beef and state aid to industry, eking out marginal advantage through preferential trade arrangements with tiny markets, engaging in fruitless competition to impose one or another's particular standards in third markets, or being tempted into beggar-thy-neighbor approaches to import surges from countries such as China, Europe and the United States could use their current primacy to invest in new forms of transatlantic collaboration that would enable them to be true pathfinders of the global economy—essentially to reposition the West as it works to integrate other major economies into mechanisms of global governance—the fourth level economic challenge facing Paris and Washington.

Task IV: Working Together to Address Global Economic Challenges

The global financial crisis and attendant recession has underscored the need for Paris, Washington and other partners to ensure that an open and liberal global trade and investment environment is guided by basic principles of global good governance. The financial crisis is also the most dramatic indicator of the growing mismatch between the scope and scale of global challenges and the ability of intergovernmen-

tal mechanisms to deal with them. Paris, Washington and their partners need to consider new forms of governance at the global level, and
to integrate rising powers in ways that give them a stake in the system.
Fortunately, today's international system—open, integrated, rules-
based—has proven to be unusually durable and accommodating. It has
facilitated the participation and integration of both established great
powers and newly independent states. Its very openness and flexibility
means that rising powers can gain full access to and thrive within this
system.

The resilient nature of the current system means that we best tackle
its excesses and omissions not by starting from scratch but by returning to first principles—reinvesting in and reinforcing those features
that encourage engagement, integration and restraint.[10] The more
open, consensual and rules-based these structures are, and the more
widely spread their benefits, the more able they will be to advance the
interests of rising powers through integration and accommodation
rather than through conflict. If Europeans and Americans want to preserve their ability to shape the environment in which rising powers can
make critical strategic choices about their engagement in the world,
they must work together to strengthen the rules and institutions that
underpin that order—giving potentially revisionist powers more
incentives for integration than opposition, making it hard for them to
be spoilers or challengers. By agreeing to abide by common rules of the
road, we gain the commitment of others to live by our standards—not
only in global finance, but in areas such as food safety, public health,
intellectual property rights, environmental and labor protection. We
also establish the means to measure compliance.

Returning to first principles also means ensuring that global governance is also *good* governance. Global mechanisms and institutions
must be grounded in the rule of law and norms of transparency, non-
discrimination, accountability, representation and responsiveness.
These characteristics assure that effectiveness is enhanced, corruption
is minimized, and the views of minorities are taken into account. We
should apply these principles to reform in each of our major institutions of global governance.

---

[10] See G. John Ikenberry, "The Rise of China and the Future of the West," *Foreign Affairs*,
January/February 2008; Daniel S. Hamilton and Joseph P. Quinlan, *Germany and Globalization* (Washington, D.C.: Center for Transatlantic Relations, 2009).

Other nations are likely to be willing to adhere to these standards not just because they want access to our markets, but because they increasingly realize that a system based on such standards is key to their own ability to benefit from globalization. And that can give them a stake in quelling conflict, working towards equitable economic development, and promoting sustainable use of national resources.

As the series of G-20 summits scheduled to address global economic ills continues, a wholesale revision of global governance seems less likely than incremental adaptation, supplemented by a strengthening of informal governance mechanisms, modelled on the stellar—yet informal—cooperation between central banks during the fall of 2008. Such informal mechanisms might include a strengthened Financial Stability Forum and such initiatives as a college of supervisors. The G20 is likely to supplant the G8 as a vehicle to guide such efforts, which could be a useful innovation. Yet as Paris and Washington agree to the G20 format, they might simultaneously consider a return to the original consultations that eventually gave rise to what has become the G8—informal, personal contacts and meetings between the leaders of the Western core—the U.S., France, Britain, Germany, and perhaps others. That core may no longer sufficient to guide global economic governance, but it remains necessary.

A related challenge is to revive the Doha Development Round of multilateral trade negotiations. In July 2008 negotiations on a framework to complete the Doha round collapsed, due to the complexity of the negotiation, insufficient substance in the likely deal and the political climate and calendar. WTO Secretary General Pascal Lamy estimated that failure to secure a deal cost the world $130 billion in potential tariff savings. Yet in the context of global recession prospects for rapid progress are dim.

Summary

Taken together, these four challenges offer a full yet daunting agenda for cooperation between Paris and Washington. As this agenda is advanced, it will be imperative for opinion leaders on both sides of the Atlantic to resist protectionist temptations, avoid superficial notions of decoupling and transatlantic drift, and recall what still makes the transatlantic partnership distinctive: when we agree across the Atlantic, we remain the core of any effective global coalition; when we disagree across the Atlantic, no global coalition is likely to be effective. Our partnership remains indispensible. But today it is insufficient to a range of challenges no nation will be able address effectively alone. As we face financial turmoil and global recession, our challenge is to reposition our domestic economies, our transatlantic partnership, and our mechanisms of global governance, so that each is more inclusive, more effective, and more responsive to the challenges of the century unfolding before us.

Part Two:

Strategic Perspectives

Chapter Three
Strategic Challenges, 2009–2012

Bruno Tertrais

Summary

Franco-American relations in the strategic realm are currently very positive, but three questions could cause tensions between Paris and Washington: American demand for an increased military presence for NATO in Afghanistan; a radical change of attitude toward Iran; and the pursuit of a "nuclear free world" by the United States.

The Euro-American Relationship on Strategic Questions: The State of Affairs

At a moment of political change in Washington, there exists a solid relationship between the two banks of the Atlantic on strategic questions. Close to twenty years after the end of the Cold War, the NATO countries once again share a common strategic perspective. The existence of Article V of the North Atlantic Treaty has not been questioned, and there is a general agreement on the idea that the Alliance must be capable of leading peace operations in the zone of the treaty. The member nations are dependent on the Strategic Concept adopted at the Washington Summit (1999), and on the political directive adopted at the Riga Summit (2006). After September 11, 2001, NATO invoked Article V for the first time in its history, and initialized joint operations aiming at patrolling the skies of the United States and at surveying Mediterranean waters. Most of the members of the Alliance immediately pledged their agreement to participate in *Operation Enduring Freedom*, including at sea.[1] NATO then took change of stabilization forces in Afghanistan. The publication of a Common European Security Strategy (2003) reconciled tensions in the transatlantic community regarding political strategies. After a "chasm" of many

---

[1] Allied Combined Task Force 150, which patrols around the Horn of Africa, is the most important operation to the German navy since the end of the Second World War.

years resulting from the Iraq crisis, European people have a new favorable image of NATO.[2] Terrorism and nuclear proliferation are recognized as the two most immediate threats to security, Iran is considered as a particularly troubling potential menace. Finally, all surveys show that international terrorism is systematically considered to be the primary threat according to public opinion, on both sides of the Atlantic.[3]

Who would have thought, in the era since the Berlin Wall, that twenty years later the member nations of the Alliance would again share a common vision? This irrefutable fact is more remarkable in light of an almost complete change in political and intellectual elites during the interval.

The next president of the United States immediately benefits from a positive *a priori* in European opinion, for the simple reason that he is not George Bush. But it is not evident that the Atlantic alliance will remain cohesive in light of new strategic challenges.

Rising Strategic Challenges

Russia and China

There exists a shift in perceptions between Europe and the United States on Russia and on China. The establishment of democracy in Russia is viewed with concern by most Americans (70 percent), but not as much in Europe (58 percent).[4] As for China, it is considered to be a potential menace by less than most Americans (48 percent), opposed to 29 percent of British, who represent the highest proportion of all major European countries in this regard.[5] And 20 percent of Americans even see a Chinese "enemy," a proportion that does not have an equivalent in Europe, except in Turkey (25 percent).[6]

---

[2] *Transatlantic Trends 2008*, The German Marshall Fund of the United States, September 2008.

[3] See for example *Transatlantic Trends 2008*, The German Marshall Fund of the United States, September 2008; TNS Emnid poll for the Bertelsmann Stiftung, October 22, 2007; Harris Interactive Survey for France 24 and the *International Herald Tribune*, March 20, 2008.

[4] *Transatlantic Trends 2008*, The German Marshall Fund of the United States, September 2008.

[5] Harris Interactive Survey for France 24 and *The International Herald Tribune*, March 28, 2008. The Proportion in France is 16 percent.

[6] 24-Nation Pew Global Attitudes Survey, The Pew Global Attitudes Project, June 12, 2008.

So because of the American insistence for a rapid admittance of Georgia or Ukraine into NATO, relations between Washington and Moscow have become strained once again, transatlantic tensions could also result from this issue. In spite of intervention in Georgia, Europe is reluctant follow the United States in a hard line toward Central and Eastern European policy. Of average public opinion, only the British consider Russia as a potential enemy, but this is not the case for the majority of the other significant members of NATO.[7] The reaction regarding a possible aggravation of the crisis in the Caucuses, for example, could be a real test of solidarity for the Atlantic alliance.

Afghanistan

President Obama is ready to reinforce the United States military commitment (by sending 21,000 extra men) and to demand extra efforts from the European allies for a common effort in Afghanistan.

But the control of combat operations against the Taliban continues to profoundly divide the opinions of the members of the Alliance: 76 percent of Americans find it favorable, against only 43 percent of Europeans.[8] And in certain NATO countries (Turkey, Poland, Spain, France, Germany), there exists a majority in support of a retreat of manpower from the Alliance.[9]

The announcement of the closure of Guantanamo prison—a cherished symbol in the eyes of many Europeans—has not sufficed in persuading parliaments for the Allied countries to authorize supplemental deployments in large numbers for military operations still often perceived, wrongly, as an American adventure.

The Iranian Crisis

The Iranian crisis will remain, in ensuing months and years, one of the most important and sensitive strategic challenges for the transatlantic community, from the opinion of governments and the public.

---

[7] Harris Poll n° 19, February 20, 2008. The United Kingdom is equally the European nation in which one finds the strongest proportion of opinion (31 percent) that considers Russia to be a potential military threat (Harris Interactive Survey for France and *The International Herald Tribune*, March 28, 2008).

[8] *Transatlantic Trends 2008*, The German Marshall Fund of the United States, September 2008.

[9] 24-Nation Pew Global Attitudes Survey, The Pew Global Attitudes Project, June 12, 2008.

Iran is unanimously perceived as the most threatening country according to public opinion in the member nations of NATO.[10] The proportion of those who are opposed to the acquisition of nuclear weapons by Tehran varies between 83 percent (Bulgaria) and 97 percent (Germany).[11] A nuclear Iran will be considered as a direct and serious threat by a large majority, from 65 percent of Bulgarians to 87 percent of Italians.[12]

As a candidate, Barack Obama did not wish to exclude the option of military action against Iran, and all believed that this was a real proclamation, even if its realization in the short term remains improbable (without an enormous Iranian provocation, or an incontrollable escalation of the continuing situation in the Gulf). Indeed, the elected President will certainly demand a "short lived reexamination" of Iranian provocation, and a look at potential options. In addition, Washington could address the problem of Iranian presidential elections in June 2009 as a starting point for reexamining their choices.

If President Obama decides on military action against Iran, it will undoubtedly provoke a serious transatlantic crisis. Even if an absolute majority in the United States is not in favor of military operations against Iran (47 percent support the idea), most Europeans are even more opposed (only 18 percent believe that the option should be maintained).[13] According to another study, executed in October 2007, "only diplomacy" (without sanctions) received the approval of only 36 percent of Americans, opposed to, for example, more than 50 percent of Spanish, Italians, and Germans: and the military option is supported by 21 percent of Americans against 7 to 8 percent of Germans, Italians, French, and Spanish.[14]

On the contrary, an American president tempted by a policy of unconditional overtures toward Tehran, despite the common stance displayed by the Group of "Five plus One" since 2005, could foster hostility with the European governments that are the most attuned to the subject—as is the case for France. The possibility of a strange

---

[10] Harris Interactive Survey for France 24 and *The International Herald Tribune*, March 28, 2008.

[11] 47-Nation Pew Global Attitudes Survey, The Pew Global Attitudes Project, June 27, 2007.

[12] 47-Nation Pew Global Attitudes Survey, The Pew Global Attitudes Project, June 27, 2007.

[13] *Transatlantic Trends 2007*, The German Marshall Fund of the United States, September 2007.

[14] Harris Interactive Survey for France 24 and *The International Herald Tribune*, November 9, 2007.

political configuration exists, that in many ways is the reverse of the present—very improbable—where in the four years ahead, major political evolutions continue to deteriorate in Iran, suggesting support for terrorism. Indeed, in such a case the United States would be less inclined to be preoccupied with Iran's nuclear program than the European governments, but the question would continue to be posed in the same terms. For America, it is the same nature of the Iranian political regime that poses problems, rather than for Europe, where it is first and always the impact of a crisis on the issue of nuclear non-proliferation as a whole.[15]

Finally, the simple pursuit of a current line that consists in requiring the suspension of nuclear activities before the start of formal negotiations will not collect a necessary consensus on both sides of the transatlantic community. The approval of this line diminished a little everywhere in the world between 2006 and 2008.[16] In the absence of Iranian provocation, the positions of Washington, Berlin, London and Paris will find themselves increasingly isolated.

Antimissile Defense

The development of a site of intended interceptors against long-range missiles is another possible subject of contention.[17] There is not a fundamental divergence of appreciation of the threat; according to NATO Secretary General Jaap de Hoop Scheffer, "there exists without contest a common perception of the threat between the Allies. The Allies are always in agreement that ballistic missiles are a threat."[18] In fact, the declaration made by the member states at the time of the NATO Bucharest Summit (2008) indicates "the proliferation of ballistic missiles represents a growing threat for the forces, the territory, and the population to the Alliance."[19] Certainly the Allies have officially given their blessing to the American Project: "Anti-missile

---

[15] On this theme, see Bruno Tertrais, "A Fragile Consensus," *The National Interest*, Spring 2006.

[16] Globe-scan poll for the BBC World Service, February 2008.

[17] The site will have just 10 interceptors at two levels (Ground Based Interceptors). Steven A. Hildreth & Carl Ek, *Long-Range Missile Defense in Europe*, CRS Report for Congress, Congressional Research Service, January 9, 2008, p. 4.

[18] Jaap De Hoop Scheffer, Press Conference, April 19, 2007.

[19] Bucharest Summit Declaration, published by the Heads of State of the participating governments at the NATO meeting on April 3, 2008, Press release (2008), 49.

defense lies within the scope of a large and visible response to counter threats. We recognize that the substantial contribution by the United States to install a midrange antimissile defense in Europe will bring protection to the Allies against long range ballistic missiles."[20] But opinions have remained very reticent. The majority of Europeans are opposed (notably 71 percent of Germans), although approximately half (49 percent) of Americans are in favor of missile defense.[21] The subject has taken on a new dimension since August 2008 as a result of the Georgian crisis. The Polish government confirmed its willingness to acquire a site of interceptors, and signed an agreement with the United States that confirmed its intention to construct this site, but on the condition that the defenses be effective, and at an affordable cost. In addition, it is specified that the timetable for its development be in accordance with the threat; also said, the approach is meant to be pragmatic and not ideological.

The Future of Nuclear Arms

Many factors will complicate the issue of nuclear politics in the coming years; it will be an important element of transatlantic debate.

The revision of NATO's Strategic Concept, that will be decided on at a summit in 2009 will be the occasion to reopen the question of an American nuclear presence in Europe. The member nations of the Atlantic alliance will want to more actively pursue success at the next conference that examines the Nuclear Non-Proliferation Treaty (NPT), which will take place in spring 2010—and will hopefully be more meaningful than the preceding conference in 2005, which has already proved to be a complete failure. In addition, it is found that, for technical reasons (replacement of aging carrier aircrafts), the "host countries" of American nuclear weapons will have to make decisions in 2010-2020 regarding the maintenance or dissolution of their air capabilities to transport nuclear arms.[22] Finally, it is toward 2012 that the first ele-

---

[20] Bucharest Summit Declaration, published by the Heads of State of the participating governments at the NATO meeting on April 3, 2008, Press release (2008), 49.

[21] Harris Interactive Survey for France 24 and *The International Herald Tribune*, March 28, 2008.

[22] According to open sources, five non-nuclear countries have acquired American nuclear arms: Germany, Belgium, Italy, the Netherlands, and Turkey. The United Kingdom has them as well, for a long time, nuclear arms intended for American bombers; but the only recent source, says these arms have been retired. See Hans Kristensen, "U.S. Nuclear Weapons Withdrawn from the United Kingdom," FAS Strategic Security Blog, Federation of American Scientists, June 26, 2008.

ments of a NATO antimissile defense system could become deployed. It hardly makes sense to doubt that the question "can NATO protect nuclear arms and defense missiles at the same time?" will be asked.

The transatlantic debate that addresses this question will be complex, and will not necessarily be approved by Europe in favor of or against the vantage point of the United States.

The United States currently affirms their full subscription to the objective of a "world free of nuclear weapons." Such an evolution is positively appreciated by the majority of NATO governments—even if certain among them find it less than favorable. Similarly, the probable ratification of the Comprehensive Test Ban Treaty (CTBT) will certainly be applauded by all. Finally, Mr. Obama claims to wish a continuation of the reduction of America's nuclear arsenal, and this position has not been affected by the recent thawing of relations with Russia.

But the strongest gesture by the United States in this domain indicates a true fault in the Atlantic alliance. The retreat of American arms from Europe or the adoption of a politics of "first non-employment" of nuclear arms (conceived under the Obama presidency, numerous experts close to him are favorable to this opinion) would indeed be perceived negatively by the countries that are the most proximate to Russia (Poland, the Baltics), and likewise Turkey.

Ankara, although its strategic relationship with the United States has become complex, is questioning the value of NATO's security guarantee.[23] The advance of the Iranian nuclear program worried Turkey. Turks are 57 percent worried about an Iranian nuclear program, opposed to, for example, 21 percent of the French.[24] If the American "umbrella" would appear to have retreated in the eyes of Turkey, the proposal of a Turkish national nuclear program would not be possible.[25]

---

[23] Not less than 70 percent of Turks consider the United States as an "enemy." 24-Nation Pew Global Attitudes Survey, The Pew Global Attitudes Project, June 12, 2008.

[24] 47-Nation Pew Global Attitudes Survey, The Pew Global Attitudes Project, June 27, 2007.

[25] Actually, Turkey is starting a civil nuclear program, but has not installed the necessary facilities to create nuclear materials. Turkey already has, at this point, an installation for enriching uranium and a dedicated plutonium engine. The production of fissile material in installations of this type implies a retreat from NPT. A Turkish national nuclear option will not be conceivable unless three conditions are met: a sever crisis of confidence between Ankara and Washington, a collapse of NPT, and finally pessimism toward the chances of Turkey ever entering the European Union. It indeed seems inconceivable that the Union would accept them with a new nuclear power.

Perspectives for the Next Four Years

As one can see, it would be unreasonable to believe that the next American presidential term will be a new European-American honeymoon.

It is hardly doubted that the first months of the next administration will lend themselves favorably to a revival of European-American strategic cooperation. The probable closing of Guantanamo prison camp, the announcement of the closing alone, even the departure of combat forces from Iraq, the pursuit of nuclear reduction and the possible ratification of the Comprehensive Test Ban Treaty—all these events should facilitate transatlantic cooperation in the years 2009-2010, as underscored by the 60th Anniversary of NATO Summit and the announcement of the French return to the integrated command structure.

The arrival of Barack Obama to the White House, in spite of the fact that he was the preferential candidate of Europeans, has not resolved transatlantic tensions. The demand for larger military support in Afghanistan did not meet the approval of all European nations. It is the same for certain problems not mentioned above, like the issue of NATO enlargement to include Ukraine and Georgia, where American demand is much stronger than European demand. Finally, the maintenance of the military option against Iran will continue to make the majority of European governments and public opinion uncomfortable.

Also, the diplomatic positions announced by Barack Obama on Iran—with whom he envisions a direct dialog, with only a minimum of conditions—could obstruct the policy of certain European governments.

In addition, even if Congress stays in Democratic hands, there will not be a sufficient Senate majority to ratify some of the treaties that Europeans have assigned a particular importance (Test Ban Treaty, Convention on Landmines, Treaty Establishing the International Criminal Court, etc.)

Finally, Europeans sometimes tend to forget that certain traits that are the most frequently associated with American politics will remain consistent under Obama despite the departure of Bush. For example, this is the case with the United States' willingness to act unilaterally, Washington's mistrust of treaties that bind American freedom of decision-making, its preference for a national prerogative at the detriment of international norms, support for Israeli politics, or the lobbying in favor of a rapid accession for Turkey into the EU.

This is why it is important to approach this new phase of transatlantic strategic relations with realism, and not with excessive optimism.

The Franco-American Dimension

In this context, the Franco-American relationship could constitute an anchoring point for transatlantic relations. It indicates an extraordinarily cooperative phase on strategic questions. This is certainly not the first time the two countries knew such a "honeymoon," but what started in May 2007 appears to be particularly durable.

France intends to return to its central place in the "Western family," as indicated by the expression of affection for the United States by Sarkozy and his advisors. This decision is currently justified by the fact that in a time of transition to an "era of relative power," it is necessary for France to more clearly affirm its essential values and interests.[26]

Certainly, reintegration into NATO's military structure caused debate in French political circles, but the opposition did not choose to go to battle. It is true that, contrary to what one would expect, the Atlantic alliance remains popular in France (55 percent of French support its maintenance... against 54 percent of Americans).[27] In addition, the clear support and openness of the Bush administration for the development of European defense, which appeared during the election of Mr. Sarkozy—a policy that seems the "opposite" of a French return to the integrated structure of NATO—satisfied French diplomats.

The Middle East

Undoubtedly on questions relative to close relations—and to the Middle East—the convergence of views and Franco-American cooperation is the most visible. The entrance of Sarkozy, accompanied by declarations of agreement toward Israel, and the voyage of Minister for

---

[26] Nicolas Sarkozy, Speech by the President of the Republic, 16th Conference of Ambassadors, August 26, 2008.

[27] Harris Interactive Survey for France 24 and *The International Herald Tribune*, March 29, 2008.

Foreign Affairs Bernard Kouchner to Iraq (August 2007), inaugurated a new atmosphere in Franco-American debates on these questions.

If the French decision to initiate a dialogue with Syria has caused frowns to fade in Washington, the United States itself has addressed this policy by inviting Damascus to participate in the Annapolis Conference (November 2007). As a result, the United States and France are engaging as co-partners in the future of direct negotiations between Syria and Israel. In addition, on Lebanon, the United States and France have been cooperating since 2004, and continue to research together methods of guaranteeing the independence of the country.[28]

For example, the intelligence services of the two countries maintain a good working relationship in the domain of counter-terrorism (a relationship that has hardly been affected by the rift in bilateral relations from 2001-2008). The persistence of the jihadist threat from the Middle East and North Africa (France is particularly interested in Al-Qaeda's actions in the Maghreb region) makes the pursuit of cooperation particularly important.

Iran

In connection with Iran, the term "alignment" with the United States was sometimes employed to qualify the French position since 2007. However, the positions of the two administrations have already been largely convergent for the last two or three years; the language used by the President of the Republic is already as strong as that of its American counterpart. Both have stated that it would be "unacceptable" for Iran to acquire nuclear weapons. Sarkozy and Kouchner have again reiterated the theme of "alternative catastrophes" (an Iranian bomb or the bombardment of Iran), a theme that was evoked for the first time by John McCain.[29] Certain choices for Obama could potentially cause tensions between Paris and Washington. Until he was a candidate, Barack Obama had decided in favor of a diplomacy excluding traditional restrictions employed when engaging Iran (self-defeating

---

[28] See Joint press conference with George W. Bush, President of the United States of America, Palais de l'Élysée, June 14, 2008.

[29] Nicolas Sarkozy, Speech by the President of the Republic, 16th Conference of Ambassadors, August 27, 2008.

preconditions).[30] However France, like its European partners, insists on respecting the formal suspension of talks with Iran until certain conditions are met. Obama additionally insists, as previously stated, on the fact that the military option must remain a possible choice—an option that France will not support without a UN mandate.

Nuclear Power

Questions in the politics of nuclear power, under the Bush administration, were a strong point of consensus between the United States and France. Paris' traditional conservatism is this domain was well matched to the concerns of the American administration. But this consensus could be weaker under the new administration. Barack Obama clearly supports, in the discourse on this issue, the goals of a "nuclear free world." This new insistence on nuclear disarmament that originated as an intellectual movement in America in January 2007, made Paris uncomfortable.[31] On the other hand, the eventual ratification in the United States Senate of a Comprehensive Test Ban Treaty would be applauded by Paris. Barack Obama is engaged in the promotion of this ratification and the creation of a bipartisan consensus for its approval; France will encourage the new American President to rapidly move in this direction, notably on the passing of the Comprehensive Test Ban Treaty by spring 2010.

In addition, France will certainly recapture the American demand for cooperation in the domain of "reducing the nuclear threat," announced as an absolute priority of the administration to combat the risks of nuclear terrorism. The United States boasts a unique experience in this domain (from its history with the ex-Soviet Union) and as an active participant in the G8 initiative toward disarmament in Kananaskis in 2002.

Antimissile Defense

The installation of a defensive anti-missile site in Europe is not popular with the French (58 percent are against it), but the issue rarely

---

[30] Barack Obama, Investigation of the American-Israel Public Affairs Committee, June 4, 2008.

[31] George P. Shultz, William J. Perry, Henry A. Kissinger, Sam Nunn, "A World Free of Nuclear Weapons," *The Wall Street Journal*, January 4, 2007.

received press, and Paris has adopted an attitude of measured support for this initiative.[32] It has been stated, that Barak Obama is not opposed to the installation of this site, but he refuses to deploy it hastily and supports the condition that the system must demonstrate its efficiency. Obama does not want to incite new divisions in Europe. It is doubted that this theme will be a major subject of debate between France and the United States in the future, Paris will prefer to avoid focus on the second line of this question — the opposite of the case during the years 1999-2000, when France opposed the American project for *National Missile Defense*, because of the fear of a reinvigorated armament. In addition, the systems of antimissile defense will probably be affected by the likely spending cuts that will need to be made to the American defense budget.

Russia

On relations with Russia, France has adopted a prudent attitude that will guarantee an absence of major divergence with the Obama administration. However, this issue may create pressure on the Allies to accelerate the accession process for Georgia and Ukraine to NATO: France does not favor this, although it does not totally reject it, at this stage, the completion of the Membership Action Plan (MAP) by the two nations will have to be the first stage of the accession process.

On the other hand, France does not have any problem with adhering to the idea of a new weight to Article V of the Washington Treaty, for the new allies that are threatened by a resurgent Russia. In fact, at the same time for non-NATO members, France has always insisted on the fact that collective defense was and will continue to be the first mission of the Atlantic alliance.

Afghanistan

Finally, allied engagement in Afghanistan is part of the few problems that could cause tension between the two countries. Indeed, since spring 2008, with the decision to reinforce the presence of the French in Afghanistan, announced at the Bucharest Summit, French engage-

---

[32] Harris Interactive Survey for France 24 and *The International Herald Tribune*, March 28, 2008.

ment in this country has become a theme of domestic politics. (At the time of the debate in the National Assembly, the Socialist party submitted a vote of no confidence.) Although this has not altered French engagement, President Sarkozy is trying to convince the allies of the need to revise the transatlantic strategy at the Bucharest Summit. But the domestic political situation has changed with the ambush on August 18, 2008 that cost the lives of ten soldiers. In addition, because of constitutional reform, Parliament has already committed to prolonging external military operations, which render more tribute to the context of domestic politics.

However, the majority of the French are already opposed to continued national engagement in Afghanistan.[33] And Parliament itself is today divided, with more supporters than opposition. There is not any doubt that France will stay engaged in Afghanistan. Sarkozy employs terms of engagement that for example would please George Bush, signified by the decision to slowly reinforce the French contingent; it was raised to 2,800 men from 2,008.[34] In addition, he decided that in spring 2009 French troops would be sent to aid in the formation of an Afghan army, and that France would augment its civil aid to the country. It will be undoubtedly difficult for Sarkozy to do more without causing a serious problem with his political supporters.

In short, if Franco-American relations in the strategic domain are positive today, many questions could cause tensions between Paris and Washington in the next four years: NATO operations in Afghanistan; the Iranian nuclear crisis; and engagement; and an increased engagement by the United States for a "nuclear free world."[35]

---

[33] 62 percent according to an inquiry BVA/Orange/L'Express executed from 12-13 September 2008. Cited in Jean-Dominique Merchet, "The Afghanistan Debate in Parliament," *Libération*, 22 September 2008.

[34] *"What is the alternative? A military retreat would cause the return of the Taliban and Al-Qaida, and without doubt the destabilization of Pakistan. It is not conceivable. It is clear: France, a permanent member of the Security Council, will assume its responsibilities. She will not yield to terrorists. She will fight them, everywhere they are found, with the conviction of the Afghan people, supported by its Allies, to end barbarism and bring progressivism."* (Speech by the President of the Republic, 16th Conference of Ambassadors, Wednesday August 27, 2008.)

[35] One also has to consider probable tensions in relation to issues with the defense industry, the democratic camp that is showing itself to be more and more drawn to protectionism. This question is not treated here since it is a commercial issues rather than a strategic problem.

Paradoxically, although the entire world celebrated the election of Obama, the Franco-American relationship on strategic questions could be a little tenser in the next four years than they were in the last two. And the absence of good personal relations between the two Presidents will not contribute to mitigating the tensions and eventual disagreements. Let us recall in this respect that relations between the two countries are sufficiently volatile, suggesting that forecasts in this realm should be made with caution. Let us remember, indeed, that relations were very good after the election of Jacques Chirac in 1995, but resumed their contentiousness under the same French President seven years later.

Chapter Four

Euro-Atlantic Security Relations and U.S.-French Cooperation

Leo Michel

As the world has become less divided, it has become more intercon-nected. And we've seen events move faster than our ability to control them—a global economy in crisis, a changing climate, the persistent dangers of old conflicts, new threats and the spread of catastrophic weapons. None of these challenges can be solved quickly or easily. But all of them demand that we listen to one another and work together; that we focus on our common interests, not on occasional differences; and that we reaffirm our shared values, which are stronger than any force that could drive us apart. That is the work that we must carry on. That is the work that I have come to Europe to begin.

—President Barack Obama in Prague, April 5, 2009.[1]

Four months after President Obama's inauguration and in the wake of his visit to Europe, officials and commentators on both sides of the Atlantic have praised his tone in dealing with *le Vieux Continent*. But savvy Americans and Europeans are also wondering when the "honeymoon" will end.

It is easy to understand why. During this same period, numerous developments have underscored the difficulties of formulating and sustaining effective transatlantic responses to challenges mentioned by the American President. Just a few examples:

- Russia—after flexing its military, energy, political and intelligence services' muscles in what President Medvedev termed its "regions of privileged interest"—remains camped in neighboring Georgia, having effectively redrawn, perhaps indefinitely, the borders of a U.S. partner and aspirant for NATO membership.

---

[1] Speech accessible at: http://www.whitehouse.gov/the_press_office/Remarks-By-President-Barack-Obama-In-Prague-As-Delivered/.

- In Afghanistan, a mix of Taliban, al-Qaeda, and other insurgent forces are demonstrating their rising ambition and improved coordination, prompting the United States to increase its military engagement there as part of a new strategy to "disrupt, dismantle, and defeat al Qaeda and its safe havens in Pakistan."

- Meanwhile, the Pakistani government's apparent willingness to cede effective control over parts of its territory to armed Islamic militants recently led Secretary of State Hillary Clinton to warn that "Pakistan poses a mortal threat to the security and safety of Americans and the world."

- Elsewhere in the "arc of crisis," Iran continues to defy efforts to end its suspected nuclear weapons-related activities; Iraq (despite successful provincial elections and improved security conditions) remains violence-prone; and the Middle East Peace Process appears frozen while simmering tensions between Israel, the Arabs, and Hamas-controlled Gaza threaten to boil over with little or no warning.

- Against this somber security background (which omits *inter alia* humanitarian crises in Darfur, Somalia, Zimbabwe and the Democratic Republic of Congo), the United States and its G-20 partners face the world's most serious economic crisis since the Great Depression, forcing Washington and European capitals to launch national stimulus plans of dizzying proportions and to work together to reform the world's financial systems.

Compounding these current challenges are more tectonic shifts. Last year, Francis Fukayama—whose 1989 essay "The End of History?" held that "liberal ideas had conclusively triumphed at the end of the Cold War"—acknowledged the reality of Fareed Zakaria's "post-American" world wherein "America's unimpeded influence will decline."[2] For their part, leading French strategists already had foreseen a long-term redistribution of global power and influence away from the problematic *hyperpuissance*. The French *White Book on Defense and National Security*, published in June 2008, cautioned against underestimating American dynamism, but predicted three dominant trends over the next 15 years: a relatively diminished U.S. capacity to shape

[2] Francis Fukayama, "They Can Only Go So Far," *The Washington Post*, August 24, 2008; and Fareed Zakaria, "The Rise of the Rest," *Newsweek*, May 12, 2008.

global events, due in part to the rising influence of China and a more assertive Russia; a shift in American focus from Europe toward pressing crises in the Middle East and Asia; and, albeit less certain, a more inward focus among part of the American population.

Exactly how the relatively new Obama Administration will fare in its efforts to tackle these problems and trends, not to mention future surprises, remains to be seen. Nevertheless, it is safe to assume that the United States and France will be obliged to work together to advance common and/or parallel interests where they exist, while limiting the fallout of diverging priorities and/or policies when they inevitably arise. Here, then, are some of the key strategic questions they will face, particularly in the area of transatlantic defense and security cooperation, and a few suggestions on where they might work bilaterally to reinforce broader Euro-Atlantic partnership.

NATO Under Strain

NATO, backed by strong U.S. military and political commitments to the Alliance, has been the primary guarantor of Europe's defense from armed attack since 1949. With the end of the Cold War, NATO assumed new roles: building defense and security partnerships with new democracies in Central and Eastern Europe that prepared many for Alliance membership; offering dialogue and cooperation on political-military issues to Russia, Ukraine, and other states of the former Soviet Union; and leading complex military operations in the Balkans and Afghanistan. Throughout its six decades, NATO also has performed the vital job of promoting intra-European as well as transatlantic collaboration regarding threat assessments, political-military strategy, defense planning, equipment standards and interoperability, and training and exercises.

Most Europeans want to preserve robust political-military links through NATO that are reinforced by various basing, information-sharing, and other bilateral ties to the United States. Yet NATO's "uni-polar moment" has passed. This is due, in large measure, to two overarching trends. First, with memories of the Cold War fading, many Europeans no longer view the most pressing threats to their security, or the tools needed to address them, as predominantly military. Second, while public opinion polls indicate a modest recovery in positive European views of the United States since the Iraq-related nadir of 2003-4, Europeans arguably remain less confident than a decade ago that U.S. interests, strategy, and policies closely match their own.[3] Their confidence in American military competence and standards of treatment for captured extremists—sensitive points at a time of combined military operations—also has been shaken.

Europeans are not alone in questioning previous assumptions. Over the past year, intense discussions on NATO's future have proliferated within Washington's influential "think tank" community, where non-government experts—including retired top diplomats and military officers—rub shoulders with serving government officials. That reassessments of NATO have taken place is not unusual or necessarily alarming. After all, for decades the transatlantic dialogue has been punctuated by tensions. Suffice it to recall the debates over Germany's rearmament and the Suez affair in the 1950s; France's withdrawal from NATO military structures in the 1960s; differing approaches to détente in the 1970s; deployment of intermediate nuclear forces in the 1980s; and NATO's interventions in the Balkan wars during the 1990s. Ultimately, the Alliance proved to be strong and resilient because its members did not allow their differences ever to rival, in scope or in depth, their shared interests and values. But fewer American experts are confident these days that the past will be prologue. Instead, they are increasingly worried that the Alliance might not adapt quickly enough to the changed security environment.

The Challenge of Afghanistan

For many Americans, NATO's solidarity and effectiveness will be decided in the caldron of Afghanistan, where European Allies and Partners contribute approximately 28,000 of the nearly 59,000 troops (including nearly 26,000 Americans) in the International Security Assistance Force (ISAF.)[4] European and American leaders broadly

---

[3] See, for example, European Views of U.S. Leadership in World Affairs, in "Transatlantic Trends 2008", a study of European attitudes by the German Marshall Fund of the United States, available at: http://www.transatlantictrends.org/trends/doc/2008_English_Key.pdf.

[4] Source: NATO figures as of April 2009. NATO Ally Canada and Australia (not a NATO member) provide 2,830 troops and 1,090 troops, respectively. Some 10,000 additional U.S. military serve in Afghanistan under Operation Enduring Freedom's Combined Joint Task Force 101. Since late 2008, all U.S. forces in Afghanistan report to ISAF's Commander, U.S. General David McKiernan.

agree that if Afghanistan were to become a failed state, terrorist networks would re-establish themselves there, posing an increased threat to the European and American homeland. But whereas American public support for the Afghanistan mission remains strong, the European public's support for the ISAF effort is wavering.

European Allies and Partners have promised to increase their ISAF contingents by a total of approximately 5,000 soldiers in the run-up to the Afghan presidential election this August, but further reinforcements are unlikely. Indeed, some Allies have announced plans to scale down or terminate their ISAF role over the next two years, especially in southern Afghanistan where, contrary to initial expectations, combat missions frequently have overshadowed peacekeeping and reconstruction tasks.

NATO's difficulty in meeting ISAF's force requirements extends beyond troop levels. Some Allies continue to invoke "caveats" that restrict how and where their nation's forces can be employed by the ISAF commander. Most European government and military leaders understand the inherent dangers of a "two-tier" NATO. Still, certain important ISAF contributors would face serious domestic opposition if their governments were to propose shifting their focus from the relatively stable northern and western regions to higher-risk operations in the south and east. Indeed, among some Allied publics, the aversion to seeing their "peacekeeping" troops attack opposition forces is almost as strong as their reaction to casualties among their own contingents.

In addition, the costs associated with ISAF are taking a heavy toll on several European troop contributor nations. Under standard NATO practice, nations must absorb the lion's share of expenses associated with their participation in operations. This is a particular disincentive to Allies who have the political will to sustain or increase troop contributions in the most demanding missions but lack sufficient budget resources to do so. However, several Allies resist suggestions to increase NATO's common funding for operations or to acquire more collective assets. Some seem unwilling to improve capabilities, fearing they might be called upon to use them. Others, faced with low and relatively stagnant defense budgets, probably worry that greater NATO common funding would come at the expense of their national programs.

Afghanistan also raises hard questions about NATO's role in long-term stabilization missions. The "comprehensive" and "regional" approach agreed at NATO's 2008 Bucharest Summit and updated at its recent Strasbourg-Kehl Summit aims to join international civilian and military assistance to the Afghan government to: recruit, train and equip capable security forces; develop the economy; improve governance and rule of law; and tackle the narcotics problem. Europeans, however, have not taken a common approach regarding their militaries' engagement in reconstruction, counter-narcotics and other non-traditional roles. Moreover, their ability and/or willingness to provide civilian experts to assist in building Afghan development and governance capacity—either through national programs or under European Union (EU) auspices—has disappointed many in Washington. For their part, some European officials privately worry that United States intends to steer NATO to build its own civilian capabilities for use alongside the military in stabilization operations—a move those officials fear would duplicate and undermine efforts by the United Nations, EU and other international actors.

U.S. frustrations with the European Allies have been growing for some time now. Last December, an unnamed U.S. military officer voiced the prevailing sentiment, commenting: "There are those (in Washington) who would say, 'Kick NATO to the curb—let's get it done.' But NATO is the reality in Afghanistan, and we need [the Allies] to be successful."[5] The United States has strong incentives to try to strengthen the Alliance's commitment in Afghanistan rather than revert to a "coalition of the willing" approach (as once favored by many in the Bush Administration.) After all, without underestimating the aforementioned challenges in Afghanistan, the ability of the Allies to sustain and even increase their ISAF commitments over recent years testifies to the value of Alliance structures for consultations, planning, decision-making, capabilities development, and mutual support in difficult operations.

Yet the questions are legion. Will the U.S. decision to increase its forces in Afghanistan by at least 21,000 over the coming year succeed in stabilizing the security situation? Will the troop increase reinforce perceptions in Europe that this is an "American war," thereby strengthening pressures within some Allied countries to draw down their military participation? And if the Europeans' military commitments to

---

[5] "Officials work toward best Afghanistan strategy," American Forces Press Service, December 12, 2008.

ISAF begin to erode, will they really follow through on promises to contribute more to non-military aspects of the "comprehensive approach"—for example, in police training and mentoring, funding for an expanded Afghan National Army, finding sustainable development alternatives to the opium poppy culture, and capacity-building for struggling civilian ministries and regional governments?[6]

The recent swift deterioration of the situation in Pakistan could heighten intra-Alliance strains. Following the Strasbourg-Kehl Summit, NATO's engagement with Pakistan might be enhanced through increased military-to-military coordination, improved high-level engagement, and expanded training for Pakistani officers in Europe. Unlike the United States, however, none of the European Allies seems prepared to contemplate any form of military involvement inside Pakistan, despite the acknowledged problems posed to ISAF by the insurgent sanctuaries. (In fact, some worry that increased U.S. military pressure against insurgent sanctuaries in Pakistan will further inflame regional tensions.) Moreover, with a few notable exceptions, most Europeans are not prepared to expand their relatively limited political, economic, and development ties with Pakistan. While perhaps understandable, this hesitation carries the risk that many Europeans might blame Washington if the Pakistani state were to collapse.

The Russia Factor

NATO's deepening engagement in Afghanistan has raised questions in several European capitals regarding overall Alliance strategy and priorities. Specifically, Russia's behavior in Georgia and elsewhere in the former Soviet space—in combination with menacing statements of intent, such as Medvedev's vow "to protect of the life and dignity of (Russian) citizens, wherever they are"—has refocused attention on NATO's collective defense role.

Sorting out relations with Russia will be a major strategic challenge for the United States and Europe.[7] Those who believe, as does Secretary of Defense Robert Gates, that "the Georgia incursion will, over time, be

---

[6] NATO's "comprehensive approach" strategy toward Afghanistan is described in the Bucharest NATO Summit declaration, accessible at: http://www.nato.int/docu/pr/2008/p08-052e.html.

[7] See also Celeste Wallander's chapter focusing on Russia.

recognized as a Pyrrhic victory at best and a costly strategic overreach" are likely to be proven right—provided Europe and the United States can forge a new consensus on policy toward Russia "as durable and agile as containment was in the Cold War."[8] For now, however, there is no common assessment between Americans and Europeans on Russian motivations or strategy; nor, indeed, is there internal agreement within the United States or Europe. Some see Russian actions in Georgia as largely a "one off" action—an opportunistic show of force to destabilize a weak but impetuous neighbor and prevent further NATO enlargement. Others divine a more deliberate and comprehensive Russian strategy that extends from discouraging investments in southern energy pipelines to intimidating Ukraine and other neighbors where Russia's "near abroad" live and, over time, to sowing disagreement within Europe and division between Europe and the United States.

To be sure, Russia does not represent the type of existential threat posed by Soviet Union, and no Allied government openly advocates a return to Cold War models of territorial defense. But many officials fret that NATO might lose its *raison d'être* of collective defense—and vital parliamentary and public support—by focusing on expeditionary missions that seem disconnected from threats that are closer to home.

Hence, some Allies—including, not surprisingly, those closest to Russia—are looking for reassurance of NATO's ability to back up its Article 5 (collective defense) commitments; specifically, they want to see an updated Alliance threat assessment and increased NATO contingency planning and exercises relevant to deterring and, if necessary, responding to any future military intimidation by Russia. Other Allies who are further removed from Russia seem less anxious about near-term military threats to their security and might see such steps as needlessly provocative. Among the latter group, certain countries also are keenly aware of their significant dependence on Russian energy supplies.

The United States must be responsive to the concerns of both those groups, but it has additional strategic concerns, as well. These include securing Russian cooperation on non-proliferation issues—for example, Iran and North Korea—and, where possible, on fighting terrorism and extremism. (For example, Russian cooperation is important to

---

[8] Gates speech to Oxford Analytica, UK, September 19, 2008; and Jim Hoagland, *Washington Post*, August 17, 2008.

establish a reliable and flexible logistics network to support operations in Afghanistan, given recent developments in Pakistan and Kyrgyzstan.) In addition, Washington and Moscow will soon begin formal negotiations on a replacement for the 1991 Strategic Arms Reduction Treaty, or START-1, before it expires in December 2009. Finding a judicious balance between cooperation with Russia where possible and resisting its bad behavior when necessary is no doubt sound strategy—but this does not guarantee agreement within the Alliance on tactics to apply to specific circumstances.

EU Seeking to Define Its Role

As non-traditional threats to European security gain more prominence, NATO will increasingly need to share the stage with the EU as a security provider. Nearly a decade after its formal launch, the notion once floated by a few European officials that European Security and Defense Policy (ESDP) would develop into a "counterweight" to American influence in Europe and beyond has been largely discredited. But while EU governments frequently differ over the priorities and resources they are prepared to assign to ESDP, even the most "Atlanticist" among them have come to accept it as a legitimate pillar of the EU's global influence.

Hence, ESDP is now firmly rooted within the EU's legal and institutional frameworks, with civilian and military decision-making structures that roughly parallel NATO's (albeit with much smaller staffs.) It is supported by a European Security Strategy document, promulgated in 2003 and updated during last year's French EU Presidency, that sets out a broad vision of threats, policy objectives, and general guidelines for collective action. The record of nearly two dozen ESDP military and civilian operations undertaken to date—all of which have taken place under UN Security Council resolutions approved by the United States—is generally positive, although most of these have been modest in size, of limited duration, and relatively low-risk.

Within the EU, debate regarding ESDP largely revolves around the appropriate balance between military and civilian tools for crisis management and how best to generate additional military and civilian capabilities. ESDP's initial focus was largely military, relatively ambitious, and heavily influenced by "lessons learned" from Europe's inability to handle on its own the Balkan conflicts of the 1990s. With its 1999 "Helsinki Headline Goal," for example, the EU pledged to develop, by 2003, the ability to deploy, within 60 days, some 50,000-60,000 military personnel to crisis spots thousand of miles from Europe, and to sustain them for at least one year for tasks ranging from humanitarian operations to peacekeeping and separating warring parties.

Faced with substantial capabilities shortfalls, however, the EU shifted its attention in 2004 to creating some 15 "battle groups" of reinforced battalions (approximately 1500 troops); two such formations serve in alert status for six month periods and, in theory, would be able to deploy within ten days of an EU decision and sustain operations for up to 120 days. (To date, the EU has not operationally deployed a battle group, but European officials cite Africa as the most likely venue for any future use.)

Some EU governments—France, in particular—continue to prioritize the development of "autonomous" military aspects within ESDP. They favor the periodic conduct of increasingly challenging "autonomous" military operations—that is, operations without NATO assistance through the 2004 "Berlin Plus" arrangements—to demonstrate ESDP's practical value and build habits of intra-European cooperation. They also seek to encourage higher defense spending and a more robust European defense industrial base through joint research, development, pooling and acquisition programs managed by the EU's European Defense Agency (EDA).

That said, in recent years the limits of such efforts have become clearer. As for military operations, the first ESDP maritime mission—a naval and marine patrol aircraft effort to protect vessels off the coast of Somalia—has been underway since last December. The EU force is part of an international anti-piracy effort, including ships from NATO and partners such as China and India. The EU force has captured some pirates and no doubt deterred some attacks, but EU officials acknowledge that the real solution lies with restoring a measure of security and stability ashore under Somali government authorities—a potentially huge task that the EU (like other international organizations) would prefer to avoid. Elsewhere in Africa, the recently completed year-long ESDP mission in Chad and the Central African Republic was arguably successful in meeting its limited mandate, but the effort—heavily promoted and supported by the French—proved more difficult and expensive than anticipated. Indeed, operational fatigue among EU member states no doubt was an important reason why the French EU Presidency turned down the UN Secretary General's plea last fall to dispatch another EU force to reinforce some 17,000 UN "blue helmets" in eastern Democratic Republic of Congo. Meanwhile, as several EU member states who are also NATO Allies are finding it hard to sustain or marginally increase their contributions to ISAF, they likely will be reluctant to take on additional EU military commitments.

Similarly, the EU's disappointing record in capability development is catalogued in a July 2008 report by former EDA Chief Executive Nick Witney.[9] As he points out in the report's summary:

> Nearly two decades after the end of the Cold War, most European armies are still geared towards all-out warfare on the inner-German border rather than keeping the peace in Chad, or supporting security and development in Afghanistan. European defense resources still pay for a total of 10,000 tanks, 2,500 combat aircraft, and nearly two million men and women in uniform—more than half a million more than the U.S. hyper-power. Yet 70 percent of Europe's land forces are simply unable to operate outside national territory, and transport aircraft, communications, surveillance drones and helicopters (not to mention policemen and experts in civil administration) remain in chronically short supply. This failure to modernize means that much of the €200 billion that Europe spends on defense each year is simply wasted.

That European defense budgets remain stubbornly low in turn limits the possibilities of significant new investments in EDA programs, especially if such programs are seen by some members as duplicative of NATO efforts or biased to advantage another member's defense industry.

Increasingly, many EU members look toward their civilian capabilities—including police mentors and experts in justice, corrections, customs, and public administration—as key tools to be deployed in

---

[9] Nick Witney, "Re-energizing Europe's Security and Defence Policy," European Council of Foreign Relations, July 29, 2008, available at www.ecfr.eu/content/entry/european_ security_and_defence_policy.

crisis prevention or crisis management operations. These capabilities can be used in conjunction with EU financial and developmental assistance and, in theory, alongside an ESDP military component.[10] But as Witney suggests, recruiting, training, and deploying qualified civilians for these purposes has not been easy, especially in cases where the EU finds itself, in effect, competing with its member governments.

European governments will remain careful to protect national prerogatives in the conduct of foreign, defense, and security policies. As Witney points out, no EU member "will allow itself to be forced to enter conflict, or to change how it spends its defense budget, by 'Brussels'—whether an EU institution, or a majority of its partners."[11] However, the past decade's trend toward greater coordination within the EU is unlikely to be reversed and might even be accelerated if the EU can overcome the setback to ratification of the Lisbon Treaty occasioned by its defeat in the June 2008 Irish referendum.

Toward a More Flexible Defense and Security Architecture

From an American perspective, the strains evident within NATO and the EU, coupled with mounting international demands for their services, strengthen the argument for closer cooperation between the two organizations. Fortunately, most Europeans no longer contest this point. The operational demands on Europe's relatively limited pool of deployable forces, combined with projected low levels of defense spending, serve as a powerful brake on impulses within either organization to expand existing missions or create new and potentially duplicative structures. And when it comes to doctrine, training, and equipment interoperability, European military commanders understand that inconsistent practices within NATO and the EU would increase the inherent risk of military operations.

There are some tentative signs that NATO-EU cooperation might work better in practice than in theory. In Kosovo, the 14,000-strong NATO Kosovo Force works well with the EU's rule of law mission (EULEX) of some 1900 international police officers, judges, prosecu-

---

[10] To date, however, most ESDP military operations have not been accompanied by a significant EU civilian component, in part because such operations have been relatively short.

[11] Ibid.

tors and customs officials. (Under an October 2008 agreement, some 100 U.S. police trainers and mentors work within EULEX—an unprecedented and promising arrangement.) In Afghanistan, some 200 European police trainers and mentors (EUPOL) complement the much larger U.S.-led training coalition, and the EU recently agreed to double EUPOL's size. Pragmatic cooperation in these two operational theaters is constrained, however, by the absence of formal agreements between the two organizations and their limited dialogue at senior levels in Brussels.

A number of steps would help remedy this situation, including: more frequent and better structured meetings between NATO's North Atlantic Council and the EU's Political and Security Committee, permitting the two organizations to have a real consultation on questions of mutual interest beyond their cooperation in Bosnia; a NATO-EU joint planning mechanism focusing on a more systematic development and application of the "comprehensive approach" as opposed to the *ad hoc* and improvised arrangements seen in Afghanistan and Kosovo; and improved practical cooperation on capabilities development. Of note, Washington reacted positively to the French suggestion in 2008 to create an informal high-level group—including the NATO Secretary General and EU High Representative, the chairmen of the respective military committees, the principal military operational commanders of each organization, and representation from the European Commission—to meet at the early stages of discussion and planning of a new operation.[12]

While some European security experts have suggested a formal "division of labor" between the two organizations, this is unlikely for the foreseeable future. EU governments would find it as difficult to agree on a fixed "ceiling" for ESDP military operations—in terms of types of missions, force composition and capabilities, and deployment regions—as NATO would find it difficult to set a "floor" for its involvement. Similarly, neither organization will or should be expected

---

[12] In a statement issued at the conclusion of the EU Summit on December 11-12, 2008, the European Council "reaffirms the goal of strengthening the strategic partnership between the EU and NATO in order to address current needs, in a spirit of mutual enhancement and respect for their decision-making autonomy. To this end, it backs the setting up of an informal EU-NATO high-level group to improve cooperation between the two organisations on the ground in a pragmatic manner." To date, no action seems to have been taken to actually set up this group.

to subordinate its decision-making autonomy to the other; nor should either seek to systematically inject itself into missions under consideration or conducted by the other.

That said, certain notional differences in each organization's level of ambition already exist. For example, none of the EU members is prepared to engage in large-scale combat operations without the United States, although only the United Kingdom has been willing to state this explicitly. On the other hand, many Europeans believe the EU has a comparative advantage, thanks to its array of developmental and civil-military tools, in crisis prevention and crisis management in parts of Africa. As evidenced by high-level U.S. statements in early 2008, Washington does not dispute that point.[13]

The long-term objective of the NATO-EU relationship should be to ensure transparency, avoid contradictions in their respective approaches and, more positively, to develop new capabilities and bring "added value" to conflict prevention and crisis management. By adapting the military's concept of "interoperability" (for example, in doctrine, equipment standards, and operational practices) to the NATO-EU relationship, the two would have better tools in place to cooperate if and when a political decision is made to do so, making their coordinated effort more timely and successful.

At the same time, Euro-Atlantic security cooperation cannot be limited to the NATO-EU relationship. Globalization has blurred the dividing lines between "external" and "internal" (or "homeland") security. The latter problems of greatest concern to European publics fall under the purview of EU structures that have little or no connection to ESDP instruments; among these are illegal immigration, so-called homegrown extremism, transnational crime, critical infrastructure protection, and environmental security. And while such problems can have serious impact on transatlantic relations, many have limited, if any, direct connection to NATO's core competencies. Not surprisingly, many European and American analysts therefore advocate a more developed U.S.-EU relationship.

---

[13] See, for example, the statement of the U.S. Permanent Representative to NATO, Ambassador Victoria Nuland, in Paris in February, 2008, accessible at: http://nato.usmission. gov/Article.asp?ID=21A35613-E9D6-431D-9FD5-36FDD1389EB0.

In fact, an important and growing bilateral U.S.-EU relationship already exists in areas such as law enforcement, counterterrorism, counter-narcotics, transportation security, and non-proliferation. Other areas of cooperation, such as the delivery of humanitarian assistance, should be developed. And since the EU increasingly serves as the Europeans' venue for strategic discussions and decision-making on security issues that do not involve military commitments—for example, dealing with Iranian nuclear ambitions—the United States will want to ensure that its views are taken into account before EU policies are set in stone. This, in turn, will periodically pose a difficult policy question for Washington: where does it draw the line between discussing strategic questions at NATO, where there is a U.S. seat at the table, and at the EU, where the United States and "Europe" sit across the table from one another?

Another looming policy question involves the suggestions by some European officials and analysts that, given political blockages in NATO-EU relations, the United States and EU should enlarge their bilateral ties to include defense matters. There are, however, inherent limits to bilateral U.S.-EU relations insofar as defense matters are concerned. One factor is the obvious mismatch of memberships: while 21 of 27 EU members are also NATO Allies, the United States will not put at risk its military and political relationships with the non-EU Allies (Canada, Turkey, Norway and Iceland) by circumventing NATO councils to consult, plan, and operate with the other Allies who are EU members. A second factor, albeit less obvious, is equally important: NATO's strength and effectiveness derive, in large part, from the multinational (and multi-layered) nature of its civilian and military structures where Americans, Canadians and Europeans sit side by side to discuss, plan, decide, and implement a broad range of political and military tasks. A bilateral U.S.-EU relationship would not include those structures—it is hard to see how they could be compatible with the EU's emphasis on "autonomous" decision making and capabilities—and there is no obvious rationale for duplicating them as they already exist in NATO. A third factor goes to the heart of ESDP's *raison d'être*: if the EU is serious about creating new capabilities that it is able to use "autonomously," it makes little sense to encourage an EU dependency upon U.S. assets and capabilities to accomplish EU operations. This need not close the door to some modest and case-by-case coordination—for example, between the U.S. Africa Command and

Europeans who provide concrete and valuable assistance in Africa — but this would not warrant dedicating U.S. military assets to work regularly with the EU (as is the case with NATO.)

Ideas for the U.S.-French Cooperation Agenda

Washington and Paris share important interests in strengthening transatlantic defense and security ties encompassing NATO, the NATO-EU relationship, and bilateral cooperation.

In terms of operations, the French and American militaries cooperate today—most importantly, in Afghanistan and Kosovo—and no doubt will cooperate in the future in diverse missions, theaters, and frameworks inside and outside Europe. To do so, they must be able to communicate, exchange information, train together, offer mutual support, and, when needed, fight side by side. Extensive cooperation between the United States and France also exists in an array of non-military areas important to the national security of both countries, including intelligence, counterterrorism, and emergency response to civil disasters.[14]

Moreover, French defense and national security policies and capabilities influence, directly or indirectly, those of other key Allies and Partners. Political or tactical differences between Washington and Paris periodically surface in NATO, NATO-EU relations, and operational theaters, as they do, on occasion, with other European countries. Yet overall U.S. interests are better served by a more capable, responsive, and cooperative French defense and national security structure that encourages fellow Europeans, through deeds as well as rhetoric, to increase their military capabilities and make them available for NATO as well as EU missions. It would be an overstatement to suggest that the U.S. route to a more capable European partner goes through Paris, notwithstanding the latter's clout in the EU. But it would be wrong to underestimate the benefits of greater convergence between American and French approaches to defense issues.

In Afghanistan, for example, the increased French participation in combat operations since mid-2008 helps to reinforce Alliance solidarity

---

[14] See, for example, Dana Priest, "Help from France Key in Covert Operations," *The Washington Post*, July 3, 2005.

in what will likely be an operation that continues for several more years. In this context, it is noteworthy that in an October 2008 interview, France's Chief of the Defense Staff, General Jean-Louis Georgelin, declared:

> I regret that in an international coalition, some nations place caveats that significantly restrict the ISAF commander's freedom of action. Imagine that a temporary but extremely strong action is needed in southern Afghanistan while the situation in the north is rather calm. Yet the force commander does not have the latitude to swing forces from the north to help those in the south because of a caveat. There is no total freedom of action, therefore; caveats are akin to a poison of international organizations.[15]

U.S. commanders no doubt share General Georgelin's sentiment, which is all the more interesting in view of his example and the fact that France's close partner, Germany, commands the bulk of forces in the north.

As for NATO, the United States has welcomed the increased French participation announced by President Sarkozy at the Strasbourg-Kehl Summit for several reasons. An influx of talented French officers and non-commissioned officers into the integrated military structure will bring additional command and planning skills that stand to improve NATO's performance in its increasingly demanding and complex operations. And while French officials have not publicly floated their vision of a new headquarters and command structure, they appear sympathetic to a realignment and reduction of NATO military staffs, opening the possibility of close cooperation with the United States and other Allies anxious to improve efficiency and equitably redistribute responsibilities and burdens. On the civilian side, as part of the Defense Planning Committee, France can help improve the coherence of the force planning process through which NATO identifies its military requirements to meet the overall level of ambition set by its political leadership.

---

[15] Interview on Public Sénat, Jeu de dames, le 8 octobre 2008. Accessible at: http://www.defense.gouv.fr/ema/commandement/le_chef_d_etat_major/interventions/interviews/08_10_08_interview_du_cema_sur_public_senat.

Contrary to the opinion expressed by some French politicians and commentators in the run-up to President Sarkozy's decision, these are not merely symbolic moves or "concessions" to the United States. Every step taken by France to improve the cohesiveness and efficiency of NATO will, sooner or later, benefit ESDP. This is true in terms of capability development, interoperability (in doctrine, training, and equipment), and performance in actual operations. Keeping in mind the large overlap between NATO and EU memberships and the fact that each of those members has one set of forces and one defense budget, NATO is not simply a means for France to cooperate with the United States; it also serves as a vital mechanism for intra-European cooperation. When he unveiled the *White Book on Defense and National Security*, President Sarkozy was correct to admonish his compatriots: "(NATO) is of course an alliance between Europeans and the United States. But it also is—and it is not said enough—an alliance among the Europeans, themselves."[16]

France's decision to "take its full place" in the Alliance should facilitate an expanded strategic dialogue with the United States on the subjects of nuclear deterrence in the 21st century, its relationship to nonproliferation, and missile defense. In his companion essay, Bruno Tertrais wonders if the Obama Administration intends to emphasize the goal of a "nuclear weapons-free world," suggesting that this would clash with France's "traditional conservatism" on nuclear matters. At first blush, his concerns might appear to be justified by the American President's speech in Prague, where he declared: "(T)he United States will take concrete steps towards a world without nuclear weapons. To put an end to Cold War thinking, we will reduce the role of nuclear weapons in our national security strategy, and urge others to do the same." But it is important here to note the President's next sentence: "Make no mistake: As long as these weapons exist, the United States will maintain a safe, secure and effective arsenal to deter any adversary, and guarantee that defense to our allies—including the Czech Republic."[17]

In my view, a good indicator of the new Administration's approach in this area is found in the remarks of Secretary of Defense Robert

[16] "Speech of the President of the Republic on Defense and National Security", June 17, 2008, available at: http://www.elysee.fr/documents/index.php?mode=cview&press_id=1568&cat_id=7&lang=fr.

[17] op. cit., Prague speech.

Gates, the only Bush cabinet official whom President Obama asked to stay in office. As Secretary Gates stated in October 2008:

> There is no way to ignore efforts by rogue states such as North Korea and Iran to develop and deploy nuclear weapons, or Russian or Chinese strategic modernization programs. As long as other states have or seek nuclear weapons—and potentially can threaten us, our allies, and friends—then we must have a deterrent capacity that makes it clear that challenging the United States in the nuclear arena—or with other weapons of mass destruction—could result in an overwhelming, catastrophic response.... Try as we might, and hope as we will, the power of nuclear weapons and their strategic impact is a genie that cannot be put back in the bottle—at least for a very long time. While we have a long-term goal of abolishing nuclear weapons once and for all, given the world in which we live, we have to be realistic about that proposition.[18]

This is a sensitive topic to be sure, but the United States and France—along with the United Kingdom—will want to avoid becoming progressively isolated (or nearly so) within the transatlantic community on the need to preserve credible and safe nuclear forces. Should French officials conclude that European political support for nuclear deterrence is under serious strain, they might reconsider the merits of joining a NATO body where nuclear issues can be discussed. This might involve renaming and restructuring the existing Nuclear Planning Group (one of the NATO committees that France has not joined to date) to include a remit on counter-proliferation and missile defense policy—areas where France has keen interests despite some differences with the United States. In this way, France could help sustain a European consensus on the need for a nuclear component as part of a broader NATO deterrence and defense strategy.

In principle, this could be done without crossing any of the *White Book's* "red lines" regarding respect for French nuclear "independence" and "autonomy." In this regard, UK policy on nuclear issues might be

---

[18] Speech to Carnegie Endowment for International Peace, October 28, 2008. Accessible at: http://www.defenselink.mil/speeches/speech.aspx?speechid=1305.

a relevant model for France, as it underscores that "decision-making and use of the [nuclear] system remains entirely sovereign to the UK [and] only the Prime Minister can authorize the use of the UK's nuclear deterrent, even if the missiles are to be fired as part of a NATO response."[19]

The Russian question is another area where the U.S.-French strategic dialogue could play a helpful role in developing a stronger Euro-Atlantic consensus. Here, Washington's attitude regarding the French EU Presidency's role in the Russian-Georgian conflict might prove instructive. Despite some tactical differences between Paris and Washington, the latter agreed, in effect, to step aside without stepping back as President Sarkozy brokered a cease-fire between the parties and mobilized EU support for a civilian monitoring mission in Georgia. True, it proved to be an imperfect arrangement, but had the United States tried to lead those efforts, the results might have been even more problematic. At the same time, the quick dispatch of American humanitarian and civilian reconstruction aid to Georgia, as well as the high-level U.S. visits to Tbilisi following President Sarkozy's conclusion of the cease-fire, kept the United States in the picture in a way that projected overall solidarity, not competition, with the EU's efforts. This might not be a perfect model for transatlantic cooperation in the future, but it seems like a step in the right direction.

In all such endeavors, the tone of U.S.-French relations will be of vital importance. Many Americans ritualistically refer to U.S. "leadership" of the Alliance, thinking this concept is essentially an accurate reflection of objective facts—in particular, the real disparities in military capabilities between the United States and our Allies. But for many in France—and no doubt elsewhere in Europe, as well—the notion of "American leadership" has sometimes been received as an outdated Cold War notion or, worse, an irritating expression of dominance by an imperfect *hyperpuissance*. It is worth considering whether Washington might best achieve its long-term goals with fewer rhetorical invocations of its "leadership" role and more of what it has often (but not always) done so well: consulting, listening, and acting resolutely—always in a spirit of true partnership—as a catalyst, builder,

---

[19] Ministry of Defence, "The Future of the United Kingdom's Nuclear Deterrent: Defence White Paper 2006," available at www.mod.uk/DefenceInternet/AboutDefence/CorporatePublications/PolicyStrategyandPlanning/HeFutureOfTheUnitedKingdomsNuclearDeterrentDefenceWhitePaper2006cm6994.htm.

and ultimate defender of a democratic and prosperous transatlantic community. This would oblige Americans, from time to time, to leave more space and accord more confidence to our European Allies. As evidenced by their statements in Europe, President Obama and his top national security advisors seem inclined to do just that.

At the same time, French leaders will need to be realistic about their national capabilities and vision of European defense. They also will need to continue—within the Alliance, the EU and in bilateral relations with the United States—to work for pragmatic and "win-win" solutions even when these might not be the most politically flashy. In the long run, an approach that genuinely reflects President Sarkozy's appreciation that NATO is "an alliance among the Europeans, themselves" will strengthen France's partnerships and stature within Europe as well as its relations with the United States.

Part Three:

Regional Perspectives

Chapter Five

American Priorities for a Transatlantic Strategy on Russia

Celeste A. Wallander

President Barack Obama faces high expectations and deep concerns for U.S.-Russia relations. Relations between the two countries had reached their worst point since the end of the Cold War—perhaps even worse than during its last years, when the Soviet Union (under Gorbachev) and U.S. (under first Reagan and then Bush I) were successfully negotiating a broad and deep array of agreements in the security/defense, political, economic, and social/cultural spheres. Not only did arms control stall, it stood at risk of being unraveled: existing strategic arms treaties are set to expire, Russia threatens to withdraw from the Intermediate-range Nuclear Forces Treaty, it has suspended its membership in the Conventional Forces in Europe Treaty, and there is a small but dangerous risk that the U.S. and Russia may be embarking on a new arms race in anti-ballistic missile systems, the avoidance of which was one of the most important security achievements during the Cold War.

On the political security front, the Russian leadership has made clear that it views one of America's central global security commitments—NATO—as incompatible with and even a threat to Russia's national interests in Eurasia. The Russian leadership posits a U.S. policy of encirclement that is meant to contain, weaken and perhaps dismember the Russian Federation. The American expert and policy community, for its part, is increasingly of the view that Russian security objectives are at least the neutralization—and perhaps even the subordination—of its neighbors in the former Russian/Soviet empire. Quiet concern that Russia has been using political, economic, energy, and cyber instruments to subvert the independence and sovereignty of its neighbors escalated to sharp warnings with Russia's willingness to use force in August 2008—invading and occupying the neighboring country Georgia. It may be that these are just a series of misperceptions and insecurities, but there is increasingly reason to believe that

Russia and the U.S. are locked into incompatible security conceptions of Eurasia: an American view that sees security in terms of Euro-Atlantic and global integration, and a Russian view based upon a zone of its "privileged interests" in which neighbors are not free to choose their security, political, economic, or other relationships.

In the economic sphere, there is a somewhat less dire situation, but only because the thinness bordering upon emptiness of U.S.-Russia economic relations means that there is little of direct conflict of interest. The U.S. has still failed to graduate Russia from the Jackson-Vanik Amendment despite the fact that the reason for that trade restriction (Soviet restrictions on Jewish emigrants) is entirely moot, and in face of the absurdity that the U.S. executive branch has to issue a waiver of the restriction each year. Russia is still not a member of the World Trade Organization. Both of these restrictions rankle the Russian leadership (and public) who view them not without reason as gratuitous political sanctions from a country that preaches non-political economic and business theories.

The conflict between Russia and Georgia did not cause this sad state of affairs: the war and the ongoing dispute about its resolution exemplify how deep is the problem and illustrate the danger of continuing to take the challenge of Russia seriously. Getting the relationship back on a pragmatic cooperative path will be critical to the future security of Europe, since the worsening U.S.-Russia relationship has complicated European policies with Russia as well. An effective U.S. policy on Russia must have a transatlantic dimension, and an effective European relationship with Russia is more likely if the U.S. and Russia are working to solve security, political, and economic problems.

The Russia We Face

Russia is not a democracy: its elections are not free and fair, political campaigns are not contested by political parties with competing or alternative policies, and the counting and conduct on election day is not monitored by credible or professional independent domestic or international observers. Why the Russia leadership is unwilling to allow free and fair elections is far from clear: with approval ratings in the 70-80 percent range it is highly likely that Vladimir Putin (and the political party he now leads, United Russia) would win even in genuine elections. Perhaps the Russian leadership knows something that we do not, but in any event the election process in Russia does not leave the results to chance.

The lack of a professional independent media capable of reporting on government deeds or misdeeds makes it essentially impossible for Russian citizens to hold their government accountable for policy and performance. Even without direct control and ownership, the atmosphere of intimidation is such that even independently-minded journalists tend to practice self-censorship. Editors and reporters understand that there are stories and issues that should not be pursued, and that if they are they could be consequences. While this does not stop all independent reporting, it has severely limited it.

Limits on contestation extend beyond political competitors or the media. Business and civil society are allowed to exist and operate, as long as they neither challenge political authorities nor make demands of them. Demonstrations by pensioners in early 2005 against the monetization of social benefits were striking precisely because they turned out to be so unusual. Business interests are active in Russian politics, but not as independent actors making claims on the leaders who represent them or seek their support. Instead, it is business interests and successful individuals who depend for their assets on their adherence to the rules and demands of political leaders, leading some to characterize Russia as a corporatist state.[1]

Yet while Russia is not a democracy (nor even the nascent pluralism of the 1990s) it is also not the totalitarian political system of the high Soviet era, nor the repressive authoritarianism of the declining Soviet system of the 1970s and 1980s. Russia is an authoritarian system, but one that functions through corruption and selective threat rather than ideology or comprehensive political control. The government is not accountable to its citizens/society, and it rules by sharing power, privileges, and wealth within a narrow elite. This is a fundamentally brittle political system, not a strong state. Its legitimacy lies in performance in the simplest sense: as long as Russian citizens have a basic sense of stability and rising prosperity, they are willing to tolerate the leadership and its corruption.

---

[1] Leon Aron, "21st Century Sultanate," *The American* (online), November 14, 2008 (http://www.american.com/archive/2008/november-december-magazine/21st-century-sultanate).

The other key to legitimacy of the system is the danger of foreign enemies. The Putin (and now Putin-Medvedev) leadership justifies the measures it has taken to limit accountability and political freedoms by claiming external enemies seek to threaten Russia from abroad, and weaken it from within. To justify close controls on NGOs, for example, the Russian government cited external funding and foreign agents seeking to challenge the Russian political system. To justify its strategic sectors law, which restricts foreign ownership of substantial swaths of the Russian economy, the Putin leadership warned that Russia's wealth should not be owned or controlled by foreigners who would wield that ownership to weaken the country. Russia's political leadership seeks participation in the international economy and in international political structures for the access to wealth and political influence that the global world affords, but meaningful integration would undermine the role of the Russian state in business by bringing in multiple players not subject to Russian political power and operating by western business practices. To justify the leading role of the state at home, the Russian leadership warns of a hostile world abroad.[2]

The shift toward a corporatist authoritarian state has rested on Russia's high-yield but vulnerable economy. On the high-yield side, Russia's economy has been one of the most successful in the world over the past decade. Its growth rates have ranged from 6 to 8 percent annually, and GDP per capita has quadrupled. Russians increasingly travel, have been able to buy their own homes and cars, and live a modern, European, middle class life. Until this fall, Russia held reserves foreign currency reserves of $600 billion, ran a current account surplus, had government budgets with 5 percent and higher surpluses for several years, and enjoyed a stock market that was among the highest performing among emerging economies

However, the Russian economy has been fundamentally dependent on energy production and exports for these impressive numbers. World Bank figures showed real growth in other sectors of the Russian economy over the past few years, notably in construction and in consumer sectors, but the funds that fueled this growth originated in huge flows of income from the energy sector. Russia's massive reserves have helped

[2] Celeste A. Wallander, "Russian Transimperialism and its Implications" in *Global Powers in the 21st Century: Strategies and Relations*, edited by Alexander T.J. Lennon and Amanda Kozlowski (Cambridge MA: The MIT Press, 2008), pp. 217-235.

it to manage the effects of the global financial crisis, but those effects have nonetheless been severe and have driven economic decline in 2009. The Russian government has already spent more than $190 billion of its reserves to provide liquidity to its strapped banks and to defend the value of the ruble. The stock market has lost two-thirds of its value since August—*Gazprom* is now worth 25 percent its July 2008 peak value. The World Bank has downgraded its estimate for Russian growth to 4.5 percent in 2009, and predicts a further growth in capital flight as investors seek more secure markets. Unemployment is rising as major growth industries—particularly construction—have seen a virtual halt because of liquidity problems as well as a decline in consumption.[3]

Russia is of course far from alone in facing serious consequences from the global financial crisis and potential global recession. However, because of its resource export dependence, failure to diversify the economy, dependence on foreign investment (that is to say, debt) in recent years, and the large backlog of inadequate infrastructure investment, Russia is more vulnerable than many other major economies to the difficult economic times of the next year or two.

The World Bank reports that this is all the more reason for the Russian government to get serious about diversification, encouraging foreign investment, and moving quickly to WTO membership and other liberalizing policies that that Russia can gain the benefits of global integration and institutionalizing liberal policies that will form the basis for future growth. The Russian leadership may or may not ultimately heed this advice, but so far Prime Minister Putin and President Medvedev have tended to blame the international community in general and the United States in particular for the crisis.[4] It is unclear whether the Russian leadership will decide that it needs the U.S. and Europe more to manage the next difficult economic years, or whether it will attempt to isolate the country from global financial effects and increase state intervention.

Russia will have less wealth and a slowing economy at home, which may cause Russia's citizens to question their support for the current

---

[3] World Bank, "Russian Economic Report , no. 18" (Moscow: World Bank Russia Country Office, March 2009).

[4] See "Putin promises economic strength; blames crisis on U.S.," *International Herald Tribune*, November 20, 2008 (http://www.iht.com/articles/ap/2008/11/20/business/EU-Russia-Financial-Crisis.php).

leadership. If global recession leads to difficult times at home, the government may become less popular and have fewer resources to make the case that it is delivering. It is striking that Russian officials have insisted that the Russian ruble will not be devalued (this was a primary theme in Dmitri Medvedev's speech to the Council on Foreign Relations in Washington, D.C. in November 2008 during the G20 summit), and that the Russian Central Bank has expended nearly one-third of the country's reserves to defend its value. For Russians, the searing memory of the crash of the ruble, devaluation, and default in August 1998 made Yeltsin so unpopular. If the Putin-Medvedev leadership's legitimacy is tied to the value of the ruble, it may face devaluation as well.

The global economic situation coincides with a crucial period for Russia's future as Eurasia's largest energy producer. The World Bank reports that foreign investment in Russia's energy sector has already been declining as the Russian state has increased its control of that sector, and with the passing of Russia's strategic sector law limiting foreign investment. With Russian oil production growth now shrinking and Russia unable to meet its contract commitments for natural gas deliveries without its own purchases and re-deliveries of Central Asian natural gas, Russia's rule as Europe's major supplier of oil and natural gas is reaching a turning point. Either Russian investors themselves will have to begin to seriously develop new fields, or foreign investors will have to be allowed to make the massive and complicated investments necessary to develop new oil and gas fields. A weakened and more vulnerable Russian economy might be the motivation for the Putin-Medvedev leadership to re-think their short-term timeframe and increase Europe's ability to negotiate more effectively with a Russian energy sector less able to dictate terms.

Or, it might make Asia a real competitor for future energy development investment in Russia. In late October 2008, Russia and China signed an agreement by which China would lend $20-25 billion to Russian oil companies to assist in their debt repayment to western banks and investors. In exchange, Russia's Transneft would build a pipeline spur to China that the Russian government had until the agreement resisted, with guaranteed delivery of Russian oil from far eastern fields to China as repayment for the loan. Energy analysts have explained Russia's preference for energy relations with Europe in terms of their relatively low costs and high yields, based upon existing pipeline infrastructure and the relative ease of negotiating with individual European countries and companies. In contrast, to produce energy for China Russia will have to undertake massive investments in new pipelines and new field development, as well as negotiate with a single bargainer that has resisted paying high prices for natural gas. Partly as a result, China has turned to negotiating directly with Central Asia, and is nearing completion of an oil pipeline from Kazakhstan as well as agreement on a parallel gas pipeline that may extend also to Turkmenistan. The prospect of losing its monopoly position on Central Asian gas may force a re-structuring of Russia's energy policy—if Europe proves to be positioned to re-think its strategic energy relationship with Russia as well in light of shifting geopolitical dynamics and new constraints on the Russian economy.

By 2009, the Russian foreign policy built on these domestic components was one of confident assertion of power and privilege combined with resentment and multi-dimensional insecurity. Russia simultaneously sent strategic bombers and a naval task force to Venezuela, while claiming that a deployment of ten missile interceptors in Poland poses an existential threat to Russia's 2000+ strategic nuclear weapons. Russian foreign policy is strikingly different from that of two other rising global powers. China and India have nurtured foreign policies and relationships meant to create external space for each country's focus on internal development and growth. China seeks to reassure great powers, and particularly the United States, by pursuing a strategy of participation in international institutions and avoidance of confrontation. Similarly, India's foreign policy in an era of extraordinary growth has been one of avoiding challenge and bluster, avoiding confrontation and challenge, finding the space to grow.[5]

Russia's foreign policy, in contrast, has sought to challenge American power and the rules-based system of international institutions rooted in a combination of the post-World War II order and in the European Helsinki process that remains one of the enduring achievements of détente. Whereas the United States has now elected a new president whose success and leadership was based in large measure on his message that the American war in Iraq was a mistake and that he would lead the U.S. back to the path of a responsible leadership that exercises power through institutions and in cooperation's with friends and allies,

[5] Fareed Zakaria, *The Post-American World* (New York: W.W. Norton, 2008), chapters 4 and 5.

Russia's leadership defiantly refuses to acknowledge that it violated international law by invading Georgia, unilaterally recognizing Abkhazia and South Ossetia, and failing to live up to the ceasefire commitments Russia's leadership made to the EU (represented by France) in August and September. That the unilateral exercise of military power and disregard for reasonable leadership and responsibility undermined America's ability to achieve security objectives seems to have been lost on Russia's leaders.

So dealing with this Russia is not going to be simple. President Medvedev welcomed President-Elect Obama's election victory with a speech on November 5 threatening to deploy Russian short-range missiles in Europe (that is Kaliningrad)—not exactly a speech signaling Russia's willingness to step up to a new chapter in U.S.-Russia relations. All the more reason to begin the work immediately in 2009, and to have a meaningful and robust transatlantic strategy to begin to build the basis for effective problem-solving and building trust.

Interests and the Potential for an Effective Transatlantic Partnership on Russia

The list of American interests in Russia is relatively straightforward—and strikingly constant over time:

- The security of Russia's nuclear weapons, materials, and technologies

- Russia's constructive participation in Eurasian geopolitics, including restraint in conventional weapons deployments and sales

- The stability and sustainability of Russia's energy supply

- Russia's constructive participation in global economic and financial markets

- The evolution of Russian domestic politics toward a more stable, inclusive, and sustainable system.[6]

---

[6] Adapted from the excellent analysis by Eugene Rumer, "Mind the Gap: Russian Ambitions vs. Russian Reality," in *Strategic Asia: Challenges and Choices*, edited by Ashley J. Tellis, Mercy Kuo, and Andrew Marble (Washington, D.C.: The National Bureau of Asian Research, 2008), pp. 167-196, at p. 190.

While the priority ordering might be different for Europe, it should be apparent that there is nothing on this list that contradicts European interests in Russia. Transatlantic relations went serious wrong on many dimensions in the past eight years, and serious disagreements on Russia were among the most damaging and problematic areas of dispute within the transatlantic community. However, the problems were rooted in leadership choices and disagreements about strategy and priorities, not in these fundamental interests.

In addition to disagreements about policies, however, the U.S. and Europe (and Europeans among themselves) have been uncertain about Russia's commitment to common interests and Western integration. It was easier to have a constructive transatlantic policy when there seemed to be great clarity in Russia's commitment to integration. During the 1990s, Russian leaders seemed committed to the promise of democratic reform, free markets, and Western integration. Indeed, as Stephen Sestanovich demonstrates in a careful review of the first years of Putin's presidency, the potential for Russian-American cooperation was very great, and there was a series of successes and agreements. The Putin leadership did not view NATO as a hostile force, and succeeded in gaining a stronger role in joint deliberations on security problems that Russia and NATO saw a common interest in resolving. Despite disagreement with the Bush Administration's abrogation of the Anti-Ballistic Missile Treaty, Russia and the U.S. concluded a new strategic arms treaty in 2002, all of this contributing to constructive progress in Russian-European relations.[7]

The United States and Russia have many mutual interests, and Russia has the potential to become a constructive stakeholder in the international system. But Russia's choices through 2008 risk the potential for security and prosperity based upon cooperation and international rule of law. Where do we go from here? A new American strategy to pursue our security, political, and economic interests with Russia should be based on four key components:

1. establish the terms for security in Eurasia (most fundamentally, reaffirming independence and sovereignty of all the post-Soviet states)

---

[7] Stephen Sestanovich, "What has Moscow Done? Rebuilding U.S.-Russian Relations," *Foreign Affairs*, vol. 87, number 6 (November/December 2008), pp. 12-28.

2. anchor Russia in Europe in close coordination with European allies

3. develop a common transatlantic approach to the politics of energy in Eurasia

4. launch effective bilateral and multilateral arms control negotiations.

These goals have to be achieved in a manner consistent with our values, at a time when values/interests priorities are a complicating issue in transatlantic relations. Integrating Russia and the other countries of the former Soviet Union into a peaceful, prosperous and rules-based community of nations remains an American strategic interest. Russia still has the potential to emerge as an important partner and a contributor to solving some of our most urgent global and regional challenges. The U.S. has a strong interest in signing a commercial nuclear agreement with Russia and in seeing Russia as a member of the World Trade Organization (WTO) and the OECD. But to enjoy the benefits of membership, Russia must accept in full the terms and responsibilities. Closer cooperation between NATO and a democratic Russia, including membership, should remain a long-term strategic goal.

The U.S. should not preclude the potential for Russia to choose to reengage with the international community responsibly and credibly, and the progress made toward agreements for the U.S.-Russia summit in July 2009 suggests that this strategic pragmatic approach has some promise. This is Russia's choice to make, but it America's responsibility to continue to make possible. Although the challenge is much greater than it appeared two decades ago, the right strategy is a recommitment to meaningful and effective Russian integration. And only a transatlantic approach can make such a strategy effective.

Chapter Six

Dealing with Russia: Challenges for France, the European Union, and the United States

Maxime Lefebvre

Abstract

Since the end of the Cold War, Russia and the West have not suc-ceeded in constructing a solid partnership. The period of relative cooperation in the 1990s was followed by a period of increasing con-frontation; the Georgian crisis was a low point in the relationship.

We must consider the lessons of the Georgian conflict and recon-struct a united transatlantic policy regarding Russia. The new U.S. Administration needs to take a fresh look at the issue, and at the same time intra-European differences need to be overcome.

Three major reflections can help us advance in this endeavor: upholding a strategy of cooperation rather than of confrontation; con-solidating a European security architecture; and including Russia in the treatment of international concerns.

A Lesson to Consider: The Inability of the West and Russia to Construct a Solid Partnership Since the End of the Cold War

The Failure of Western Offers Towards a Weakened Russia

Between the fall of the Berlin Wall in November 1989 and the implosion of the USSR in December 1991, the entire Soviet empire collapsed. Western policies at the time combined optimism and pru-dence. A facile belief prevailed in the West that democracy would suc-ceed communism in a developing "new world order." Yet through a realist approach, it strove primarily to handle the threat of instability by targeting the removal of Russian troops in former "people's democracies" (achieved in 1994); the denuclearization of non-Russian republics of the former USSR (1992-1996); and nuclear and conventional disarmament agreements (the treaty on conventional weapons in Europe in 1990, revised in 1992; the treaties START I and START II in 1991 and 1993, respectively), which seemed to herald a new security order in Europe.

Russia, however, did not resign itself easily to the contraction of its state boundaries or its strategic borders. Russia did abandon foreign territories (the Baltic states, Ukraine, Kazakhstan, etc) in which large Russian-speaking populations live—approximately 20 million "red feet." This situation will not end, like in Yugoslavia, in bloody military confrontations. But Russia maintains strategic influence outside of its borders. In 1992-1994, it imposed itself as a mediator in the conflicts that exploded in Moldova (Transniestria), in Georgia (Abkhazia and South Ossetia), and between Armenia and Azerbaijan (Nagorno-Karabakh). Russia maintains a military presence in Sevastopol, sharing the waters of the Black Sea with Ukraine, and it has encouraged autonomy for Crimea. Khrushchev attached Crimea to Ukraine in 1954 (for the occasion of the 300th anniversary of the union between Russia and Ukraine), although it is inhabited primarily by Russian speakers. Russia also attempts to promote itself as an organizing force in the post-Soviet space, which it calls its "near abroad" (the creation of the Community of Independent States in December 1991 and the Collective Security Treaty Organization in 1992; the project of a customs union with Belarus and Kazakhstan in 1995).

The years that followed saw the clash of two opposing trends of unequal force in Europe. On one side, the European Union (1993) then NATO (1994) launched policies of enlargement, aiming to consolidate the democratic stabilization of eastern Europe. On the other side, Russia maintained a privileged influence in the former USSR, but without succeeding in putting in place a model of effective integration. Westerners, without being turned from their objectives, tried to put in place a cooperative and trustworthy relationship with Moscow, despite the indignation caused by the first Chechnya War (1994-1996). The participation of Russia in the "Contact Group" on the Balkans strengthened pressure from the international community on the Serbs during the Bosnian war, which led the latter to accept the Dayton Peace of 1995. And the decision to enlarge NATO to include Poland, Hungary, and the Chechnya Republic in 1997 was accompanied by the conclusion of the "Founding Act" between NATO and Russia, which aimed to reassure Moscow and bring Russia into the fold of NATO policy.[1] Moreover, Russian troops participated with NATO peacekeeping forces in Bosnia. And the trust was reinforced by mutual declarations regarding the disarmament of nuclear missiles.

A first crisis nevertheless occurred with the Kosovo affair. Russia, weakened more and more by its post-communist transition (as evidenced in the great financial crisis of 1998) took Belgrade's side but was unable to affect the course of events, outside of its ability to block the UN Security Council. Westerners, convinced that they could only stop the new waves of ethnic cleansing under Milosevic by force, used NATO to declare war on Serbia, despite the absence of United Nations authorization. However, Russia resigned itself to rejoin the game to put an end to the conflict, in the capacity of the G-8 and of the Security Council (Resolution 1244), in going through a kind of compromise: In June 1999 Kosovo was extracted from the authority of Belgrade and put under the protection of the United Nations and NATO, but the territorial integrity of Yugoslavia (Serbia-Montenegro) was reaffirmed. Moreover, the explosion of the second Chechnya war, which lasted from 1999 to 2005, further worsened the climate between Moscow and the West.

The crisis of 1999 was overcome during the first years of the G.W. Bush Administration. The Bush administration claimed to have "read the soul of Putin in his eyes" and allied with Russia in the War on Terror. Moscow supported the American military intervention in Afghanistan and was not offended to see Americans installed in military bases in former Soviet territories in Central Asia. A NATO-Russia charter was concluded in 2002, even though NATO decided to enlarge by including seven new former-communist states (of which three were Baltic countries, who were annexed by the USSR and included important Russian minorities). But if the West offered Russia an advanced relationship characterized by partnership and cooperation, it would not go

---

[1] In this same year, 1997, the "partnership accord of cooperation" signed by the EU and Russia in 1994 came into force, which was due to begin after ten years, but automatically renewed from year to year.

as far as to offer Russia a potential membership that would give it a veto right. Trust has its limits.

2003-2008: Growing Confrontation

If NATO membership is seen by the West and by the eastern European states which aspire to it as a means through which to reinforce stability and democracy in Europe, it is perceived by Russia as a hostile operation aiming to isolate and narrow its sphere of influence. After the enlargement of 2002, NATO shared a long border with Russia and former USSR countries. The enlargement of NATO preceded and accompanied the enlargement of the European Union: the latter occurred effectively, May 2004, from 15 to 25 member states (and then to 27 in 2007).

This "bond towards the East" of "Euro-Atlantic" institutions narrowed the buffer zone with Russia, which from then on was reduced to Belarus, Ukraine, Moldova, and the three Caucasus countries. These three countries are covered by a "Neighborhood" policy launched by the European Union since 2003, which offered them, not membership, but a maximum rapprochement with the EU. And yet it is precisely in this buffer zone that the "color revolutions" occurred, which installed in Georgia (the 2003 "rose revolution") and in Ukraine (the 2004 "orange revolution") pro-Western regimes suspicious of Russia.

Moscow is hostile toward these changes. Perhaps the changes contribute to the authoritarian and nationalist tightening that is taking place there: President Putin, comfortably reelected in 2004, restored the authority of the Russian state (the "vertical power"), depended on "special services" (ex-KGB, of which he himself is heir) and on power structures to govern, brutally suppressed the Chechnyan revolt and the terrorist attacks (Moscow in 2002, Beslan in 2004), nationalized Russia's petroleum riches by expropriating the oligarchs, limited the liberty of the press and of NGOs, and has taken increasingly nationalist stances critical of the West. This return to order has been popular in Russia, as it has been seen as putting an end to the anarchic period of the Yeltsin years, and was accompanied by a veritable economic turnaround, facilitated more by an increase in the price of energy exports than by a true diversification of the economy.

The tension between the "West" (taken as a whole) and Russia did not develop all at once. In 2002-2003, while the Bush administration half-heartedly launched its war on Iraq in a fit of unilateralism, France and Germany were governed by leaders who had sympathy for a Russia under Putin's sway and were suspicious of the then new American leaders. The three countries—France, Germany, Russia—put aside their differences to attempt to prevent Washington from attacking Iraq. And since France was the one that opposed the attack the most overtly, it was to France that Condoleezza Rice, then National Security Advisor to President Bush, focused her ire after the victory against Iraq (her watchword was thus "pardon Russia, ignore Germany, punish France"). The force of the Paris-Berlin-Moscow axis is such that the European Union launched, in 2003, a Franco-German proposition, a negotiation of "four spaces" of EU-Russian cooperation (economic, internal security, external security, culture, education and research), which ended in 2005 with the devising of four leaves of road (beneath the label of concrete cooperation). This EU-Russia partnership, parallel to the NATO-Russian cooperation track, perhaps contributed to reassuring Russia regarding the enlargement of Western institutions, towards the East.

The situation changed, however, after 2005. The second term of President G.W. Bush opened with a revival of the transatlantic partnership under the banner of a crusade for liberty. Washington depended on anti-Russian sentiment in the "new Europe" (which had supported Washington without fail during the Iraqi crisis) to establish the schema for a united transatlantic partnership against a common enemy, indeed a common menace. Support for Ukraine and even more for Georgia became a credo for the tenants of this Washingtonian line, which one also finds in western Europe, including France at times, indeed even Germany. Even energy policies do not escape this schema: Washington pushes its energy diversification projects, which would allow it to protect Europe's Achilles' heel (its energy dependence on Russia), while allowing Washington direct access to the hydrocarbon resources of the Caspian (via pipelines crossing the Caucasus, extended notably by the Nabucco gas pipeline, which crosses the Balkans).

It would be an oversimplification to think that the "new Europe" was swayed by this policy. Switzerland has participated in it with increasing energy, despite never having been in NATO or in the Russian orbit. Poland played a dynamic role solely by placing its veto—between the end of 2006 and the spring of 2008 — on the launch of negotiations for a new framework agreement between the European Union and Russia, intended to succeed the agreement on partnership and cooperation. Poland and the Czech Republic are moreover the closest countries to Washington, such that they did not hesitate to brave Moscow's ire in receiving elements of American anti-missile shields within their borders. Lithuania has shown itself to be increasingly active in hardening EU policy toward Russia, and reinforcing its engagement on the borders of Georgia. Estonia and Lithuania are equally possessed of a keen sensitivity in relationships with Moscow. Nonetheless, countries such as Hungary, Slovakia, Bulgaria and Slovenia adopted a much more moderate strategy, allowing the renewal of their gas supply contracts.

These differences are likely explained by a gradation of feelings of vulnerability: the Czechs, the Poles, and the Balts were subjected much more strongly to former Soviet imperialism as well as to past Nazi imperialism. Their borders are, moreover, historically less secure (Czech and Polish territories were formerly inhabited by Germans; there is a strong minority Russian-speaking presence in the Baltic countries of today). As a result, it is not surprising that they have/feel more the need to rely on the guarantee of an international and European order, rather than merely an American order.

The Georgian Crisis: A Turning Point

The conflict in Georgia is less the manifestation of a new Russian imperialism than the angry and brutal reaction of a power that was pushed too hard into a corner. It is true that Russia did nothing to change the status quo in Georgia, which assured it two guarantees in the Caucus, and in particular on its small Georgian neighbor. But it is also true that Russian aggression was woken by the "rose revolution" and the "orange revolution" (which evoke memories, *mutatis mutandis*, of the "Cuban revolution" of 1959, which took place within an American sphere of influence), and even more by the increasingly asserted willingness of Georgian and Western leaders (the United States in particular, and its closest allies in the "New Europe") to force the reintegration of Abkhazia and of South Ossetia into Georgia. The recognition of the independence of Kosovo, which Moscow had clearly and publicly considered as a possible precedent for the settlement of other conflicts suspended in the former Soviet Union, along with the promise of NATO (April 2008), evidently played a role in the eventual integration of Georgia. Historians can debate extensively to what extent Georgia's decision to reconquer South Ossetia was a reaction to the increasingly menacing posture of Russia, and to what extent it was Russia who reacted to an increasingly bellicose Georgian position. In any case, the facts themselves are not in question; the Russian offensive against Georgia occurred the day after the Georgian military offensive in South Ossetia.

It is necessary to draw out all lessons from the Georgian conflict.

First lesson: Russian policy demonstrated that it continues to think as a nationalist state, in spheres-of-influence, zero-sum geopolitical terms. Russia has not gone as far as to reverse the regime of President Saakashvili, but it refused to abandon control of South Ossetia and Abkhazia. While wanting to conserve and consolidate its position, Russia shows itself unable to propose a relationhip of regional integration and of cooperation with the European Union, which would allow it to overcome conflict with its neighbors. Russia's proposal to amend the Helsinki Final Act (which has directed rules for a peaceful coexistence in Europe since 1975) seemed, moreover, to target more the consolidation of strategic positions than to open the way to true pan-European cooperation beneficial to all. This behavior poses a fundamental challenge to the West: can it influence Russia's perception and behavior, and if so, how?

Second lesson: Western policy. The Bush Administration, at the very least, showed itself to be imprudent in encouraging (or in not discouraging) President Saakashvili in his offensive posturing: the Bush administration's incapacity to come to the aid of its ally while the latter was invaded by the Russian army revealed that the emperor, as the saying goes, was not wearing any clothes. The European Union, in its own words, emphasized its preference for diplomacy, stability, soft power. The EU could have stopped the conflict through mediation, but did not avoid a consolidation of the on-the-ground Russian position, since the entirety of South Ossetia and Abkhazia escaped Georgian sovereignty. Lastly, NATO saw its credibility undermined, as its promise to Georgia regarding Georgian membership (in addition to Ukrainian membership), had the effect of kindling Russian aggression rather than reinforcing Georgian security.

Third lesson: regarding the questions surrounding "common neighbors" in our relationship with Russia. The August 2008 conflict created a *fait accompli* that will be difficult to reverse, while Russia recognized the independence of two new "states." At best one can anticipate a situation similar to that of Cyprus, which will be frozen for some time to come. In the worst case one can anticipate the multiplication of on-the-ground incidents in which European observers risk finding themselves involved, and which could lead to a resumption of hostilities. The options are limited and it must be decided, as much for the United States as for the Europeans, which is the most desirable. But other potential conflicts can degenerate in the post-Soviet space; for example in Transniestria, which Russia will not allow to reunify with Moldova without extracting a guarantee from the countries of a federal statute of neutrality; and in Ukraine, where important Russian-speaking minority populations inhabit one fifth of the total population. The Georgian conflict must remind us that, taking into account Russian positions in the region, all escalation scenarios risk ending in a tragic and counter-productive conflagration.

The Relationship with Russia: What Interests Are at Stake in the Transatlantic Partnership?

We must analyze points individually from the American point of view as well as the point of view of the European Union and its member states.

From the American Point of View

In considering the American point of view, we must ask ourselves what position Russia should occupy in the Obama Administration's global agenda.

Since the end of the Cold War, the world is no longer dominated by its relationship between two Great Powers. The United States has for some time still maintained a privileged partnership with Russia, notably in the realm of nuclear parity and disarmament agreements, but this relationship has steadily declined, while American strength became more and more apparent, and while other centers of power emerged (Europe, China, India, etc).

But even if the United States is no longer inclined to see in the Russo-American relationship a global partnership essential to global stability, the United States still needs Moscow in many projects: the management of its still-considerable nuclear arsenal, the struggle against proliferation, and all the global stakes for which a cooperation between the great powers remains indispensable (maintaining peace in the United Nations, the management of energy access, protecting the environment and combating global warming, etc). The Obama Administration justifiably began a dialogue with Russia emphasizing common subjects of interest (disarmament and non-proliferation, Iran, Afghanistan), rather than subjects known to raise tensions (Georgia, anti-missile defense, or human rights).

At the same time, for now Washington will likely stay the course regarding the fundamentals of its policy *vis-à-vis* Russia—essentials that are more less the same as those that guided its policy toward the former USSR; in particular a strong suspicion of this too-undemocratic power that dominates "Eurasia;" and a policy of containment, all the while consolidating Euro-Atlantic stability and security through NATO.

From the European Point of View

From the European point of view things are much more complex, as the last few years have shown the difficulty in defining a united policy with regards to Russia (as mentioned, for example, the vote put by Poland and then by Lithuania at the start of the negotiations of a new Russia-EU partnership agreement).

Schematically, we could consider that there are in fact two Russian policies in the European Union. A policy that constitutes, more or less, the "old Europe" (France, Germany, Italy, Spain, Benelux, Greece, Cyprus, Finland, etc.) and the "new Europe (including the United Kingdom and Sweden, but not necessarily all the new member states, as we saw earlier). An "old Europe" policy prioritizes economic interests and the problem of stability; a "new Europe" policy is eager to see in Russia a menace that must be confronted with a firm stance.

This division reflects, imperfectly, the traditional geopolitical opposition between maritime and continental countries. It particularly reflects the positioning of EU member states with respect to American

policy and its strategy of containment: the United Kingdom is traditionally attached to a strong transatlantic partnership; the "new
Europe" was the iron spear of the democratic crusade of the Bush
administration (along with Turkey, the RFA, Japan, and South Korea
during the Cold War, it was part of the *rimland* "land ring" on which
the American maritime power depended to contain Russia); Sweden,
since it is not a member of NATO, has a singularly difficult position
with regard to Russia, explained more by its history (the ancient Russo-
Swedish antagonism), its commitment to human rights and the environment, and by a true sense of moral superiority, to which it adds a
more temporary political factor.[2]

These classifications are imperfect and not static. Russian policy is
cause for debate within various countries: in Germany, for example,
the Left tends to be more pro-Russian (as we saw with the Schroeder
chancellery) and the CDU is more Atlanticist; in Poland, the departure of one of the Kaczynski brothers resulted in a softening of Warsaw's policy toward Russia. Nevertheless, the similarities are striking,
from the Italian Left to Right, or from Chirac to Sarkozy, who claimed
to be departing from the policy of his predecessor but who hastened to
establish a privileged position with Moscow. The desire for good relations with Moscow did not otherwise prevent a sincere attachment to a
solid and effective transatlantic partnership: Italian policy is consistent
on that point as well, and it is more marked in the Spanish and German
Right than the Left, while French preferences often ignore political
cleavages (there is a continuum from De Gaulle to Chirac in passing by
Mitterrand on the United States and Russia, and a certain Atlanticist
inflection on the part of Sarkozy, as the return to the NATO military
structure demonstrated).

Nevertheless, the Bush Administration was so polarizing that it
could only become deeper entrenched in its own position. What will
the Obama Administration do? It enjoys a favorably predisposed opinion in Europe, and its first initiatives (pressing the "reset" button in
relations with Russia, as the American Vice President Joe Biden
announced during the annual Munich security conference, the *Wehrkunde*) offer the opportunity to reconstruct a new and more effective

---

[2] The current Swedish government, and notably its foreign minister Carl Bildt, is clearly
more Atlanticist than the Social Democrats, which traditionally dominated this country.
The Social Democrats could return to power in the 2010 legislative elections.

policy with regards to Russia that will perhaps permit it to transcend prior disparities.

How to Construct a Renewed Transatlantic Agenda on Russia?

Three fundamental questions need to be addressed.

Will we Change Russia through Confrontation or Cooperation?

For certain, we can consider that Russia itself distanced itself from democratic tenets: that is what the defenders of a hard-line approach maintain, in clearing the West of all responsibility in the authoritarian hardening of Russia.

It is essential to begin a fair and balanced, rather than ideological analysis, of realities. Russia today, while it may claim to reflect deeply on the territorial integrity and independence of its immediate neighbors, is not the USSR of 1945-1948. It likely has neither the desire nor the means to launch an imperial project anew. Its economic situation is fragile (technologically backward, corrupt, dependent on primary export products and on several isolated economic sectors, such as armaments or space). Its demographic situation is still more fragile (it loses between 0.5 and 1 million residents per year, even though Putin was able to revive feelings of Russian nationality). Of course, if Russia becomes more menacing, the question of a deterrence strategy will again arise. This scenario cannot be completely excluded. But one must not assume or encourage such a view in order to avoid it becoming a self-fulfilling prophecy. The lesson of the Georgian conflict must be considered with this in mind; in wanting to force the issue, one plays the role of sorcerer's apprentice.

The question of democracy and human rights is difficult and will remain as such, as do the old debates regarding the appropriate role of morality in international politics. Russia is not the only problem-child with respect to this question. But in contrast to a vision of a despotic country that can never function otherwise, we can add a more optimistic vision (perhaps too naive?) of an authoritarian transition that was perhaps necessary in order to take control of a situation characterized by political and economic anarchy, but that tomorrow could result in a veritable process of economic, social, and political modernization. Do not the Russian youth of today have the desire to travel and to open themselves up, as do the Westerners of their generation? The liberalization of the visa regime is moreover one of the rare subjects on which the Russian authorities show themselves to be veritable beggars with respect to the European Union.

The choice between confrontation and cooperation must be considered. With Russia, keeping the playing field level by showing a strong arm from time to time is inevitable, and dialogue on the part of the European Union and of the United States does not have to be interpreted as a sign of weakness in the defense of our interests and our values. But confrontation is a risky strategy that could fuel the return of authoritarianism and nationalism, while dialogue, opening, and cooperation offer a perspective of progressive modernization of the economy, of society, and of the Russian elites. Some say that we will have a Russia that we deserve; in either case, it could be beneficial to not lock ourselves into a Manichean vision of partner/opponent, and to try to put it in its place, to understand it, to deepen dialogue, difficult as it may be. The United States and the European Union could try to together define the terms of such an engagement, with the condition of returning to a realistic and reasoned approach. And the European Union could begin by drawing inspiration from the American approach, by identifying subjects of mutual interest with Russia (for example, energy, cross-border cooperation, or cooperation in research) to reestablish a relationship characterized by trust and cooperation.

How to Reconstruct Security in Europe?

Today the European security architecture rests primarily on two pillars.

The OSCE is the legacy of the Helsinki conference (1973-1975). It potentially offers the legitimacy of a pan-European security framework, but its effectiveness is very limited at present. It mostly does electoral observation, which generates tension between Western democrats and countries distanced from democratic tenets (Russia, Belarus, Central Asia...). Today the OSCE still plays a role in issues regarding national minorities. Its arms control regime is in crisis, due to the disagreement regarding the location of Russian troops in "frozen conflicts," to the dispute over anti-missile shields, and to Russia's suspension of the CFE treaty.

NATO has played a growing role by significantly occupying the space left empty by the death of the Warsaw Pact, and by transforming itself into an organization charged with maintaining peace (initially in the Balkans, and since 2003 in Afghanistan, which is outside its traditional geographic location). NATO did not judge that Russia was a sufficiently reliable partner to merit the prospect of membership, which would give Russia paralyzing veto rights. But we must not be astonished then, *a contrario*, if Russia perceives NATO as an organization that is at best a stranger, at worst, hostile.

The European Union itself developed an increasingly self-declared mandate to maintain peace through its "European security and defense policy" (ESDP) in the Balkans and in Africa, but also in other places (Indonesia, Iraq, Palestine). However the autonomy of the European Union compared with NATO is limited, as the territorial defense of Europe rests primarily on NATO (Article 5 of the Washington Treaty), and the strength of NATO's military structure is such that all significant operations of the European Union must in truth depend on it.

The collective situation in Europe is unstable, to a slightly larger extent in the Balkans, and even more so in the post-Soviet space. There are, in fact, two possible scenarios that describe how the situation could develop. The confrontation scenario could see the reinforcement of NATO's mandate of territorial defense in order to prepare against the threat that Russia still embodies, which would translate into a revived arms race in Europe; a growing dependence of the European Union on NATO and the United States under the banner of security; and a cold war or even armed confrontations in conflict zones of Russian influence (Caucasus, Moldova, Ukraine).

The other scenario, the stabilization scenario, consists in restoring a relationship of trust and cooperation with Russia. It would work through a halt in NATO's policy of enlargement to include Georgia and Ukraine, by the revival of disarmament discussions in Europe (including Russo-American discussions regarding nuclear disarmament and anti-missile systems), and by an increased role for the European Union. The European Union, in reinforcing its relations with its eastern neighbors but also with Russia, can play a major role in shaping an atmosphere of trust. The European Union is more a source of hard security (territorial defense, heavy army interventions). The establishment of a veritable partnership between the EU and Russia in the domain of ESDP, as well as the reestablishment of a NATO-Russian cooperation in the maintenance of peace, would bring us further away from a cold war in Europe, and would bring us closer to cooperative management of security arrangements, not only in Europe by way of a revitalized OSCE, but also in the world through the United Nations. This could facilitate the resolution, negotiated with Russia, of certain frozen conflicts such as that of Transniestria or Nagorno-Karabakh.

The second scenario is indeed possible, but it assumes sufficient desire on the part of several key countries in Europe (primarily France and Germany, but also the United Kingdom) as well as the good disposition of Washington. One can only bet whether or not Russia fundamentally wishes a confrontation in which it has much to lose, and therefore one must discuss and be prepared to listen to its security interests. In this regard, the Medvedev proposition for a European security treaty can offer the opportunity of a more cooperative path, as the dialogue in the OSCE framework demonstrated.

How to Create a Global Strategy Partnership with Russia?

This question is linked, quite simply, to the future of multilateralism. For the Europeans, the choice is clear-cut and simple: if the European Union recognizes its debt to the United States, with whom it shares fundamental similar, Western, and democratic values, in addition to a shared destiny, the EU is itself a multilateral being, and it will be made more strong as multilateralism at the global level becomes stronger. This choice is expressed as clearly as can be in the 2003 European security strategy, at a time when the United States was won over by the "neo-conservative moment," and was reaffirmed when the security strategy was revised at the close of 2008. For the United States, things are less clear: its power gives it choice; its attachment to the multilateral system will not go so far as to deprive it of the means that allow for unilateral action. But one has reasons to hope that an Obama Administration will show itself to be more universalistic and more multilateralist than the preceding Administration.

This must occur through a rediscovery of global issues: disarmament and the struggle against proliferation; the reestablishment of a global system of collective security (as symbolized by the debate over enlargement of the UN Security Council), the consolidation of a universal base to defend human rights and to fight against poverty; better regulation of globalization in all its aspects (economic, finance, primary commodity markets, organized crime, the environment). In all these domains, Russia is a partner that cannot be ignored. Russia is, along with the United States, the European Union, China, India, and Japan, one of the great world powers. Its stature as an energy giant (having a quarter of the world's gas reserves, but also petrol and nuclear power) makes it an indispensable partner to secure supply on a European and indeed worldwide scale. One must try hard to include Russia in shared rules, to not try to exclude it from the G-8, and to start the process of including it as a member of the World Trade Organization, which was already belated. Russia's participation in the G-20 meetings for the global financial crisis is a first step in the right direction.

A strategy to integrate Russia in the world economy would be beneficial in three ways: to combat common challenges; to reestablish an atmosphere of trust and cooperation; and to open and modernize the Russian economy and society.

The Europeans and the new American administration are, as much as Russia itself, faced with a fundamental choice. We can contribute to a heightened hardening of attitudes. But we can also, together, modify the course of events. Politics is, after all, realism's power struggle but also freedom of choice. The majority of Europeans fundamentally prefer cooperation to struggle. The United States made this choice at certain points of the Cold War, and the stance taken by the Obama Administration shows that the U.S. is again able to appreciate the distinction and opportunity. There is thus material, today, to redefine a strategy of lucid, if not resolute, engagement with regards to Russia.

Chapter Seven

Strategic Priorities in the Mediterranean and the Middle East

Ian O. Lesser

For decades, crises and flashpoints in the Middle East and the Mediterranean have had a central place in American foreign policy, and have absorbed a great deal of political energy through successive administrations. Developments on Europe's southern periphery have also become increasingly central to transatlantic relations. With a new Administration in Washington, it is unlikely that challenges across the region will lose their saliency. The crisis in Gaza underscores this reality. But the American capacity for engagement and the dynamics of partnership, from Morocco to the Gulf and beyond, may change substantially over the next few years. The new regional agenda is likely to see growing interaction between Washington and Paris, with new incentives for closer policy coordination. There will also be an opportunity for more explicit cooperation on "Mediterranean" strategy—a longstanding French interest, but a relatively underdeveloped aspect of American foreign policy.

An Expanding Middle East

Traditionally, American policy toward the Middle East has focused on a limited number of core issues, above all the Arab-Israeli dispute, and stability and energy security in the Gulf. North Africa and the Levant have not been absent from the equation, but they have rarely had the weight given to these sub-regions in European policy. Or they have simply been seen through the lens of the Middle East peace process. This has certainly been the case with Lebanon. The close U.S. relationship with Morocco has, more often than not, been driven by Rabat's moderate stance and willingness to serve as an intermediary in Arab relations with Israel. Over the last decade, several factors have served to broaden the scope of Middle East policy and the American concept of the region as a strategic space. The September 11th experience strongly reinforced a pre-existing tendency to emphasize the trans-regional character of challenges that, though they might have the Israeli-Palestinian conflict as a center of gravity, affect the security equation across a far wider area. Crises of governance and political legitimacy, the rise of Islamic politics, terrorism and political violence, and unresolved state-to-sate frictions, have encouraged American strategists to think of the region in terms of an arc of crisis stretching from "Marrakesh to Bangladesh." It has become fashionable to refer to the "broader" Middle East, and this notion became imbedded in the Bush Administration's Middle East Partnership Initiative. The Obama administration may well take a less vigorous line on democratization and transformation, opting instead for a more traditional human rights agenda, but this expansive geopolitical approach to the Middle East is likely to remain, even if the vocabulary changes.

This evolving mental map of the region could actually encourage a convergence of American and French perspectives, even if this proved elusive over the last eight years. For Europe, Middle East policy has never been limited to the Levant and the Gulf. For France, and especially for southern European countries, North Africa and the Mediterranean have been leading parts of the strategic environment, and the future of these areas is interwoven with Europe's own security and prosperity. This is Europe's near abroad, and an area where disengagement is not an option. By contrast, across much of the broader Middle East, the U.S. will have the option of a reduced political and security posture. With the important exceptions of the Middle East peace process and the challenge of Iran, the current high level of American engagement cannot be taken for granted over the next decade. Competing strategic requirements in Asia and economic stringency could well produce an environment in which there is actually *too little* American presence for European taste. This is not the most likely scenario, but under current conditions, it is one worth considering.

Reinvigorating the Peace Process

As the Gaza crisis demonstrates, the Israeli-Palestinian conflict is now central to transatlantic security concerns in a way that has not been seen since the heyday of Palestinian terrorism in Europe in the 1970s and 80s. Without question, a comprehensive settlement, incorporating a two-state solution, will remain the ultimate diplomatic prize for Washington. Successive American administrations have come to office committed to reinvigorating the Arab-Israeli peace process. In practice, new administrations have been reluctant to risk their reputation on Middle East diplomacy until conditions seemed ripe, or until events on the ground forced a more active approach. When the U.S. has been actively engaged, there has been a strong preference to keep control of the process, minimizing the role of other actors, whether regional or European. Arguably, U.S. policymakers have lost some of their resistance to a more active European role—especially with regard to funding—but reservations persist even in more progressive circles.

It remains an open question whether Washington will be willing to see the Quartet and Annapolis-style multilateralism as the way forward if a comprehensive settlement appears within reach. The Obama Administration inherits a legacy of peace process diplomacy in which, with some rare exceptions, the U.S. has been reluctant to cede the initiative and equally reluctant to press the parties beyond traditional limits. Even if the new Administration is inclined to break with tradition and engage itself rapidly in Israeli-Palestinian diplomacy—and the ongoing security and humanitarian crisis in Gaza may leave little choice—the parties are unlikely to be in a position to agree on final status questions any time soon. In this case, transatlantic strategy may need to focus on continued containment of the consequences of no-peace, encouraging regional détentes (e.g., with Syria) even as the core issues remain unresolved. The growing ability of more distant actors such as Iran, and even Pakistan, to play a role and to threaten the security of Israel directly and via proxies, will have increasingly important implications for the notion of "end of conflict." In this sense, both Washington and Paris will confront a peace process conundrum that has expanded alongside the definition of the Middle East as a strategic space.

Disengaging from Iraq

Far more than September 11th, Iraq has been a watershed in transatlantic and, above all, Franco-American relations. The Iraq war continues to be a source of policy disagreements between Washington and virtually all of America's international partners. More significantly, differences over Iraq have fueled a far more serious and continuing debate about the nature of American power among publics as well as leaderships across the Atlantic. To be sure, this debate was well under-way before 2003. But the Iraq War crystallized the critique of Ameri-can power and leadership in new and powerful ways. At the same time, the Iraq experience has spurred America's own reflection on foreign policy style and priorities. Within Washington's foreign policy com-munity, the invasion of Iraq has long been regarded as a colossal failure of intelligence and judgment—a miscalculation with far-reaching strategic consequences. Disengagement from Iraq is now a leading pri-ority. Containing if not repairing the consequences of the Iraq adven-ture will not be easy, and it will be impossible without the active coop-eration of regional actors and key allies.

If the Obama Administration adheres to its stated timetable, and if Iraqi pressure to accelerate an American withdrawal mounts, Baghdad will face a serious near-term test of its ability to provide minimum conditions of security in the country. Over the longer-term, the ability of Iraq to maintain itself as a unitary state cannot be taken for granted. The Kurdish north of Iraq is already poised to emerge as an independent entity, even if the rest of the country remains unified and chaotic. Under these conditions, Turkey will face very difficult challenges of adjustment. The management of a post-occupation Iraq, and avoiding the wider destabilization of the region, will require more serious regional diplomacy of the kind envisioned in the "Baker-Hamilton" report, but never seriously attempted. It may also require a larger role for international organizations inside Iraq. Both initiatives would be greatly strengthened by a concerted transatlantic approach with a solid UN mandate.

Engaging or Containing Iran?

The stage may now be set for a greater degree of Franco-American convergence on Iran policy. The Obama Administration has made clear its willingness to explore a strategic dialogue with Iran, and an Iranian-U.S. détente is not out of the question over the next few years. In Europe, concern about the consequences of a nuclear-armed Iran is also growing, driven in large measure by vulnerability to Iranian bal-listic missiles of trans-Mediterranean range. That said, it is likely that Washington will remain highly sensitive to the prospect of a nuclear Iran—progress on this issue will remain a key test for any dialogue with Tehran—and the potential for a military strike against Iran's nuclear infrastructure is undiminished. France as well as the U.S. (and Israel) would be exposed to the immediate and longer-term consequences of such an action.

It is also possible that Tehran may opt for a prolonged near-nuclear posture, delaying the development of a deployable capability until conditions seem propitious and minimizing the adverse diplomatic and security consequences in the Gulf and elsewhere. A scenario of this kind—intransigence on nuclear development short of provoking Western intervention—would compel the U.S., France and others to think in terms of a durable containment strategy. This might extend to new multilateral security assurances in the Gulf, or to Israel, and would benefit greatly from progress in the Middle East peace process. Tehran would presumably work strenuously to undermine the process in Gaza, Lebanon and elsewhere.

The European stakes in containing Iran's nuclear ambitions may be as high, and perhaps more direct than those of the U.S. Washington will have a systemic interest in preventing the emergence of a new nuclear power. But Europe, including France, will be more tangibly exposed to the strategic consequences of a nuclear-armed Iran. Ballistic missile reach is part of the equation. But Europe will also have to reckon with the possible cascading effects of a nuclear, or even a nuclear-ready Iran. Heightened proliferation incentives across the Middle East could produce changes in military balances across a wide region, from the Aegean to Central Asia. Russian strategy, already highly dependent on nuclear forces, could move further in this direction, at a time when NATO will be reassessing and recasting its own strategy and doctrine. A nuclear or near-nuclear Iran would have a variety of negative consequences for the strategic environment on Europe's eastern and southern periphery. If arms control issues are set to reemerge on the transatlantic agenda, the content of this new debate is likely to include Middle Eastern dynamics to a far greater extent than in the past.

Pakistan—on the far reaches of the Mediterranean hinterland—will also be part of this equation. A highly unstable nuclear-armed state on the brink of economic collapse, Pakistan presents a formidable and proximate risk for crisis management with a nuclear edge. Unlike Iran, Pakistan offers a more straightforward case of convergent security

interest on both sides of the Atlantic. Given the precarious political
dynamics and existing nuclear arsenal (how secure?) in Pakistan, there
is considerable reason to ponder the potential requirement for a coalition operation, involving the U.S., France or others, to secure the Pakistani arsenal under chaotic conditions. Not a Middle Eastern or Mediterranean action in the strict sense, perhaps, but one that would have
important political and security echoes across adjacent regions.

The Mediterranean Dimension

The U.S. has been a Mediterranean power for over two hundred
years. But despite this long history of presence, American policy
toward the Mediterranean remains fragmented and diffuse. There is
little in the way of a Mediterranean consciousness of the kind found in
France, Italy and elsewhere in southern Europe. The EU has a Mediterranean strategy in place, even if this strategy falls short in critical
respects. New initiatives, including the French-inspired Union for the
Mediterranean, reflect a well-developed notion of the Mediterranean
and its hinterlands as an identifiable strategic space. By contrast, the
U.S. continues to divide the region, intellectually and bureaucratically,
along rigid regional lines: Europe, on the one hand, and the Middle
East and North Africa on the other. Key sub-regions and issues,
including the Balkans, the Aegean, the Israeli-Palestinian dispute, and
Turkey, are rarely placed in an explicit Mediterranean frame. This
basic asymmetry in French and American perspectives is likely to persist, even as the future of North Africa and functional issues in the
Mediterranean become more central to transatlantic cooperation.

American interests in the area are diverse, with policymakers
attuned to the Mediterranean as an aspect of European security (the
dominant aspect during the Cold War); as a logistical gateway to areas
such as the Gulf (e.g., the role of Suez and Incirlik airbase); and as a
focal point for crisis management (e.g., the Western Sahara, Cyprus or
Lebanon). Washington's political engagement is still driven largely by
close bilateral relationships, such as those with Morocco and Israel,
rather than a sense of Mediterranean policy *per se*. One exception has
been the trans-regional purview of American military commands such
as EUCOM, which has spanned Europe and Africa (AFRICOM now
constitutes a separate command whose responsibility includes the

Maghreb, although still located in Germany). The Sixth Fleet has also had a trans-Mediterranean outlook.

Looking ahead, several issues are likely to drive transatlantic stakes in the Mediterranean, and may offer new incentives for Franco-American cooperation. First, North Africa has become more central to the strategic concerns of Europe and the U.S. The Maghreb is closely linked to Europe by virtue of its position as a source and conduit for migration, its uncertain economic and political prospects, and links to political violence and terrorism affecting Western interests. The renewal of the Barcelona Process, including the new Union for the Mediterranean, will be an integral part of the EU's evolving approach to the wider European neighborhood, and one where the U.S. will have an important stake. For all of the skepticism regarding the Union for the Mediterranean, it is noteworthy that the initiative attracted an unusual amount of attention in Washington where it now a fashionable topic for debate. A reflection of growing American attention to North Africa and the Mediterranean perhaps, but the French dimension cannot be discounted at a time of mounting interest in rebuilding Franco-American ties.

Washington and Paris (and Rome) will be among the leading actors in political and economic relations with North Africa, including the challenge of reintegrating Algeria and Libya; the former after over a decade of instability and violence, the latter after decades of diplomatic isolation and international sanctions. Neither task will be easy. Algeria faces a slow-moving crisis of governance and development, and a resurgence of terrorism and criminality. Algeria's unreconstructed nationalism and sovereignty consciousness will continue to complicate European, American and Russian relations with Algiers. With Washington, Libya is literally starting from a blank page, and even with Europe, there is the potential for relations to take new and different forms. The reintegration of these states as regional actors will be critical to the larger effort to encourage closer cooperation along south-south lines; a priority when seen from either side of the Atlantic.

Second, terrorist networks with roots in North Africa are likely to be a significant concern for French and U.S. planners over the next few years. These will be a leading source of risk for Europe, and an element in the outlook for stability around the southern Mediterranean. Substantial numbers of Maghrebi and Egyptian fighters have appeared in

Iraq, and may now be moving to Afghanistan. They could emerge as a durable element in the security equation in the Middle East and South Asia, and their return to North Africa or Europe could vex intelligence and security services for years to come.

Third, energy security will be another driver of transatlantic interest in the Mediterranean, with very different characteristics from the Gulf and Central Asia. The proliferation of new gas, oil and electricity transmission lines is leading to the emergence of a Mediterranean energy market, with potential importance in offsetting European dependence on Russian gas. Algeria and Libya are key actors here, but Morocco, Tunisia and Turkey are playing leading roles in energy transit. Clearly, France and southern European partners will have a more direct stake in the Mediterranean energy security equation than will the U.S. But as the market for natural gas continues to expand, the U.S. stake should continue to increase. Today, the American debate about energy security is overwhelmingly about oil, and largely focused on the Gulf. The European debate, by contrast, is first and foremost about gas. This asymmetry in perspective may shape transatlantic discussions about energy security strategy for some time to come.

Fourth, the Mediterranean is already a multi-polar environment, and could become even more visibly multi-polar with the return of Russia as a commercial, political and security actor. It is probably too soon to judge the real scale and significance of Russia's modest re-entry into the region as a naval power and defense partner for Algeria, Libya and Syria. But a more difficult strategic relationship between Moscow and the West could well include more open competition around the Mediterranean. At the same time, China, India and the Gulf states are acquiring economic interests around the Mediterranean and its hinterlands, sometimes in direct competition with Europe and the U.S. The global economic crisis could well slow or interrupt this trend, but the general outlook favors a diversification of ties among regional and extra-regional actors. In the future, Europe and the U.S. could well face a more competitive atmosphere in relations with southern Mediterranean partners.

Fifth, and from an American perspective, the evolving strategic relationship with France will be a leading influence on U.S. policy in the Mediterranean. Unlike more distant areas, the Mediterranean basin is a place where American and French engagement and capabilities are relatively balanced, and interests *should* be broadly convergent. Habits of defense cooperation in the region are well-developed and longstanding. If France returns to NATO's Integrated Military Command, this cooperation could become more intensive and explicit. A decade ago, some American policymakers might have been uncomfortable with this idea. Today the notion would be welcomed in many quarters and could go some way toward revitalizing NATO's purpose and capabilities on the European periphery.

Turkey as a Transatlantic Issue

Finally, Turkey should also be part of a new Franco-American discussion on strategic priorities, not least because of Ankara's growing activism and capacity for power projection in the Levant and the Gulf. Washington will undoubtedly continue to support Turkey's EU candidacy for strategic reasons, although the U.S. capacity to make this argument and to influence European decision-making is declining. The quality of transatlantic relations will be an important factor here, but structural and technical issues also matter, and these have become more prominent in Turkish-EU relations over time. As President Sarkozy's prompt and critical response to President Obama's statements on Turkey's EU candidacy in April 2009 made clear, the Turkish question remains a potential source of transatlantic friction. At base, the American interest in Turkey-EU relations is not membership *per se*, but rather Turkey's continued convergence with European norms in various sectors, from governance to security. At this level, French and American interests in Turkey are entirely compatible.

On key functional questions such as energy and defense, the scope for purely bilateral cooperation with Ankara is narrowing, and in most instances a transatlantic approach makes sense for all sides. As Turkey seeks new partners and reassurance *vis-à-vis* instability on its Middle Eastern borders—including the future of Iraq—multiple partners will be the order of the day. President Obama's decision to visit Turkey early in his administration was significant, not least because he chose to make the visit as part of a European rather than a Middle Eastern tour.

Some Strategic Priorities

The enlarged definition of the Middle East as a strategic space, including the Mediterranean dimension, holds the potential for more explicit Franco-American partnership. A sharp change in American foreign policy style, and a more expansive approach to French and European interests on the periphery of the continent, will create the basic conditions for closer cooperation. Economic stringency and pressures for a re-nationalization of foreign and security policies on both sides of the Atlantic could work against this objective, as could unforeseen crises in Asia or elsewhere. A short list of shared strategic priorities should include:

- Stability in Gaza and reinvigoration of Middle East peace process diplomacy early in the new U.S. administration, with fewer reservations about European engagement, fewer fixed ideas about who can be a broker (the Oslo model) and multilateral security guarantees where required;

- A common approach to regional diplomacy in support of U.S. disengagement from Iraq, including strategies to hedge against chaos and the collapse of the unitary state;

- Planning to address the challenge of a nuclear Iran, possibly including a sustained strategy of containment if Tehran opts for a prolonged near-nuclear posture;

- Development of a more explicit Franco-American approach to development and security in the Mediterranean, both inside and outside the NATO frame. Encouraging greater south-south integration should be a key theme in a more concerted policy toward North Africa.

The prominence of these issues in the strategic calculus on both sides of the Atlantic, and their location in places Europe can reach, will make policy toward the Mediterranean and the Middle East a key near-term test of commitment to a revived transatlantic relationship.

Chapter Eight

For a Defused Franco-American Dialogue in the Mediterranean

Jean-Pierre Filiu

Abstract

President Obama renewed Washington's engagement toward a durable solution to the conflict in the Middle East. Such a solution would emerge through the establishment of a Palestinian state bordering Israel. France, in proposing its own contribution to the renewal of direct negotiations between Israel and Syria, encourages this American desire for a revival of a genuine peace process. Confronted by a challenge of such scope, Washington and Paris must also deal with the diffusion of global jihadist networks in the Mediterranean. Generally speaking, the United States should take into greater account the legitimacy of a French involvement in the Middle East, while French prejudices regarding American policies in the Maghreb should be reconsidered. In this respect, academic exchanges, as well as cooperation between legislative institutions, can create new space for dialogue.

For France as well as for the United States, the Mediterranean and the Middle East represent a place in which each affirms a certain idea of what is French and what is American, respectively, and of their world view. This privileged projection of power can mobilize priority resources in Washington and Paris. As a result, this projection of power will not be reduced to the sum of diverse French and American interests in the region, as their strategies are as much political and economic, as symbolic. In addition, Washington is regularly tempted by a unilateralism that scorns international law or efforts to work through the United Nations in the Middle East, while successive French presidents have seemingly wanted to break free of European references and disciplines.

Beyond Annapolis and Paris

This fundamental political dimension lends significant importance to presidential initiatives, as well as to national and international public opinion regarding such initiatives. Nicolas Sarkozy chose the very night of his election, May 7, 2007, to launch his Mediterranean Union project, and the Arab-Israeli conflict was one of the most highly debated topics during the American presidential campaign.

It is for this reason that a comparison of the two summits between the heads of state of France and the United States in 2007-2008 is enlightening. For George Bush, the goal of the summit was to attain a decisive contribution to the Arab-Israeli peace, suspended since 2001, in order to secure his second presidential mandate. For the French president, a new political dynamic needed to be deployed in the Mediterranean:

The Middle East peace conference, convened by George W. Bush in Annapolis on November 27, 2007, involved 49 countries and international institutions. Honored invitees included Prime Minister Ehud Olmert and President Mahmoud Abbas, while Saudi Arabia was represented only by its Minister of Foreign Affairs, and Syria only by its second highest ranking diplomat. The White House hoped to open a new round of Israeli-Palestinian negotiations with the prospect of establishing an independent and viable Palestinian state before the close of 2008. However, the declaration adopted at Annapolis remained too vague regarding the elements of a final agreement, and Washington refused to adopt an active mediating role between the Israeli and Palestinian camps, calling on each to negotiate directly with the other. During the donor conference for the Palestinian state held in Paris on December 17, 2007, the international community committed up to $7.4 million over a span of three years. However, the Israeli-Palestinian negotiations became mired, and no significant break was made after Annapolis.

The launching summit for the Union for the Mediterranean (UFM), hosted in Paris July 13, 2008, under the co-presidency of Nicolas Sarkozy and Hosni Mubarak, effectively brought together 43 partners, the 27 members of the European Union, and their 16 associates from the surrounding Mediterranean area. Only Libya boycotted the initiative, to which the countries of the Southern Bank of the Mediterranean, with the notable exception of Morocco, generally responded with the highest levels of official participation. Present also were the General Secretaries of the United Nations, of the Arab League, of the African Union, of the Arab Maghreb Union, and of the Organization of the Islamic Conference, as well as Qatar, representing the Council of Cooperation of the Gulf. The profile of the UFM meeting was also raised by the tripartite French-Israeli-Palestinian summit, and the announcement of the establishment of diplomatic relations between Damascus and Beirut. Nevertheless, much needs to be done to develop the UFM; the initial project, for instance, was already modified to take into account the success of the Euro-Mediterranean process in Barcelona.

The last weeks of the Bush administration were marked by an offensive of unprecedented violence by the Israeli army in the Gaza strip, which nevertheless did not significantly weaken the Islamist Hamas movement; Hamas' dominance in this Palestinian territory is still uncontested. This "War of 22 Days," from December 27, 2008 to January 17, 2009, also did not spare Tzipi Livni, successor to Ehud Olmert as the head of the Kadima Party, from electoral defeat. The tight Israeli general elections of February 10, 2009 led to laborious negotiations, resulting in a government led by Benyamin Netanyahu (Likud), with Ehud Barak (Labor) as head of Defense, and Avigdor Lieberman (Israel Beitenou) as head of Foreign Affairs—a government that questioned the Annapolis principles. The political impasse and the military escalation thereby strengthened radical options, rendering it both necessary, and making more complex, an international intervention to overcome the deadlock.

Soon after his inauguration, Barack Obama expressed a commitment to the establishment of a Palestinian state next to Israel. Hilary Clinton underlined the President's policy in the Middle East; the designation of a Special Emissary from the White House, George Mitchell, further confirmed the mobilization of political will at the highest levels of the U.S. administration. The French-American collaboration was remarkable at the time of the Sharm el-Sheikh conference, March 2, 2009, under the co-presidency of Hosni Mubarak and Nicolas Sarkozy. Participants were engaged to contribute $4.5 million for the reconstruction of the Gaza strip, devastated by the Israeli offensive. However, the violence of the "War of 22 Days" also resulted in profound diplomatic repercussions and the suspension the UFM processes, at the initiative of the Arab party.

The challenge for the United States, as for France, is to reinvigorate the processes initiated in Annapolis and in Paris, to profit in this regard from the formidable potential of a mobilized international community (and this, despite the palpable 'donor fatigue') and to promote a top-down exit approach from such an unfavorable regional context.

Divided Interests

The United States and France share the same deep and strategic interests concerning both the Mediterranean and the Middle East:

- Stability, which alone can guarantee the enduring settlement of the Arab-Israeli conflict in all dimensions. Washington and Paris, both irrevocably attached to Israel's security, are nevertheless convinced that peace depends on the establishment, next to the Jewish state, of a viable and independent Palestinian state. In the Maghreb, the Western Sahara question is the key to a genuine regional detente.

- The development of the southern bank of the Mediterranean, as this sea is traversed by some of the greatest income disparities in the world. Such disparity encourages migratory pressure, as well as more or less populist social movements. These are the tens of millions of jobs that must be created in the South to absorb the potential labor force.

- The democratization of regimes marked by a troubled permanence (the most senior head of state in the region, Colonel Qaddafi, has been in power since 1969), while the more and more wealthy middle class, and the more and more educated youth, have difficulty translating their aspirations into the political field.

The new American administration must manage the weighty failure of the Bush presidency. The image of the United States is strongly tarnished in the Arab world, where the United States is accused, following the circumstances, of leading a politics of aggression, of practicing the two influences/measures in favor of Israel, or of not championing democratic advances when they favor those who oppose American policies. Out of this a potential basis is formed for hatred of Western countries, which could give credence to the notion of a "clash of civilizations," which should be avoided. This possibility was appreciably aggravated by the management of the media during the "War of 22 Days" in Gaza: the ban, supported by Israel, on foreign press effectively deadened the impact of the offensive in Western minds, but the massive diffusion of filmed images by Arab television, during the worst of the bombardment, aroused a veritable wave of horror and indignation.

Thankfully, Barack Obama took the initiative as soon as he took office. His speech on the satellite channel "Al-Arabiyya", his declarations regarding the Palestinian state, and his official visit to Turkey succeeded in confining growing anti-American sentiment. The rejection of the term "Global War on Terror," the announcement of the closing of Guantanamo Bay, and the refusal to tolerate torture, were all measures welcomed with great expectation. The task faced by Washington and its partners is, however, immense. France, because of its historic and political credit in the Arab world, will be a determined ally in the indispensable enterprise of reestablishing the image of the West in general, and of the United States in particular.

The grand neo-conservative design of a "Greater Middle East," or the democratization by force of Arab regimes ("the road to Jerusalem runs through Baghdad") must treat the Palestinian question carefully. To do otherwise is to risk sinking without return. Paris, because of its capacity to suggest and to initiate, can accompany Washington in a return to the principal basis of an Arab-Israeli peace process, one of exchange of land in return for peace. A territorial conflict is by definition open to resolution, in contrast to a conflict based on oil or on identity. And the United States will need all the support it can get as it finally rises to the challenge of the occupation and the colonization of the West Bank.

But the most calamitous legacy of the Bush administration is the transformation of Iraq into centers of attraction and of mobilization for a new generation of transnational jihadists. After the "Afghans" of the 1980s and the "Chechnyans" of the following decade, this century opened with the diffusion of "Iraqi" networks in the entire Mediterranean, from Fath al-Islam in Lebanon to the transformation in Algeria of the Salafi Group for Preaching and Combat (GSPC) into al-Qaeda in the Islamic Maghreb (AQMI). France is specifically targeted by this new-found menace, and is designated as the fiend of the American "crusade."

Generally speaking, France wishes for neither the isolation of the United States in the region, nor the reversal of American policy; France demonstrated that its warnings concerning the Iraqi situation were also relevant from the point of view of American national interests, and that it opposes isolationist attempts to the benefit of an American engagement, structured and measured. But Paris is perfectly justified in demanding of Washington the right to weigh in on decisions that, in the Middle East, affect France's security.

The Syrian-Lebanese Strategy

Next to the United States, Paris controls the most established network in the region, and its diplomacy is, after that of the United States, the most active and consistent in the area. France's cultural and commercial presence certainly does not rival that of the United States, but it remains vital. Hundreds of thousands of French citizens live and work in the zone. There, France conducts ambitious operations of cooperation with almost all countries, and this regional policy, a contributor to its international image, gives it credibility and support.

France and the United States have for some time actively cooperated regarding Lebanon. Without revisiting the time of the Multinational Force in Beirut in 1982-84, one recalls that Paris and Washington sponsored from 1996 to 2000 an indirect arrangement between Israel and Hezbollah, which proscribed civil targets and which neutralized the escalation of [numerous] crises. Since 2004, the United States and France worked together to accomplish the end of the Syrian occupation of Lebanon. It was with the help of Washington that the Interim Force of the United Nations in Lebanon (FINUL) rose in power in August of 2006, with an important French investment on the border with Israel. And the French experience of dialogue with Syria is full of lessons for the Obama administration, which can only with difficulty exclude Damascus, while reaching out to Tehran. This Syrian equation is so crucial for Paris and Washington that the crisis in Gaza torpedoed indirect negotiations between Israel and Syria, under the aegis of Turkey.

President Sarkozy wanted to open a new era of Franco-American cooperation, regarding the Middle East among others things, in a reasoning that is not without recalling the determination of Francois Mitterrand, in 1981, to raise the Paris funds towards the Camp David process. France mobilized itself without depending on the success of the Annapolis meeting; in the month immediately after France convened an international conference of backers for the Palestinian state, concerning which France assured an attentive monitoring follow-up. In the end, French diplomacy is available to ensure, next to the United States and when the time comes, the co-sponsoring of direct negotiations between Israel and Syria.

Clichés and Ulterior Motives

Despite the intensity of daily communication between Paris and Washington in the region, there remain numerous American leaders who consider the Franco-American dialogue to be above all a means by which to neutralize the French capacity to be a nuisance, while contemptuous and destabilizing clichés of the United States are still prevalent in Paris. Among the tenacious prejudices that continue to plague a true shared vision, two kinds of stereotypes can be placed before both sides of the Atlantic.

Seen from Washington, French action is caricatured as being profoundly conservative, supporting existing regimes regardless of their dictatorial character, with a guiding principle to defend the status quo and historic funds. This caricature is aggravated by a projection of Anglo-Saxon communitarianism onto the reality of French sociopolitics. This is how the presence in France of the largest Muslim population in Europe (approximately five million people, comprising some eight percent of the French population) is put forth to "explain" the so-called leanings of French diplomacy, regarding the Iraqi conflict for example. Along the same lines as ideas, it is the important Armenian presence in France that serves as automatic justification for the Parisian funds used for the admittance of Turkey into the European Union.

Seen from Paris, the United States is at times described as being engaged in a systematic politics of exclusion and of elimination of all competing powers, even friendly powers, and this aggressive hegemonism in the Middle East was met soon after with an anti-French campaign in North Africa, more so in Algeria than in Morocco. The supposed desire to drain the historic position of France in the Maghreb was joined by encouragements, more or less discreet, directed toward

Islamist Arabs. Lastly, Turkey is reduced to a "Trojan horse" of American influence, of which its absorption into the EU completes the European alignment, led by the inclusion of east European members.

Four Common, Large Challenges

France and the United States are faced with four common, large challenges in the region; the responses they choose would be enhanced by, at least in part, coordination or consultation:

- The road to the establishment of a Palestinian state must be reopened, with clear guidelines commensurate with time and space/land requirements. It is important to no longer question the humanitarian record as an end in and of itself, and to thus register aid to the population in a long term political process. The training of Palestinian youth should consequently resume as a clear priority of investment into the future. In addition, the support for the Palestinian Authority or for the schools of the United Nations, sufficient for primary and secondary education, no longer meets the needs of largely private universities. It is in these universities that lie the fundamental stake for a generation of cadres who consciously refused the option of expatriation.

- The stability of the northern border of Israel and the southern border of Lebanon are contingent on a settlement of the Israeli-Syrian conflict, and thus on negotiations of the Golan. The bone of contention of the so-called "farms of Chebaa" enclave—Lebanese according to Beirut, Syrian according to Israel (that maintains the occupation as an extension of the Golan), links the Lebanese element and the Syrian element of the conflict with Israel. France imagined the placement of this enclave under the guardianship of the United Nations; UN forces already guarantee the cease-fire of southern Lebanon and in the Golan. This could be the first step to a universal settlement, where France—like the United States—would have its role to play.

- The collapse of the "Great Middle East" left longstanding legacies and created strong resentment against the instigators; only the promotion of a new shared perspective will be able to overcome it. Such a new perspective can, for the United States, be a major attraction of the Union for the Mediterranean, just as an inclusive perspective and a rigorous equality between partners of the North as for the South can be.

- The diffusion in the Mediterranean of global jihadist networks, particularly in the form of al-Qaeda in the Islamic Maghreb (AQMI), represents a major security challenge. However, two pitfalls should be avoided: that of "all-security", indeed that of "all repressive", that is at times counter-productive since the target sighted is too large, and which often obscures the upstream work (of potential jihadists) and the downstream work (of former terrorists); and that of Western interference, a factor of nationalist resentment. It is important to not forget that, in the Mediterranean as elsewhere, civil Muslim societies live on the front lines of al-Qaeda and that pay the highest price for its terror.

Seven Paths of Dialogue

Failing a revival of a formal French-American cooperation in the region, a new spirit could prevail and be based on a reciprocal appreciation of interests and expertise; Washington must consider French interventions in the Middle East as legitimate and take into account the advice of its experts, while France must at the same time respect the initiatives and the analyses of the United States in the Maghreb. Outside of this generally more favorable climate, seven paths of more practical dialogue may be outlined:

- American Members of Congress and French parliamentarians do not do, and do not know, enough regarding these high profile issues of domestic policy. The bilateral channels between the two administrations would benefit from a more active parliamentary diplomacy, and thus would benefit from encouraging the development of exchanges between the Congress, the National Assembly, and the SenateFrance developed an incontestable academic expertise in the Middle East that could be better disseminated in the United States by way of translations and invitations, while American experts on the Maghreb merit seeing their work better known in France, with the possibility of joint projects with relevant offices or with French research centers in north Africa.

- The United States and France should together consider of how to definitively settle the Saharan conflict, the persistence of which compromises all Maghreb development efforts and cooperation across North Africa. Spain can effectively be associated with such a joint consideration, indeed even with a concerted reasoning on this matter.

- Al-Qaeda in the Islamic Maghreb (AQMI) is a priority theme in Franco-American counter-terrorist cooperation, not only because the only "franchise" of Bin Laden poses an offensive threat, but also because of its interaction with the Iraqi theater, catalyst of the mutation of the Salafist Group for Preaching and Combat (GSPC) into AQMI, and the traditional intervention space of the GSPC.

- France and the United States should work together toward the viability of a long term future Palestinian state, which depends on the quality of its cadre training, and thus on the solidity of academic institutions in the West Bank and in Gaza. Paris and Washington together can bring better integration of Palestinian universities into the international engagement in favor of a Palestinian state.

- France can facilitate U.S. recognition of the United Nations as a viable judicial reference framework and of eventual intervention in the Middle East. With the continuation of "blue helmet" deployment on the Israeli-Lebanese border, the placement of contested territory of the "farms of Chebaa" under guardianship of the United Nations can be studied, by way of experience to make the most of the Syrian element, indeed of the Palestinian peace process.

- France already promised an original vision, voluntarist and dynamic, of the Mediterranean at the heart of the UPM. France can interest the United States in the ambitious design of a Euro-Gulf space of cooperation, in which the Mediterranean would constitute the center, and where the formidable resources of the Gulf could promote development and exchanges.

The revival of Franco-American relations, encouraged by President Sarkozy, has had an undeniable effect on American decision makers in the Administration as well as in Congress. President Obama enjoys exceptionally high public opinion ratings, which can only reinforce goodwill on either side of the Atlantic. However, there is still a serious trend in Washington of too often rejecting French suggestions regarding the region, without taking the time to evaluate or to discuss the ideas. The new Administration, encouraged by Paris to engage resolutely in the Middle East, can surmount these bureaucratic reflexes. On the French side, the French contribution in the region is not in question, but it would be improved by greater strength and greater visibility each time that it makes an impression on the European process. The time of anger and resentment thankfully seems to be over, and the Franco-American dialogue can henceforth improve in substance in the Mediterranean.

Chapter Nine

African Dynamics

Nathalie Delapalme

Summary

At the beginning of a new century, as the large western democracies have been unsettled by the general experience of the recession, the frightening disorder of financial systems, and the preoccupation with the stagnation of the conflicts in Iraq and Afghanistan, the acceleration of African dynamics demands a profound reappraisal of the situation on the African continent and perspectives for its future, as well as a redefinition of the nature of our relations with African nations.

Many fundamental evolutions characterize Africa: the continuation of a strong population increase, in reverse relation to the rest of the planet; the development of an average economic growth rate superior to other developed economies; and the end of many historical conflicts that most observes consider definitively finished. Nations across European continent are concerned with African developments in the context of risks accruing from a globalized world, and recognition that the pursuit of durable and equal growth is essential to global security. Globalization embodies a vast spectrum of contemporary risks — terrorism, emerging epidemics, environmental catastrophes, uncontrolled mass migrations, the trafficking of drugs and weapons, hostage crises and piracy. But globalization also offers a vital potential for the pursuit of growth by developed economies, due to issues related to natural resources and the formidable market potential bound to the demographic perspectives of the developing world. The recent surge of numerous new partners on the African continent attests to the breadth of the stakes. The competition exerted there will become strong from now on. The time of Western monopoly over the political balances and economic perspectives of Africa has ended.

The stakes for Europe, Africa's immediate neighbor and aging meddler, can seem more acute than those for the United States, which is more distant geographically. In fact, with the adoption of the December 2007 EU-Africa Joint Strategy at Lisbon, Europe is now becoming interested in constructing concrete partnerships relating to topics of mutual interest, like migration, energy, or climate change. But closer examination of the stakes and the risks in a globalized world render the apparent differences between the United States and Europe smaller. The election of Barack Obama in particular appreciably modifies the impact of an American message on our African interlocutors and increases the consequences of American responsibility, at a moment when, in the context of new competition, the traditional European partners appear handicapped by their colonial past

In this profoundly agitated context, it is essential for the Western partners — the United States and Europe — of the African continent to attentively measure the stakes on one hand, and the evolution of "competition" on the other, in order to define a new strategy that develops in accordance with their interests, meaning their comparative advantages and their complementary potentials.

Too frequently, the African continent appears as the gloomy, almost cursed relative of the global family, sentenced to poverty without a future, to unending civil war, to unremitting epidemics. In fact, the approach of developed countries from this perspective, resulting from political leaders or especially public opinion, rests too frequently on a logic defined by compassion, moral obligation, or the loyalty of temporarily shared history. While at the same time the general experience of the recession, the frightening disorder of the financial systems, and the preoccupation with the stagnation of the crisis in Afghanistan, in Iraq or the Middle East shakes the major Western developed countries, the acceleration of African dynamics is an emblematic illustration of significant geostrategic evolutions underway in the contemporary world. The situation demands profound reconsideration of the situation and the perspectives of this large continent and, in this context, a new definition of ways Africans can relate to the Western powers.

Towards the Abatement of African Conflicts?

The last ten years were marked by the nearly unbelievable termination of many serious conflicts, spanning many decades, that seemed endless: Angola, ex-Zaire, Burundi, Sierra-Leone, Liberia, Southern

Sudan. Admittedly, the situation remains fragile in the Democratic Republic of Congo. Admittedly, new popular fronts are on the rise. At the edge of the border between the African continent and the Middle East, the dramatic conflict in Darfur is a major crisis. It reflects the risk of implosion in Sudan and sparks interest in the conclusion of an agreement on Southern Sudan. It threatens neighboring Uganda and, beyond that, the Great Lakes region, as well as the eastern Sahelian tribes, who are increasingly fragile, to the west, from Mauritania to Eritrea, including Nigeria, Central Africa, and Chad. The Horn of Africa, in particular Somalia, remains a serious source of instability. Old "champions" long cherished by the West, like the Ivory Coast or Kenya, are now handicapped by a profound political crisis that carries heavy economic consequences.

Nonetheless, a new trend is apparent, driven by two essential evolutions. The first is a dawning realization by the local players that the economic interests of the country can henceforth exceed interest in war. Consequently, the practical incentive to end conflicts that had resulted in such failures during the last quarter of a century seems to be beginning to prevail.

The second evolution, stemming in part from the first, is the rise of determined regional actors motivated by a cynical analysis of their most basic interests and under pressure by declarations made at the United Nations. The concept of African responsibility for repairing these great conflicts is now understood to be the key element to success, the element that is impossible to circumvent. Since the crisis of the Ivory Coast slowly began its termination, there is less grace in the determination of the Western community—who has sometimes made things more difficult—that because of the ensuing implication created by Burkina-Faso, that consequently measured that the international community would not disentangle itself from its neighbor, has yielded the conclusion that it is better to work cooperatively than divisively. In the same manner, the solution of the Darfur crisis rests primarily on accommodation of the political interests of Presidents Omar Bechir and Idriss Delay, and on a constructive attitude by their different neighbors or regional godfathers, notably Eritrea, Ethiopia, Egypt, and Libya. Again the drawback in the positions of the Western partners relate to the complications of exiting. As a result some parties seem to choose a stagnant position rather than engage in a solution.

African Dynamics

The occurrence of economic growth on the African continent constitutes another fundamental evolution that marks the passing of the
21st century. During the most recent six years, from 1995 to 2007,
average economic growth was superior at 5 percent, meaning triple the
average growth in the eurozone during this same time period (which
was about 1.4 percent). The significant isolation of the African continent, which was largely forgotten by the major global financial networks, attenuated the spread of the financial crisis that has shaken the
developed economies and could even demonstrate a comparative
advantage for Africa. In fact, according to the analysis of the IMF[1] for
2008 and 2009, which was strongly revised on account of the financial
crisis, there will be a subsequent deceleration of global growth, and
this decline will persist, with the entrance of the eurozone and the
United States into recession. African growth, in contrast, will only
subside slightly: +1.5 percent in 2009 then +4 percent in 2010 for Sub-
Saharan Africa, compared to -4.2 percent, then 0.4 percent for the
eurozone, and -2.8 percent, then 0 percent for the United States.

Emergence of a Middle Class

Admittedly, this starts from a small foundation. Admittedly, the
total number of impoverished people is increasing, and consequently
demographic growth continues to outpace economic growth. But the
trend is there. Most of all, the growth of Africa's average income,
which started at an average of 90, is accelerating and enlarging. In
2007, 39 African countries recorded an increase in GDP growth per
person, against 27 in 2000.[2] In 10 years, from 1997 to 2007, 23 countries reported an average growth rate of 5 percent with more than 50
percent of real GDP per an inhabitant, and an even higher average
growth of 25 percent for 12 countries in this grouping.[3] Even though
an additional indication is the obvious reinforcement of inequalities in
the standard of living, this new middle class now accounts for a third
of approximately 900 million Africans. The major data, already visible

---

[1] FMI—Perspectives on the global economy and Perspectives on regional economies—
April 2009.

[2] FMI—Perspectives on regional economies—Sub-Saharan Africa—October 2008.

[3] 25 percent to 50 percent: Burkina Faso, Gambia, Ghana, Madagascar, Mali, Sao Tome,
Tanzania; superior growth at 50 percent: Chad, Mozambique, Nigeria, Sierra Leone.

in the majority of African cities, will weigh necessarily on the economic evolution but also on the political stability of African countries, as it did in Asian countries.

Significant Demographic Variation

More fundamental than the unhooking of the dynamics of growth is that the extraordinary demographic burst in Africa will profoundly change the economic and political equilibrium, both at center of the continent and for its partners simultaneously. By 2050, one generation from now, the African population will more than double, passing 900 million in 2000 to 1,937 million, growing from an estimated 14 percent to 21 percent of the world total. Europe, during this time, will decline from 488 to 472 million (7.5 percent to 5.2 percent of world total). The United States, thanks to the assumed continuation of strong immigration, will grow from 297 to 409 million.[4]

Currently, two thirds of the African population is only 25 years old, a statistic that is nearly the inverse of the European continent. Basically, as of now, our African partners consider their demographic weight to be less of an obstacle in their economic development than an essential element to consolidate their political force in a globalized game. Finally, the "yes we can" attitude that has just hoisted a black president to the head of the United States obviously perpetuates this belief, as shown by reactions in the press and the African streets notably in the younger generation.

The Fragility of Traditional Interlocutors and Generational Conflict

These evolutions are accompanied by a sensible modification in the inward equilibrium of the continent. One noticeable change is the appearance of risks associated with the fragility of the "large" states on the continent, notably the longtime privileged partners of the Western developed world—meaning the excellence of their international image threatens the internal strength of these states, the potential exists that they are or will be, shortly, like the other turbulent African states for

---

[4] United Nations—Department of Economic and Social Affairs—Perspectives on the global population—last revision 2006.

this reason—notably Algeria, Gabon, equatorial Guinea, Cameroon, Libya—all confronted by difficult successions. The rising powers on the continent, like Ghana, Tanzania, or Mozambique, are currently intermediate-sized countries, which are privileged by the diversification of their relationships, well beyond the only Western members of the Security Council or the G8.

In fact, this fragility reflects the impact, new to a traditionally respectful continent of age and of seniority, inevitable with the acceleration of demographic renovation and the new weight of the media and the Internet. It is a phenomenon of generational conflict, which will be defined by an increased requirement for a true change of generation (of dynasty...?) of most African political officials.

The Center of African Gravity Shifting Toward the Arab and Asian Worlds

This rebalancing also is translated by a sensible shifting of the center of gravity of the African continent toward the East—immediately apparent with the Gulf countries, more remote with China and India, whereas seeming to distend, with the ancient European colonizers, and to a line forged by history, more than by joint geographic ownership. Significantly, whereas globally the total number of air passengers stagnated in 2007, the aviation routes between the African continent and the Middle East have continued at a rate close to 7 percent and with Asia close to 10 percent.[5]

China is already, behind France and after the United States, the second commercial partner of Africa[6], and imports a third of its current oil needs from Africa. In 1960, Europe represented two thirds of African exports.[7] In 2006, it did not represent any more than 40 percent. At the same time, Asia's share passed from 6 percent to 16 percent.

---

[5] IATA—International Air Transport Association.
[6] In 2005: $32.1 Million for China, $60.6 Million for the Unites States, and $56.4 Million for the European Union.
[7] WTO—World Trade Organization.

But Africa is also a strategic reservoir of resources for China: energy, mines, forests, and even agriculture.[8, 9] It is an essential outlet for an active population, a significant market for China's enterprises, a new terrain for its military presence,[10] an aspect of its privileged partnership for its financial system. In short, Africa represents a major political holding in the reshuffling of cards underway in the international game. The itinerary chosen by President Hu Jintao for his mid-February 2009 trip to Africa—his sixth visit—is significant: Mali, Senegal, Tanzania, Maurice, and Saudi Arabia: three of these countries will naturally become "strategic partners."[11]

Less explicit and less known, India's strategy follows the same objectives of ensuring the security of energy and mining resources, the reinforcement of outlets, and representation on authoritative international bodies. Finally, relations with the Muslim oil countries, Gulf monarchies, but also Iran and Malaysia are reinforced in a marked way in the commercial and financial realm, as well as in the area of military cooperation. Arabian sovereign funds concentrate particularly on the control of the infrastructures of outlets. This, until the present in parts of Djibouti, Dakar, Cape Town, *Dubai World Ports*[12] is showing interest in Comoros and in Algeria.[13]

Geostrategy

This major evolution in Africa is not limited to economic or commercial interests. It is conveyed in a long-term political strategy that includes, exactly as with the Western powers in the preceding century, consideration of the balance of power in a multilateral world. China

---

[8] In Tanzania, the group "Chongqing Seed" acquired 300 hectares of land and invested $143 million to cultivate rice. China predicts to create fifty of the same times of zones on the African continent.

[9] Hu Jintao aims to install three specialized economic zones in Africa: the first in Zambia for metals (copper, uranium, diamonds), the second in Tanzania for transports from the port of Dar es Salaam, and the third in Maurice dedicated to commerce and financial services.

[10] With 1,628 soldiers, police, or military observers on the land, China is by far the top contributor of blue soldiers in Africa, a priority since it positions there 75 percent of its deployed personnel (against 40 percent for France).

[11] "We will seek China-Africa pragmatic relationship and promote the fuller development of our new strategic partnership"—Hu Jintao—Dar es Salaam—February 16, 2009.

[12] Subsidiary company of Dubai World, it holds the authority of the Emirates government.

[13] Tanzania, who leads to the Indian Ocean, could serve as a base or facility for the Chinese navy.

now looks more frequently to African voices on the Security Council than France. On issues such as the Ivory Coast, Zimbabwe, and Sudan, many African nations are clearly against Western positions in Council debates. Increasingly, in Africa's collective fora, notably the African Union, on the most important and frequently broached subjects—climate change, international migration, control of urbanization, prospects for employment, allocation of water—the Arab world tends to take a position counter to Western opinion. Qatar has actively participated in summits and meetings since the origin of the African Union. In fact, the Security Council or the European Union has become indispensible in calling attention to a number of important African issues, notably Darfur and Mauritania. But despite Western efforts, in the difficult negotiation of the Darfur crisis the African Union preferred an association with the Arab League and the Organization of the Islamic Conference over ties with the West.

In this profoundly altered framework, it is essential for Africa's Western partners to carefully measure the risks on the one hand, and the evolution of "growth" on the other, to define a new strategy that simultaneously develops the interests, comparative advantages, and the complementary potential of the West and Africa.

In the context of globalization at the start of the century, the traditional divide between wealthy northern countries and southern poorer countries is no longer as prevalent. Now the new divide is between countries that are growing old, and are mostly preoccupied with their own security and stability, and younger countries obsessed with their futures and defined by unpredictability. Consequently, the true challenge is balancing the security concerns of the older countries with the contradictory aspirations of the newer nations. The security of the developed world, and its capacity to maintain strong and durable growth, depends in an immediate and acute way on the development and stabilization of Africa.

From this standpoint, the challenge for Europe, the most immediate and oldest neighbor of Africa, seems more acute than the challenge for the United States, which is more geographically distant but closer to Africa in its demographic makeup. But a closer look at the gains and the risks of globalization diminish this apparent difference.

Africa–The West: Shared Risks

In fact, in the context of the new geostrategic theater, the African continent's primary concern is not its own territory, despite all the risks of the contemporary world. The security risk is demonstrated by the fact that more than ten years before September 11, 2001, the first terrorist attacks were on African soil—UTA Flight 772 crashed over the desert of Ténéré in 1989, then Dar es Salaam in Tanzania and Nairobi to Kenya in 1998. Already, on a continent that serves as a joint breeding ground for terrorism and a lawless security risk, the potential for a new attack aimed at Western symbols and interests is high. An example is the recent transformation of the GSPC (Groupe Salafiste pour la Prédication et le Combat), a group initially oriented exclusively on Algeria in AQMI (Al Qaida Maghreb Islamique), to extend is activities to the Sahelian region and to increase it military modes of operation. Beyond the terrorist threat loom important threats such as illegal trafficking of drugs from the Southern Region of South America to Africa, the development of maritime piracy and financial laundering, risks to information security, and the constant arrival of new armaments sourced from the East.

Health risks are also a significant challenge on a continent that has the highest concentration in the world of transmittable diseases—AIDS, certainly, but also the spread of tuberculosis, meningitis, and other rapidly emerging epidemics—SARS, avian and swine flu, and chikungunya.

The environmental risk is demonstrated by the already obvious advancement of desertification, the stagnation of the great rivers combined with the flooding of their deltas, uncontrolled crowding of urban zones, deforestation, and rising risks to plant health in a region that is dependent on agricultural production. Despite being the smallest "polluter" among the continents, Africa is the apparent first victim of climate change. The new High Commissioner for Refugees Antonio Gurerres has registered a visible and worrying rise in climatic refugees, a trend that underscores the challenge of balancing economic development without exaggerating existing environmental challenges.

A Considerable Potential

If Africa holds major risks, it also holds considerable potential. Africa is home to 12 percent of global oil production and 10 percent of known oil reserves—in addition to zones that are yet to be explored. Also, in near monopoly in conjunction with Australia or Russia, Africa holds most of the metals and minerals essential for continued industrial growth and the development of new technologies: close to 90 percent of known resources of platinum, chrome and copper, 60 percent of reserves of magnesium, 30 percent of reserves of gold and phosphates, cobalt, uranium and bauxite, and 25 percent of titanium reserves. While pressure on demand, notably from Asia, will be problematic in the long term, the potential for gain rests largely on the underexploited, resulting from insufficient infrastructures for production and commercialization and the crises that continue to shake certain oil producers, causing the freeze of exports in times of conflict. In fact, as we have seen, the abatement of conflicts in Angola, Democratic Republic of Congo, and in Southern Sudan have opened up new perspectives—and gained attention from numerous "new friends" to Africa.

Especially, strong demographic growth that predicts Africa will have the youngest population on the planet suggests acute economic, social, and political risks for countries concerned with domestic stability, and neighboring European regions will contend with massive migrations stemming from this young population. But Africa also represents a significant potential market in terms of high consumption. For Western economies challenged by the current recession and financial crisis, in conjunction with an aging population that is causing a shift in trends of demand, the potential economic contributions from the African population will become vital to the health of Europe.

A New Growth

The recent increase in new partners to the African continent alters the significance of its potential. Growth that is already present is becoming stronger. The time of Western monopoly over Africa's political equilibria and economic perspectives has ended.

In the nearly ten years between the first European Union-African Summit in Cairo in 2000 and the second meeting (end of 2007) at Lisbon, a result of the British embargo on Zimbabwe, other large global players have formalized contact with Africa: in 2006 the first African-Chinese Summit and the first African-Latin American Summit were held, a second Summit with the IBSA[14] countries and a fourth TICD[15] meeting in Japan occurred in 2007, and the very first African-Indian Summit was held in 2008. The marked presence of Hugo Chavez and Iranian President Ahmedinijad, who were honored invitees to the African Union Summit of July 2006, constituted an important signal. In fact, looking to the examples of China, India, Venezuela, but also Brazil—and like Iran in the past—Africa seems to be following their economic and political strategy. Since 2000, commercial exchanges between Brazil and Africa multiplied by a quarter; additionally, Brazilian President Lula went on seven trips to the continent and opened a dozen new embassies there. Like India, Brazil has developed cooperation in very specific sectors: tropical agriculture, generic prescriptions, and bio-fuels. Russia itself, a new arrival on the continent, is developing a growing interest in Africa; its strategy is to control energy supplies, but also a balancing of power. Finally Turkey, which is regularly invited as an honored guest to African Union Summits, has reinforced its links to Africa while readily underlining its geostrategic position "at the global crossroads."

The Emergence of Non-State Actors

Beyond classic state-to-state relations, the landscape is being modified by unofficial partnerships and the development of non-public partnerships. The Lebanese, Islamic, Indian, and Chinese diasporas play a growing role in Africa, complemented by African diasporas outside of the continent. The emergence of large investors, for example foundations—like the Gates Foundation or the Aga Khan Foundation, which spend more money each year on the health of Africa than the WHO—are already impacting the organization of industries on the periphery of the continent and in the Sahelian band. Sovereign funds are becoming major actors,[16] without which Western financial backers would lack capital. The World Bank has already partnered

---

[14] India—Brazil—South Africa.

[15] Tokyo International Conference on Development.

[16] Today estimated at $3 billion, by the *Abu Dhabi Investment Authority*: $875 million, *Kuwait Investment Authority*: $213 million, *State Administration of Foreign Exchange* (China): $311 million.

with an assembly that could carry 1 percent of actual estimated returns from sovereign funds, a portfolio of nearly $30 million, i.e. close to the equivalent of the total amount of foreign direct investment (FDI) in Africa for 2007 (...and the equivalent of bonuses distributed in 2007 by Western banks). Islamic banks, with the support of the Gulf countries and Iran, are becoming important partners and privileged voices of the local banks and investors. There is also a growing role for African expatriates, recently evaluated to be worth more than $700 million by the British Parliament.

French Priorities

Since the very beginnings of an international presence in Africa, the French have been privileged brokers in settling African debt and installing financial innovation with the goal of global integration. French engagement in Africa has always highlighted the indispensible balance between development and conflict resolution. In recent years France was resolutely engaged in the ending of African crises, including military intervention in Iturbi with operation Artémis in 2003 and in the Ivory Coast with operation Licorne during 2002. With the RECAMP device, France contributed in an essential manner to the formation of African forces to maintain peace on their own continent. France opened a new European Facility, which has aided since 2004 in the funding of peace operations carried out by the African Union, excluding the resources not used by the EDP (European Development Fund).

The stress is already laid on the resolution of African regional issues—economic, political, and military—and on the partnership between the European Union and the African Union as a privileged forum for the treatment of shared problems: notably immigration, climate change, and energy security. Lastly, the support of the private sector as an essential factor in economic growth and in guaranteeing development is a key element of President Nikolas Sarkozy's political agenda.[17]

Evolving Problems

In the context of domestic preoccupation with economic growth and social stability, evolutions in Africa generally prompt public criti-

---

[17] Speech in the Cape (South Africa)—February 28, 2008.

cism or misunderstandings that see efforts to improve "stability" in Africa as pointlessly expensive undertakings to prop up corrupt regimes. An alternate criticism is that the emphasis on "African self-sufficiency" and the development of "mutual interest" seems to represent Western abandonment of regional partnerships. These hesitations are obviously confronted by the new rejection—frequently angry, sometimes violent—of the ancient colonizers by the younger generations of Francophone countries, and exacerbated by the development of global media and the rise of the Internet.

Our shared stakes in the development and stabilization of the largest continent on the planet must be considered, even though this is rarely done. In this respect, the arrival of Barack Obama permits the emergence of considerably new perspectives. The perception of African issues by the new administration is more important: Barack Obama is an American who will defend the interests of his country as a priority, but will be sure to guard a positive perception of the United States by Africans. The fact that the majority of American people chose to elevate a black man to the head of the United States profoundly modifies African perspectives and gives Africa a new willingness to listen to American positions.

Security and Development: The Key Link

Within this framework, there are many joint or complementary tracks for action that could be evoked to nourish a new transatlantic partnership on African issues.

The first track is the necessary acceleration of the resolution of outstanding conflicts and the recognition of the existing relationship between crisis and development. The link between peace and development, highlighted by the work of Paul Collier,[18] must be confronted and interpreted from the two perspectives. Not because development without peace and security is certain, but because a durable security cannot occur without development, or without an end to crises and the convincing of leaders that economic issues are important. In fact, intervention by Western partners in the resolution of African crises would stand to gain from the abandonment of efforts at political mediation, which has become unproductive, even counterproductive, in

---

[18] Paul Collier, *Breaking the Conflict Trap*, and *The Bottom Billion*, 2007.

favor of efforts at economic sustainability that would showing warring leaders that there is more to be gained from peace. The recent agenda established by the United Nations Commission for the Consolidation of Peace could be aided by a stronger alliance with the major international financial institutions, other major international organizations and aid agencies, and regional banks for development.

Moreover, if the Western states really wish to make African peace a priority, financial support should be given to the African Union for the formation of regional forces that also must be complemented by investment in effective means of communication and surveillance and transport, notably helicopters, to cover the vastness of African theaters of war—as demonstrated by the case of Darfur.

In any event, acute attention must be paid to the grey zone that continues to prevent the advent of a prolonged stage of peace—nearly $5 million are devoted each year to the OMP (Operation to Maintain the Peace) in Africa, and the commitment is meant to last ten years. There is clearly a humanitarian urgency to improved development.

The Reform of Public Aid

The second track relates to the necessary evolution of public aid for development in the context of reduced aid budgets from the biggest donors, for example from the CDAC (Development Aid Committee) of the OECD. The Paulson Plan intended to devote, in diverse forms, $700 million backed by Western banks, which is about ten times the amount promised at the 2005 Gleneagles Summit by the G8 nations, who have pledged but have yet to increase their annual aid to Africa by 2010. The obvious lethargy of the realization of the Millennium Goals for Development,[19] of which a preliminary assessment is planned for 2010, weighs on the relations between the developed countries. There is a debate about the best way to allocate funding to such a tumultuous region.

Improved coordination and complementarity is becoming a priority objective between the donors and the recipients of funding.[20] The

---

[19] Report on reflections regarding the late realization of development goals—World Bank—2008.

[20] Today the count for aid donation from only institutional donors, 280 bilateral donors, 242 multilateral programs, 24 banks for development, 40 UN agencies.

principles of "good behavior" established in the Paris Declaration of March 2007[21] should be broadened to non-member countries of the DAC of the OECD. Associating with private actors, such as the large foundations and sovereign funds, is essential. These principles must be equally extended to the problem of debt, meaning the real risks of running a massive deficit that is unregulated by the external creditors of the Paris Club—the first of which is China, while at the same time helping the debt of African countries exceeds the budget allocated to health concerns in 52 of 54 African countries. In comparison, with the massive effort that remains underway by the members of the Paris Club, particularly France, there is a considerable stake in effectively processing African debts.

The coordination of public and private financial backers must also be coordinated with better coordination between donors and recipients. This enhanced coordination is logical to both sides of the partnership. It also permits an improved sharing of responsibility to counter results that have in the past been considered insufficient. In particular, the granting of aid needs to be paired with effective governance. The current insufficiency of governance explains the limited impact of current aid programs, more than a deficiency in the amount of aid donated.

In fact, the emphasis will have to be on the identification of results in the countries that have positively benefited from aid. Donors need to engage more concretely to serve as partners in improving the allocation of funding, instead of as "witnesses" to the process of African development. Economic growth needs to serve as the primary motor for development, complemented by aid and its allocation to priority sectors for growth.

The Conditions for Equal and Durable Growth

An essential emphasis on growth implies that a more consistent attention must be paid to development from the private sector and the factors that support it: control of the allocation of energy sources, the development of communication infrastructures—highway networks and regional airports, but also access to new technologies and broadband internet—installation of solid banking structures to secure the

---

[21] CF OECD—DAC: *2006 Survey on Monitoring the Paris Declaration.*

savings of migrants, the utilization of the capital of diaspora and expatriate communities, and most importantly the integration of African countries into global financial circuits. A successful result to the recent Doha round from this perspective is a priority. But if the successes of African exports and trade increases are to be translated into domestic growth, they will have to be supplemented by the improvement, transformation and commercialization of production infrastructures.[22]

Priority attention will finally have to be brought to food safety and African agricultural development, the potential of which could be considerable. These sectors are already handicapped by productivity delays and the diverse constraints on American and European markets, in addition to the consequences of climate change. In fact, the necessity to preserve environmental and ecological equilibria will have to be prioritized ahead of strategies for growth. The near disappearance of public funding for agriculture—from 16.9 percent in 1982 to 3.5 percent in 2004—must be reversed, with a particular effort paid to rural infrastructures, inputs, farming methods and information about markets and regulations.

The Inescapable Reform of the Architecture of Global Governance

All of these recommendations and conclusions additionally imply the need for an educational effort to improve public opinion about Africa. Stereotypes need to be abandoned that represent Africa as perpetually in crisis, as necessitating military operations to maintain peace, as unable to carry out fair elections, and as starved for humanitarian intervention.

A joint reflection will have to be carried out to address many symbolic measures—democracy, governance, human rights, and international justice. In effect, on the subjects that remain priorities for favorable public opinion, the West is now confronted by the positions of other forceful partners in Africa, chiefly China, which does not face restrictions over its actions and engagement from domestic public opinion. This gives these rival powers a real comparative advantage in the context of new growth.

---

[22] CF CNUCED: Economic Development in Africa 2008—Results of exportation and the liberalization of commerce—Trends and perspectives.

Beyond, this shared reflection that will have to be brought to the international community, who should not limit themselves to the designs created in 1945, except in seeing itself, *horresco referrens*, and from now on qualified by a certain "cannibalistic command."[23] The G20 summits attest to the breadth of the importance of rebuilding the architecture of global governance. The election of Mummar Gaddafi to the head of the African Union foreshadows a revitalization of the project of the United States of Africa. In total, in an altered context, the most significant African issues—notably stabilization of conflicts in the grey zones, the capacity to compete on the global market, improved security, local employment, and the reinforcement of capacities for governance—could be the privileged subjects of a renewed transatlantic partnership.

---

[23] Jean Ziegler.

Chapter Ten

Africa Policy in an Era of Franco-American Cooperation

Gwendolyn Mikell

Overview

As the administration of President Barack Obama comes on line, the U.S. and France have a new opportunity to redefine the directions they should take toward Africa. In doing so, they should be guided by an understanding of the complex local and global realities that both Africa and the larger global community now face. My years of research on Africa incline me toward seeing policy formulation as well as national interest in terms of a continual challenge to keep eyes on the social context and on how Africans and Americans perceive the changes in their lives. In the recent past, unilateralism, anti-terrorism and security/defense concerns drove much of the American agenda toward Africa. However, Secretary of State Hillary Clinton said that U.S. policy must be a marriage of principles and pragmatism—"there are three legs to the stool of American foreign policy: defense, diplomacy, and development—and two of those reside at the State Department and the U.S. Agency for International Development."[1] Hopefully this means that even given the difficult current global economy, the State Department and the Obama Administration will examine policy challenges and multilateral possibilities within broader institutional, integrated social contexts, and multilateral frameworks than in the past.

My goal here is to examine prospects for Anglo-Francophone cooperation by contrasting it with the past, exploring the dynamics of the strategic players, outlining the security/peacekeeping and governance challenges that are playing out in Africa, and hinting at the opportunities presented by new Diaspora constituencies for Africa. Despite

---

[1] Hillary Rodhan Clinton, "Nomination Hearing to be Secretary of State," January 13, 2009. Also, Mark Silva, "Hillary Clinton: Its Going to Be Hard," *Chicago Tribune: The Swamp*, February 22, 2009.

ongoing conflicts, many African states are moving past the civil wars and rebel conflicts of the 1990s, armed with new knowledge about how to defuse militarized conflict and fight diseases like HIV/AIDS. The crises of the 1990s evoked a flowering of civil society organizations determined to offer critical commentary on the process of nation-building. The West has played a critical role in providing support for this civil society evolution, but the tasks are far from complete. The concern with global terrorist networks that could exploit the vulnerabilities of young African states has placed new burdens on these African polities. Fortunately, most African states, including those with majority Muslim populations, have moderate religious-political cultures, and they have not bought into the terrorist enterprise. Now, we need development approaches that reinforce this moderate stance, rather than derail it. These approaches would help encourage a positive trajectory for African states and the African Union (AU), and require that the U.S., France and the European Union work together in sensitive and effective ways to sustain it.

The Bush Administration approach to Africa was primarily a unilateral one that focused on military/security, trade, and the fight against HIV/AIDS. It acknowledged the historical military and trade relations of France with francophone Africa, saw this as potentially limiting American influence on the continent, and sought to counter it through bilateral relations on trade, development, and security. The Obama Administration's approaches are still embryonic, but claim to emphasize "strengthening democratic institutions, preventing conflict, fostering economic growth, and partnering with Africa to combat global threats."[2] While substantively this sounds similar to prior approaches, there are suggestions that stylistically it may differ, and that there may be opportunities for the U.S. to work more collaboratively with France and other EU countries. This will involve breaking old behavioral molds so that multilateral initiatives are more in sync with African needs and developments on the ground.

American Policy in the Past

Initially, the U.S. did not have a coherent Africa policy, relying instead on Cold War strategies and European spheres of influence in

---

[2] Tami Hultman, "Africa: Carson Outines Obama Administration's Policy Priorities," *allAfrica.Com*, April 29, 2009.

Africa. The only historical American relationships were with Liberia and South Africa, although from the 1960s onward the U.S. had ties to the harsh regime in Congo/Zaire under President Mobutu Sese Seko, and fluctuating strategic relations with Ethiopia, and Somalia.[3] With the end of the Cold War, the U.S. preferred to rely on the U.N. to address the expansion of violent conflicts in Africa, in spite of its difference with the UN over budget and dues. Following the unsuccessful American interventions in Somali in 1992, the U.S. was concerned about 'mission-creep,' and more reticent to engage with Africa on security, political or development issues. The Administration of President Bill Clinton crafted a new economic diplomacy for Africa operating through the Departments of Commerce and Transportation in the 1990s. The earlier reticence to engage on political and military issues continued to haunt U.S. policy, and as the Rwandan genocide unfolded in 1994 U.S. failure to act severely damaged U.S./African relations. Americans were content to rely upon the UN as the major actor, and upon the French, Belgians and the UN in Rwanda, although clearly these proved inadequate to the task of stemming the conflict.[4]

In 1994, the American focus was on South Africa as it cast off apartheid and went through its democratic elections. Using the bi-national conferences for South Africa, Vice President Al Gore oversaw a set of exchanges and conversations between our Foreign Service Institute, and our Departments of Commerce, Agriculture, Transportation, and Education with their South African counterparts. During the regime of General Sani Abacha in Nigeria, the U.S. withdrew most diplomatic resources and deliberately funded pro-democracy civil society organizations which became vocal advocates for the restoration of democracy. When the Abacha regime ended, the process of matching of development assistance to specific needs of the new government, and the pairing of political and security assistance through a bilateral relationship (such as in South Africa) was replicated in 1999 as President Obasanjo assumed office. Post-election Nigeria was a more complicated process for the U.S., which involved restoring diplomatic resources,

[3] Marguerite Michaels, "Retreat from Africa," *Foreign Affairs*, 1992/3. Elliott P. Skinner, *African Americans and U.S. Foreign Policy Toward Africa, 1850-1924: In Defense of Black Nationality*. Washington, D.C.: Howard University, 1993.

[4] Victoria K. Hult and Moira K. Shanahan, "African Capacity-Building for Peace Operations: UN Collaboration with the African Union and ECOWAS" http://www.stimson.org/fopo/pdf/Africa_Capacity-building.pdf.

navigating the Muslim-Christian tensions within the country, reinforcing Nigeria's capacity to play a central role in ECOMOG conflict
resolution, targeting funding toward women's civil society groups, and
addressing HIV/AIDS as a civilian and military issue. However, stronger U.S. relations with Nigeria have not yet translated into stronger
democratic development in that country.[5]

The competitive economic focus of both American and French relations with Africa appears consistent throughout the 1990s, but they
often yielded mixed results for Africa. The U.S. and France relied on
Nigeria and Angola for sweet crude oil exports, and were supportive of
corporate relationships with both countries. In Angola, the U.S.
backed Jonas Savimbi, the rebel leader of the war against the socialist
government for 30 years; and only after Savimbi's death in 2002 did the
U.S. strengthen relations with the Angolan government, and support
the democratic transition.[6] In comparison, France had supported the
separatists of Angola's Cabinda province after independence, but sub-
sequently backed French arms sales to President dos Santos to fight the
rebels in the 1990s. Likewise, France's oil giant Total has the largest
concessions in Sudan, and France has significant interests in the Chad-
Cameroon Pipeline project, making it supportive of government stability, despite the ongoing conflicts in those countries. While U.S.
companies have significant oil interests in Sudan, the U.S. has focused
on fighting human rights violations in Sudan in response to pressures
from its religious and civil society groups.

American public pressure has had an impact on emerging Africa
policy, and the same may be true in France. The roots of the African
Growth and Opportunity Act (AGOA) were laid during the 1998-
2002 transition period as U.S. civil society agitated for coherent legislation designed to lift tariff restrictions on African imports into the
U.S. and broader African trade. President Bush is credited with tri-
pling overseas development assistance (ODA) to Africa, and he signed

---

[5] Gwendolyn Mikell, "Players, Policies, and Prospects: Nigeria/U.S. Relations," in Ade-
keye Adebayo and Abdul Raufu Mustapha (Ed), *Gulliver's Troubles: Nigeria's Foreign Policy
After the Cold War*, Scottsville SA: University of KwaZulu-Natal Press, 2008, pp. 281-313.
See also, Gwendolyn Mikell and Princeton Lyman, "Critical Bilateral Relations in Africa:
Nigeria and South Africa," Chapter 6 in J. Stephen Morrison and Jennifer Cook, eds.,
Africa Policy in the Clinton Years: Critical Choices for the Bush Administration, Washington,
D.C.: CSIS Significant Issues Series, 2001.

[6] Fred Bridgland, "Ghost of Savimbi haunts Angola," February 22, 2003, *NEWS.scotland.
com*. "Angolagate: les principaux acteurs de l'affaire," *Le Figaro*, March 28, 2007.

renewed AGOA legislation into law during his first months in office in 2001. In addition, Americans have been concerned about humanitarian and health crises in Africa.

What earned President Bush an 85-plus percent approval rating from Africans was not his security initiatives, but his eagerness to travel to varied African countries to assess trade and development as well as humanitarian projects, his willingness to talk with ordinary Africans about democratic processes, his joy in 'dancing' as he did in Liberia and Ghana, and his passionate commitment to fighting HIV/AIDS and other diseases in Africa. He proudly asserts that he more than doubled development assistance to Africa relative to its level in 2004, and that he worked on partnering with African leaders to overcome poverty by growing their economies. His policy initiatives included the signing of the African Growth and Opportunity Act (AGOA-2001), the African Education Initiative (2002), the Millennium Challenge Corporation grants totaling $3 billion to democratic and liberalizing African countries (2003), and the President's Emergency Fund for AIDS Relief (PEPFAR-2003). PEPFAR was controversial within the U.S. because of its ABC (abstinence, be faithful, and condoms) approach, and its reliance upon support from religious groups which backed the initiatives. 'Just say no,' which was a holdover Republican mantra, found its way into PEPFAR. Yet, even critics have to grudgingly congratulate Bush on the impact of the antiretroviral drugs and counseling that are changing the face of HIV/AIDS in many African areas.[7] These successes and failures point to new possible U.S./French/EU collaborations, especially if they move beyond the treatment component to deal with the health systems and health education components, which are key to health success.

Bush's initiatives included the President's Malaria Initiative (2005), Multilateral Debt Relief Initiative (2005), five new investment funds supported by the Overseas Private Investment Corporation (OPIC), the African Global Competitiveness Initiative (AGCI-2006), and training over 39,000 African peacekeepers in 20 countries (especially ECOWAS), in addition to working with local partners to address security challenges and peace prospects in Africa. The U.S. is the largest

---

[7] Giles Bolton, "How is America's Extra Aid Being Spent?" in *Africa Doesn't Matter: How the West has failed the Poorest Continent and What We can do about It* (NY: Arcade Publishers, 2008) p. 279.

donor to the Office of the High Commissioner for Refugees (UNHCR), which gave more than 40 percent of that funding to Africa in 2007; and also "the largest contributor to the Global Fund for HIV/AIDS, Malaria, and Tuberculosis, pledging over $3.5 billion and providing over $2.5 billion since 2001.[8] On receiving an honor from Africare for his Africa policies, especially his African health initiatives, President Bush proudly noted: "People across Africa now speak of a Lazarus effect: communities once given up for dead are being brought back to life."[9]

The Bush Administration's stated policy of 'African solutions to African problems' and of relying on regional powers to handle the security demands, was viewed more critically within Africa; and there was increased pressure for the U.S. to be a more involved advocate for multilateral peacekeeping at the U.N. President Bush's U.S. Security Strategy of 2002 and 2006, which took preemptive approaches to combating terrorism, and which sought to "expand the circle of development by opening societies and building the infrastructure of democracy"[10] was initially quite controversial. Yet, Bush's African initiatives increasingly recognized Africa's geo-strategic importance, and by-and- large they were deemed successful. In West Africa, the U.S. gradually acquiesced to greater support for Nigeria's role in ECOWAS peacekeeping in Liberia and Sierra Leone, albeit the security strategies were less successful elsewhere on the continent.

There is pressure for the Obama Administration to expand PEP-FAR to include health systems more broadly, and to remove the preferential treatment for religious groups in project funding. Likewise, the Obama Administration may continue and deepen support for security issues in Africa, perhaps best symbolized by the new African command (AFRICOM) that was proposed in 2007 and formalized stood up in October 2008. Some of the security issues and critiques are fleshed out more below.

---

[8] Fact Sheet: U.S. Africa Policy: An Unparalleled Partnership Strengthening Democracy, Overcoming Poverty, and Saving Lives. *White House News*, February 1, 2008.

[9] PEPFAR has supported treatment for approximately 1.7 million Africans, and it was increased by $48 billion in 2007 after being extended by Congress. See Brian Kennedy, "Top U.S. Charity Lauds Bush Africa Policy," *AllAfrica.Com*, November 17, 2008 Washington, D.C.

[10] *The National Security Strategy of the United States of America*, George W. Bush, The White House, March 16, 2006.

Core Countries and Strategy in the Horn, East, and Central Africa

Each era has its policy interest and needs, as well as its distinct awareness of national interests. The terrorist assaults of September 11, 2001 within the U.S., when seen against the backdrop of the bombing of U.S. embassies in Nairobi Kenya and Dar es Salaam Tanzania in 1998, strengthened American concern about security and President George W. Bush's commitment to pre-emptive diplomacy. From 2002 onward, Bush began to establish a new set of relations with Africa, initially based on the traditional security and trade emphases of Republican administrations, but gradually with a determination to help prevent African countries from becoming sites exploited by Islamic militants and global terrorist networks. With the growing African and global commitments to ending civil wars and to conflict resolution, perceptions of how economic and conflict dynamic are integrated have increased. Yet, greater awareness and sensitivity in Western strategic approaches is necessary.

First, there is the need for sophisticated regional and country-specific analyses that are fine tuned to conditions on the ground in the Horn. The Horn of Africa continued to be a major concern, especially as anxiety about transnational networks operating in Somalia fed American advocacy for 'draining the swamps,' fueled Ethiopian and American collaborations, and as African tensions heightened in the region.[11] The French Parliament also debated how to approach policy in the Horn, especially in its dialogue with representatives from the region, but no productive conclusions emerged.[12] More recently, the phenomenon of piracy off the coast of Somalia had cemented the conclusion that policy for this area is not just a unilateral issue, but must be the outcome of collaborative American, Francophone, and United Nations discussions about how to fight the poverty that may feed piracy off the Horn of Africa.[13]

---

[11] Princeton Lyman and J. Stephen Morrison, "The Terrorist Threat in Africa," *Foreign Affairs*, January/February 2004. See also "Draining the Swamp: The Financial Dimension," Council on Foreign Relations, The American Response to Terrorism series, March 25, 2002; and "Why Ethiopian and American Interests Conflict on Somalia: Commentary," *Ogaden Online Editorial Board*, January 15, 2002.

[12] "France Renews Ties with the Horn of Africa," *Ethiomedia*, February 6, 2004.

[13] "Pirates force the world to see sad plight of Somalia," *Irishtimes.com*, October 29, 2008.

Clearly the Obama Administration must devote more focused attention to resolving issues such as Somalian piracy, the Sudanese Civil War, and DRC post-conflict rebuilding. In the case of Somalia piracy, the recent rescue of the American captain and crew apprehended by pirates off the coast provide a demonstration of American naval and military ingenuity in the face of maritime criminality. Nevertheless, our approaches must become more systematized and involve less loss of life or we will escalate the violence along the Somali coast. Simpkins has rightly points out weakness in international peacekeeping processes there; insisted that despite our history of problems in Somalia, that country must become a priority for U.S./Africa policy; and urged us to work through Inter-Governmental Authority on Drought and Development (IGAD) to stem small arms flows and potential terrorist cells.[14]

It is obvious that international law on piracy provides little comfort—no one wants to bring the pirates back to the U.S. or Europe for trial, incurring enormous domestic and international legal and financial difficulties. Therefore, in addition to international maritime approaches and multilateral agreements, our attention must turn to a better understanding of the local conditions that enable piracy and to a search for local solutions that involve the use of Somali and African social and cultural capital. Piracy in the Gulf of Aden is easy, and it is an economic strategy born of coastal anger about colonial-cum-international infringement on Somali territory and waters that is not being addressed. Pirates operate as an extension of on-land networks based on lineage/kinship, friendship, and patron-client relations to provide food, jobs, and other critical resources to people living in a crisis-ridden non-existent state. Since they function in the shadows of older political authority networks, I believe that the solution is to be found on land.

The suggestion that African leadership is critical in resolving the piracy problem must be taken seriously by the U.S. and France. Some have suggested that Somali piracy will not end until appeals have been made to local leaders of the areas from which the pirates come; and there is some precedence for expecting that local Islamic leaders can help resolve conflict and end killings in the area.[15] I suggest that the

---

[14] Gregory B. Simpkins, "Raising the Level of Engagement between America and Africa: A Leon H. Sullivan Foundation White Paper, Washington, D.C., April 2009.

[15] Abdi Samatar, "The Road Ahead: Violence and Reconciliation in Somalia, Council on Foreign Relations, podcast, *http://www.cfr.org/publication/13209/road_ahead.html*.

solution must initially involve the use of both Somali and broader African social capital. It is time to strategize about a development strategy for Somalia that provides occupational incentives that preclude piracy as an economic strategy. African institutional approaches must be expanded to include other African regional judicial/ tribunal frameworks to deal with piracy. Therefore, working with IGAD is an essential, but probably not a sufficient strategy. Whether the Somalia solution should include the creation of a Horn-of-Africa tribunal, or a new institution that deals with economic/security issues is the question.

In essence, 'African solutions' without accompanying Western support and partnership is not the answer. G8 support must be constructed thoughtfully and collaboratively. While the creation of the Rwandan tribunal of the International Criminal Court was innovative and essential, it short-circuited other possible African conflict resolution approaches, and triggered Anglo-Franco tensions. In retrospect, we also see the unanticipated problems created in Swahili coastal communities by the pursuit of Kenya/Tanzania bombing suspects; and the legal proceedings against al-Qaeda suspects teach us that issues of justice must be informed by local African and global standards in order to withstand scrutiny.[16] Our security approaches must involve awareness of local impacts, and engage local partnerships. It is essential that the U.S., France, and the EU find common ground in addressing security in the Horn of Africa and East Africa, especially since the possibility of using UN authority here is still distant.

Global security crises have increased the importance of African areas for the U.S., since roughly 22 percent of African sweet crude oil imports into the U.S. are derived here.[17] Now, Muslim populations in these oil-producing areas are sensitive to how we deal with security issues in Muslim countries.[18] There are the issues of strengthening and

---

[16] Susan F. Hirsch, *In the Moment of Greatest Calamity: Terrorism, Grief, and a Victim's Quest for Justice*, Princeton University Press, 2006. Also, "What if Torturers Go to Trial and Win?" *Yglesias*, April 28, 2009. See http://yglesias.thinkprogress.org/archives/2009/04/what-if-torturers-go-to-trial-and-win.php.

[17] "African Crude Exports to the U.S. Jump," *Energy Tribune*, April 18, 2007. See also, David Shin, "China, Africa, and Oil," Center for Strategic and International Studies, Washington, D.C., 2006.

[18] Ibrahim Addo Karawa, "Exploring Mutual Perceptions: Dialogue between U.S. and Northern Nigerian Opinion Leaders," January 27-28, 2003. See also, Gwendolyn Mikell, "America's Response to Terrorism: Fundamentalist Movements in Africa," Council on Foreign Relations, Washington, D.C., December 5, 2001.

rationalizing the military institutions in Africa, dealing with conflict resolution, increasing public diplomacy and outreach to the African Islamic world, as well as heightening the support that U.S. defense institutions could provide for civil-military relations in Africa. These initiatives, combined with the 2002 U.S. national security strategy[19] of defending and preserving the peace, the promotion of democracy, preventive assaults on terrorist networks, and disrupting the financing for terrorism, have had significant impacts on Africa. The Obama Administration must now respond to this.

Darfur/Sudan now poses problems which require the use of African social and cultural capital in peacekeeping and conflict resolution capacity building. Clearly the hybrid United Nations/African Union (UNAMID) force is not working for myriad reasons. In addition to the lack of financial and institutional resources necessary for African Union to provide sufficient peacekeeping troops for UNAMID, there is the lack of political will on the part of the Security Council members to fund, staff, and provision a mission that could provide the requisite protection for Darfur refugees; suspicion about American desires to use the ICC to control a Muslim country; as well as conflict within the AU about the political wisdom of the UN holding President al-Bashir and Sudanese officials to account for atrocities.

The question is whether France is restrained in using its moral authority to help resolve the Sudan regional crises. The military intervention to reinforce President Idris Dirby of Chad demonstrate the importance of France in regional affairs in Fall 2008, but raise the issue of French national interest.[20] The ICC warrant for the arrest of President Omar al-Bashir—a sitting head of state—is considered unprecedented, and this has angered North African leaders as well as the AU heads-of-state writ large. While AU leaders either deny or abhor the Darfur atrocities, they appear to fear interventions in Sudan that challenge state sovereignty, anticipating that their acquiescence would divide the AU. This division is a real possibility, given the role that President Muamar Qadaffi of Libya and others have played in leveraging financial assistance to African countries as a means of con-

---

[19] President George W. Bush, "National Security Strategy of the United States," *New York Times*, September 20, 2002.

[20] Mark Tran, "France Threatens Military Action against Chad Rebels," *The Guardian*, Tuesday, February 5, 2008. http://www.guardian.co.uk/world/2008/feb/05/france.sudan.

trolling the dynamics of the AU. The end result is AU support to President al-Basir, which insulates him from the global threat and preserves his control over Sudanese politics.

This quagmire poses enormous problems for the U.S., the UN, and for the AU, and the solution cannot readily emerge from Africans themselves. President Obama has already appointed a special envoy on Sudan—General Gracian, and there is hope for some progress. However, it may be time for Americans to sit down with members of the G8 to discuss the effectiveness of strategies on Sudan. The G8 approach means utilizing a forum outside the United Nations, but one in which the Chinese and other P5 members would be involved. China is key to a resolution on Sudan, yet UN Secretary General Ban ki-Moon had already utilized a little of his moral authority to urge Chinese cooperation on Sudan, and there may be limits on how much this can yield. Former Secretary-General Kofi Annan was not reticent about attending the Summit meetings of the AU, or using his bully-pulpit to help shift AU language and normative behavior on conflict resolution, governance, and other issues. It may be time for this Administration to begin to work with the EU, Canada, the Scandanavians, and the UN to encourage new venues within Africa at which these issues could be discussed. Together, they could propose a special G8 Conference on Sudan occurring on the margins of an upcoming AU Summit.

The creation of the new AFRICOM command now alters the security dialogues. In 2007 both Africa and many U.S., groups were suspicious of the Bush Administration's creation of the U.S. Africa Command, and thus what they perceived as a 'militarized foreign policy.' At that time, AFRICOM had development components that were alternatively criticized as inadequate and more appropriate for USAID. However, since that time it has resolved many of these issues. A more positive American response emerged after AFRICOM's stand-up in October 2008, and as the AU reflected on AFRICOM's more consultative agenda and its decision to build a base in Stuttgart, Germany rather than on the African continent for the foreseeable future.[21] There are lessons here for both the U.S. and other Western countries that will be

---

[21] "African Union Rejects America's AFRICOM Military Base," *Ligali*, February 19, 2008. "AFRICOM: Assessing the African Perspective," Council on Foreign Relations, Washington, D.C., October 1, 2008. See also Gwendolyn Mikell, "U.S. Academics and the Security Sector: Issues and Concerns," Plenary Paper for the AFRICOM Symposium, The Africa Center for Strategic Studies, National Conference Center, June 10, 2008.

explored more fully later: post-Cold War security-focused approaches usually do not take sufficient note of the fact that terrorist challenges are often predictable results of failing to address development needs and give poor people options.

The competition between the U.S. and France, which tended to dominate relations in the 1990s, is weaker now but still colors security relationships with African countries. Like the U.S., France also has gone through different phases in its foreign policy—albeit, with less publicity than have American because of the nature of our Congressional and political party systems. France has had a century of deeply developed entrenched economic and military relations with Sub-Saharan countries like Senegal, Mali, Niger, Nigeria, Burkina Faso, Cote d'Ivoire, Chad, Central African Republic, Gabon, Zaire/DRC, Rwanda, and Burundi.

The more than 250,000 French citizens residing in Africa, and the economic ties through trade and investment in African oil and metals, had increased France's stake in ties with its former colonies.[22] Yet over the last decade, global dynamics encouraged the Africans in francophone areas to be pragmatic, to cross borders to work, to take advantage of education and opportunities, and to participate in social movements for change outside this orbit. The de-linking of the African franc (CFA) from the French franc in 1994 created dislocations, but it was the difficult military relationships in Rwanda in 1994 and Zaire/ DRC in 1997 that have further intertwined the relations of Anglophone and Francophone African countries. Since 2000, France has seems inclined to move away from bilateral military engagements in favor of multilateral cooperation in peace and humanitarian assistance, but the French still engaged in military interventions in Chad in 2007/8, CAR in 2006, and in Cote d'Ivoire in 2005-6.[23] Perhaps the intense dynamics of globalization have further sped up France's search for a new type of relations with African countries. Hansen quotes Andre Dulait, the parliamentarian as saying that "The African continent is our neighbor, and when it's shaken by conflict, we're shaken as well" (2008). Yet, many French citizens and officials have begun to rethink their strate-

---

[22] Andrew Hansen, "The French Military in Africa," *Backgrounder*, February 8, 2008

[23] Ibid. See also, David Gauthier-Villars, "Continental Shift: Colonial Era Ties to Africa Face a Reckoning in France," *Wall Street Journal*, May 16, 2007.

gic and military priorities in Africa relative to their long-held interests in Asia, or their emerging interests in South America.

2009 brings a special opportunity for change to both the U.S. and France, because the post-Cold War transition in Africa has ended, and a new phase of continental and global dialogue has begun. Will the EU countries look beyond their borders and be poised to try to make a difference? Will the U.S. and France work together in the G8 and within the UN Security Council to offer common approaches to Africa? People everywhere have a more nuanced view of 'global terrorism' than they did seven years ago. There are many African immigrants who, as new citizens in both the U.S. and France, do vote and register their desire to see a nuanced and pragmatic policy emerge with their chosen candidates. In this new phase, African countries are assuming greater control over their own destinies, trying to create the regional and continental mechanisms to deal with the many crises they face. How the Western countries collaborate with Africa on these challenges will affect the global outlook.

The Emerging Strategic Players in Africa

The African Union's development—especially institutional, economic, political-legal, and security infrastructure—is the first strategic consideration, and therefore critical to the continent's future. The ground has shifted, and the former colonial divisions that emerged from the Berlin Conference are dissipating, but Africa's emerging understandings of its collective strategic interests have not yet kept pace. The American assumption that Africa belonged to the Europeans has disappeared, to be replaced by confusion over when and where the U.S. should intervene, and how to respond to African requests for assistance without increasing international tensions. Over the last two decades, driven largely by economic and security interests, the U.S. and France have competed for influence in every corner of the African continent. On both economic and security issues, real collaboration among the big power players has yet to happen, perhaps because of historical competitions, tensions within the UN General Assembly, or different priorities despite the dialogues and commitments surrounding the G8 African Agenda. Some have argued that the U.S./French competition which played out in the search for economic trade and protection agreements has negative regional impacts especially for SADC. Trade with South Africa is the prize, guaranteed to bring American or French products to an enormous national and regional market. However, the impact on the smaller neighbors in SADC could be devastating, say many concerned southern Africanists.[24]

The New Partnership for African Development (NEPAD) reflects Africa's determination to coordinate regional and continental development. The U.S., France, and the EU have yet to craft a coherent policy response to NEPAD's development agendas, and the global economic downturn may not be advantageous. Western countries have tended to pursue their own national/strategic interests to the neglect of multilateral initiatives. There are enormous economic issues that await discussion, especially how to focus attention on sustainable agriculture, which must be at the core of poverty alleviation in the coming years. Neither AGOA nor other initiatives have sufficiently addressed the importance of encouraging local agricultural production and agro-industry to sustain local communities, as strategies for decreasing poverty as they balance global market dynamics. Nor have they been sensitive to the gender component in rural development, despite the fact that women's roles will be critical to African national and regional economic sustainability. Indeed, there is a need to see the Millennium Challenge Corporation's initiatives integrate broad concerns for poverty alleviation and gender equity, if the U.S. is to support movement toward achieving the Millennium Development Goals by 2015.

The AU is now debating the eventual amalgamation of African states into the 'United States of Africa,' and collaborative approaches will be essential in the future. The three different positions taken by African states within the Great Debate' on Pan-Africanism at the 9th Summit of the AU was emblematic of the difficult challenges facing Africa[25]—how to blend states that are at different levels of develop-

---

[24] Margaret C. Lee, "The 21st Century Scramble for Africa," *Journal of Contemporary African Studies*, Vol. 24, No. 3, September 2006, pp. 303-330 (also to be published in *Africa in Global Power Play: Debates, Challenges and Potential Reforms*, Behekinkosi Moyo, ed., London: Adonis & Abbey Publishers, Ltd (forthcoming) 2007). See also "European Union-South Africa Free Trade Agreement: In Whose Interest?" *Journal of Contemporary African Studies*, Vol. 20, No. 1, 2002, pp. 81-106.

[25] The three positions are: Instantivism (unity now), Gradualism (regional integration first), and Opposition (national sovereignty only). See T. Murithi, "Institutionalizing pan-Africanism: Transforming African Union values and principles into practice. ISS Paper, No. 143, 2007. Also, James Butty, "Analyst suspects Khadafi phobia in Summit Outcome," Ngwane, http://www.gngwane.com/2007/07/analyst-suspect.html.

ment, have different institutional and constitutional capacities, have widely different international networks and partnerships, and widely differing economic realities and potentials. Africans are becoming convinced that the Francophone, Anglophone, and Lusophone divides of the colonial past are of lessening relevance to their lives, and that they must find national policies and foreign policies that meet their needs, no matter from where their origins and with whom they forge alliances. These new possibilities require the U.S., France, and the EU to be more collaborative than they have been in the past, and more creative in imagining how local initiatives and their economic, political, security, and development policies in general, can be integrated in more productive and efficient ways.

China's entrance onto the global stage changes the strategic dynamics. First, it alters the economic balance sheet, offering new opportunities and approaches to some African states, and new competitions for African resources. The first Tokyo International Conference on African Development (TICAD) suggested that Japan would be the Asian partner of note,[26] but this had changed tremendously by 2000 as the global economy shifted and Japan mobilized its relations throughout Asian on behalf of global trade and aid. This emergence of Asia has created trauma and anxiety for many in the West, given the possibility of U.S./Chinese/ French interests. It has not yet been possible to negotiate with China regarding the impact of their trade and concessional loans on poverty and growth in African areas, but this should not be ruled out as a possibility in the current difficult global economy. Do Chinese imports and exports serve to increase Africa's dependence without assisting with longer-term growth strategies? Does Chinese trade benefit disproportionately from African debt relief by absorbing capital that might be used for development purposes, or occupying development space that?

These concerns have been raised by researchers who focus on China's increased penetration in Africa, in terms of 'trade links, investment in the petroleum sector, infrastructural projects, diplomatic gains,

---

[26] TICAD.

and participation in peacekeeping missions."[27] Whether described as 'oil diplomacy' or as the 'new scramble for Africa,'[28] many say:

> Clearly what is demonstrated in most of the case studies is that the economies of the African states are quickly becoming overly dependent on commodity exports to China, while at the same time ignoring the need to devise robust and coherent national industrial policies.[29]

The 'oil and weapons' link figures centrally in their analysis, especially whether China's lack of concern for human rights in countries with which they trade is having a negative impact on democratic governance. In the context of Sudan and Zimbabwe, China initially protested that it did not mix politics and business.[30] Their subsequent defenses have included statements about China's policy of non-interference in the domestic affairs of another country, despite the uproar created by their shipment of arms to the Zimbabweans and the Sudanese.[31] Initially, the UN Security Council was unable to mobilize sufficient pressures on China to help persuade Sudanese President Bashir to accept UN and AU troops, and the prolongation of the Darfur crisis reflected this lack of political will to resolve the crisis. But now China has begun to move on the Darfur issue, and we need to understand better how Bashir was convinced to accept the hybrid UNAMID force in 2008.[32]

---

[27] Ray Gilpin, "China in Africa: An Analysis of Recent Developments," *The Africa Center for Strategic Studies*, October 2006.

[28] Margaret C. Lee, "Uganda and China: Unleashing the Power of the Dragon," in Margaret C. Lee, Henning Melber, Sanusha Naidu, and Ian Taylor, *China in Africa*, Nordic Africa Institute, Current African Issues 35, Uppsala, Sweden: Nordic Africa Institute, 2007, pp. 26-40.

[29] Kweku Ampiah and Sanusha Naidu, eds., *Crouching Tiger, Hidden Dragon? Africa and China* (Scottsville SA: University of KwaZulu-Natal Press, 2008), pp. 11-12.

[30] China/Sudan Fact Sheet, http://www.savedarfur.org/newsroom/policypapers/china_and_sudan _fact_sheet/.

[31] Lloyd Sachikonye, "Crouching Tiger, Hidden Agenda? Zimbabwe-China Relations" in Ampiah and Naidu, eds., *Crouching Tiger, Hidden Dragon? Africa and China*, Scottsville SA: University of KwaZulu-Natal Press, 2008. Hilary Anderssen, "China is Fueling War in Darfur," *BBC News*, July 13, 2008. See also, "South African Union Refuses to Unload Chinese Arms Headed for Zimbabwe," *Reuters*, April 18, 2008.

[32] "China Presses Sudan Over Darfur," Reuters, *New York Times*, Asia-Pacific, June 12, 2008.

The new strategic players add complexity to the political and economic equations. There are many lessons to be drawn from the Sudan crises, including ones about the complexity of AU deliberations, the alliances between Libya, Sudan, and other Arab countries in approaching UN negotiations on Sudan, and the difficulties that Sub-Saharan Africans feel in questioning African 'brotherhood' by pressuring Bashir on Darfur. But other important lessons are that China may be poised to become a more integrated partner in global alliances, and perhaps coordinated pressures from Western countries can begin to discourage a Chinese arms trade linkage that the world finds repugnant. The U.S., France, and the EU must work on finding ways to increase the collaborations with China on Zimbabwe,[33] and to draw China more fully into the security and governance dialogues so that there is greater coordination in multilateral conflict resolution, and more moral resources available to support African democratic initiatives.

India is another new global player in Africa, who is not really new. Indians have had a presence in East Africa for the last one hundred years, but the presence of state relationships is the new factor. The Africa-India Forum Summit in Delhi in April 2008 served notice that ties would be strengthening between these two areas over the coming decades. Through relations with the COMESA countries (Kenya, Tanzania, Southern Africa), India seeks to find new markets to their products like machinery, transport equipment, petroleum and timber products, textiles, metals, agricultural products, technology, and pharmaceuticals.[34] In addition, India has a significant technical and agricultural cooperation program with African countries of over a billion dollars, and focused on tele-education and tele-medicine.[35] Their shared concerns related to the Indian Ocean commerce, maritime relations, and ecological developments where Western interests will meet and clash or harmonize with Asian ones. While the U.S. might be able to play a mediating role between China, Indian, the Middle East, and Africa in these relationships, thus gaining relative to its European colleagues, global partnerships may hold the greater potential.

---

[33] Adekeye Adebajo, "An Axis of Evil? China, the United States, and France in Africa," Ampiah and Naidu, op. cit.

[34] "India — Boosting Trade with Africa," Africa Business Pages, http://www.africa-business.com/features/india_africa2.html.

[35] "India to offer Duty Free Access to Products from Africca," Africa Business Pages.

Security and Governance Transitions in West and Southern Africa

If foreign policy periodically recalibrates with realities on the ground, then the American and French security and governance relationships with Africa should become less militarized and more focused on human security[36] during the terms of President Obama and the EU Presidencies of France and Czechoslovakia. With few exceptions, over the last decade West Africa has moved away from the crises of the immediate post-cold war period, and has demonstrated excellent ECOWAS regional collaboration in conflict resolution, national rebuilding of state institutions after civil war and regional collaboration on oil and gas projects with support from international financial institutions. Even within the successes, it is possible to see the problems that African states have experienced in finding the resources necessary to face the military/security challenges posed by civil war and rebel action, to deal with the difficulties of balanced 'nation-building' after conflicts end, to protect and empower women, to rebuild agricultural and trade economies so that poverty reduction and food security are achieved, and then to deal with the burden of HIV/AIDS at all levels.

Let us remember that in the area of peacekeeping, peace enforcement, and conflict resolution West African neighbors to Liberia and Sierra Leone have often had their hearts in the right places, and enthusiastically supported peace dialogues, negotiations, and agreements. However, African leaders (Cote d'Ivoire, Ghana, Nigeria, Senegal, ECOWAS as well as the OAU) generally lacked sufficient tactical/political strength and economic resources to handle the peace processes alone, and reliance on the regional hegemon (Nigeria) proved inadequate. The emphasis must always be on African ownership of peace processes. Yet, the West African experiences highlight questions about the kinds of bilateral and multilateral (UN) commitments that are essential to make African peace missions really work. Therefore, two examples and sets of suggestions are contained here — one about

---

[36] Kofi A. Annan, *In Larger Freedom: Toward Development, Security, and Human Rights for All.* United Nations, March 2005. See also, *Human Security in Africa*, Office of the Special Adviser on Africa (OSAA), United Nations, Dec. 2005, http://www.un.org/africa/osaa/reports/Human%20Security%20in%20Africa%20FINAL.pdf. See also, African Human Security Initiative 2: *Enhancing the Delivery of Security in Africa: Complementing the African Peer Review Mechanism*, London: DFID, http://www.african review.org/.

peace processes, and the other about collaboration on civil-military relations in Africa.

The goal of creating AU Standby Forces that can move rapidly to an emerging crisis must be addressed, because while the AU has the desire to deal with African conflicts, it lacks the financial and logistical capacity to do so. Now Africans ask why AFRICOM's stand up in late 2008 has not been balanced by support for the AU stand-by force. Throughout the 1990s, Americans were largely unwilling to put 'boots on the ground' to help stop the fighting. Many professed distrust that the UN was able to handle the funding and the execution of peace missions, and they did not lobby Congress or the State Department to obtain additional funds and support for these missions. Conflicts were lengthened as a consequence, and the Liberian and Sierra Leonean people paid an enormous price in lives and social capital.

But Western countries all have different capacities and strengths which can be joined with African strengths if the political will exists. In Darfur for example, some can supply tanks, and others can supply troops, others can provide training, and others can supply operational funds. The lesson is that the U.S., France, the Netherlands, Germany, Canada, and the UK among others, must provide coordinated and engaged support to African states in military retraining and capacity building. We must find innovative ways to help support the AU and regional initiatives in peace missions, and must be enthusiastic cheerleaders for multinational support within the General Assembly of the UN.

In the Liberian and Sierra Leonean conflicts, Nigeria bore the brunt—providing the largest numbers of troops as well as the financial burden of payment for soldiers and equipment.[37] After President Obasanjo's election in 1999, Nigerians were unwilling and unable to go further without Western support of the process, and Nigeria withdrew from ECOMOG and UNOMSIL in Sierra Leone in May 2000. Just as in Liberia with UNOMIL, the Sierra Leonean UNOMSIL mission was too small and unarmed with only a Chapter VI mandate, rendering it unable to stop the re-entry of rebel forces into Freetown in Janu-

---

[37] Margaret A. Vogt, ed., *The Liberian Crisis and ECOMOG: A Bold Attempt at Regional Peace Keeping*, Lagos: Gabumo Publishing Co., 1992. See George Klay Kieh, *Ending the Liberian Civil War: Implications for United States Policy Toward West Africa*, Washington, D.C.: TransAfrica Forum, 1996.

ary 1999. Olonisakin says that although Canada, the Netherlands, the United Kingdom, and the U.S.—in that order—provided some funding for the new UNAMSIL mission, initially it was inadequate. [38] While UNAMSIL could not function without Nigerian troops and influence or without Chapter VI authorization to use force, it also could not have pushed the Rebels out of Freetown without the bilateral IMATT troops supplied by the United Kingdom. UNAMSIL alone could not have conducted the negations that led to the Nigerian facilitated Abuja agreement; nor could it have won the 'hearts and minds' of Sierra Leoneans without the humanitarian initiatives that were grafted onto the original UNAMSIL mission in 2000.

Only in 2000, under the new leadership provided by Sir Jeremy Greenstock of the UK, and the engagement of the new U.S. Permanent Representative to the UN Richard Holbrooke did we see a major shift. Holbrooke's efforts led to a change of heart within the American Congress on UN funding for UN-DPKO Africa missions, increased support within the UN Security Council for the Sierra Leonean peace mission, and the expansion of UNAMSIL troop strength to 17,500 spread over much of the country. UNAMSIL became a model of what effective peacekeeping could be, although its reputation also suffered from accusation of child and female exploitation by UN troops.

There is also another story here, about the Security Council's initiative in creating a joint UN-Sierra Leone Special Court—which did not have Chapter VII authorization—to try cases of war crimes and crimes against humanity, exactly two years before Sierra Leone established the Truth and Reconciliation process (TRC-2002) outlined at the Lome Agreement of 1999. Many Sierra Leoneans angrily pointed out that the Special Court was a creation of the UN Security Council and General Assembly in which American influence was pronounced or that it appeared to contravene the Constitution of Sierra Leone, [39] while the TRC grew out of Sierra Leonean and African negotiations and agreements. Conflict also ensued from the fact that the Special Court could hand down indictments and sentences—some of which punished lower level persons more than those higher up, some of which

---

[38] Funmi Olonisakin, *Peacekeeping in Sierra Leone: The Story of UNAMSIL*, NY: International Peace Academy, 2008.

[39] Abdul Karim Bangura, Sami Gandi-Gorgla, and Abdul Razak Rahim, "An Appeal to Discontinue Funding the Special Court for Sierra Leone," and "An Open Letter to Sierra Leone's Parliamentarians," The Sierra Leone Working Group, 2004.

threatened to reignite conflict within the country, and some of which contradicted understandings that Africans on the ground had about justice and penalties (as in the transfer of Charles Taylor from Nigeria to the Special Court, and then to the Hague). While few condoned Taylor's brutal actions, the process leading to his extradition has been controversial.

The above example demonstrates that national advocacy for African peace and justice processes can have an enormous impact on the ground, but we must make sure that it is overwhelmingly positive. Only when Holbrooke succeeded in engaging the Americans with the UN peace issues did we see effective movement forward. The issue is whether such advocacy, welcomed and potentially productive as it might be, is also calibrated to work well with African derived institutions and processes for peace and justice, many of which were promoted by women's initiatives. African women worked hard to bring to fruition UN Security Council Resolution 1325 of 2000, which calls for integrating women into conflict resolution strategies and mechanism. But African women and others note that we have not yet seen the monitoring to ensure that women's initiatives are included or that women's rights in conflict situations are protected.[40] As we contemplate working more in tandem over the coming years, it would stand us in good stead to seek out information on what the Africans themselves have in mind, what institutions and agreements of their construction are already in operation, how to achieve gender equity and balance in these initiatives, and how bilateral or multilateral activism could increase the effectiveness of consensus approaches.

Where does military preparedness to prevent terrorism clash with the concern for supporting positive democratic civil-military relations in Africa? Despite initial African skepticism of the 1996 American proposal of an African Crisis Response Force,[41] the 1997 African Crisis Response Initiative (ACRI) sought to train African militaries to respond effectively to peacekeeping or humanitarian relief operations

---

[40] Gwendolyn Mikell, Jeanne Maddox Toungara, and Vivian Lowery Derryck, *Empowerment of Women in Africa: Gender Equality and Women's Leadership*, British Embassy and DFID Policy Paper, April 2008; and *Empowerment of Women in Africa: Impact of the Changing Global Outlook*, Conference at the National Geographic, May 8, 2009. See also, Gwendolyn Mikell, *African Feminism: The Politics of Survival in Sub-Saharan Africa*, Philadelphia: University of Pennsylvania Press, 1997.

[41] Newsmaker: Warren Christopher, *Lehrer News Hour*, October 15, 1996.

on the Continent in response to UN, AU, or ECOWAS requests.[42] Whether through ACRI or ACOTA, the U.S. made significant contributions to peacekeeping between 1997 and 2004 in Sierra Leone and in Central African Republic, although much more was needed.

The tensions over global terrorism and the Iraq War, have left a legacy that the U.S. and France will have to overcome in the coming period. AFRICOM was widely perceived as pursuing America's strategic interests so that weak states could not be exploited by Islamic terrorists. Few people understood the objectives of the initiative, and U.S. military leaders themselves had not initially thought through AFRICOM's mission, responsibilities, location, its relationship to African militaries, as well as relationship to civil society both African and American.[43] The AU rejected notions of an AFRICOM base in any country on African soil; and Liberia's president Ellen Sirleaf-Johnson and Ethiopia's president Lucha were the only two Heads of State to extend a welcome and a request the AFRICOM base. For the most part, African leaders did not see AFRICOM as a unique counterpart of the U.S. regional commands that existed for other parts of the world. In addition to a combatant functions, AFRICOM officials have emphasized that it would work in conjunction with USAID to respond primarily to the humanitarian and development needs voiced by Africans. More recently AU representatives have reflected an openness to dialogues on AFRICOM,[44] especially since its base in Stuttgart, Germany will allow sufficient time to work out collaborative relations with Africans.

Nor was the U.S. alone in encountering such suspicions. Many Africans had seen the Linas-Marcousis Accords emerging from the Roundtable convened by France in January 2003 as threatening to Cote d'Ivoire's constitutional sovereignty before the UN intervened.[45] In

---

[42] "African Crisis Response Initiative; African Contingency Operations Training and Assistance," *Global Security.Org*, Military. http://www.globalsecurity.org/military/agency/dod/acri.htm.

[43] Gwendolyn Mikell, "Academics and the Security Sector: Issues and Concerns," Presentation at the ACSS/AFRICOM Seminar, Dulles VA, June 12, 2008.

[44] Ambassador Amina Salum Ali, dialogue on AFRICOM, Council on Foreign Relations, Oct 2008.

[45] J. Peter Pham, "Forgotten Interests: Why Cote d'Ivoire Matters," *World Defense Review*, 3 August 2006. See also, J. Peter Pham, AFRICOM: Ready to Roll, October 2, 2008, website http://www.familysecuritymatters.org/ publications/id.1340/pub_detail.asp. See also "AFRICOM: The Poisonous Fruit of the Mercy Industrial Complex," *The Zaleza Post*, November 15, 2007.

this process, both the U.S. and France have learned an important lesson—the need to engage in public relations campaigns, civic education, and the exchange of ideas about policy initiatives in a systematic and thorough way, with many civil society groups and constituencies, before, during, and after policy implementation.

Many conflicts have been as much about governance problems—political and/or financial—as much as they have been about conflict resolution. In the DRC conflict, the weak Congolese state was used as a base for attacks against Rwanda, and it suffered retaliatory incursions onto its soil by surrounding states also seeking to exploit the vast Congolese resources. No matter how surrounding states justify incursions onto DRC territory, it appears that that the conflicts benefit corporations that extract resources from DRC. There are few state pressures for accountability in that political climate. It may be time for the U.S. to join with the international community in find a strategy for discussions about a regional framework for peace and development in DRC, and to initiate a conversation about the link between development and conflict. There is a need a new set of 'Sullivan Principles' that deal with the contemporary business-state interface in weak states that cannot or will not control borders or violence, such as in the DRC and in the coastal communities of the Niger Delta.

Important governance questions emerge: how much room is there for African civil-military relations training that broadly connect these constituencies in a dialogue that explicitly links governance and military preparedness issues? Concern for the professionalization of the African military, must involve thinking about issues related to civilian oversight of the military.[46] It is important to note that both the U.S. and France have evolved their own institutional processes for dealing with the military institutions in Africa, especially in terms of education and training. Although many conflicts have ended, and more countries have gotten aboard the democratic bandwagon, the legacy of military rule lingers often lingers on in the form of weakened state institutions in comparison to the military, the persistence of a militarized and gendered culture.

---

[46] Claude E. Welch, No *Farewell to Arms? Military Disengagement from Politics in Africa and Latin America*, Boulder CO: Westview Press, 1987; and *Military Role and Rule: Perspectives on Civil-Military Relations*, North Scituate MA: Duxbury Press, 1974.

Education and training on the role of human security and civil society development should be a priority. Since 1999, Africa Center for Strategic Studies (ACSS) of National Defense University has provided training senior seminars for military and security leaders and dialogues with members of civil society organizations in countries undergoing democratic transitions. Between 2000 and 2006, ACSS functioned with a mix of military and civilian employees, American, African, Anglophone and Francophone. However, as ACSS has been integrated more fully under military leadership and oversight, it has evolved in a direction that has aligned it more closely with U.S. national security concerns. This places the countering of ideological support for terrorism as primary, followed by harmonizing views on security challenges, and promoting institutional partnerships to address fundamental defense and security challenges facing Africa. Now, there is a need to seek balance in terms of human security and civil society development, and engendering civil-military training.[47] Given that civilian dialogues are occurring across the Anglophone/Francophone areas on human security issues, this would appear to be an arena in which collaboration between the French and the Americans could usefully occur.

Since 2000, one aspect of the governance issues relates to intrastate ethnic and religious tensions that have exploded in the post-Cold War and globalization period. At their worst, they yielded Rwanda and Burundi type genocidal crises. But for the most part, they have manifested as ethnic/religious conflicts (Cote d'Ivoire, Sudan, Chad), constitutional issues related to term limits (Nigeria, Ghana), and what I have called 'ethnic entrepreneurs' who sought to capture power and destabilize fragile or emerging democracies (Liberia, Sierra Leone).[48] As the conflicts subside, African countries express need for institutions and processes that serve as early-warning signals of impending conflicts or that could have prevented the conflicts, but the resources to handle this are often hard to come by. One Ghanaian institution— CHRAJ—serves as an example of this anticipatory function: Ghana's Commission on Human Rights and Administrative Justice (CHRAJ) works to enhance good governance, democracy, respect for human

---

[47] African Defense Attaché Seminar, Africa Center for Strategic Studies, November 17-25, 2008, www.africacenter.org.

[48] Gwendolyn Mikell, "Ethnic Particularism and New State Legitimacy in West Africa," *Tulsa Journal of Comparative and International Law*, Vol. 23, No. 1, 1997.

rights, and transparency, and tries to head-off conflicts before they explode.[49] CHRAJ is sharing its conflict resolution experience with other ECOWAS countries. Elsewhere, African Parliamentarians for Peace have strategized about how to marshal constituencies to resolve the conflicts.

Another aspect of the governance issue relates to rebuilding state institutions—parliamentary, legal, police, etc—so that they can offset the historical strength of military institutions in Africa. Strong state institutions allow government to protect property rights, protect women's rights and the rights of vulnerable populations, and make laws that protect national resources against appropriation and abuse. Significant American resources have been poured into democracy-support and institution-building in Africa, through the National Democratic Institute and the International Republican Institute which work with Parliament, the Judiciary, the police forces, and NGOs. This area is ripe for Americans and French collaboration, especially on how to provide critical resources and support in a way that also enhances local ownership and initiative. There must be a rational division of labor that transcends the former Anglophone/Francophone or Lusophone divides, that emphasizes multilateral initiatives, and that acknowledge the important roles that new strategic player like China and India could play in regional collaborations.

A third governance issue related to the importance of electoral transitions, and finding exit strategies for African leaders and presidents. Sub-Saharan African states are still in their infancy, and thus, do not yet have the institutional, constitutional, and processual strengths of older western states. Presidential two-term limits often are challenged as incumbents seek to change constitutional limits in order to serve longer. This is predictable, given insufficient leadership opportunities for retiring leaders, and weak public consciousness about the dangers of a life-time-term-of office. African Elders chairing the Mo Ibrahim Prize for Achievement in African Leadership mark a new level of seriousness in governance advocacy. It succeeds the African Presidential Archives and residential fellowship initiative at Boston University (2002) that recognizes and reward African leaders who set examples of good governance. Likewise former Nigerian Senate President Ken

---

[49] "Ghana: CHRAJ calls for Tolerance as Election Day Approaches," *Accra Mail*, November 19, 2008. See also, Ghana Commission on Human Rights and Administrative Justice website.

Nnamani's leadership helped stop the movement toward a 3rd term in Nigeria, and it provides an African example of support for good governance and exit strategies.[50] The consistent message in these initiatives is that good governance is the wave of the future,[51] and they need reinforcement in Anglo-Francophone collaborations.

Recent evidence suggests that formerly stable African democracies that made great strides in the last decade still are vulnerable to internal schisms and political upheavals—Nigeria, South Africa, and Kenya, for example. Only the emboldened Nigerian civil society and a tough international community push-back prevented a conflagration there. The electoral transition in Kenya threatened to explode into violence, and had already generated ethnic clashes that produced internally dislocated populations and refugees spilling out into surrounding countries. Only through the invitation of the AU, and the committed engagement of former Secretary General Kofi Annan and other Western partners did a negotiated settlement to the conflict emerge. Even Ghana, where four relatively successful democratic elections have been held since 1992, threatened to flounder on the shoals of party and presidential privilege this year, when the possibilities of a transfer of power to a new party emerged. Only systematic dialogue through Ghana's public and civil society organizations, pressure and support from Western partners, and systematic monitoring seemingly kept the election on track.

Support for democratic transitions even in relatively stable African countries like South African needs to rank high on the agenda of any Franco-American partnership. To the surprise of many, the rancor within South Africa's African National Congress between President Mbeki and Prime Minister Zuma which burst into conflict in 2008 suggested that there was much work to be done to make sure that this country stays on track. With successful 2009 elections now behind us, the U.S., France, the UK, and the EU are challenged to offer the kind of moral support and reinforcement that address both domestic tensions and regional issues. South Africa must rebuild regional confidence in its role within SADC, and provide the space that allows Zim-

---

[50] Ken Nnamani and Sam Amadi, *Nnamani's Third Way: Selected Speeches on Legislative Leadership and Democratic Transformation in Nigeria*, Princeton NJ: Sungai Books, 2007.

[51] Celia Drugger, "Botswana's Former President Wins Prize for Good Governance," *Herald Tribune*, October 21, 2008; "Joaquim Chissano Wins the Largest Prize in the World," *Southern Africa Trust*, 22 October 2007; Celia Drugger,

babwe to recover. Mugabe now shares power within the unity government, and the country is reconstructing its economy and stabilizing its parliamentary system, prior to reworking constitutional/legal structures, and dealing with the land issues that may revive agriculture. Zimbabwe is sorely in need of focused and subtle western consensus and strategies, in order to off-set the heightened tension that Mugabe has fostered about Western intentions.

Of course, there are weak, ethnically fractious or unconsolidated states in the Horn of Africa (especially Somalia) that are struggling to evolve approaches to democracy that are tailored to their ethno-histories. These 'ungoverned spaces' pose a thorny problem for the West. The U.S. devoted significant resources to the Horn of Africa initiative, with modest results,[52] perhaps because security/ anti-terrorism was the single operative notion and concern over radical Islam was dominant. The missing ingredient was knowledge about how people in this region understood good governance, and what they saw as ideal approaches to governance. Neither the Americans nor the French have been very successful in their attempts to deal with these states, and it may take combined attention to find solutions. I suggest that it is time to develop a G8 Agenda for on the Horn of Africa—perhaps starting with a conference at which regional and AU representatives are invited to offer their suggestions as to what governance and development initiatives for the area might be.

The Diaspora Connection

Both the U.S. and France have internal diasporas that are well-springs of knowledge about Africa, and that seek engagement on African policy issues.[53] In the U.S. they are African-Americans, Ethiopians, Ghanaians, Nigerians, Sierra Leoneans, South Africans, and Sudanese, among others; and in France, they are Algerians, Congolese, Senegalese, Ivorians, Moroccans and West Indians. The U.S. is poised to undergo a dramatic shift in Africa policy during Obama's Presidency depending on how the U.S. State Department and the White House treat African

---

[52] J. Swan, "U.S Policy in the Horn of Africa," U.S. Department of State, August 4, 2007; and James Butty with Terrence Lyons, "Avoiding Conflict in the Horn of Africa," *VOA News*, 22 December 2006.

[53] See Mel Foote, Gregory Simpkins, Gwendolyn Mikell, African American Unity Caucus Plenary, *Africa: Suggestions to the Obama Admin.*, April 16, 2009.

issues. Yet after three months State Department priorities have been on Europe, Asia and the Middle East, and the White House has not tried to marshal American knowledge about Africa to inform a coherent Africa policy. Yet, the expectations of those many constituencies and civil society groups that supported his Presidential campaign are that he will elevate African issues.

As we wait to see what priorities emerge, it is instructive to think about Skinner's description of the use of symbolic power by African-Americans in pushing recalcitrant American policy makers to forge ties with Africa in the late 19th century.[54] Hopefully, the mass organizational power that brought about Obama's election will cause Congressional and State Department officials to think longer and look deeper as they craft new policies for Africa. The Obama administration could build on the economic and conflict resolution achievements of previous administrations,[55] they might refocus Bush policies for poverty reduction, and they must challenge Congress to live up to promised foreign aid to Africa.[56] Hopefully, they will remember Tanzanian President Kikwete's advice to President Obama to "be as good a friend of Africa as President Bush has been."[57]

It is possible that American and the Francophone directions will converge on some African issues, given growing symbolic and formal pressures from new constituents. There is pressure for the Obama Administration's policies to be more sensitive to conditions on the ground in Africa, maximize diplomatic resource in African countries, utilize more subtle diplomacy in dealing with difficult situations like Darfur and Zimbabwe or DRC, and to be more responsive to the public pressure. But will the same be true in France and in the wider EU community over the next few years? Balancing the formal foreign policy, public diplomacy, and unofficial advocacy regarding Africa will be

---

[54] Elliott P. Skinner, *African Americans and U.S. Policy Toward Africa, 1850-1924: In Defense of Black Nationality*, Washington, D.C.: Howard University Press, 1992, pp. 1-19.

[55] "Obama Presidency Would Bring New Dimension to Africa Policy; Africa Specialist Howard Wolpe discusses future of U.S.-Africa relations," http://www.america.gov/st/elections08-english/2008/October/20081022083943WCyeroCO.2450067.html.

[56] Giles Bolton, "Make Them Pay: What They Promised and By When," in *Africa Doesn't Matter: How the West has failed the Poorest Continent and What We can do about It*, NY: Arcade Publishers, 2008:156-7.

[57] Bush Confronts Africa Policy Critics," AFP, Sunday February 17, 2008, http://rawstory.com/news/afp/Bush_confronts_Africa_policy_critic_02172008.html.

an exciting yet challenging process for Franco-American relations in the coming years.

Recommendations

The need for in-depth conversations between the U.S. and the French on Africa policy on the above issues are obvious. As a consequence of the arguments made, the following broad issue areas are identified for possible cooperation and collaborations:

1. Despite the global economic decline, the U.S. should continue and expands African policies through AGOA, the Millennium Challenge Corporation, or PEPFAR, as well as other initiatives.

   • What are areas of French strength in development that could be brought to the American/French development collaborations in Africa?

   • How can Franco-American collaboration strengthen the impact on the ground of multilateral initiatives like the Global Fund for HIV/AIDS, Malaria, and TB?

   • How can the U.S. and France strengthen diplomatic resources in Africa?

2. What new development initiatives for the Horn of Africa are possible?

   • How can Americans and the French work together on cutting the links between resources and conflict in Africa?

   • How does Franco-American trade competition affect regional development, regional cohesion, and regional problem solving?

   • What should be done to enlist greater Chinese engagement and dialogue on the links between trade, resources and conflicts?

3. What differences prevent the U.S. and France from being more collaborative on security and peace issues for Africa?

- What would make U.S. and France more collaborative within the UN Security Council on multilateral peace mission in Africa?

- What divisions of labor could make such collaborations more effective?

- What interesting mechanisms might exist for U.S./ French collaboration on military training, civil-military relations, and human security issues writ large?

- How do you educate Western publics on the importance of military issues and military commands? How do you make the military more responsive to public concerns about African military issues?

4. Post-conflict, how can justice mechanisms must be more finely tuned to address challenges and utilize existing African social capital in resolving conflict?

- What joint initiatives can be created to stem gender violence in post-conflict zones?

- What new initiatives could be supported by France and the U.S. to stem piracy that would also make use of AU frameworks, and utilize African social capital?

- Using Rwanda, Sierra Leone, and Darfur as examples, how can the U.S., France, and the EU help make courts, Special Courts, and Tribunals more responsive to local ownership, more gender sensitive, and derived from local initiatives?

5. On governance issues, what additional supports for democratic institutions and leadership performance should be pursued across Africa?

- What mechanisms for cultivating democratic governance would be of interest to Congress and the EU Parliaments? The Chinese? The Indians?

- What additional supports for political party education and development could be pursued across Africa?

- How can the U.S., France, and the EU work collaboratively on this?

6. What concerns exist among the diaspora communities in the U.S. and France that could provide clues to productive issues and directions for policy collaboration?

  - What strategies could be used to engage African diasporas in policy dialogues?

La France, l'Amérique et le monde : une nouvelle ère dans les relations Franco-Américaines ?

Dirigé par
Michel Foucher
et
Daniel Hamilton

Remerciements

Dans cet ouvrage, des experts français et américains analysent les principaux défis auxquels doivent faire face la France et les Etats-Unis et font des recommandations pour des actions conjointes ou complémentaires qui pourraient par ailleurs relancer la relation bilatérale.

Le groupe stratégique franco-américain, dont les travaux se sont déroulés de l'été 2008 au printemps 2009, avec deux séminaires à Paris et Washington, était motivé par le souhait d'améliorer les relations bilatérales et le partenariat euro-américain. Il compte dix auteurs français et américains et deux co-directeurs, tous ayant une expérience gouvernementale, académique ou dans des think-tanks. Ils partagent une vision opérationnelle des thèmes suivants : la France et les Etats-Unis face aux défis stratégiques majeurs ; les approches face au Moyen-Orient et à la Méditerranée ; l'engagement auprès des nations africaines ; les options stratégiques face à la Russie ; et les responsabilités incombant aux Etats-Unis, à la France et à l'Europe pour faire face aux défis économiques mondiaux. Ce groupe stratégique propose aux lecteurs les outils nécessaires pour une coopération franco-américaine renouvelée et efficace.

Le groupe stratégique franco-américain a été soutenu par la Fondation Robert Schuman et le Centre des relations transatlantiques de la Paul H. Nitze School of Advanced International Studies (SAIS). Nous remercions Jean-Dominique Giuliani et Pascale Joannin, respectivement Président et Directeur général de la Fondation Robert Schuman pour leur soutien à nos travaux et pour leurs propres contributions à la discussion. Nous remercions également les nombreux hauts responsables et experts qui nous ont rejoints dans nos délibérations, et notamment Jean-David Levitte, conseiller diplomatique du Président Nicolas Sarkozy, Pierre Vimont, Ambassadeur de France aux États-Unis, Jean François-Poncet, ancien ministre français des Affaires étrangères et sénateur et Jim Hoagland, éditorialiste au *Washington Post*. Nous souhaitons aussi remercier Thierry Chopin et Florence Moingeon à la Fondation Robert Schuman ainsi que Gretchen Losee et Katrien Maes du Centre des relations transatlantiques pour leur aide. Nous remercions également Mathilde Durand, à la Fondation Robert Schuman, pour son aide et ses travaux de traduction et de relecture. Nous remercions enfin Esther Brimmer, qui avait initié ce projet lorsqu'elle travaillait au Centre des relations transatlantiques, avant de rejoindre le Département d'Etat américain. Tous les auteurs s'expriment à titre personnel et n'engagent pas leur institution.

Daniel Hamilton et Michel Foucher
Co-directeurs du groupe stratégique franco-américain

Introduction

Une nouvelle ère dans les relations franco-américaines ?

Daniel Hamilton et Michel Foucher

La France est le plus vieil allié des Etats-Unis. Cependant, cette relation a toujours eu sa part de tensions, qui ont peut-être culminé lors de l'invasion de l'Irak par l'administration Bush en 2003. La volonté de voir cette relation revenir sur le droit chemin a certainement été l'une des raisons pour lesquelles l'opinion publique et les leaders d'opinion français ont suivi d'aussi près la campagne électorale américaine de 2008. Mais ce n'était clairement pas la seule raison. La France, comme la plupart des pays européens, a tout d'abord été intriguée, puis réellement enthousiasmée par la perspective de voir Barack Obama devenir le nouveau président américain. En fait, si les Français avaient pu voter lors de cette élection américaine, ils auraient massivement voté en faveur de Barack Obama.

Toutefois, Obama avait à peine scellé sa victoire que les experts commençaient déjà à chercher de potentiels points de convergences ou de tensions entre la « future » administration et le vieux continent. Les critiques ont rapidement argué du fait que quel que soit le futur président, le partenariat transatlantique avait manifestement perdu l'importance qu'il avait eu, que les valeurs et intérêts des Européens et des Américains semblaient avoir divergé et que nombre d'institutions transatlantiques étaient peu pertinentes pour les défis du 21ème siècle. D'autres estimaient que le président élu n'avait aucun lien personnel profond avec l'Europe et serait donc plus enclin à se tourner vers d'autres partenaires pour contribuer à la résolution des problèmes des Etats-Unis.

Avant même d'être entré en fonction, le comportement du président Obama a balayé de telles suspicions. L'équipe chargée de la sécurité nationale nommée par le président était fortement favorable à l'Europe, y compris le vice-président Biden et la secrétaire d'Etat Clinton, tout comme le conseiller à la sécurité nationale James Jones, ancien commandant suprême des forces alliées en Europe, qui parle couramment français et a passé une partie de sa jeunesse en France. Immédiatement après la prise de fonction, des ordres ont été donnés pour fermer le centre de détention de Guantanamo, qui constituait une source considérable d'acrimonie entre les Américains d'une part et les Français, mais aussi les Européens d'autre part. Des consultations ont ensuite été lancées de part et d'autre de l'Atlantique sur la manière de faire face à la crise économique mondiale, sur la conception d'une nouvelle stratégie en Afghanistan et sur l'élaboration de nouvelles approches au Moyen-Orient. Les voyages du président en France en avril et en juin 2009 ont souligné l'intérêt des deux rives de l'Atlantiques à relancer un partenariat plus efficace.

Ces signes d'ouverture, probablement favorables à une relance de la relation franco-américaine, soulèvent des questions plus fondamentales. Comment l'administration américaine va-t-elle traiter les nombreux défis nationaux et internationaux qui lui sont lancés, et comment envisage-t-elle de travailler avec la France et l'Europe ? La France et ses partenaires européens ont-ils la volonté et la capacité d'engager les États-Unis dans un nouveau partenariat ambitieux, malgré leurs préoccupations liées à la construction européenne et aux défis importants qu'ils doivent relever en Europe ? Les États-Unis et la France vont devoir réexaminer les meilleures solutions qui soient pour faire progresser leurs intérêts communs, quand ils existent, tout en limitant les conséquences des divergences de priorités, quand elles ne manquent pas d'apparaître. Nos auteurs se sont penchés sur cinq domaines clés qui devraient constituer de véritables tests pour une relation franco-américaine revigorée.

« C'est toujours l'économie, idiot ! »

Peu de questions sont susceptibles d'être aussi déterminantes pour les relations euro-américaines en général, et plus particulièrement franco-américaines, au cours des prochaines années, que la crise économique mondiale. Cet événement marquant a levé tout doute sur le degré d'interconnexion de l'économie transatlantique. Plus cette grande dépression s'aggrave et se prolonge, plus il faut craindre, des deux côtés de l'Atlantique, l'apparition de politiques protectionnistes. Notre défi commun consiste à montrer aux citoyens américains et aux millions de citoyens du monde qu'il est possible de profiter des avantages de la mondialisation tout en rendant les coûts supportables pour ceux qui sont les plus directement touchés, sans succomber à la tentation du protectionnisme. Pour cela, il faut plus que d'importantes incitations fiscales et monétaires. La réflexion et l'action doivent être audacieuses. Le krach financier et la récession qui en découle obligent les Européens et les Américains à reconsidérer leur économie et leur relation bilatérale et l'Occident lui-même à faire face aux défis économiques du 21ème siècle ; mais ils constituent aussi une opportunité.

Pour la France et les États-Unis, l'une des meilleures manières de faire face aux défis économiques mondiaux et de profiter des avantages d'une économie mondiale ouverte consiste, pour chacune des parties, à se réorganiser sur le plan interne, à se repositionner comme une économie ouverte, résistante et adaptée à la mondialisation. De manière générale, la France doit contrebalancer ses dispositions sociales avantageuses en se dotant d'une économie plus souple et plus flexible, tandis que les États-Unis doivent contrebalancer leur flexibilité manifeste en renforçant les mesures d'aide sociale pour offrir aux Américains le réconfort et le soutien qui leur est nécessaire pour pouvoir rivaliser dans une économie mondiale ouverte. Le défi commun des responsables de chaque pays consiste à montrer à leurs citoyens qu'il est possible de tirer profit de la mondialisation tout en rendant ses coûts supportables pour ceux qui sont les plus directement touchés.

Les deux partenaires doivent ensuite tirer parti de l'intérêt fort et croissant qu'ils ont réciproquement dans la réussite économique de l'autre. Les liens économiques bilatéraux entre la France et les États-Unis constituent une illustration manifeste du degré d'intégration qui caractérise les relations commerciales transatlantiques et une véritable preuve que les intérêts économiques et la prospérité future des États-Unis et de la France n'ont jamais été aussi interdépendants et intégrés qu'aujourd'hui. 2 millions de travailleurs français et américains doivent leur emploi aux bonnes relations économiques entre les deux pays.

Troisièmement, une grande partie de l'agenda économique des Etats-Unis avec la France s'organise en fait avec l'Union européenne. Les marchés transatlantiques comptent parmi les plus ouverts du monde, même si diverses barrières non-tarifaires empêchent l'émergence d'un marché transatlantique plus prospère. Compte tenu de la taille de ce marché, même les plus petits changements destinés à harmoniser les législations nationales pourraient entraîner des gains économiques bien plus importants que la poursuite des réductions des tarifs douaniers transatlantiques.

Enfin, pour paraphraser un vieil adage chinois (emprunté à plusieurs reprises par le chef de cabinet du président américain, Rahm Emanuel), « une crise est trop précieuse pour être gâchée ». Les récessions économiques sont des invitations au changement, aux nouvelles idées. Le climat économique actuel est prêt pour le changement, et c'est donc le moment idéal pour les États-Unis, la France et les autres partenaires européens de travailler conjointement sur de vastes initiatives telles que la sécurité énergétique, le développement économique durable et le changement climatique mondial. L'innovation dans ces domaines pourrait générer, sur le long terme, d'importantes périodes de croissance et de prospérité. L'Europe et l'Amérique du Nord sont mieux placées que la majorité des autres économies pour rompre le lien entre création de richesses et consommation de ressources. Rompre ce lien constitue un défi historique, mais aussi une opportunité d'évoluer vers des modèles de consommation et de compétitivité complètement différents. La coopération transatlantique et l'innovation pourraient ouvrir la voie.

Jean-François Jamet reprend aussi ces idées mais prend également en compte d'autres considérations. Le défi social créé par le chômage et la récession économique générale constitue le cœur de la crise. Grâce aux programmes sociaux dont elle dispose, la France est bien armée pour relever ces défis à court terme mais l'absence de flexibilité de son marché du travail devrait la confronter à des difficultés à long terme. De leur côté, les États-Unis sont plus à même de faciliter la mobilité sur le marché du travail mais ne peuvent pas fournir à leurs citoyens le filet de sécurité sociale suffisant pour faire face à la crise. Les deux pays doivent investir davantage pour améliorer l'éducation et la formation : les États-Unis devraient améliorer leur éducation primaire et secondaire tandis que l'Europe devrait investir davantage dans l'enseignement supérieur et améliorer la gouvernance dans ses universités.

J.F. Jamet est également préoccupé par le niveau de la dette découlant des dépenses de relance ambitieuses de l'administration Obama ; il s'agit là d'un bon exemple des différences franco-américaines en termes de gestion économique. J.F. Jamet s'inquiète de la spirale inflationniste et des déséquilibres globaux qui pourraient prolonger la crise. Il pense que la thésaurisation du capital en Chine constitue l'un des principaux défis et propose deux solutions pour y remédier : diminuer la dette des États-Unis et encourager la consommation chinoise par la création d'un système d'assistance sociale plus solide.

Jean-François Jamet estime que la coopération euro-atlantique sera essentielle pour relever les défis actuels de l'économie mondiale. Il suggère que la coopération étroite entre les banques centrales européenne et américaine soit élargie dans plusieurs directions : la structuration et l'encadrement prudentiel du marché des dérivés de crédit ; la supervision des banques et des assurances actives au niveau international ; l'adaptation des normes comptables, la transparence des bilans, la régulation des bonus ; ou encore l'obligation faite aux banques de constituer des provisions plus importantes chaque année pour parer aux risques de liquidité et de solvabilité. Dans le domaine de l'environnement et de l'énergie, J.F. Jamet souligne la nécessité pour les États-Unis et l'Union européenne de trouver un accord lors du sommet de Copenhague sur le changement climatique en décembre 2009, de partager les meilleures pratiques, de définir des normes communes et d'adopter une stratégie commune en vue du développement de technologies propres. Il recommande aux États-Unis et à l'Europe d'abandonner les objectifs chiffrés et les subventions concernant les biocarburants car en l'état actuel, cette technologie renchérit les prix de l'alimentation, est coûteuse et relativement inefficace.

En termes d'amélioration de la gouvernance économique mondiale, Jean-François Jamet ne recommande pas seulement une coordination plus étroite, mais il appelle l'Union européenne à adopter une représentation commune à la Banque mondiale et au FMI, comme c'est déjà le cas à l'OMC. Le rôle du FMI devrait, en même temps, être revu pour qu'il se concentre sur la certification des comptes financiers des États, sur la prévention des crises financières, sur l'aide aux Etats exposés à des crises de change et sur les études macroéconomiques, tout en cessant ses programmes d'ajustements structurels et les prêts non destinés à des situations d'urgence qui devraient rester la compétence exclusive de la Banque mondiale. Enfin, tout en s'engageant à conclure le processus de Doha, il serait intéressant que les États-Unis et l'Union européenne examinent ensemble la possibilité de recourir à des accords plurilatéraux ouverts à tout signataire et permettant à ceux qui le souhaitent de poursuivre l'intégration commerciale.

Questions stratégiques

Bruno Tertrais présente les prochains défis stratégiques : la Russie et la Chine, l'Afghanistan (où Washington n'a pas obtenu l'engagement militaire attendu des Européens), l'Iran (où la nouvelle approche américaine mérite un dialogue concerté avec les capitales européennes afin que les efforts puissent se renforcer mutuellement), le système de défense antimissiles (pour lequel une attitude pragmatique et non plus idéologique des Américains servirait les intérêts européens), l'avenir des armes nucléaires (qui nécessite un dialogue discret et approfondi entre Washington, Londres et Paris). B. Tertrais estime qu'il existe un fort potentiel de coopération franco-américaine sur les questions stratégiques, le danger d'un désaccord sur la manière de traiter la crise afghane et sur la question du désarmement nucléaire constituant de dangereux défis.

L'avenir de l'OTAN constitue une autre des questions stratégiques majeures auxquelles la France et les Etats-Unis devront faire face. Pour de nombreux Américains, la solidarité et la réussite de l'OTAN seront évaluées à l'aune de l'Afghanistan, où l'administration Obama double la taille du contingent militaire américain. Leo Michel met cependant en garde contre l'injection de troupes américaines supplémentaires qui pourrait renforcer les erreurs de perception dans certaines régions d'Europe, qui la considèreraient comme une « guerre américaine », et renforcer les appels à une diminution de la participation européenne. Il reconnaît que l'OTAN en tant qu'institution pourrait survivre à une issue ambiguë en Afghanistan mais il s'interroge sur l'efficacité de son fonctionnement en cas de récrimination mutuelle des Alliés.

Leo Michel note également que le comportement de la Russie en Géorgie et dans les autres anciennes régions soviétiques a recentré l'attention sur le rôle de défense collective de l'OTAN, notamment chez les Européens de l'Est et du Nord. Il souligne toutefois que le « moment unipolaire » de l'OTAN est dépassé. Selon lui, la Russie actuelle ne représente plus le type de menace existentielle posé par l'Union soviétique. Plus généralement, pour de nombreux Européens, les principales menaces pesant sur leur sécurité ou les outils nécessaires pour y faire face ne sont plus considérés comme essentiellement militaires. Par ailleurs, les sondages indiquent que les Européens restent moins confiants qu'il y a 10 ans sur la compatibilité des intérêts, de la stratégie et des politiques américaines avec les leurs.

La relation de l'OTAN avec l'Union européenne constitue également un défi stratégique. L'Union européenne a fait d'importants progrès en développement sa Politique européenne de sécurité et de défense (PESD). Cependant, les budgets de défense européens restent relativement faibles et certaines des opérations militaires de la PESD se révèlent plus difficiles et plus onéreuses que prévu. De plus en plus, de nombreux Etats membres de l'UE considèrent leurs capacités civiles, et notamment l'encadrement de la police, les experts judiciaires, les maisons d'arrêt, les douanes et l'administration publique, comme des outils vitaux à déployer lors d'opérations de prévention ou de gestion de crises. Selon Leo Michel, l'un des avantages attendus de l'approche plus positive du président Nicolas Sarkozy à l'égard des relations entre l'OTAN et l'Union européenne et de son intention déclarée de renforcer la participation française dans les structures de l'OTAN serait d'améliorer la mise en œuvre d'une « approche globale » en Afghanistan, au Kosovo ainsi que la gestion des crises futures et des efforts de stabilisation lorsque les deux organisations sont impliquées.

Leo Michel estime que l'objectif de long terme d'une relation plus étroite entre l'OTAN et l'Union européenne ne devrait pas conduire à diminuer l'autonomie de prise de décision de chaque organisation, ni à tenter de définir une division formelle du travail, ni à encourager une organisation à s'immiscer systématiquement dans des missions conduites par l'autre organisation. Cette relation plus étroite devrait au contraire garantir la transparence, éviter les approches contradictoires et permettre de bénéficier de synergies positives.

Toutefois, il apparaît de plus en plus nettement que la coopération euratlantique en matière de sécurité ne peut être limitée à l'OTAN ou à la relation OTAN-UE. La mondialisation a brouillé les lignes de démarcation entre la sécurité « extérieure » et « intérieure »). Heureusement, il existe une relation bilatérale Etats-Unis/Union européenne forte, et qui ne cesse de se renforcer, dans des domaines comme la lutte contre le terrorisme, la sécurité dans les transports, la non-prolifération et la lutte contre le crime transnational. L'Union européenne étant de plus en plus souvent le théâtre des discussions stratégiques et de la prise de décision sur les questions de sécurité, comme par exemple la politique à l'égard de l'Iran, Leo Michel note que les Etats-Unis vont vouloir s'assurer que leur point de vue est bien pris en compte avant que les politiques européennes ne soient figées.

Leo Michel conclut que de manière générale, Washington et Paris ont tout intérêt à renforcer les relations transatlantiques de défense et de sécurité qui passent par l'OTAN, la relation OTAN-UE et la coopération bilatérale. Actuellement, sur le terrain des opérations, les militaires français et américains coopèrent, principalement en Afghanistan et au Kosovo, et il ne fait pas de doute qu'ils coopéreront à l'avenir dans des missions, des théâtres d'opération et des structures de nature diverse à l'intérieur et à l'extérieur de l'Europe. De plus, les politiques de la France relatives à la défense et à la sécurité nationale ainsi que ses capacités influencent, directement ou non, celles d'autres alliés ou partenaires de premier plan. Les intérêts des Etats-Unis sont globalement mieux servis par une structure de défense et de sécurité nationale française plus compétente, plus réactive et plus coopérative qui encourage ses compatriotes européens, en pratique comme en théorie, à accroître leurs capacités militaires et à les mettre à la disposition des missions de l'OTAN et de l'UE.

Dans tous ces efforts, le ton des relations Etats-Unis/France sera d'une importance vitale. De nombreux Américains font régulièrement référence au « leadership » américain au sein de l'Alliance, pensant que ce concept reflète fidèlement des faits objectifs, et notamment les disparités réelles en termes de capacités militaires entre les Etats-Unis et leurs alliés. En revanche, pour beaucoup en France, et sans aucun doute aussi ailleurs en Europe, la notion de « leadership américain » est parfois considérée comme une notion désuète de la Guerre froide, ou pire comme l'expression, par une « hyper-puissance » imparfaite, d'une domination qui énerve. Selon Leo Michel, les Etats-Unis pourraient mieux atteindre leurs objectifs à long terme en faisant moins référence à leur rôle de « leadership » et en faisant davantage ce qu'ils ont souvent si bien fait, mais pas toujours, à savoir consulter, écouter et agir résolument, toujours dans un esprit de véritable partenariat, comme un catalyseur, un constructeur et un défenseur ultime d'une communauté transatlantique démocratique et prospère. Ainsi, les Américains seraient obligés, de temps en temps, de laisser davantage de place aux alliés européens et de leur accorder une plus grande confiance. Parallèlement, les dirigeants français devront être réalistes concernant leur vision de la défense européenne et continuer, dans le cadre de l'Alliance et des relations bilatérales avec les États-Unis, à chercher des solutions pragmatiques et « gagnant-gagnant » même si, politiquement, elles ne sont pas les plus visibles.

Le Moyen-Orient et la Méditerranée

Concernant les défis liés à la sécurité régionale, Ian Lesser note que la crise de Gaza a souligné l'importance des évolutions au Moyen-Orient et en Méditerranée pour la nouvelle administration Obama, et pour l'Europe. Mais il suggère également que la capacité d'engagement américaine et la dynamique du partenariat, du Maroc jusqu'au Golfe et même au-delà, pourraient changer considérablement au cours des prochaines années. Le nouvel agenda régional est susceptible de voir des interactions croissantes entre Washington et Paris, avec de nouvelles incitations en faveur d'une meilleure coordination politique. Il estime qu'il existe là une possibilité de coopération plus explicite sur la stratégie « méditerranéenne », qui est un intérêt français de longue date mais qui restait relativement peu développée dans la politique étrangère américaine.

Ian Lesser présage que le changement manifeste de style de la politique étrangère américaine dont fait preuve l'Administration Obama, associé à une approche plus imaginative des intérêts français et européens à la périphérie de l'Europe, pourrait créer les conditions favorables d'une coopération plus étroite. Sa courte liste de priorités stratégiques communes comprend notamment la stabilité à Gaza et la relance rapide d'une diplomatie favorable au processus de paix, avec moins de réserves américaines sur l'engagement européen ; la coopération visant à promouvoir la diplomatie régionale afin de soutenir le désengagement américain d'Irak, ce qui inclut des stratégies de protection contre le chaos et le séparatisme ; la coopération visant à répondre ensemble au défi de l'accession de l'Iran au statut de puissance nucléaire, et comportant éventuellement une stratégie durable d'endiguement si Téhéran choisit de prolonger son statut de quasi-puissance nucléaire ; le développement d'approches bilatérales plus explicites en Méditerranée ; et enfin une amélioration de la productivité des discussions franco-américaines sur l'importance croissante de la Turquie.

Selon Jean-Pierre Filiu, les actions menées jusqu'à présent par Barack Obama ont satisfait la France. B. Obama a utilisé les mots que les Français attendaient d'un président américain : la volonté de s'engager auprès du monde musulman et la fin de la rhétorique de la « guerre contre la terreur ». Il a par ailleurs commencé à faire ce que la France attendait de lui : s'engager en faveur d'une solution à deux Etats pour Israël et la Palestine et fermer le centre de détention de Guantanamo.

Jean-Pierre Filiu pense que l'administration Obama a réitéré l'engagement de Washington de trouver une solution durable au conflit au Moyen-Orient via l'établissement d'un Etat palestinien. La France ne peut qu'encourager la volonté américaine de revenir à un véritable processus de paix et sa disposition à engager un dialogue renouvelé et ambitieux, notamment en contribuant aux négociations directes entre Israël et la Syrie et aux efforts continus pour soutenir le dialogue politique interlibanais. Jean-Pierre Filiu considère que la faiblesse des partis nationaux constitue le problème principal du Moyen-Orient, ce qui permet à Al-Qaïda d'exercer son contrôle sur un certain nombre de nations. Il estime que les Etats-Unis et la France doivent coopérer pour disperser les réseaux terroristes, notamment en contrôlant les sites internet des jihadistes et le développement d'un réseau terroriste électronique à l'échelle mondiale. Les gouvernements de Paris et Washington sont tous deux confrontés à l'expansion des réseaux jihadistes mondiaux dans la région méditerranéenne. Les Etats-Unis semblent prêts à s'engager de nouveau pour trouver une solution commune et sont conscients que pour des raisons historiques et géographiques, la sécurité européenne est concernée par ce qui se passe sur les rives méridionale et orientale de la mer Méditerranée.

L'Afrique se lève

Nathalie Delapalme estime que la France et les Etats-Unis ont des intérêts similaires en Afrique, les deux pays souhaitant mettre fin au danger que représentent les Etats défaillants et exploiter le potentiel économique de la région. L'intégration de l'Afrique dans l'économie mondiale lui fait connaître actuellement d'importants changements. La population a été multipliée par deux, les classes moyennes augmentent et la population migre vers les villes. Ces changements portent en eux un potentiel économique mais posent également d'importants risques sanitaires liés aux installations sanitaires insuffisantes, aux ressources limitées, à l'anarchie, aux maladies et au trafic de drogue. Pour relever tous ces défis tout en aidant l'Afrique à développer ses ressources nationales et à moderniser son économie, Nathalie Delapalme recommande de faire de la politique africaine une priorité de l'Union européenne. En outre, l'Europe et les Etats-Unis doivent créer un lien plus fort entre sécurité et développement, et réformer la structure mondiale de l'aide au développement afin d'améliorer l'efficacité de l'aide extérieure.

La France et les Etats-Unis doivent convenir qu'ils partagent, tout comme leurs nouveaux concurrents sur ce continent que sont la Chine, l'Inde et les pays du Golfe, certains intérêts et avantages dans cette importante arène stratégique en raison des dangers, des enjeux et du potentiel du continent africain qui se trouve au seuil de l'Europe. L'Afrique abrite tous les types de dangers inhérents au monde moderne en termes de sécurité, de santé et d'environnement. Mais elle offre aussi un fort potentiel pour la croissance mondiale. La France dispose d'une expérience unique concernant l'engagement en faveur de l'aide au développement et la gestion des crises, malgré les questions soulevées par l'opinion publique et l'émergence de concurrents importants. Paris souligne notamment l'interaction entre le développement et la résolution des conflits, et note l'importance du renforcement des organisations régionales africaines. Nathalie Delapalme note que l'élection de Barack Obama a envoyé un message d'espoir que les Africains sont prêts à écouter. Un agenda commun franco-américain devrait reposer sur un renforcement des efforts de résolution des crises, notamment en développement les propres capacités de l'Afrique, sur une approche économique basée sur la réalité des intérêts africains et la croissance plutôt que sur la compassion, sur des efforts pour encourager les progrès en termes de gouvernance et de respect des droits de l'Homme, et sur des efforts concertés pour intégrer les acteurs africains au système international.

Alors que les Etats-Unis et la France s'interrogent sur l'attitude à adopter à l'égard de l'Afrique, Gwendolyn Mikell estime que les deux pays doivent d'abord comprendre les réalités locales et mondiales complexes auxquelles l'Afrique doit actuellement faire face. Les politiques africaines de l'administration Obama devront prendre en compte les contextes sociaux des différents pays africains ainsi que la manière dont les populations perçoivent l'influence de ces politiques sur leur vie. Par conséquent, les politiques africaines doivent s'éloigner des pratiques passées et ne pas être motivées uniquement par la sécurité mais aussi par une reconnaissante et une utilisation efficace de la diplomatie et du développement qui constituent les trois piliers de la stratégie mentionnée par la secrétaire d'Etat Hillary Clinton.

G. Mikell estime qu'au lieu de se focaliser uniquement sur la lutte contre le terrorisme ou sur le Centre de commandement des États-Unis pour l'Afrique (AFRICOM), il convient de se préoccuper davantage de la manière de répondre aux nécessités et aspirations des citoyens africains et de la société civile, de lancer leurs initiatives et de renforcer les institutions démocratiques qui contribuent à faire face aux crises et à les prévenir. Alors que les États-Unis et la France doivent poursuivre leur engagement en faveur du développement, les deux pays doivent réfléchir à la manière de renforcer la lutte contre le VIH/Sida et autres maladies afin qu'ils puissent contribuer à la reconstruction de systèmes de santé dans les pays d'Afrique, en offrant aux Africains la capacité de faire face à ces problèmes dès leur apparition. Compte tenu de la nature relativement modérée de l'Islam sur le continent africain, il est néces- saire de développer des approches qui renforcent cette position modé- rée, et non qui la radicalisent. L'administration Obama devrait soute- nir des initiatives de coopération visant à prévenir l'exploitation des vulnérabilités des Etats africains par le biais de partenariats straté- giques avec ces Etats et les organisations régionales, ainsi qu'avec l'ONU. Cela implique de rompre avec les anciens comportements uni- latéralistes afin que les initiatives multilatérales correspondent davan- tage aux besoins et aux évolutions de l'Afrique sur le terrain.

Un « nouveau départ » avec la Russie ?

Celeste Wallander note que le président Obama devra faire face à un double défi : les relations États-Unis/Russie suscitent de fortes attentes et parallèlement de fortes préoccupations. À la fin de l'administration Bush, les relations entre les deux pays n'avaient jamais été aussi mau- vaises depuis la fin de la Guerre froide. Les États-Unis et la Russie ont de nombreux intérêts communs et la Russie dispose du potentiel néces- saire pour devenir un acteur essentiel du système international. Néan- moins, ses dernières prises de position constituent une menace poten- tielle pour la sécurité et la prospérité basées sur la coopération et l'Etat de droit international. Celeste Wallander suggère qu'une nouvelle stra- tégie américaine visant à satisfaire ses intérêts sécuritaires, politiques et économiques avec la Russie soit basée sur 4 éléments clés : établir les conditions de la sécurité en Eurasie en réaffirmant l'indépendance et la souveraineté de tous les Etats postsoviétiques ; ancrer la Russie en Europe en étroite collaboration avec la France et les autres alliés euro- péens ; développer une approche transatlantique commune pour la politique énergétique en Eurasie ; et lancer des négociations bilatérales et multilatérales sur le contrôle des armes.

Selon elle, la satisfaction de ces objectifs doit se faire conformément aux valeurs américaines, à une période où les priorités de valeurs/d'intérêts compliquent les relations transatlantiques. L'intégration de la Russie et des autres pays de l'ex-Union soviétique dans une communauté de nations pacifique, prospère et fondée sur des règles reste un intérêt stratégique américain. La Russie dispose toujours du potentiel lui permettant de devenir un partenaire important et de contribuer à la résolution de certains des défis mondiaux et régionaux à relever d'urgence. Les États-Unis ont un intérêt manifeste à signer un accord commercial sur le nucléaire avec la Russie et à voir ce pays adhérer à l'Organisation mondiale du commerce (OMC) et à l'OCDE. Mais pour profiter des avantages de l'adhésion, la Russie doit accepter l'ensemble des règles et des obligations. Une coopération plus étroite entre l'OTAN et une Russie démocratique, voire son adhésion, devrait rester un objectif stratégique de long-terme.

C. Wallander souligne que les États-Unis ne devraient pas exclure la possibilité, pour la Russie, de choisir de réintégrer la communauté internationale de manière responsable et crédible. C'est un choix que doit faire la Russie, mais c'est de la responsabilité des États-Unis de faire en sorte qu'il reste possible. Le néo-endiguement ne constitue pas la bonne stratégie. Bien que le défi soit bien plus important que ce qu'il semblait être il y a 20 ans, la bonne stratégie consiste en un réengagement en faveur d'une intégration russe sérieuse et efficace. Et seule une approche transatlantique peut rendre cette stratégie efficace.

Maxime Lefebvre estime que depuis 1989, la Russie et l'Occident n'ont pas réussi à développer un partenariat fort et que les relations russo-occidentales sont particulièrement tendues depuis 2003/2004. Il évoque les principaux moments de la détérioration de cette relation, à savoir la mission américaine en Irak, l'élargissement de l'OTAN, la proposition de mettre en place des boucliers antimissiles en Pologne et en République tchèque1, le récent conflit en Géorgie et la crise énergétique de 2008. Il estime que malgré le retour à une Russie autoritaire, l'Union européenne doit conserver son partenariat stratégique tout en trouvant, pour les pays européens situés à son voisinage, d'autres solutions innovantes que la politique européenne d'élargissement qu'il considère comme non viable actuellement. Maxime Lefebvre pense que l'Union européenne et les Etats-Unis doivent coopérer avec la

---

[1] Finalement le président Obama y a renoncé le 17 septembre 2009

Russie en l'intégrant dans les structures européennes de sécurité et les structures économiques telles que l'OMC. L'ouverture d'un dialogue par l'administration Obama sur des sujets d'intérêt commun (désarmement, non-prolifération, Iran et Afghanistan) est de bon augure. Les Russes utiliseront peut-être ce nouveau dialogue avec Washington pour essayer de modifier l'équilibre des pouvoirs avec l'Union européenne sur le continent, celle-ci ayant un pouvoir attractif croissant aux yeux de l'Europe orientale, et ce, afin d'essayer de renforcer sa « sphère d'influence ».

Maxime Lefebvre reconnaît toutefois que la politique russe reste un élément de discorde entre les Européens pour des raisons d'intérêts économiques, historiques et géographiques. La position française consiste à les considérer comme partie prenante d'un vaste contexte géographique comprenant naturellement l'Amérique du Nord, et allant de Vancouver à Vladivostok. La nouvelle approche américaine offre aux Européens la possibilité de redéfinir une stratégie d'engagement lucide. Celeste Wallander et Maxime Lefebvre sont tous deux d'accord pour affirmer qu'une Russie faible et se désagrégeant serait plus dangereuse que le *statu quo*. Il est dans l'intérêt de la communauté transatlantique d'engager le dialogue avec la Russie, plutôt que de l'isoler.

Conclusion

Pour résumer, nos auteurs ont souligné de nombreuses opportunités en faveur d'un partenariat renouvelé et proposé divers domaines méritant une action conjointe ou complémentaire. Ils soulignent toutefois des différences d'approche entre nos deux pays liées à des raisons historiques et géographiques ou à des divergences de conceptions ou de perspectives. Les différences apparaissent dans les moyens spécifiques recherchés par chaque pays pour faire face à la crise financière et dans les propositions en faveur de la future gouvernance mondiale ; dans l'urgence et le degré d'efforts requis en Afghanistan et dans la région avoisinante ; dans les instruments et mécanismes institutionnels nécessaires pour étendre la stabilité à tout le continent européen et faire de la Turquie un partenaire stratégique ; dans la portée et le rythme des initiatives en matière de contrôle des armes et de désarmement. Toutefois, de nouvelles synergies d'efforts semblent apparaître pour lutter contre le changement climatique et promouvoir la croissance durable ; réagir face au développement africain ; relever les défis liés à la paix et au développement au Moyen-Orient et en Méditerranée ; développer un nouveau concept stratégique pour l'OTAN et créer un véritable partenariat « stratégique » avec l'Union européenne ; et s'engager avec Moscou dans un nouveau schéma de coopération tout en respectant fermement les principes essentiels et en rassurant les alliés participant au processus. Mais surtout, il existe une possibilité de faire en sorte que ce partenariat franco-américain ou européo-américain aille au-delà des défis classiques de la stabilité européenne et qu'il repose sur une perspective plus globale. L'avenir nous dira si les Américains auront la patience de s'engager auprès de leurs partenaires européens sur cette base et si la France et l'Europe auront la volonté d'agir ensemble de manière cohérente dans ce type de partenariat.

Première partie :

points de vue économiques

Chapitre un

La France et les Etats-Unis face aux défis économiques mondiaux

Jean-François Jamet

Résumé

Crise économique, financière et désormais sociale, risques énergétiques, environnementaux et alimentaires, montée des inégalités et tentation du protectionnisme : les défis auxquels est confrontée l'économie mondiale sont nombreux et simultanés. Compte tenu de l'ampleur de ces défis, le lien transatlantique est extrêmement précieux et doit bénéficier d'un élan politique fort. Pour dépasser les défis actuels et futurs, les administrations américaine et européenne devront définir des objectifs partagés et des actions communes dont nous donnons ici de nombreux exemples. Elles pourront ainsi promouvoir la stabilité de l'économie mondiale, la compétitivité de leurs économies et le soutien des citoyens à l'ouverture internationale. La France, traditionnellement méfiante vis à vis de la mondialisation et des États-Unis, peut jouer un rôle important dans ce rapprochement et en faire l'un des éléments de la promotion d'une mondialisation mieux régulée.

L'économie mondiale est en crise. Le choc est d'autant plus brutal que le monde a connu une croissance forte au cours de la période récente (4% entre 2001 et 2007), favorisée par le développement des échanges internationaux et l'émergence des BRIC (Brésil, Russie, Inde et Chine). Elle est aujourd'hui déstabilisée par plusieurs phénomènes majeurs : la crise immobilière et la titrisation des créances ont été à l'origine de la plus grave crise financière aux États-Unis depuis 1929, rapidement communiquée à l'Europe ; la crise économique qui s'en est suivie est partout la cause d'une vague de défaillance d'entreprises et d'une augmentation brutale du chômage ; le commerce mondial recule ; les prix des matières premières ont largement augmenté, entraînant en 2007-2008 une crise alimentaire et un choc pétrolier ; la pression sur les ressources écologiques s'est accrue et les inégalités restent très

**Figure 1   Evolution des marchés boursiers 2000–2009
(base 100 = janvier 2000)**

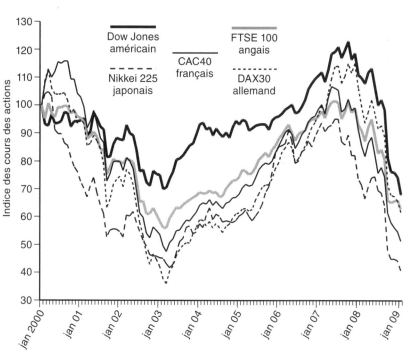

Sources : Eurostat et Données réunies et mises en forme pour la fondation
Robert Schuman, ©FRS.

fortes à la fois à l'échelle mondiale et au sein des pays. Ces bouleversements ont pour conséquence d'accroître le malaise face à la mondialisation et l'incertitude face à l'avenir des acteurs économiques.

Dans ce contexte, les États-Unis, la France et l'ensemble des pays
développés cherchent des solutions à la fois pour le court et le long
termes. Pour que ces solutions soient efficaces, il est essentiel qu'elles
soient coordonnées : un repli des économies sur elles-mêmes plongerait l'économie mondiale dans un marasme prolongé. Si la France a
engagé des réformes structurelles internes nécessaires au redressement
de sa compétitivité, elle est aussi liée sur le plan de sa politique économique à ses partenaires de la zone euro et de l'Union européenne. Une
coopération européenne est notamment nécessaire pour aider les Etats
membres les plus affaiblis. C'est également à ce niveau qu'il faut penser

la relation transatlantique en matière économique. Les liens commerciaux et surtout financiers sont en effet très forts entre les deux principales économies de la planète. Dans un monde qui se régionalise en même temps qu'il se mondialise, il est important de développer le marché transatlantique, la taille du marché domestique étant un atout essentiel dans la compétition internationale. La coopération transatlantique doit également permettre d'élaborer des réponses communes aux défis économiques actuels.

Des défis communs

La propagation de la crise financière à l'ensemble de l'économie

L'économie mondiale connaît depuis juillet 2007 une crise financière dont le coût est estimé par le FMI à 4000 milliards de dollars. Cette crise est d'abord née de l'explosion de la bulle immobilière aux États-Unis. Son effet s'est communiqué à l'ensemble du système financier du fait de la perte de valeur brutale des crédits hypothécaires à risque, les subprimes, et des produits dérivés associés. La crise des subprimes a ensuite fragilisé les banques, précipité la chute des indices boursiers (figure 1) et déprimé l'économie réelle aux États-Unis et en Europe à travers différents canaux de transmission, notamment l'intégration des marchés financiers[1] : en 2009, le PIB devrait reculer de 3% en France et de 2,8% aux Etats-Unis.

Les banques sont devenues brutalement réticentes à prêter, non seulement aux particuliers et aux entreprises, mais aussi entre elles. Cette situation où les banques détiennent des créances douteuses et font face à une crise de liquidité a plongé les marchés dans l'incertitude sur l'étendue des pertes. De ce fait, plusieurs établissements de crédit et banques ont fait faillite ou n'ont pu être sauvés que grâce à l'intervention publique ou à leur rachat par d'autres banques moins touchées ou par des fonds souverains. En outre, les sociétés non-financières ont à leur tour été touchées par la contraction du crédit. Les défaillances d'entreprises et le chômage augmente rapidement : en 2010, celui-ci devrait atteindre 10,1% aux Etats-Unis (contre 4,6% en 2007) et 10,3%

---

[1] Pour une analyse de la crise financière, voir *Crise financière : analyses et propositions*, numéro spécial de la Revue d'économie financière et de Risques, juin 2008.

Figure 2   Taux de croissance du PIB réel (en %) en 2007, 2008 et 2009 : comparaisons internationales

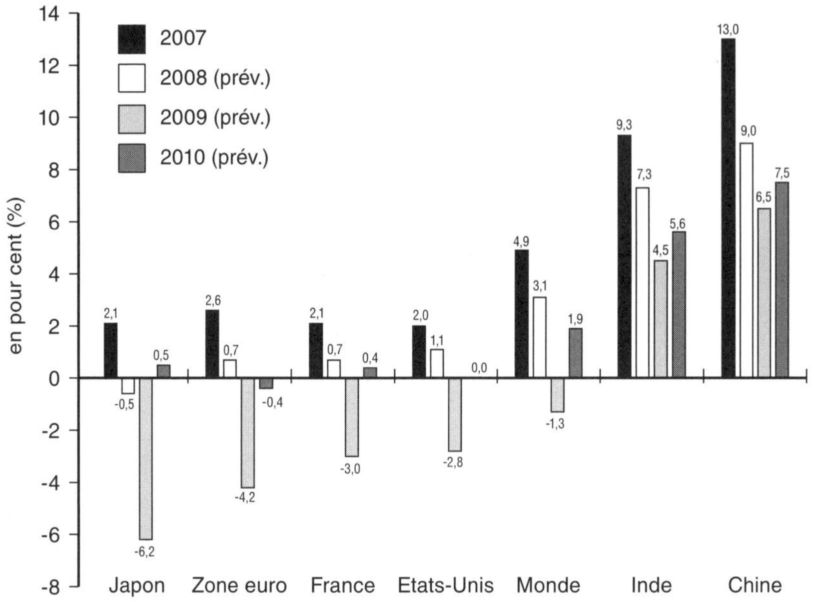

Source : Banque mondiale et OCDE.

en France (contre 7,3% en 2008). Dans ce contexte extrêmement troublé, le commerce mondial diminue (-13,2% prévus en 2009), amplifiant la crise. L'économie mondiale est désormais en récession dans sa globalité : le PIB mondial reculera de 1,3% en 2009 selon les prévisions (figure 2) malgré le maintien d'une croissance relativement élevée dans les pays émergents[2].

Si la Fed et la BCE ont coordonné leurs interventions et élargi leurs instruments d'intervention pour permettre au marché du crédit de continuer à fonctionner, les réponses européenne et américaine à la crise ont d'abord divergé. Aux États-Unis, la Fed a baissé ses taux de façon spectaculaire (figure 3), tandis que le Trésor et le Congrès amé-

[2] Une contagion plus forte de la crise financière à ces pays (par exemple via le ralentissement des échanges commerciaux ou via la sphère financière) plongerait l'économie mondiale dans une crise encore bien plus grave, notamment lorsque l'on sait que les pays riches sont parfois importateurs nets de capitaux, l'épargne chinoise étant, par exemple, largement investie aux États-Unis.

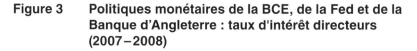

Figure 3 **Politiques monétaires de la BCE, de la Fed et de la Banque d'Angleterre : taux d'intérêt directeurs (2007–2008)**

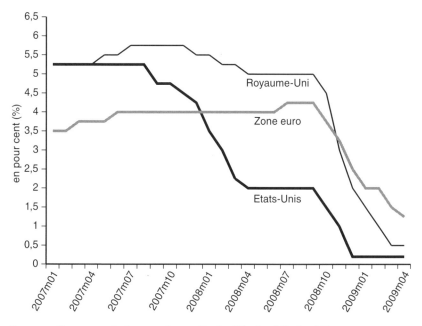

Sources : Banque centrale européenne, Bank of England, Federal Reserve

ricain ont orchestré d'abord une relance budgétaire en janvier 2008 puis, en septembre, sont parvenu à un accord sur le plan Paulson, destiné à récupérer plusieurs centaines de milliards de dollars d'actifs liés aux subprimes. Enfin, le président nouvellement élu, Barack Obama a annoncé en janvier 2009 un plan de relance de 775 milliards de dollars. Le déficit américain devrait ainsi dépasser 10% en 2009 et 2010, portant la dette publique à 87% du PIB en 2009 et 97% en 2010. Les États-Unis ont ainsi fait le choix de substituer de l'endettement public à l'endettement privé pour éviter l'effondrement de l'économie et une dépression prolongée. Cet effort est rendu possible par la préférence des investisseurs pour les obligations d'Etat (perçues comme peu risquée) et des faibles taux d'intérêt auxquelles elles sont donc émises. Cependant, le risque existe que la situation change lorsque l'économie repartira, avec la possibilité d'un krach obligataire et d'une augmentation des taux d'intérêt applicables à la dette publique. De ce fait, il est essentiel que les mesures de relance soient réversibles et il faudra préparer soigneusement la sortie de crise. En particulier, de grandes quantités de liquidités ont été mises en circulation qui pourraient alimenter une forte inflation au moment de la reprise. Or, il est important de noter que l'inflation a surtout pris au cours des quinze dernières années la forme d'une bulle financière et immobilière. Il sera donc très important de veiller à limiter la masse monétaire au cours de la reprise pour ne pas générer une bulle qui pourrait conduire à une nouvelle catastrophe dans quelques années.

Dans la zone euro, l'inflation a longtemps empêché la BCE de baisser ses taux à l'image de la Fed (figure 3). Des plans de sauvegarde du système bancaire ont été adoptés par les Etats membres sur le modèle britannique, allant parfois jusqu'à la nationalisation des établissements en difficulté. La coopération a été plus difficile pour ce qui est des plans de relance : l'opportunité de plans de relance a été examinée au niveau national selon la situation et les contraintes propres de chaque État. La Commission a certes proposé en décembre 2009 que l'ensemble des pays européens adoptent un plan de relance budgétaire à hauteur de 1,3% de leur PIB[3] mais l'ampleur des moyens mobilisés et la nature des plans varient considérablement d'un Etat à l'autre (figure 4). Ceci s'explique pour partie par le niveau variable des marges de manœuvre d'un pays à l'autre : ainsi des pays comme l'Italie ou la Hongrie n'ont pas de marge de manœuvre en raison du niveau déjà trop élevé de leur dette publique, et la détérioration des finances publiques de l'Irlande en raison de l'ampleur considérable de la récession contraint ce pays a une politique de rigueur.

Le retour de la rareté

Si la mondialisation permet de faire baisser les prix de certains produits en augmentant les capacités de production et en faisant baisser les coûts, il n'en va pas de même des produits pour lesquels l'offre est intrinsèquement limitée, en particulier les ressources naturelles. La croissance mondiale a ainsi contribué à l'augmentation spectaculaire des prix de l'énergie et de l'alimentation.

Les prix du pétrole sont passés de 20 dollars le baril en janvier 2002 à 146 dollars en juillet 2008, avant de revenir à 38 dollars fin 2008

---

[3] Communication de la Commission au Conseil européen, *Un plan européen pour la relance économique*, 26 novembre 2008 — COM(2008) 800.

Figure 4   Les plans de relance budgétaire face à la crise (montant des sommes engagées sous forme de baisses d'impôt ou de dépenses additionnelles pour la période 2008–2010, en % du PIB de 2008)

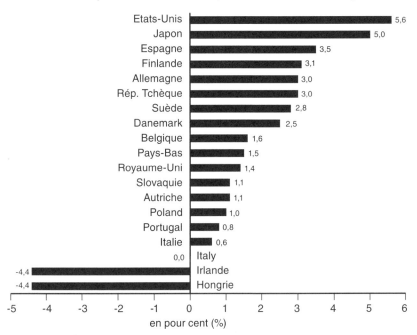

Source : OCDE.

(figure 4). Cette hausse a été favorisée par le sous-investissement dans les capacités de production et de raffinage ainsi que par l'instabilité politique dans de nombreux pays producteurs. Elle a des conséquences négatives sur la croissance des pays importateurs[4] mais elle a également d'autres implications, par exemple l'importance croissante de la « géopolitique du pipeline » qui accroît l'insécurité énergétique.

Le prix des aliments a, quant à lui, augmenté de 95% entre 2001 et 2008 (figure 4). Les causes sont multiples : croissance rapide de la consommation des pays émergents, augmentation des prix du pétrole (qui affecte les coûts de production), mauvaises récoltes liées à des conditions climatiques défavorables (sécheresses, inondations), déve-

---

[4] Voir par exemple Jean-Francois Jamet, « L'impact de la hausse des prix du pétrole sur la croissance de la zone euro », *Questions d'Europe — Policy Papers de la Fondation Robert Schuman*, janvier 2008. http://www.robert-schuman.org/question_europe.php?num=qe-85.

Figure 5   Augmentation des prix du pétrole et de l'alimentation dans le monde 2001–2009 (Indice 2001 = 100)

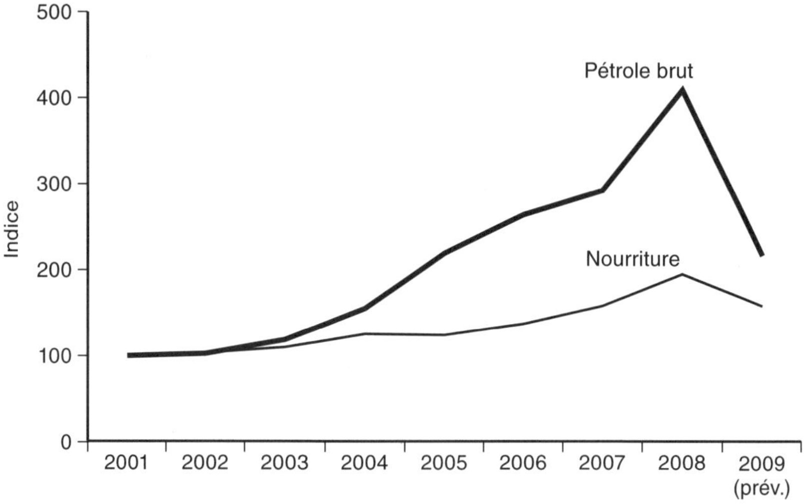

Sources : FMI, Department of Energy et calculs de l'auteur.

Notes : Prix du baril de pétrole — moyenne annuelle. Indice des prix de l'alimentation (basé sur le prix des céréales, des huiles végétales, de la viande, du poisson, du sucre, des bananes et des oranges) — moyenne annuelle.

loppement des biocarburants qui tend à indexer les prix de certaines matières premières agricoles sur l'énergie[5], ou encore difficultés locales propres à certains pays pauvres (capacités de stockage insuffisante et piètre qualité des infrastructures).

Enfin, la pression sur les ressources écologiques pose de multiples problèmes environnementaux : réchauffement climatique augmentant la fréquence des événements climatiques extrêmes, épuisement des ressources en eau et des ressources halieutiques, pollutions multiples, recul de la biodiversité. La liste est longue et le coût économique et humain potentiellement considérable.

---

[5] Voir Juan Delgado et Indhira Santos, "The New Food Equation: Do EU policies add up?", *Bruegel Policy Brief*, Juillet 2008 (http://www.bruegel.org/8105). Les travaux de recherche conduits jusqu'ici ne permettent pas d'incriminer la spéculation.

Tableau 1   **Part dans le PIB mondial, croissance et niveau de vie : comparaisons internationales (pour cent)**

	Part du PIB mondial (PPA), 2008	Part du PIB mondial (PPA), 1997	Part du PIB mondial (prix courants), 2008	Taux de croissance annuel moyen, 2001–2007	PIB par habitant, 2008 (en euros (€) PPA)
France	3,1	3,7	4,8	1,7	25765
Euro zone	15,8	18,6	22,6	1,8	25479
UE27	22,3	25,5	30,9	2,3	23233
Etats-Unis	20,9	23,2	23,1	2,4	35363
Japon	6,4	8,5	7,8	1,6	25944
Chine	11,4	6,4	6,8	10,1	4469
Inde	4,8	3,4	2,0	7,3	2096
Brésil	2,8	3,1	2,7	3,3	7744
Russie	3,2	2,7	2,9	6,6	12153
Monde	100,0	100,0	100,0	4,0	N/A

Sources : FMI et calculs de l'auteur.

La pression sur les ressources devrait continuer à augmenter dans les prochaines années : avec une population mondiale qui va passer de 6,5 milliards en 2005 à 8,3 milliards en 2030, les besoins mondiaux en énergie primaire vont par exemple augmenter de 55%.[6] En outre, la tentation est grande pour les pays producteurs de constituer des cartels : la Russie est par exemple ouvertement favorable à la création d'un cartel du blé et a d'ores et déjà posé les bases d'un cartel du gaz.

Le nouveau visage de l'économie mondiale... et ses déséquilibres persistants

La croissance mondiale est désormais tirée par les BRIC (figure 5). En 10 ans, leur part dans le PIB mondial est passée de 15,6% à 22,2% (en PPA), leur part dans les échanges internationaux de biens et services de 5,8% à 11,5%. Si les BRIC ont fait entrer dans l'économie

---

[6] *La France dans quinze ans : tendances et ruptures, opportunités et risques*, Rapport du Conseil d'analyse économique, avril 2008. http://www.strategie.gouv.fr/IMG/pdf/CAE_Prospective2025-avril__3.pdf.

mondiale un nombre sans précédent de travailleurs, ce sont également des marchés considérables avec 2,8 milliards d'habitants. Enfin, ce sont des puissances politiques avec lesquelles il faut désormais compter dans la gouvernance de l'économie mondiale. La transformation du G7 en G20 et l'engagement pris en avril 2009 d'accroître le poids décisionnel des pays émergents au FMI et à la Banque mondiale vont dans ce sens.

L'économie mondiale est aussi marquée par des déséquilibres importants : les pays asiatiques sont structurellement exportateurs nets de capitaux tandis que les Etats-Unis sont importateurs nets du fait de leurs déficits jumeaux (déficit de la balance commerciale et déficit public). Cet état de fait correspond au fait que les Etats-Unis épargnent moins que ce qui serait nécessaire pour financer leurs emprunts. Le différentiel est apporté par l'épargne étrangère, en particulier asiatique, laquelle a permis aux Etats-Unis de bénéficier de taux d'intérêt particulièrement faibles dans les années 1990 et 2000 et de financer ainsi une économie fondée sur un accès aisé au crédit mais aussi sur un endettement de plus en plus élevé. Dans un régime de change flottant, ceci aurait du se traduire par une dépréciation du dollar face aux monnaies asiatiques, qui permettrait en retour un rééquilibrage des flux de capitaux et de la balance commerciale américaine[7]. Or, cela ne s'est pas produit car certains pays asiatiques, notamment la Chine, souhaitent conserver une croissance fondée sur les exportations et refusent de voir leur monnaie réévaluée : ils maintiennent un taux de change fixe ou quasi fixe face au dollar en utilisant les réserves de change de leurs banques centrales (très importantes du fait des excédents commerciaux de ces pays). La crise actuelle met en évidence la nécessité d'un rééquilibrage, qui peut prendre différente voies : augmentation de l'épargne américaine (laquelle a commencé avec un effet récessif sur la consommation), réévaluation des monnaies asiatiques (peu probable), recul du taux d'épargne en Asie (au profit de la consommation), ou monétisation de la dette américaine (financement de la dette par l'émission de dollars par la Fed, avec pour conséquence une augmentation de l'inflation qui réduira la valeur réelle de la dette américaine). Chacune de ces voies est étroite et implique une répartition des coûts entre les pays asiatiques et les Etats-Unis. Mais plus l'ajustement est retardé, plus il risque d'être brutal, comme en témoigne déjà le recul de la consommation aux Etats-Unis.

---

[7] Voir Olivier Blanchard, Francesco Giavazzi et Filipa Sa, "The U.S. Current Account and the Dollar", Brookings Papers on Economic Activity, 2005, 1-66.

L'autre déséquilibre persistant de l'économie mondiale est celui des inégalités et de la pauvreté. Malgré la croissance rapide des pays émergents, les inégalités sont restées stables au niveau mondial[8] en raison de l'augmentation des inégalités au sein des pays. Entre le début des années 1980 et le milieu des années 2000, la part des revenus du percentile le plus élevé dans le revenu national est ainsi passée de 10 à 20,9% aux États-Unis et de 7,6% à 9% en France.[9] Il existe en effet des gagnants et des perdants à la mondialisation et au changement technologique au sein de chaque pays, du fait de la réallocation internationale du travail vers les secteurs et les sites les plus productifs. Les transitions peuvent être particulièrement douloureuses pour les salariés concernés. Enfin, les chiffres rappellent que la lutte contre la pauvreté dans le monde est loin d'être gagnée : en 2005, 1,4 milliard de personnes disposaient de moins de 1,25 dollar par jour.[10]

Face aux crises, la tentation du repli protectionniste

Les crises actuelles et les ajustements suscités par la mondialisation renforcent la tentation protectionniste. Elle s'est manifestée dans le contexte de la crise alimentaire avec la mise en place de taxes à l'exportation ou d'interdictions d'exporter certaines denrées alimentaires. Elle s'est aussi traduite par le blocage du cycle de Doha, un accord n'ayant pu être trouvé entre les États-Unis et l'Inde sur la clause de sauvegarde autorisant l'application de tarifs douaniers agricoles spéciaux dans les pays en développement en cas d'augmentation trop forte des importations ou de baisse des prix excessive.

Dans les pays développés, les difficultés de certaines industries (par exemple l'industrie automobile aux États-Unis et l'industrie textile en Europe) ainsi que la peur des délocalisations ou des fonds souverains étrangers ont conduit à une résurgence des discours protectionnistes. En Europe, des voix se sont élevées pour utiliser la préférence communautaire contre ce qui est présenté comme le dumping social, environ-

---

[8] Voir Branco Milanovic, "An Even Higher Global Inequality than Previously Thought: A Note on Global Inequality Calculations Using the 2005 ICP Results", *World Bank Policy Research Working Paper Series*, 2007 (http://papers.ssrn.com/sol3/papers.cfm?abstract_id=1081970). En 2002, le coefficient de Gini des inégalités de revenu dans le monde était de 0,7, ce qui reste plus élevé que dans n'importe quel pays pris individuellement.

[9] Jean Pisani-Ferry. "Progressive Governance and Globalisation: the Agenda Revesited", *Bruegel Policy Contribution*, Avril 2008. http://www.bruegel.org/6715.

[10] Source : Banque mondiale.

nemental et fiscal des pays émergents. Aux Etats-Unis, l'administration Obama a promu une clause « Buy American » dans son plan de relance pour aider son industrie métallurgique. Aux Etats-Unis comme en Europe, plusieurs secteurs manufacturiers souhaitent que des quotas soient imposés aux importations en provenance de Chine.

Si les difficultés rencontrées par les salariés d'industries en déclin ne doivent pas être ignorées et si la lutte anti-dumping est justifiée, il est important de rappeler que le protectionnisme est dangereux. Il aurait pour conséquences de renforcer les tensions sur les marchés mondiaux, avec le risque de lancer une guerre tarifaire et d'aggraver la crise, comme ce fut le cas dans les années 1930. Il est dores et déjà acquis que le commerce international reculera en 2009 pour la première fois depuis plus de 25 ans. Or, l'Europe reste le principal acteur de la mondialisation des échanges de biens et services, elle serait donc la première perdante d'une contraction plus brutale encore du commerce international[11].

Réformer, malgré la crise : perspectives pour l'économie française

Des performances insatisfaisantes

Si la France reste la 2e économie par la taille dans l'UE et la 5e dans le monde, ses performances économiques récentes ont été relativement décevantes (figure 3): en matière de croissance, d'emploi, d'augmentation de la productivité et des exportations, la France se situe en dessous de la moyenne européenne. En outre, il y existe un certain nombre de problèmes sociaux de premier ordre comme les formes de ghettoïsation urbaine dans les banlieues ou le niveau élevé de l'échec scolaire, 15% d'une classe d'âge sortant du système éducatif sans diplôme.

Les performances récentes du commerce extérieur ont suscité des inquiétudes quant à la compétitivité de l'économie française. Alors que la France disposait d'un excédent de la balance des paiements courants à hauteur de 3,5% du PIB en 1999, elle connaît désormais un déficit de plus de 1% du PIB. Les entreprises françaises ont en effet perdu des

---

[11] Voir Jean-Francois Jamet, « La préférence communautaire ou les illusions du protectionnisme européen », *Questions d'Europe – Policy Papers de la Fondation Robert Schuman*, janvier 2008. http://www.robert-schuman.org/question_europe.php?num=qe-64.

parts de marché dans un grand nombre de ses domaines de spécialisation. Cette perte de compétitivité contraste avec les performances remarquables de l'Allemagne, premier exportateur mondial, qui a augmenté ses parts de marché. Une partie de l'explication vient de la géographie des exportations françaises, insuffisamment orientées au cours de ces dernières années vers les pays à forte croissance d'Europe centrale et orientale ou d'Asie, ainsi que de stratégies macroéconomiques différentes entre la France et l'Allemagne.[12]

Une forte méfiance vis-à-vis de la mondialisation

Les Français se montrent particulièrement méfiants vis à vis de la mondialisation: en 2008, ils étaient 66% à juger que la mondialisation est une menace pour l'emploi et les entreprises françaises, contre seulement 25% qui estimaient qu'elle est avant tout une opportunité pour les entreprises à travers l'ouverture des marchés: c'est bien plus que pour l'UE 27 dans son ensemble où 43% des sondés affirmaient que la mondialisation est surtout une menace contre 39% qui estimaient qu'elle est une opportunité.[13] D'après une enquête du German Marshall Fund[14], une majorité des personnes interrogées en France sont favorables au maintien de barrières commerciales destinées à protéger les entreprises nationales même si cela a potentiellement pour conséquence de freiner la croissance. Les Français manifestent ainsi un désir de protection particulièrement fort face aux aléas économiques et à la crainte des délocalisations. Si celles-ci n'ont représenté que 5,8% des suppressions d'emplois dans les entreprises de plus de 100 salariés entre 2002 et 2007,[15] elles marquent les esprits et sont associées au recul de l'emploi industriel en France (-8,2% entre 2000 et 2006). En outre, la

---

[12] L'Allemagne a choisi de fonder sa croissance sur les exportations, en réduisant les coûts du travail quitte à réduire la consommation intérieure. La croissance de la France a au contraire été tirée par la consommation. Or l'Allemagne est à la fois le premier client et le premier fournisseur de la France (avec 19% des importations et 15% des exportations en 2007). Il semble donc que le ralentissement de la consommation en Allemagne a pénalisé les exportations françaises, alors que la bonne tenue de la consommation en France a favorisé les exportations allemandes. De facto, entre 2000 et 2007, les importations françaises de produits en provenance d'Allemagne ont augmenté de 50% alors que les exportations vers l'Allemagne n'ont augmenté que de 25%.

[13] Commission européenne, *Eurobaromètre Standard 69*, 2008.

[14] German Marshall Fund of the United States, *Perspectives on trade and poverty reduction, a survey of public opinion*, 2007.

[15] Source : European Restructuring Monitor.

Tableau 2   Les performances économiques de la France

	France	Rang au sein de l'UE27	Moyenne UE27	Moyenne Zone euro	Etats-Unis	Japon
Croissance et niveau de vie						
Part du PIB mondial (prix courants), 2008	4,8%	2	30,9%	22,6%	23,1%	7,8%
Taux de croissance annuel moyen, 2001–2007	1,7%	23	2,3%	1,8%	2,4%	1,6%
Taux de croissance, 2008	0,7%	19	1,0%	0,9%	1,2%	-0,3%
PIB par habitant, 2008 (en euros à parité de pouvoir d'achat)	25765	11	23233	25479	35363	25944
Emploi						
Taux de chômage, fin 2009 (prévision)	9,8%	24	8,7%	9,3%	9,1%	4,9%
Taux d'emploi, 2007	64,6%	17	65,4%	65,7%	71,7%	70,6%
Taux d'emploi des jeunes (15–24 ans), 2007	31,5%	16	37,2%	38,0%	53,1%	41,4%
Taux d'emploi des séniors (55–64 ans), 2007	38,4%	19	45,1%	43,6%	41,4%	66,1%
Evolution de l'emploi industriel, 2000–2006	-8,2%	18	-5,4%	-2,2%	-15,8%	nd
Finances publiques						
Déficit public, 2009 (prévision, en % du PIB)	-5,4%	24	-4,4%	-4,0%	-10,2%	-6,8%
Dette publique, 2008 (en % du PIB)	63,9%	22	58,7%	66,1%	65,5%	196,3%
Compétitivité						
Taux de croissance annuel moyen de la productivité, 2000–2007	1,0%	22	1,8%	1,1%	1,5%	1,8%

	France	Rang au sein de l'UE27	Moyenne UE27	Moyenne Zone euro	Etats-Unis	Japon
Taux de croissance annuel moyen des exportations, 2000–2007	7,7%	23	11,6%	11,1%	5,8%	5,8%
Part dans les exportations mondiales de marchandises, 2007	4,0%	2	16,5%*	N/A	8,4%	5,1%
Classement selon la compétitivité de l'environnement économique (World Economic Forum), rang sur 131 pays, 2008	16	8	nd	nd	1	9
Economie de la connaissance						
Dépenses totales de R&D (en % du PIB), 2006	2,1%	6	1,8%	1,9%	2,6%	3,3%
Dépenses de R&D des entreprises (en % du PIB), 2006	1,1%	7	0,9%	nd	1,7%	2,5%
Nombre de brevets accordés par l'Office européen des brevets et l'United States Patent and Trademark Office, 2007 (par million d'habitants)	114,2	8	97,6	123,7	302,9	343,0
Dépenses annuelles d'éducation dans l'enseignement supérieur, 2005 (milliers d'euros PPA)	9,3	9	8,3	8,8	21,0	10,3
Taux de scolarisation dans l'enseignement supérieur, 2006	56,2%	17	nd	nd	81,8%	57,3%
Inégalité et pauvreté						
Inégalité de répartition des revenus — ratio de Gini (0=égalité parfaite, 100=inégalité parfaite), 2006	27	9	32,0	nd	47	24,9
Taux de pauvreté après transferts sociaux (seuil de pauvreté=60% du revenu médian), en %, 2006	13%	8	16%	16%	24	nd

*: à l'exclusion du commerce intracommunautaire.

Sources : Eurostat, FMI, OMC, Banque mondiale, OEB, OCDE, Groningen Growth and Development Center et calculs de l'auteur.

crise actuelle accélère les fermetures de sites industriels en Europe : or, il est peu probable que les emplois de production ainsi perdus soient recréés une fois la crise passée. Les nouvelles capacités de production seront installées près des marchés les plus dynamiques, c'est-à-dire dans les pays émergents.

La politique française face à la crise économique

Si la méfiance vis à vis de la mondialisation favorise le patriotisme économique et la politisation des fermetures de sites industriels, elle a aussi créé un désir de rendre l'économie française plus compétitive grâce à des réformes structurelles visant à accroître la concurrence sur le marché des biens, à améliorer le fonctionnement du marché du travail et de l'enseignement supérieur, ou encore à réformer la fiscalité et la fonction publique. Ces réformes ont été engagées par le gouvernement actuel, qui a annoncé son intention de les poursuivre malgré la crise. Dans le contexte de ralentissement de la croissance, le gouvernement a choisi d'engager un plan de relance budgétaire de 26 milliards d'euros, qui comprend notamment 10,5 milliards d'euros d'investissements publics, un soutien à la trésorerie des entreprises et des aides au secteur automobile. Cependant, 10 milliards des fonds prévus dans le plan de relance français consistent en un paiement accéléré de montants dûs par l'État aux PME et ne correspondent donc pas réellement à des fonds supplémentaire. L'OCDE estime ainsi que le plan de relance français pour la période 2008-2010 s'élève à seulement 0,6% du PIB. Jusqu'ici, le gouvernement a refusé de financer des mesures de relance de la consommation, estimant que l'investissement était prioritaire. Il a focalisé son attention sur une demande de moralisation de la rémunération des dirigeants d'entreprise, sur une meilleure indemnisation du chômage partiel et sur la mise en œuvre d'un « revenu de solidarité active » destiné à donner une situation décente aux plus défavorisés sans pour autant les décourager de reprendre un emploi. Compte tenu des risques de forte hausse du chômage, il serait souhaitable qu'un accord soit trouvé dans les grandes entreprises – sur le modèle d'Air France – autour de la préservation de l'emploi en contrepartie d'une mobilité professionnelle accrue en leur sein et d'efforts temporaires de modération salariale. Il serait également opportun qu'un effort spécial de requalification des chômeurs soit mis en place, ce qui bénéficierait aux chômeurs eux-mêmes mais aussi à la compétitivité du pays.

Priorités à moyen terme pour la politique économique française

L'élection présidentielle de 2007 puis les décisions du gouvernement et le ralentissement économique ont favorisé un débat économique intense au cours des deux dernières années. Il est possible d'en dégager les principales orientations :

- Se redonner les moyens de conduire une politique budgétaire contracyclique, ce qui supposera d'assainir les finances publiques à moyen terme. Depuis 1981, le déficit public n'est jamais descendu en dessous de 1,5% du PIB. Au cours de la même période, la dette publique est passée de 22% à 65% du PIB. Elle devrait atteindre 75% en 2009 et 80% en 2010. En période de croissance, il faudra donc faire passer la réduction du déficit en priorité, de façon à pouvoir relancer l'économie en période de crise, ce qui fait aujourd'hui cruellement défaut. Pour y parvenir, un code de responsabilité budgétaire pourrait être mis en place avec des procédures incitant à une gestion plus contracyclique des finances publiques. Par ailleurs, les efforts actuels de réduction de la dépense publique au niveau de l'État doivent être accompagnés par des efforts similaires au niveau des collectivités territoriales dont les effectifs et les dépenses ont augmenté rapidement ces dernières années. Une possibilité est de réduire le nombre d'échelons administratifs pour limiter les doublons et faire des économies d'échelles.

- Poursuivre la réforme du système de retraite, qui constitue une dette publique implicite qu'il faudra financer d'ici à 2020. En particulier, il serait intéressant de simplifier le système en le rendant plus transparent et en s'inspirant du modèle suédois de la retraite par points[16].

- Augmenter simultanément le taux d'emploi et la productivité. Cette politique de l'offre suppose de favoriser le travail des populations sous-employées (jeunes, femmes et « seniors »), en supprimant les dispositifs désincitatifs (par exemple les dispenses de recherche d'emploi pour les seniors) et en facilitant

---

[16] Voir sur ce point Antoine Bozio et Thomas Piketty, *Retraites : pour un système de comptes individuels de cotisations. Propositions pour une refonte générale des régimes de retraites en France*, avril 2008, http://www.jourdan.ens.fr/piketty/fichiers/public/BozioPiketty2008.pdf.

la reprise d'un emploi (par exemple en rendant plus aisée la garde d'enfant pour les mères célibataires). L'employabilité et l'augmentation de la productivité supposent également d'investir plus dans l'enseignement supérieur et la formation et d'en revoir le fonctionnement, afin d'en améliorer la qualité et le caractère professionnalisant. En France les dépenses d'enseignement supérieur ne représentent qu'1,1% du PIB contre 2,3% aux États-Unis.

• Réduire les barrières à l'entrée des professions réglementées libérales et artisanales pour favoriser le développement de l'emploi dans les services.

• Favoriser le développement des PME : la France a un déficit d'entreprise de taille moyenne (entre 50 et 500 salariés) et de petits groupes (entre 500 et 3000 salariés), qui sont pourtant ceux qui croissent le plus vite et créent le plus d'emplois. Il s'agit donc de limiter les effets de seuil réglementaire, d'encourager la diffusion des technologies de l'information et de faciliter la transmission intergénérationnelle ainsi que l'accès aux financements et aux services de conseil. Le Conseil d'analyse économique (CAE) a également proposé de fixer un taux d'impôt sur les sociétés plus bas (18% par exemple) pour le premier million de bénéfice imposable.

• Limiter la ségrégation urbaine. Pour favoriser l'intégration des banlieues pauvres, un effort important est nécessaire pour y développer les commerces, les transports publics ou privés, le microcrédit, et améliorer le logement social[17]. Il est aussi essentiel de faciliter l'accès des jeunes qui y sont scolarisés à des programmes éducatifs professionnalisant, par exemple en encourageant les formations en alternance.

L'horizon européen

Pour la France comme pour les autres pays européens, la mondialisation est d'abord une européanisation. Non seulement, l'UE représente deux tiers du commerce extérieur français, mais les décisions

---

[17] Voir à ce sujet Eric Maurin, *Le ghetto français. Enquête sur le séparatisme social*, La République des Idées/Le Seuil, 2004.

sont prises au niveau européen dans plusieurs domaines essentiels : la politique monétaire, les négociations commerciales, l'agriculture, la concurrence et le marché intérieur. En outre, la majorité des normes techniques relatives à la sécurité industrielle, à l'environnement et à la protection du consommateur sont désormais définies dans le cadre de directives ou de règlements communautaires.

Dans ce contexte, il est possible et nécessaire d'améliorer la gouvernance économique de l'Union européenne[18]. Ceci concerne la coordination des politiques économiques, la régulation financière[19], l'attribution des aides agricoles dans le cadre de la PAC[20], ou encore la mise en œuvre de la Stratégie de Lisbonne[21]. A plus court terme, face au risque de crises de change dans différents pays non membres de la zone euro (Hongrie, Lettonie, Roumanie, etc.), l'Union européenne doit garantir une solidarité économique entre ses membres. Ceci implique notamment une assurance que la BCE apportera des prêts aux banques centrales des pays exposés à des crises de change, mais aussi une coordination étroite avec le FMI, la mise en place d'un fonds de garantie européen, ou encore l'augmentation des fonds structurels. Enfin, pour favoriser le déblocage du crédit et le refinancement des grandes entreprises, la BCE pourrait créer une ligne de crédit spéciale pour l'achat de billets de trésorerie.

Un autre sujet de premier plan est la politique de change de l'euro, particulièrement controversée[22]. Depuis sa création, la volatilité de l'euro a été très forte (Tableau 2), ce qui est fortement pénalisant pour les entreprises exportatrices, notamment les entreprises industrielles, dont l'évolution des coûts devient ainsi peu prévisible. En outre, l'euro s'est fortement apprécié entre 2002 et 2008 face aux principales devises.

---

[18] Voir Jean-François Jamet, « La gouvernance économique de l'Union européenne : controverses et pistes de réformes », *Questions d'Europe - Policy Papers de la Fondation Robert Schuman*, juillet 2007. http://www.robert-schuman.org/question_europe.php?num=qe-67.

[19] Voir Jean-François Jamet, « Quelle peut être la réponse européenne face à la crise financière ? », in *Crise financière : analyses et propositions*, Revue d'économie financière, 2008.

[20] Voir Nicolas-Jean Bréhon, « L'agriculture européenne à l'heure des choix : pourquoi croire à la PAC? », *Notes de la Fondation Robert Schuman*, n°44, novembre 2008.

[21] Voir Yves Bertoncini, Vanessa Wisnia Weill, « La stratégie de Lisbonne : une voie européenne dans la mondialisation », *Notes de la Fondation Robert Schuman*, n°41, septembre 2007.

[22] Voir sur ce point le rapport du Conseil d'Analyse Economique, coécrit par Michel Didier, Agnès Bénassy-Quéré, Gilles Bransbourg et Alain Henriot, *La politique de change de l'euro*, 2008.

Figure 6   Cours de l'euro face aux principales monnaies 1999–2008 (base 100 = janvier 1999 ; février 2000 pour le yuan)

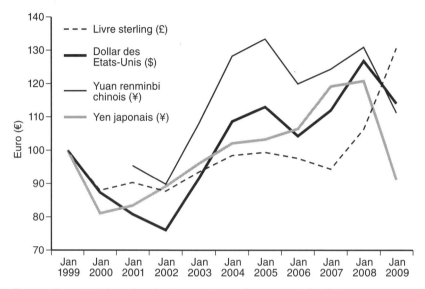

Source: Eurostat et Données réunies et mises en forme pour la fondation Robert Schuman, ©FRS.

De ce fait, il serait souhaitable que l'Eurogroupe définisse des orientations pour la politique de change, comme les Traités communautaires lui en donnent la possibilité après consultation de la BCE pour avis. Il serait notamment utile que, dans les périodes de faible inflation, la BCE prenne en compte l'objectif de change dans sa politique de taux d'intérêt de façon à éviter une appréciation trop brutale de l'euro. Ceci sera d'autant plus nécessaire en période de sortie de crise compte tenu des risques d'inflation aux Etats-Unis. Par ailleurs, une action est nécessaire pour réduire la surévaluation de l'euro vis à vis de la monnaie chinoise. Sans aller jusqu'à demander aux autorités chinoise de laisser flotter le yuan, il serait opportun de lui proposer d'adosser son taux de change à un panier de monnaies plutôt qu'au seul dollar. Ceci permettrait une transition graduelle vers un système plus flexible sans pour autant remettre en cause à court terme le statut du dollar comme monnaie de référence.

Les enjeux du partenariat transatlantique

L'économie transatlantique, cœur de la mondialisation

Les États-Unis et l'Union européenne représentent, en 2008, 54% du PIB mondial (43,2% à parité de pouvoir d'achat), 26,6% du commerce mondial de produits manufacturés et 46,7% du commerce mondial de services[23]. Ils sont également de très loin les principaux émetteurs et récepteurs d'investissements directs étrangers : ils sont ainsi à l'origine de 70% du stock d'IDE dans le monde et la destination de 60% de celui-ci.

L'économie transatlantique est également très intégrée[24], avec des barrières douanières très basses (environ 3% en moyenne). En 2007, les États-Unis ont ainsi absorbé 23% des exportations de biens et services de l'Union européenne et l'UE a été la destination de 21,5% des exportations de marchandises américaines. Cependant cette part est en recul au profit des pays asiatiques. L'intégration de l'économie transatlantique se lit plus encore dans le niveau des investissements croisés : en 2007, l'UE représentait ainsi 75% du stock des IDE reçus par les États-Unis et 46% du stock des IDE de l'UE venait des États-Unis.

Enfin, il est important de noter que la mondialisation de l'immatériel est avant tout synonyme d'américanisation dans les États membres de l'UE. Dans les secteurs du cinéma, du logiciel, de l'audiovisuel, du livre ou encore de la pharmacie, la grande majorité des importations viennent des États-Unis.[25] Ceci conduit parfois les Européens à vivre la relation commerciale avec les États-Unis comme une relation de concurrence frontale, non seulement économique, mais culturelle. Inversement, aux États-Unis, la concurrence de l'Europe dans certains domaines (aéronautique, défense, agriculture, acier, par exemple) est mal acceptée. Il est dans l'intérêt de l'UE et des États-Unis de savoir discuter ouvertement de ces questions, en acceptant les différences culturelles et en examinant les moyens de les respecter tout en promouvant les intérêts de chacun. Ceci permettrait de limiter les régle-

---

[23] Hors échanges intracommunautaires.

[24] Pour plus de détails, on se reportera utilement à Daniel S. Hamilton et Joseph P. Quinlan, *The Transatlantic Economy 2009*, Center for Transatlantic Relations, Jhu-Sais, 2009.

[25] Voir Daniel Cohen et Thierry Verdier, *La mondialisation immatérielle*, Rapport du Conseil d'analyse économique, août 2008. http://www.cae.gouv.fr/rapports/dl/076.pdf.

mentations techniques régissant le commerce et l'attribution des marchés publics de façon à ce qu'elles ne deviennent pas un instrument non avoué de protectionnisme entre les deux côtés de l'Atlantique.

Le marché transatlantique, un point d'appui à promouvoir dans la compétition internationale

Dans le contexte de l'émergence des BRIC, qui sont de larges marchés permettant aux entreprises qui y sont installées de réaliser des économies d'échelle substantielles, il est essentiel pour la compétitivité et l'attractivité des États-Unis et de l'UE de disposer d'un large marché intérieur. Au-delà de la nécessaire poursuite de la mise en œuvre du marché unique en Europe, il est donc de l'intérêt à la fois des États-Unis et de l'Europe de développer une zone de libre échange transatlantique, au bénéfice du consommateur (prix plus bas, standards technologiques communs) et des entreprises (marché plus large). Les barrières principales ne sont pas douanières mais réglementaires.

Un agenda a été défini en 2007 à l'initiative d'Angela Merkel pour réduire les barrières non tarifaires dans le cadre du Conseil économique transatlantique (*Transatlantic Economic Council*) établi à cette occasion. Le but est de pouvoir mettre tous les sujets sur la table, parmi lesquels les services, les marchés financiers, les télécoms, l'énergie, les marchés publics ou encore les cosmétiques et les produits électriques[26]. Par ailleurs, le TEC devrait pouvoir être le lieu d'un dialogue entre industriels sur les questions de standards, d'innovation et de brevets dans des secteurs comme l'énergie, les nanotechnologies, les biocarburants, la santé ou encore l'électronique. Comme l'ont mentionné les conclusions du sommet informel UE-Etats-Unis tenu à Prague le 5 avril 2009, l'arrivée d'une nouvelle administration aux Etats-Unis est l'occasion de renforcer les relations économiques entre l'UE et les Etats-Unis, en soutenant notamment les travaux du TEC. Cependant, compte tenu du changement d'administration au niveau de l'UE, il sera important que la nouvelle Commission redonne une impulsion forte au TEC à la fin 2009.

---

[26] Voir par exemple "Transatlantic integration — delivery time is now", *Current issues — Deutsche Bank Research*, Juin 2008. http://www.dbresearch.com/PROD/DBR_INTER-NET_EN-PROD/PROD0000000000225962.PDF.

Un agenda commun face aux défis actuels

Face aux défis actuels de l'économie mondiale, la coopération entre l'Europe et les États-Unis est non seulement utile mais nécessaire. Plusieurs sujets peuvent ainsi faire l'objet de concertations approfondies en vue d'élaborer des positions ou des actions communes :

- C'est d'ores et déjà le cas dans le contexte de la crise financière. Les banques centrales européennes et américaine ont par exemple travaillé en coopération étroite pour coordonner leurs interventions en vue de calmer les tensions sur le marché du crédit interbancaires. Le G20 d'avril 2009 a également permis d'avancer en accroissant de 500 milliards de dollars les moyens du FMI, en augmentant de 250 milliards de dollars les garanties au financement du commerce international, mais aussi en formalisant des engagements en matière de régulation (paradis fiscaux, agences de notation et hedge funds) et de supervision financière (avec des prérogatives étendues confiées au Conseil de Stabilité financière). Pour autant, il est essentiel que cet effort soit poursuivi dans plusieurs directions : la structuration et l'encadrement prudentiel du marché des dérivés de crédit (en particulier pour les CDS[27]), la supervision des banques et des assurances actives au niveau international, l'adaptation des normes comptables, la transparence des bilans, la régulation des bonus[28], ou encore l'obligation faite aux banques de constituer des provisions plus importantes chaque année pour parer aux risques de liquidité et de solvabilité.

- Dans le domaine de l'environnement et de l'énergie, une coopération entre les États-Unis et l'Union européenne est indispensable. Sur le plan environnemental, les États-Unis et l'Europe ont jusqu'ici eu un différend sur la stratégie à adopter (définition d'objectifs chiffrés, participation des pays émergents et en développement). Or, il est essentiel de trouver un accord lors du sommet de Copenhague sur le changement climatique en décembre 2009. Dans le cadre du paquet énergie-

---

[27] Voir sur ce point : Julien Cantegreil, Romain Rancière et Aaron Tornell, "Future régulation financière : deux règles simples", *Telos-eu.com*, 6 avril 2009.

[28] Sur l'ensemble de ces sujets on pourra se référer à "Reconstruire la finance pour relancer l'économie", *Amicus Curiae*, Institut Montaigne, Mars 2009 (http://www.institutmontaigne.org/ac-crise-3045.html).

climat adopté en décembre 2008, l'Europe s'est donnée pour objectif de réduire de 20% d'ici 2020 ses émissions de gaz à effet de serre et de porter à 20% la part des énergies renouvelables dans la consommation d'énergie de l'UE. De son côté, la nouvelle administration américaine a d'ores et déjà annoncé son souhait de fixer des objectifs de réduction des émissions de gaz à effet de serre et la mise en place d'un système de « cap and trade » (marché de quotas d'émission) qui pourrait dans le futur être lié au système européen déjà existant. Au-delà de ce rapprochement sur la question climatique, une coopération concrète entre les États-Unis et l'Europe en matière environnementale est absolument nécessaire : elle passe par le partage des meilleures pratiques, la définition de standard commun, l'identification des opportunités ouvertes à chacun par les clean techs, qui formeront probablement la base de la prochaine révolution industrielle, et l'adoption d'une stratégie commune en vue du développement de ces technologies. En matière énergétique, il est de l'intérêt commun des États-Unis et de l'Europe de réduire leur dépendance au pétrole et au gaz. Pour cela, il serait utile de mutualiser et de soutenir significativement les efforts de recherche à long terme : recyclage, utilisation de l'hydrogène, biocarburants de 3e et 4e génération, séquestration des émissions, nucléaire de 4e génération. Par ailleurs, les États-Unis peuvent bénéficier de l'expertise européenne dans le domaine de l'éolien et du solaire (pour lesquels l'Allemagne est le leader mondial) ainsi que dans le nucléaire (dont la France est le leader mondial). Enfin, les États-Unis et l'Europe doivent abandonner les objectifs chiffrés et les subventions concernant les biocarburants dans l'état actuel de cette technologie, qui renchérit les prix de l'alimentation, est coûteuse et ne constitue pas en Europe et aux États-Unis la manière la plus efficace de réduire les émissions de CO_2.

- Face à la compétition internationale et aux inégalités, les États-Unis comme l'Europe doivent investir dans l'éducation et la formation. Les études économiques montrent en effet que les inégalités dépendent pour une large part du déséquilibre entre la demande de travail qualifié dans l'économie et l'offre de travail qualifié produite par le système d'éducation et de formation[29]. Sur le plan de la formation, les États-Unis et l'Europe ont un défi commun : développer des formations adaptées aux besoins du marché du travail et capables d'aider à la reconversion des salariés des secteurs en déclin et des chômeurs. Pour ce qui est du système éducatif, il serait utile de partager les meilleures pratiques, les forces de l'un correspondant souvent aux faiblesses de l'autre : les États-Unis doivent ainsi améliorer leurs éducations primaire et secondaire tandis qu'en Europe, il s'agit d'investir plus dans l'enseignement supérieur et d'améliorer la gouvernance des universités[30]. Du côté européen, il est par exemple possible de s'inspirer de l'expérience américaine pour rapprocher universités et entreprises (pour le financement des universités, la recherche, l'apprentissage), revoir l'organisation des premiers cycles universitaires en vue de développer l'employabilité de ceux qui sortent de l'université à ce niveau, et encourager la mobilité des étudiants en Europe, par exemple en créant un « standardized European test » pour l'entrée en master.

- Améliorer la gouvernance économique mondiale. Les États-Unis et l'Europe peuvent contribuer de façon décisive à une amélioration de la gouvernance économique mondiale. La création du G20 et l'engagement pris lors du sommet de Londres de donner un poids plus important aux pays émergents dans les décisions du FMI et de la Banque mondiale ont constitué de ce point de vue une avancée significative. Elle doit être mise à profit pour mieux traiter les problèmes de l'économie globale, notamment les déséquilibre commerciaux et monétaires, et améliorer la supervision financière. De son côté, l'UE pourrait adopter une représentation commune à la Banque mondiale et au FMI[31], comme c'est déjà les cas à l'OMC. Le rôle du FMI devrait en même temps être revu pour

---

[29] Claudia Goldin et Lawrence E. Katz, *The Race between Education and Technology*, Belknap Press, 2008.

[30] Voir les recommandations de Philippe Aghion, Mathias Dewatripont, Caroline Hoxby, Andreu Mas-Colell et André Sapir, "Higher aspirations: An agenda for reforming European universities", *Bruegel Blueprint Series*, 2008.

[31] Voir Emile-Robert Perrin, « La représentation de l'Union européenne dans les institutions financières internationales : Vers une chaise unique ? », *Questions d'Europe — Policy Papers de la Fondation Robert Schuman*, février 2006. http://www.robert-schuman.eu/question_europe.php?num=qe-20.

qu'il se concentre sur la certification des comptes financiers des États, sur la prévention des crises financières, sur l'aide aux Etats exposés à des crises de change et sur les études macroéconomiques, tout en cessant ses programmes d'ajustements structurels et les prêts non destinés à des situations d'urgence qui devraient rester la compétence exclusive de la Banque mondiale. Ceci permettrait de rendre le FMI plus indépendant des pressions politiques et de recentrer sa mission. Parallèlement, il est essentiel de soumettre la Banque mondiale à des audits externes réguliers et de développer la traçabilité des aides et prêts qu'elle accorde, de façon à en accroître la transparence et l'efficacité. La FAO devrait de son côté se voir attribuer les moyens institutionnels et financiers suffisants pour être capable de faire face de façon adéquate aux crises alimentaires sans avoir à solliciter les fonds adéquats dans l'urgence. Enfin, même si les négociations y sont bloquées, l'OMC reste indispensable, notamment pour éviter les retours en arrière. Tout en s'engageant de façon concrète pour conclure le processus de Doha, il serait intéressant que les États-Unis et l'UE examinent ensemble la possibilité de recourir à des accords plurilatéraux ouverts à tout signataire et permettant à ceux qui le souhaitent de poursuivre l'intégration commerciale[32].

Conclusion

Crise économique et financière, retour de la rareté, montée des inégalités et risque de protectionnisme : les défis auxquels est confrontée l'économie mondiale sont nombreux et simultanés. Compte tenu de l'ampleur de ces défis, le lien transatlantique est extrêmement précieux et doit bénéficier d'un élan politique fort. Pour dépasser les défis actuels et futurs, les prochaines administrations américaine et européenne devront définir des objectifs partagés et des actions communes dont nous avons donné des exemples. Elles pourront ainsi promouvoir la stabilité de l'économie mondiale, la compétitivité de leurs économies et le soutien des citoyens à l'ouverture internationale. La France, traditionnellement méfiante vis à vis de la mondialisation et des États-Unis, peut jouer un rôle important dans ce rapprochement et en faire l'un des éléments de la promotion d'une mondialisation mieux régulée.

---

[32] Voir Simon J. Evenett, "Getting over those Doha blues", *Vox*, août 2008 (http://www.voxeu.org/index.php?q=node/1503).

Chapitre deux

« Ne gâchez pas une bonne crise ! » Un leadership franco-américain pour un nouvel agenda économique mondial

Daniel S. Hamilton

La crise financière mondiale et la récession qui en découle, associées aux changements politiques aux États-Unis et en Europe, fournissent à la France et aux Etats-Unis l'opportunité, mais aussi la nécessité, d'adapter leur économie, leur relation bilatérale et finalement l'Occident lui-même pour lui permettre d'affronter défis économiques du XXIème siècle.

Dans ce contexte, la France et les Etats-Unis font face à quatre missions interconnectées. Tout d'abord, les défis économiques internes auxquels sont confrontés chacun des Etats sont redoutables. Chacun doit donc investir les ressources et l'énergie politique nécessaires pour réformer sa propre économie sans succomber aux tentations protectionnistes. Deuxièmement, la France et les Etats-Unis doivent mieux mesurer leur poids respectif dans une relation économique franco-américaine forte et tout faire pour renforcer ces liens plus solidement encore. Troisièmement, l'agenda économique des États-Unis avec la France doit s'inscrire dans le contexte européen. Il est impératif que l'Union européenne et les Etats-Unis coopèrent pour renforcer les liens économiques transatlantiques. Quatrièmement, des relations fortes entre les États-Unis et la France d'une part et l'Union européenne d'autre part garantissent la coopération entre les Etats-Unis et la France, mais aussi avec les autres principaux partenaires, pour relever les défis économiques globaux.

Contexte

Peu de questions vont autant façonner les relations franco-américaines dans les années à venir que la crise économique globale. Si les

Etats-Unis ont été l'épicentre de la crise financière mondiale, les banques françaises et européennes nont étét que trop contentes de se joindre à la ruée sur les subprimes qui a secoué l'économie mondiale. La crise financière devrait lever les derniers doutes sur l'interdépendance des économies globale au cours des dernières décennies. Au début de la crise, la majorité des Français et des Européens estimaient que les problèmes financiers américains, déclenchés par l'effondrement des subprimes, étaient juste un problème américain. De nombreuses discussions ont alors porté sur un « découplage » mondial, sur la capacité de l'Europe et des marchés émergents à continuer à prospérer malgré l'affaiblissement des Etats-Unis. Le niveau de confiance était tel en Europe que la Banque centrale européenne avait opté pour une hausse des taux d'intérêts au début de l'été 2008, indiquant ainsi que la croissance de la zone euro était satisfaisante et que le véritable défi était l'inflation et non la croissance.

Tout ceci changea au début de l'automne 2008 lorsque l'Europe, France comprise, se retrouva dans les affres de la crise financière et de la récession économique issues du tsunami financier provoqué par les Etats-Unis. L'interconnexion liée à la mondialisation et l'intensité des liens transatlantiques sont tels que lorsqu'un problème surgit aux États-Unis, il se transforme rapidement en un problème pour l'Europe et la France. La mondialisation est à double tranchant : lorsque l'économie va bien, les nations ouvertes et réceptives aux flux internationaux de capitaux, de biens, d'idées et de personnes voient leurs bénéfices se multiplier alors que dans les périodes difficiles, nul n'est à l'abri.

Remarquons que beaucoup de banques en Europe, et aussi en France, étaient plus que prêtes à accepter les pratiques de prêts risquées de leurs partenaires américains, accumulant les instruments de dettes risqués pendant qu'ils comptaient sur des emprunts à court terme plutôt que sur l'épargne pour financer leurs activités. Ces pratiques, associées à une réglementation souple, à une soif croissante de risque, à la prolifération et à la titrisation de nouveaux instruments d'investissement et à de nombreux crédits peu chers ont emporté l'Europe dans la crise mondiale du crédit. Alors que les autorités, en France et ailleurs, ont réagi rapidement pour soutenir leurs secteur bancaires respectifs, l'économie réelle était touchée de plein fouet. Les Etats-Unis, la France et la zone euro connaissent une grave récession.

Ce n'est donc pas étonnant que les Français et les Américains soient pessimistes face à la mondialisation. Pourtant, la France et les Etats-Unis en ont été les grands vainqueurs. Ils disposent tous deux de nombreux atouts : diffusion rapide de la technologie, fortes opportunités commerciales, barrières limitées à l'investissement, réformes intérieurs qui ont généré d'importants flux de biens et de services, de personnes, de capitaux et d'idées au sein de la France et des Etats-Unis mais aussi entre ces deux pays et le reste du monde. De manière générale, ces atouts ont été très bénéfiques pour chacun des pays : croissance forte des exportations et importations, importants flux d'investissements entrants et sortants, meilleure diffusion de la technologie, investissements entrants de portefeuilles, afflux de travailleurs, création d'emplois et augmentation du PIB[1].

Ces bénéfices n'ont cependant pas été équitablement partagés et ne bénéficient pas directement à chaque travailleur, entreprise ou commune. Il y a des gagnants et des perdants. Les bénéfices de la mondialisation sont certes importants mais ils peuvent souvent sembler abstraits ou peu visibles. Quant aux souffrances liées à la mondialisation, elles peuvent être tangibles et traumatisantes et avoir un impact démesuré sur certaines communes ou entreprises. La mondialisation n'est pas la seule source de changements et de bouleversements économiques aux Etats-Unis ou en France, mais comme les autres sources, elle peut engendrer des coûts réels pour certains individus[2].

Des deux côtés de l'Atlantique, les citoyens et les leaders d'opinions sont conscients que leur prospérité tient à une économie mondialisée, ouverte et dynamique mais la plupart pense que les bénéfices et les souffrances générés par la mondialisation n'ont pas été équitablement répartis dans la société. Beaucoup s'inquiètent du rythme des évolutions économiques mondiales. Ils craignent qu'un emploi acquis à l'étranger soit un emploi supprimé dans leur pays, que leur prospérité difficilement gagnée puisse disparaître d'un coup. Ils appréhendent que

---

[1] Voir *La France et la Mondialisation* de Daniel S. Hamilton et Joseph P. Quinlan (Washington, D.C. : Centre pour les Relations Transatlantiques, 2008) disponible en anglais sur http://transatlantic.sais-jhu.edu/Publications/FRANCE_AND_GLOBALIZATION. pdf et en français sur http://transatlantic.sais-jhu.edu/Publications/France_face_a_la_mondialisation.pdf.

[2] Pour une analyse de la mondialisation en Europe, voir Daniel S. Hamilton et Joseph P. Quinlan, *Globalization and Europe* (Washington, D.C. : Center for Transatlantic Relations, 2008).

les futurs gagnants de la mondialisation vivent à Mumbai ou Shanghai et non à Tolède ou Toulouse.

Ces inquiétudes sont réelles, largement répandues et légitimes. Et elles sont exacerbées par les problèmes internes.

De part et d'autre de l'Atlantique, le défi consiste à contrôler intelligemment cette crise sans succomber aux pressions protectionnistes.

Premier défi : bâtir des économies nationales ouvertes et solides

L'un des meilleurs moyens, pour la France et les États-Unis, de relever les défis économiques mondiaux et de profiter des bénéfices d'une économie ouverte et mondialisée consiste à appliquer ces principes dans leur pays, c'est-à-dire de se repositionner comme économie ouverte et solide, adaptée à la mondialisation. La France et les Etats-Unis sont mis au défi d'adopter un programme audacieux de relance de leur économie nationale contribuant à favoriser les investissements d'avenir plutôt que la consommation actuelle, à préparer les citoyens aux changements climatiques plutôt que de les en protéger et à offrir aux personnes les plus touchées par la mondialisation la possibilité de participer au partage des bénéfices.

À certains égards, un tel agenda rappelle les réponses occidentales à l'effondrement de la première phase de la mondialisation qui avait conduit à la dépression et la guerre durant la première partie du siècle dernier. À la suite de ces immenses désastres, les pays occidentaux ont ré-ouvert leurs économies, mais aussi bâti des systèmes de protection sociale efficaces, aidant les citoyens les plus touchés par l'internationalisation et la persistance des évolutions économiques. Ils ont ainsi combiné ouverture et sécurité. L'équilibre n'était pas le même sur chaque rive de l'Atlantique : les États-Unis ont généralement favorisé l'ouverture tandis que la France privilégiait la sécurité. Les deux options font face aujourd'hui à de nouvelles pressions. De manière générale, la France doit contrebalancer ses dispositions sociales fortes en assouplissant et en flexibilisant son économie tandis que les Etats-Unis doivent améliorer leur protection sociale pour compenser leur très grande flexibilité, de manière à donner aux Américains le soutien et les garanties dont ils ont besoin pour être compétitifs dans une économie ouverte mondialisée. Le défi commun pour Paris et Washington est de montrer à leurs citoyens et au reste du monde qu'il est possible de récolter les bénéfices de la mondialisation tout en rendant ses coûts supportables pour les plus affectés.

Le défi américain

Les Etats-Unis doivent renforcer leur système obsolète de protection sociale. Les Américains luttent contre une vague croissante d'insécurité économique qui les assaille de toutes parts[3]. Les diverses Administrations américaines ont fait face à cette insécurité de manière partielle et fragmentée mais ces efforts n'ont pas permis de fournir aux Américains le soutien dont ils ont besoin pour faire face à ces changements économiques rapides.

La récession a clairement dévoilé les difficultés économiques auxquelles les Américains doivent faire face. D'après une étude publiée par le Bureau national de la recherche économique en 2007, au cours de la dernière génération, 95% des salariés ont vu leur salaire diminuer, après ajustement de l'inflation. 47 millions de citoyens n'ont pas d'assurance maladie, soit près d'un Américain sur 6. La peur de perdre l'accès à la couverture maladie constitue la première source de préoccupation des Américains lorsqu'ils sont confrontés au chômage. De plus, lorsqu'ils perdent leur emploi, ils n'ont qu'une chance sur trois de bénéficier d'une assurance chômage.

Les Américains ayant cherché à maintenir leur niveau de vie malgré toutes ces contraintes, ils ont emprunté de plus en plus d'argent. Le ratio de la dette des ménages par rapport au revenu disponible, qui était resté relativement stable, un peu au-dessus de 60%, entre le milieu des années 1960 et celui des années 1980, s'élève aujourd'hui à 130%.

De plus, le gouvernement américain estime que les personnes arrivant aujourd'hui sur le marché du travail occuperont sans doute, au cours de leur vie professionnelle, entre 12 et 15 emplois différents, soit près du double du nombre d'emplois que pouvaient envisager les personnes de la génération de leurs parents.

---

[3] Je suis redevable à Bruce Stokes pour son analyse succincte de ce défi. Voir par exemple Bruce Stokes, « Balance of Payments: Homeland Insecurity », *Congress Daily*, 28 février 2008. Voir aussi Gene Sperling, « A Powell Doctrine for the Economy and a Grand Bargain », *Roll Call*, 20 novembre 2008

Malgré ces changements, les Américains disposent d'une protection économique faible et inégale. Les Etats-Unis sont le seul grand pays industriel à ne pas fournir de couverture santé universelle. L'assurance chômage ne compense environ que 30% de la perte de revenus chez les travailleurs américains à bas salaire licenciés. En comparaison, le montant des indemnités chômage perçues par les ouvriers à faibles revenus des autres pays industrialisés s'élève à 55% de leur ancien salaire. De plus, Washington ne dépense qu'une faible fraction du montant dépensé par les autres pays pour la reconversion des salariés.

Les défis sont importants mais la situation n'est pas désespérée. Washington fait peut-être faillite mais l'Amérique n'est pas pauvre. Les Etats-Unis demeurent la plus grande puissance économique du monde, mais payent un lourd tribut en essayant d'esquiver des choix difficiles. Notre crise est essentiellement politique et non économique.

Au lieu de succomber aux pressions visant à protéger les Américains de l'ouverture de l'économie, ce qui serait un désastre politique et économique, les Etats-Unis doivent agir de manière à aider les Américains à faire face aux changements économiques rapides en créant un nouvel accord social global à trois dimensions : une couverture santé universelle, une assurance chômage universelle et des mesures universelles de reconversion. Une protection sociale fondée sur ces trois piliers procurera aux Américains les assurances suffisantes pour avancer dans un monde de plus en plus instable.

Le défi français

La France est divisée concernant la mondialisation. D'un côté, elle a été l'un des principaux bénéficiaires de la mondialisation et devrait en bénéficier encore plus. De l'autre, les sondages indiquent systématiquement que les Français sont profondément sceptiques, voire effrayés par la mondialisation. Le principal défi de la France concernant la mondialisation est d'ajuster le sentiment populaire aux réalités liées à l'intégration de la France dans l'économie mondiale, tout en capitalisant sur les atouts français et en aidant ceux qui souffrent de la mondialisation.

Les entreprises, les consommateurs et les travailleurs français ont tous profité de la mondialisation. Des dizaines de milliers d'emplois français sont créés et préservés chaque année grâce aux investissements américains, européens ou asiatiques. 1 Français sur 7 travaille pour une entreprise étrangère, contre 1 sur 10 en Angleterre ou 1 sur 20 aux Etats-Unis. La France est l'un des principaux bénéficiaires des investissements directs étrangers, ayant reçu 481 milliards $ entre 1997 et 2006. Elle accueille aussi de nombreux investissements de R&D d'entreprises étrangères, principalement issus des Etats-Unis ou d'Europe. Près de la moitié des entreprises cotées au CAC 40 appartiennent à des investisseurs étrangers. La France est relativement bien classée parmi les leaders mondiaux en termes d'innovation et elle dispose de bases solides pour faire face à la mondialisation : une productivité forte, une natalité élevée, des infrastructures bien développées et des services publics forts.

La France est potentiellement bien placée pour profiter de la mondialisation des services ; en 2006, elle comptait pour 4,1% des exportations mondiales de services. Les perspectives économiques de base du pays sont bonnes : ces dernières années, la production a augmenté et les finances publiques se sont améliorées. Le chômage, s'il reste trop élevé, a néanmoins chuté. La France soutient la comparaison avec la majorité des autres pays en termes d'attraction des cerveaux. Elle enregistre un flux positif d'entrées de travailleurs spécialisés et techniques et bénéficie de flux de connaissances importants. La France apparaît également comme un bénéficiaire net des relocalisations et des délocalisations. Entre 2003 et 2006, le nombre de destructions d'emplois liées aux délocalisations a été minime. D'après l'OCDE, en 2005, les délocalisations ne représentaient que 3,4% de la destruction totale d'emplois français. La majeure partie de ces délocalisations se sont faites dans d'autres nations européennes et non dans d'autres continents.

La France bénéficie d'un très bon niveau moyen d'éducation, ce qui devrait contribuer à l'adaptabilité de sa main d'œuvre aux normes internationales. Une forte proportion des travailleurs les plus jeunes sont qualifiés dans le domaine tertiaire. La mobilité régionale liée au travail est également relativement élevée par rapport aux autres pays d'Europe.

Malgré ces avantages, les sondages continuent de montrer que les Français s'inquiètent des impacts de la mondialisation sur à peu près tous les aspects de leur vie. Un sentiment diffus de pessimisme et d'insécurité menace de compromettre la capacité de la France de profiter encore plus de la mondialisation. De telles craintes ne sont malgré tout pas complètement infondées. La France a glissé de la 15ème à la 18ème place dans le classement des nations les plus compétitives établi par le Global Competitive Index et elle se classe 23ème dans celui du Networked

Readiness Index. Au cours des 25 dernières années, la France est passée de la 8ème à la 19ème place en termes de PIB par habitant. En 1991, le PIB par tête en France représentait 83% de celui des Etats-Unis, il en représente aujourd'hui 71%. La différence correspond presque parfaitement à l'écart entre le nombre total d'heures travaillées par habitant entre les deux pays. Selon l'OCDE, la France se place en deuxième position juste derrière la Norvège en termes de taux de productivité horaire, mais les Français commencent à travailler plus tard que dans la majorité des autres pays, puis le temps de travail est moins élevé et ils partent à la retraite plus tôt. De plus, le chômage est supérieur à 8% depuis un quart de siècle. Le chômage des jeunes est particulièrement élevé, atteignant 22%. Seuls 41% de la population adulte travaillent, soit l'un des taux de participation à la population active les plus bas du monde. Le sentiment des Français d'être dépassés par un certain nombre d'autres nations est objectivement vrai.

La France bénéficie à plusieurs titres de la mondialisation. Mais la rapidité des changements hors de ses frontières peut être déconcertante et démoralisante à l'heure où la France doit faire face à ses propres défis. De nombreux Français ont l'impression qu'un pouvoir d'achat limité freine la croissance. Cependant, les difficultés en termes de croissance ne sont pas dues à une faible consommation, mais aux rigidités qui entravent l'offre et affectent les exportations. Afin de répondre au besoin d'assouplissement des institutions et des pratiques liées au marché du travail, la France doit adopter des stratégies soutenant les travailleurs et promouvant les opportunités d'emplois, plutôt que de protéger certains emplois spécifiques. Le marché du travail doit gagner en flexibilité en supprimant la limitation de la durée légale du temps de travail pour privilégier les négociations entre les entreprises et leurs salariés. Le vieillissement de la population aura bientôt un impact réel sur l'évolution de la main d'œuvre et sur les finances publiques. Cet élément doit néanmoins être nuancé par la vigueur relative de la natalité française par rapport aux autres partenaires de l'Union européenne.

Si la France demeure un pays très compétitif, l'inégalité de ses performances à l'exportation est une preuve supplémentaire de l'importance de ses rigidités internes. Les entreprises françaises bénéficient de l'évolution des exportations vers les pays en voie de développement, mais n'en profitent pas encore pleinement. Des mesures destinées à renforcer la capacité d'exportation des petites et moyennes entreprises pourraient soutenir l'ensemble des exportations. Le secteur des services constitue un atout important pour les exportations françaises qui doit désormais être pleinement exploité. La France tendant à devenir une économie de services fondée sur la connaissance, elle doit conserver et améliorer sa compétitivité dans les services et les biens de haute technologie, au risque de voir son économie décliner. Cependant, de nombreux pôles micro-régionaux ou technologiques importants semblent faire défaut à la France pour pousser l'innovation et la croissance tandis qu'elle ne mobilise pas suffisamment ses ressources en recherche et développement.

Les récentes réformes engagées par le gouvernement français doivent permettre d'assouplir ces rigidités et de stimuler la croissance économique, mais elles ont été progressives et inégales et pendant ce temps, le monde évolue…

Actuellement, le président Sarkozy demande à la France de « jouer le jeu de la mondialisation » et elle s'y prête plutôt bien, même si la population a l'impression du contraire et malgré la tourmente économique actuelle déclenchée par la Grande dépression. La France a largement profité de l'accroissement du commerce international, des investissements et des capitaux, mais a bénéficié inégalement des flux de personnes et d'idées. Elle dispose d'atouts intrinsèques importants et des moyens de capitaliser les bénéfices de la mondialisation. Mais le changement se révèle compliqué pour une société habituée à ce que l'Etat fournisse les emplois, redistribue l'argent, protège contre les importations indésirables, fasse la promotion des secteurs industriels prestigieux et mette en avant la grandeur nationale.

Comme si souvent dans le passé, le débat en France devrait être la clef du débat européen. Une France ouverte et engagée au plan international peut à la fois façonner la mondialisation et en tirer largement profit ; à l'inverse une France fermée, repliée sur elle-même et morose aurait beaucoup à perdre. Compte tenu de l'intensité des inquiétudes et du potentiel de gain élevés, il est important pour la France de trouver un nouveau consensus autour de la mondialisation, même si cette tâche est rendue plus périlleuse encore par la crise économique mondiale et la récession qui en découle.

Deuxième défi : promouvoir les liens économiques bilatéraux

Dans un deuxième temps, la France et les Etats-Unis doivent prendre conscience de l'intensité et de l'accroissement de leur interdépendance dans leurs performances économiques. L'économie n'est pas forcément un jeu à somme nulle. Dans une économie en croissance, le succès des uns peut aussi être celui des autres. Les relations économiques bilatérales entre la France et les Etats-Unis sont la preuve irréfutable de la forte intégration qui caractérise les relations commerciales transatlantiques et l'évidence même que les intérêts économiques et la prospérité future des deux pays n'ont jamais été autant interdépendants et liés qu'ils ne le sont aujourd'hui.

En réalité, malgré la tendance (trompeuse) des médias à assimiler les échanges au commerce et malgré l'excitation entourant les marchés émergents, le renforcement de l'intégration et de la cohésion de l'économie transatlantique en général et des liens franco-américains en particulier a constitué l'une des principales caractéristiques du paysage économique mondial au court de la dernière décennie.

Les intérêts commerciaux français et américains sont liés par les investissements étrangers, qui constituent la forme la plus poussée de l'intégration économique, et non par les échanges commerciaux, qui sont une forme d'intégration bien connue mais plus superficielle. La primauté des investissements directs étrangers dans le soutien au commerce franco-américain se reflète dans la robustesse des infrastructures liant la France et les Etats-Unis. Ces structures commerciales se mettent en place depuis plus d'un demi-siècle, mais restent très discrètes aux yeux des décideurs et de l'opinion publique de part et d'autre de l'Atlantique. Les données suivantes offrent une meilleure image de l'intensité de la force d'intégration qui fait de la relation commerciale franco-américaine l'une des plus fortes au monde.

Produit brut des filiales étrangères

La figure 1 montre l'importance de la production totale des filiales américaines en France (près de 55 milliards $ en 2007) et des filiales françaises aux Etats-Unis (plus de 60 milliards $). Chacun de ces deux nombres est supérieur ou égal au PIB de bon nombre d'Etats.

Figure 1   Relations franco-américaines* : produit brut des filiales étrangères

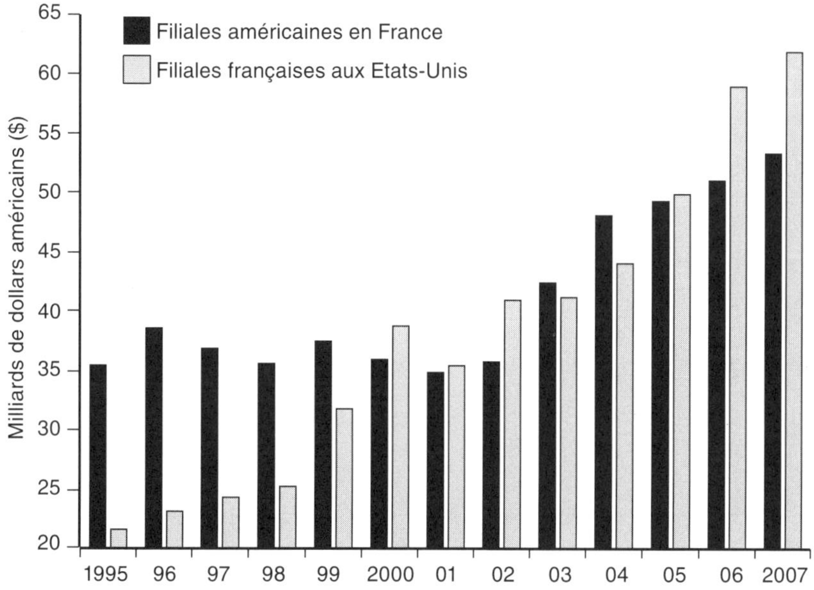

Source : Bureau of Economic Analysis.

*Données pour des filiales étrangères possédées en majorité.

Notes : Données 2006 et 2007 pour les filiales américaines en France sont des estimations du Centre pour les relations transatlantiques, données 2007 pour les filiales francaises aux Etats-Unis sont des estimations du Centre pour les relations transatlantiques.

Les actifs étrangers de filiales étrangères

La présence commerciale américaine à l'étranger, telle que mesurée par les actifs étrangers des entreprises américaines, est considérable, s'élevant à près de 10 000 milliards \$ en 2005. L'essentiel de ces actifs (62%) sont placés en Europe et plus particulièrement au Royaume-Uni, aux Pays-Bas et en Allemagne. Situés loin derrière, les actifs américains en France, totalisant près de 300 milliards \$, dépassaient les actifs américains en Amérique du Sud en 2005, et ceux de nombreuses régions en voie de développement, y compris l'Afrique, le Moyen-Orient, l'Europe de l'Est et les pays de l'OPEP.

Figure 2   Relations franco-américaines* : les actifs des filiales

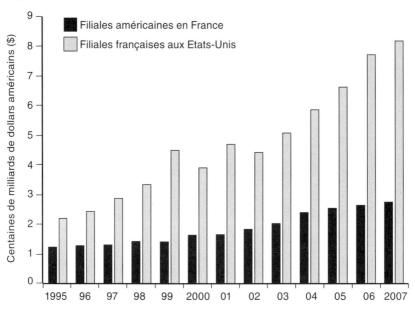

Source : Bureau of Economic Analysis.

*Données pour des filiales étrangères possédées en majorité.

Notes : Données 2006 et 2007 pour les filiales américaines en France sont des estimations du Centre pour les relations transatlantiques, données 2007 pour les filiales francaises aux Etats-Unis sont des estimations du Centre pour les relations transatlantiques.

Les Français ont investi plus de 800 milliards $ d'actifs aux Etats-Unis, comptant ainsi parmi les principaux investisseurs étrangers. Seuls le Royaume-Uni, la Suisse, l'Allemagne et les Pays-Bas font mieux. Il est intéressant de noter que les actifs français aux Etats-Unis sont près de trois fois plus élevés que les actifs américains en France. Ceci s'explique par l'accroissement des investissements directs étrangers (IDE) français aux Etats-Unis pendant la dernière décennie. Le figure 2 montre les actifs des filiales françaises et américaines respectivement aux Etats-Unis et en France.

L'emploi dans les filiales

Des milliers de salariés travaillent pour des filiales américaines en France et pour des filiales françaises aux Etats-Unis. En effet, en 2007,

Figure 3   Relations franco-américaines* : l'emploi dans les filiales

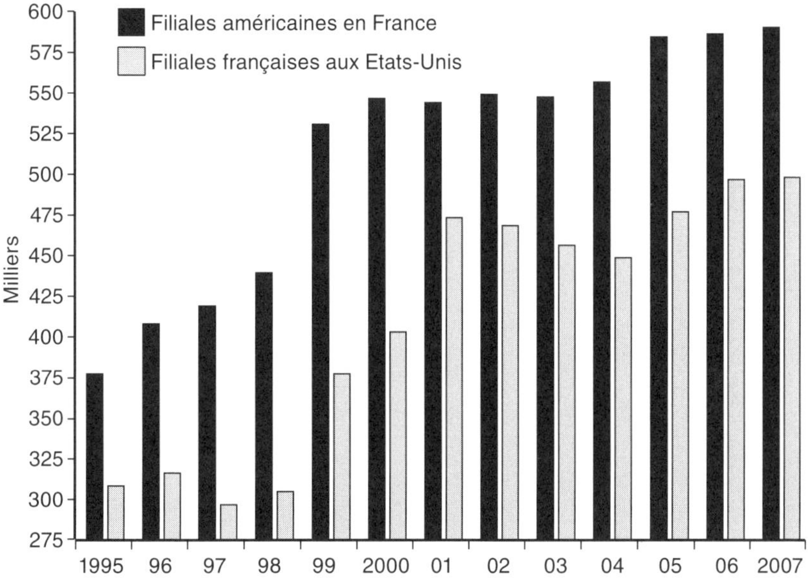

Source : Bureau of Economic Analysis.

*Données pour des filiales étrangères possédées en majorité.

Notes : Données 2006 et 2007 pour les filiales américaines en France sont des estimations du Centre pour les relations transatlantiques, données 2007 pour les filiales francaises aux Etats-Unis sont des estimations du Centre pour les relations transatlantiques.

environ 500 000 salariés américains étaient directement employés par des filiales françaises qui constituent l'un des principaux employeurs étrangers aux Etats-Unis. De plus, des dizaines de milliers d'autres emplois sont liés aux exportations américaines vers la France, bien que ces derniers soient plus difficiles à quantifier. Seules les entreprises anglaises et allemandes ont employé en 2007 davantage de salariés américains.

Les filiales américaines en France sont de plus grandes pourvoyeuses d'emplois encore : près de 585 000 emplois français en 2007. Les filiales américaines en France emploient presque 20% de salariés français supplémentaires par rapport au nombre de Chinois qu'elles emploient en Chine. Les figures 3 et 4 montrent ces effets sur les emplois, qui sont sous-estimés puisqu'ils ne prennent pas en compte les emplois français créés par les exportations françaises aux Etats-Unis et les effets des emplois

Figure 4   Relations franco-américaines* : l'emploi dans les filiales de produits manufacturés

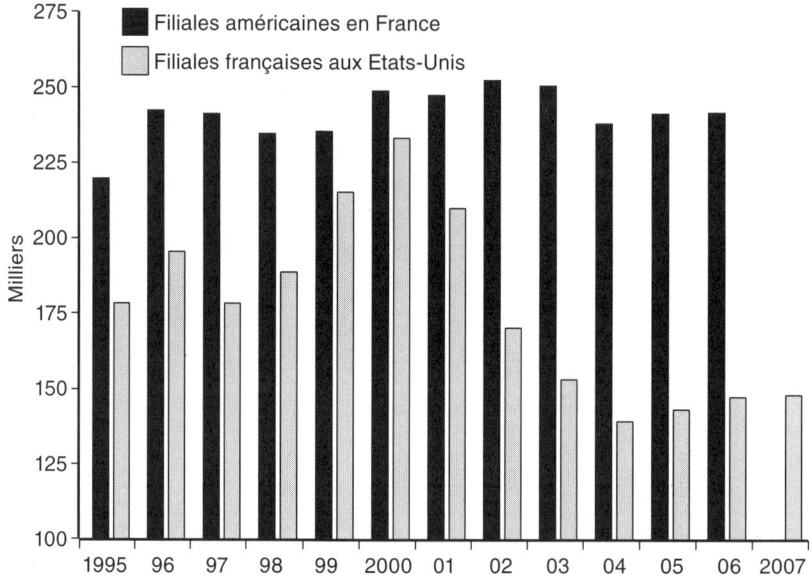

Source : Bureau of Economic Analysis.

*Données pour des filiales étrangères possédées en majorité.

Notes : Données 2006 et 2007 pour les filiales américaines en France sont des estimations du Centre pour les relations transatlantiques, données 2007 pour les filiales francaises aux Etats-Unis sont des estimations du Centre pour les relations transatlantiques.

indirects liés à des accords non mobiliers comme les alliances stratégiques, les joint-ventures ou autres relations. En bref, il est probable que deux millions de Français et d'Américains gagnent leur vie grâce aux étroites relations économiques entre la France et les Etats-Unis.

La recherche–développement (R&D) dans les filiales

Si les dépenses en recherche-développement (R&D) ne sont pas comparables au plan interne, la R&D des filiales étrangères s'est renforcée au cours de la dernière décennie. En effet, les entreprises cherchent à partager les coûts de développement, à répartir les risques et à exploiter la matière grise des autres pays. Les alliances, les licences croisées de propriété intellectuelle et les fusions–acquisitions, sous ces

Figure 5   **Relations franco-américaines* : la R&D dans les filiales**

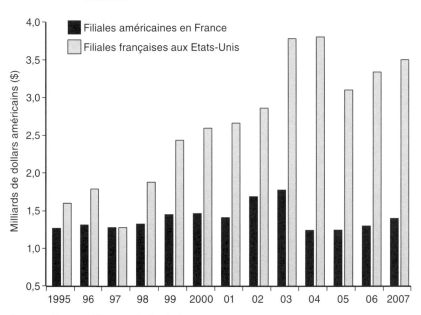

Source : Bureau of Economic Analysis.
*Données pour des filiales étrangères possédées en majorité.
Notes : Données 2006 et 2007 pour les filiales américaines en France sont des estimations du Centre pour les relations transatlantiques, données 2007 pour les filiales francaises aux Etats-Unis sont des estimations du Centre pour les relations transatlantiques.

formes de coopération ou d'autres, sont devenues les bases du partenariat franco-américain, comme en témoigne le figure 5.

Selon ce tableau, les filiales américaines investissent près de 1,5 milliard $ pour la recherche-développement en France, ce qui témoigne de la main d'œuvre qualifiée et innovante du pays et de la tendance des entreprises américaines à tirer profit des compétences où qu'elles soient dans le monde. A l'inverse, la main d'œuvre hautement qualifiée des Etats-Unis, leur culture d'entreprise et leurs excellentes universités ont été les principaux facteurs d'attractivité des capitaux français dans la R&D. Ainsi, en 2007 les filiales françaises aux Etats-Unis ont investi 3,5 milliards $ dans la recherche-développement aux Etats-Unis. Les activités de R&D des entreprises françaises aux Etats-Unis sont cruciales pour soutenir la vitalité et la rentabilité de l'économie française.

Les dépenses en R&D des filiales françaises aux Etats-Unis représentent 15% des dépenses totales en recherche-développement de la France.

Echanges intra-entreprises des filiales étrangères

Les ventes des filiales étrangères sont le premier vecteur d'échange des biens et services entre les deux rives de l'Atlantique. Les échanges en constituent le deuxième mais les deux types de transactions ne doivent pas être considérés indépendamment l'un de l'autre. Ils sont plus complémentaires qu'ils ne se remplacent car les investissements étrangers et les ventes des filiales favorisent de plus en plus les échanges. En effet, une part substantielle des échanges entre la France et les Etats-Unis est considérée comme du commerce intra-entreprise ou du commerce entre parties liées, c'est-à-dire du commerce international mais qui reste dans le cadre de l'entreprise, comme par exemple Michelin en France qui envoie des composants à Michelin aux Etats-Unis. Près de 49% des importations américaines venant de France et 34% des exportations américaines vers la France appartiennent à la catégorie élargie du commerce intra-entreprise, ce qui reflète les liens très étroits entre les maisons mères françaises et leurs filiales américaines.

Le rôle important des échanges entre parties liées explique partiellement pourquoi les fluctuations monétaires ont moins d'impact sur les liens économiques transatlantiques que ne le laisse penser *Economics 101*. Alors qu'un euro fort devrait, en théorie tout du moins, être associé à un recul de la compétitivité française aux Etats-Unis, le fait que de nombreuses multinationales françaises produisent, commercialisent et distribuent des biens de part et d'autre de l'Atlantique, les protège fortement contre des variations excessives des taux de change. Dans ces circonstances, les flux commerciaux dépendent davantage de la demande dans le pays hôte. Plus la demande est forte aux Etats-Unis, meilleures sont les ventes des filiales françaises, ce qui génère plus de demande (importations), auprès de la maison-mère en France, de certains éléments ou composants, indépendamment des variations de taux de change. Les échanges entre parties liées permettent de mieux comprendre l'intensité et l'interdépendance des relations économiques entre la France et les États-Unis et leur intérêt mutuel à relancer la croissance interne de part et d'autre de l'Atlantique.

Les ventes des filiales étrangères

Les ventes des filiales étrangères constituent le principal vecteur des entreprises françaises et américaines pour alimenter respectivement les marchés américains et français en biens et services. Ainsi, en 2007, les ventes des filiales américaines en France se sont élevées à plus de 210 milliards $, un chiffre bien supérieur aux exportations américaines en France la même année. De la même manière, les ventes des filiales françaises aux Etats-Unis étaient évaluées à près de 193 milliards $ pour 2007, très loin devant les importations américaines de France. En d'autres termes, les ventes des filiales étrangères donnent une certaine vision des relations franco-américaines, tandis que les échanges en donnent une autre.

Les échanges seuls constituent un indicateur très trompeur des relations économiques internationales, et les médias et les dirigeants font constamment cette erreur. Si l'on regarde uniquement les flux commerciaux américains, par exemple, la France se classerait loin derrière d'autres nations telles que la Chine, le Canada, le Mexique ou le Royaume-Uni. De ce point de vue, il n'est pas difficile de penser que de nombreux marchés émergents comme la Chine ou le Mexique sont plus importants pour les intérêts commerciaux américains que la France, ou que ces économies en voie de développement rapide sont devenues plus importantes pour la France que pour les Etats-Unis. Mais les choses sont complètement différentes lorsqu'on observe les ventes des filiales étrangères. Sur leur base, les Etats-Unis constituent pour la France le marché le plus important au monde et la France représente l'un des marchés les plus importants pour les Etats-Unis. Le figure 6 montre l'augmentation de ces ventes au cours des dernières années.

Les revenus des filiales étrangères

En termes de profits, l'Europe reste de loin la région la plus importante pour les entreprises américaines, comptant pour la moitié des gains totaux réalisés par les filiales américaines en 2006 et pour 55% sur la dernière décennie. En 2007, les filiales américaines en France ont engrangé plus de 6 milliards $ et les filiales françaises aux Etats-Unis près de 11,5 milliards $. Pour beaucoup d'entreprises, une forte demande dans le pays partenaire peut aider à compenser une croissance interne stagnante, montrant là encore une interdépendance.

Figure 6   Relations franco-américaines* : ventes des filiales

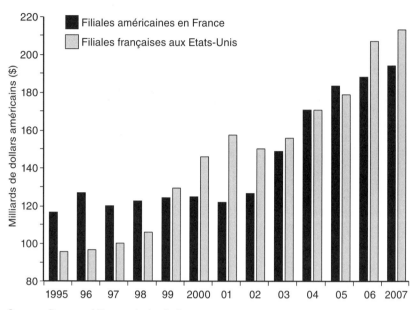

Source : Bureau of Economic Analysis.

*Données pour des filiales étrangères possédées en majorité.

Notes : Données 2006 et 2007 pour les filiales américaines en France sont des estimations du Centre pour les relations transatlantiques, données 2007 pour les filiales francaises aux Etats-Unis sont des estimations du Centre pour les relations transatlantiques.

Il est temps de saisir l'opportunité d'approfondir les liens franco-américains

Ces données fournissent une image plus complète des flux économiques internationaux que la simple mesure des exportations et des importations. Les investissements directs étrangers constituent l'armature économique du partenariat franco-américain, avec d'autres variables comme les actifs à l'étranger, l'emploi et les ventes des filiales, les échanges entre parties liées, les services et autres relations dont divergent le degré et l'intensité d'investissements. Les relations commerciales entre les États-Unis et les Français comptent parmi les plus forts du monde, les deux parties bénéficiant depuis plus d'un demi-siècle de liens d'investissements et d'échanges très importants.

Figure 7   Relations franco-américaines* : revenus des filiales

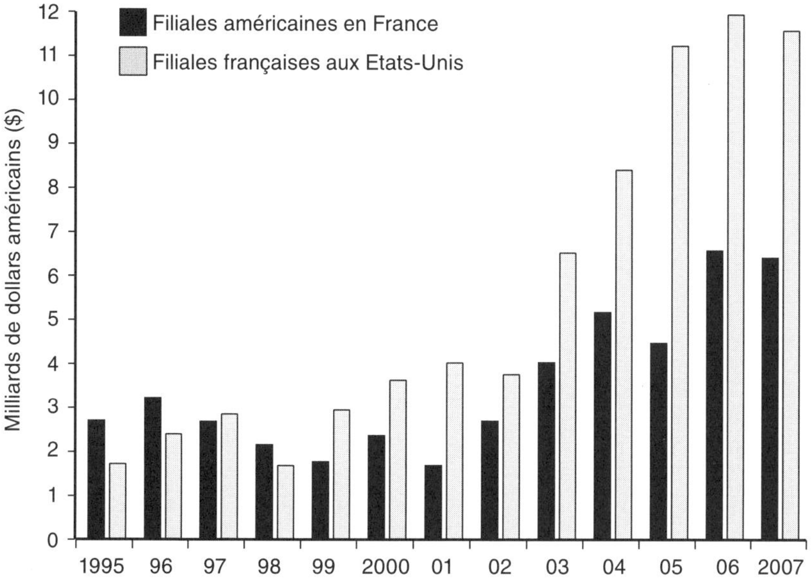

Source : Bureau of Economic Analysis.
*Données pour des filiales étrangères possédées en majorité.

L'intérêt mutuel à voir le partenaire prospérer constitue une autre des raisons pour lesquelles les réformes internes sont essentielles. Si les politiques françaises ne cherchent pas à diminuer les rigidités du travail et à engager une réforme de la fiscalité, les multinationales américaines pourraient être davantage tentées de regarder ailleurs plutôt que d'investir en France. La manière dont Paris gère ses problèmes d'immigration et d'intégration, favorise l'innovation, cherche à respecter des normes environnementales et réagit à son évolution démographique aura également une incidence sur l'avenir des flux d'investissement américains.

Aux États-Unis, les divergences de règlementations et de normes techniques, la législation de type Sarbanes-Oxley, les tentations de versements d'aides d'État à l'industrie et des mesures de sécurité trop zélées, comme la surveillance de 100% du fret, pourraient stopper ou ralentir le rythme des investissements français et européen aux Etats-Unis.

Sur les deux rives de l'Atlantique, le renforcement de l'intégration des diverses activités de services constitue un énorme potentiel. Les services constituent le « géant endormi » de l'économie transatlantique : si cette force économique se réveillait et se déchaînait, elle pourrait offrir de formidables opportunités aux consommateurs, aux travailleurs et aux entreprises en France et en Amérique. Cependant, les règlementations sont différentes et les obstacles non-tarifaires dans les deux nations et au sein de l'Union européenne ont empêché les activités de service entre les Etats-Unis et la France de croître et de devenir pleinement intégrées. Compte tenu de l'appartenance de la France à l'Union européenne, l'alignement des normes et l'élimination des obstacles commerciaux nécessite souvent une action entre les États-Unis et l'Union européenne, ce qui constitue le troisième niveau des défis économiques pour Paris et Washington.

Troisième défi : améliorer les relations économiques Etats-Unis/Union européenne

Les relations économiques franco-américaines sont à bien des égards un microcosme au sein des relations commerciales entre les Etats-Unis et l'Europe. Les Européens et les Américains sont devenus si étroitement liés que nous nous mêlons littéralement des affaires de l'autre et que nous nous possédons mutuellement. Ces liens soutiennent une économie de 3750 milliards $ qui fournissent jusqu'à 14 millions d'emplois des deux côtés de l'Atlantique[4]. Aucune autre relation commerciale dans le monde n'est aussi forte que celle qui lie l'Amérique du Nord et l'Europe. Il n'a pas deux régions dans l'économie globale qui aient autant fusionné, sur le plan économique, que les deux entités riveraines de l'Atlantique, faisant de l'économie transatlantique la plus grande et la plus riche du monde.

Les marchés transatlantiques sont parmi les plus ouverts au monde et sont pleinement intégrés grâce à des flux d'investissement denses, aux ventes des filiales et aux échanges entre parties liées. Pourtant, plusieurs obstacles subsistent, empêchant l'émergence d'un marché transatlantique libre ; il s'agit des barrières tarifaires traditionnelles, ainsi que des obstacles non-tarifaires et des réglementations qui limitent la

---

[4] Voir Daniel S. Hamilton and Joseph P. Quinlan, *The Transatlantic Economy 2009: Annual Survey of Jobs, Trade and Investment between the United States and Europe* (Washington, D.C. : Center for Transatlantic Relations, 2009).

propriété étrangère de ressources nationales, attribuent le statut de monopole à des entreprises publiques, instaurent des obstacles réglementaires importants aux investisseurs étrangers potentiels ou font de la discrimination entre les soumissionnaires nationaux et étrangers[5].

Les barrières tarifaires transatlantiques sont généralement peu élevées : elles tournent autour de 3 ou 4% du montant total du commerce transatlantique annuel. Toutefois, les niveaux tarifaires dans l'Union européenne sont plus variés que ceux des États-Unis et les droits de douane dans ces deux zones sont plus élevés sur certains produits spécifiques dans des secteurs sensibles tels que le textile, l'habillement et les produits en cuir, ou en vertu d'accords commerciaux préférentiels[6].

C'est parce que les tarifs douaniers transatlantiques sont généralement assez faibles et que les industries européenne et américaine sont fortement interconnectées que les barrières non-tarifaires représentent le principale obstacle à un marché transatlantique libre. Les barrières non-tarifaires restantes reposent essentiellement sur des réglementations intérieures, y compris les normes sécuritaires, sanitaires, environnementales ou techniques, sur des règles d'origine ou sur les exigences en matière d'étiquetage. Ces mesures sont dues en partie aux préférences et aux priorités divergentes de la société mais aussi, pour une large part, à un manque de coordination ou à de mauvais échanges d'informations entre les régulateurs et les législateurs de chaque côté de l'Atlantique, qui sont soumis à différents mandats légaux ou qui se livrent à différentes procédures de contrôle.

Ces obstacles à l'intégration transatlantique ont tendance à être concentrés dans certains secteurs économiques. En général, les obstacles

---

[5] Pour l'évaluation de ces barrières pour certaines industries, voir Daniel S. Hamilton and Joseph P. Quinlan, eds., *Deep Integration: The Changing Geography of the Transatlantic Economy* (Washington/Brussels: Center for Transatlantic Relations/Centre for European Policy Studies, 2005). Voir aussi les contributions au 2004-2005 US-EU Stakeholder Dialogue (disponible sur : http://www.ustr.gov/World_Regions/Europe_Mediterranean/ Transatlantic_Dialogue/Section_Index.html); Voir aussi : OCDE, *The Benefits of Liberalising Product Markets and Reducing Barriers to International Trade and Investment: The Case of The United States and the European Union* (*Les bénéfices de la libéralisation des marchés de produits et de la réduction des barrières aux échanges et aux investissements internationaux: le cas des Etats-Unis et de l'Union européenne*), Economics Department Working Paper 432, Paris, Juin 2005, pp. 7-10.

[6] Transatlantic Business Dialogue, "Report to the 2005 US-EU Summit: A Framework for Deepening Transatlantic Trade and Investment," Avril 2005 (http://128.121.145.19/tabd/ media/TABD2005SummitReportFINAL051.pdf); et OCDE, ibid.

pour les produits manufacturés sont plutôt limités tandis que les obstacles dans les services et l'agriculture ont tendance à être relativement
élevés. L'agriculture représentant une part relativement faible et les services un pourcentage relativement élevé de l'ensemble de la production
économique et de l'emploi transatlantiques, les gains de la libéralisation des services pourraient être très élevés par rapport à l'agriculture.

En Europe, l'OCDE indique que les services de transport, les télécommunications et en particulier l'électricité connaissent les barrières
sectorielles aux IDE les plus élevées. Aux États-Unis, les restrictions
relatives aux IDE dans les services de transport et de télécommunications sont plus élevés que dans la moyenne des pays de l'UE[7].

Avantages potentiels de la poursuite de la libéralisation transatlantique

En juin 2005, un rapport de l'OCDE estimait que la mise en œuvre,
dans l'Union européenne et aux Etats-Unis, de réformes structurelles
portant sur une réduction de la règlementation limitant la concurrence, des barrières tarifaires et des restrictions aux IDE pourrait
conduire, des deux côtés de l'Atlantique, à une hausse durable du PIB
par habitant de 3 à 3,5% et offrir des avantages supplémentaires aux
autres pays de l'OCDE pouvant aller jusqu'à 1,5% du PIB par habitant.
Rapportés à la vie active d'un individu estimée en moyenne à 40 ans,
l'OCDE estime que les revenus supplémentaires, par personne, repré-
senteraient entre 6 mois et plus d'un an de salaire.

En outre, les réformes prises en compte dans l'étude sont relativement restrictives et excluent le marché du travail, les marchés financiers et les réformes agricole ou fiscales, alors que tous ces secteurs
pourraient également renforcer l'intégration économique transatlantique et ses performances. L'étude de l'OCDE est donc mesurée dans
ses conclusions[8].

L'étude de l'OCDE insinuait que ces gains de production impliquaient des réformes ambitieuses dans les secteurs clés. Dans la plupart
des pays de l'UE-15, les règlementations limitant la concurrence
devraient être considérablement réduites dans les transports aérien,

---

[7] OCDE, op. cit., p. 19.
[8] OCDE, op. cit., pp. 5-7.

ferroviaire et routier internes, l'électricité, le gaz et les télécommunications. Quant aux États-Unis, ils devaient se concentrer sur les réformes de l'électricité et du transport ferroviaire. La plus grande réduction des restrictions sur les investissements directs étrangers aux États-Unis concernait les services relatifs aux transports, tandis que dans l'Union européenne, elle concernait la production d'électricité. Les réductions de droits de douane dans l'Union européenne devaient être concentrées sur les produits agricoles, tandis qu'aux États-Unis, elles impliquaient davantage d'ajustements des taux de protection relatifs au textile, aux vêtements et autres produits manufacturés.[9]

En résumé, compte tenu de l'ampleur et de l'intensité des interconnexions entre les économies américaine et européenne, la suppression des dernières barrières tarifaires et non-tarifaires associée à un renforcement de la coopération économique et règlementaire entre les États-Unis et l'Union européenne, pourrait être le catalyseur d'une forte augmentation de la croissance économique, de l'emploi, de l'investissement et de l'innovation sur le marché transatlantique ; elle pourrait également renforcer l'attractivité de l'économie transatlantique dans un monde globalisé et permettre aux États-Unis et l'Union européenne d'agir comme pionniers de la coopération en matière de règlementation et d'ouverture des marchés au-delà de l'économie transatlantique.

Le Conseil économique transatlantique et ses critiques

Les efforts de libéralisation des marchés transatlantiques concentrés sur les barrières internes ont débuté avec la présentation du Nouvel agenda transatlantique. Les États-Unis et l'Union européenne les ont poursuivis avec plus ou moins d'enthousiasme. La création du Conseil économique transatlantique (TEC) en 2007 en est la plus récente incarnation. Son objectif est d'améliorer la coopération règlementaire aux États-Unis et dans l'Union européenne et, si possible, de lever les barrières pour une libre circulation des biens, des services, des technologies et des idées de part et d'autre de l'Atlantique.

Dès la création du Conseil économique transatlantique, ses détracteurs ont exacerbé les critiques. La plupart d'entre eux ont confondu cette initiative avec la vieille idée, largement abandonnée, d'une zone de libre-échange transatlantique (TAFTA) entre les États-Unis et

---

[9] OCDE, op. cit.

l'Union européenne qui, selon eux, serait si grande qu'elle détruirait le système d'échanges multilatéral. Cependant, ces détracteurs se trompent sur l'objectif du Conseil économique transatlantique ou n'ont rien compris. L'initiative ne porte pas sur le commerce, et ne fait donc pas concurrence au cycle de Doha et autres initiatives commerciales, car le commerce n'est vraiment pas le problème entre les deux rives de l'Atlantique. Les querelles commerciales transatlantiques peuvent certes faire la Une des journaux mais, de manière générale, les barrières commerciales transatlantiques sont très basses. L'économie transatlantique reposant davantage sur l'investissement que sur le commerce, les obstacles économiques transatlantiques les plus importants ne sont pas les barrières douanières « aux frontières » mais les barrières nationales, « après la frontière », qui restreignent la libre circulation des capitaux, des biens et des services.

De plus, compte tenu de la taille du marché transatlantique, même de petits changements visant à aligner les règlementations nationales de chaque côté de l'Atlantique pourraient engendrer de bien meilleurs gains économiques que la poursuite des réductions tarifaires.

Désormais, la solution consiste à impliquer deux corps importants : les législateurs et les régulateurs. Une intégration transatlantique forte peut signifier que des mesures non-tarifaires nationales deviennent des barrières non-tarifaires transatlantiques. Une grande partie de ceci n'est pas délibéré ; les agences de régulation nationales ne sont tout simplement pas faites pour prendre en compte la nature fortement intégrée, mais inégale, du marché transatlantique. Certes, les autorités de régulation ont le devoir de s'assurer que certains produits spécifiques peuvent être utilisés sur le territoire où elles sont compétentes. Mais compte tenu de l'intensité de l'intégration, une amélioration de la cohérence et de la coordination de l'évaluation des risques et des procédures de surveillance de la règlementation entre les Etats-Unis et l'Union européenne peut bénéficier aux entreprises, aux consommateurs et au grand public.

Le Conseil économique transatlantique promet à cet égard de nouvelles avancées en établissant une communication régulière et des échanges d'informations sur de nombreux sujets tels que la protection sanitaire, sécuritaire, environnementale ou des consommateurs et les normes de sécurité, examinant ainsi différentes approches de la gestion des risques. La reconnaissance de « l'équivalence », sur le fond, des procédures d'expérimentation et de régulation, rigoureuses de chaque côté de l'Atlantique, pourrait être un premier effort prometteur. Plutôt que de chercher à harmoniser toutes les normes, une tâche impossible qui aurait plutôt tendance à alourdir la bureaucratie au lieu de l'alléger, chaque partie pourrait s'accorder sur la reconnaissance mutuelle de ses normes respectives, comme l'ont fait les Etats membres de la Communauté européenne dans les années 1980.

Le défi est maintenant de savoir si le Conseil économique transatlantique sera capable de développer tout son potentiel. Les résultats ont été jusqu'à maintenant décevants et restent marqués par les différences franco-américaines. A l'heure de la crise économique, une relance du Conseil économique transatlantique centrée sur la coopération transatlantique règlementaire, associée à un renforcement des discussions stratégiques entre les Etats-Unis et l'Union européenne sur la manière de sortir de la crise économique en s'appuyant sur le « leadership » transatlantique, pourrait créer de nouvelles opportunités économiques.

Ceux qui s'inquiètent qu'une initiative économique transatlantique ambitieuse puisse menacer le système multilatéral devraient envisager la possibilité de l'hypothèse inverse. Il ne fait aucun doute que les Européens et les Américains ont un intérêt commun à étendre la prospérité par le biais de la libéralisation du commerce multilatéral. Mais même l'obtention d'un accord sur le commerce mondial dans le cadre du cycle de Doha ne permettra pas de répondre aux questions pressantes liées à une « forte intégration » qui touchent les économies européennes et américaines, telles que les politiques de concurrence, la gouvernance d'entreprise, l'amélioration de la coopération règlementaire, la fiscalité, etc. Cet accord ne portera pas non plus sur les questions avant-gardistes soulevées par les scientifiques et les entrepreneurs européens et américains, qui repoussent les frontières des découvertes humaines dans des domaines tels que la génétique et la nanobiotechnologie, où il n'existe ni règles mondiales ni mécanismes transatlantiques, pour décider de compromis juridiques, éthiques et commerciaux imposés par de telles innovations. Il n'existe pas de réponse européenne ou américaine « brevetée » face à ce défi. En fait, pour la majorité de ces thèmes, aucune des parties n'a encore trouvé les questions appropriées, et encore moins les réponses.

Les marchés transatlantiques constituent le laboratoire de la mondialisation. Compte tenu de l'intensité de l'intégration transatlantique, les Européens et les Américains sont confrontés à des problématiques auxquelles ils ne font pas encore face avec d'autres partenaires. C'est la raison pour laquelle la dichotomie « multilatéralisme contre transatlantisme » est un faux choix. Les Etats-Unis et l'Union européenne devraient progresser sur les deux fronts simultanément : faire progresser la libéralisation multilatérale par le biais du cycle de Doha et d'autres canaux et faire avancer des initiatives transatlantiques dans les services, les marchés financiers, les télécommunications, l'énergie, les politiques d'innovation et autres domaines qui ne sont pas encore couverts par des accords multilatéraux.

La perspective d'une évolution de l'équilibre économique mondial au cours des deux prochaines décennies est réelle. Mais un certain nombre de « grands marchés émergents » ne partagent pas nécessairement certains des principes juridiques essentiels ou des mécanismes de base sur lesquels repose l'ouverture du commerce international. Au lieu de dépenser beaucoup d'énergie politique dans des querelles transatlantiques relatives à la banane, au bœuf et aux aides d'Etat aux industries, de chercher à obtenir des avantages marginaux par le biais d'arrangements commerciaux préférentiels avec des petits marchés, d'engager une concurrence stérile pour imposer les normes de l'une ou l'autre des entités sur un marché tiers ou d'être tentés par des approches protectionnistes pour augmenter les importations chinoises, l'Europe et les Etats-Unis pourraient utiliser leur prédominance actuelle pour investir dans de nouvelles formes de collaborations transatlantiques qui leur permettraient d'être les véritables pionniers de l'économie mondiale, essentiellement afin de réadapter l'Occident qui cherche à intégrer les autres grandes puissances économiques dans les mécanismes de la gouvernance mondiale. Il s'agit du quatrième défi auquel font face Paris et Washington.

Quatrième défi : travailler ensemble pour relever les défis économiques mondiaux

La crise financière mondiale et la récession qui en découle ont souligné le besoin pour Paris, Washington et les autres partenaires de s'assurer que l'investissement et l'ouverture en matière de libéralisation du commerce mondial sont guidés par les principes fondateurs de la bonne gouvernance mondiale. La crise financière est également le meilleur indicateur de la disparité croissante entre l'ampleur des défis mondiaux et la capacité des mécanismes intergouvernementaux à y faire face. Paris, Washington et leurs partenaires doivent envisager de nouvelles formes de gouvernance au niveau mondial et intégrer les puissances émergentes de façon à ce qu'elles soient parties prenantes au système. Heureusement, le système mondial actuel, ouvert, intégré et règlementé, a prouvé qu'il était étonnamment solide et flexible. Il a facilité la participation et l'intégration des grandes puissances traditionnelles mais aussi des Etats nouvellement indépendants. Son ouverture et sa flexibilité mêmes signifient que les puissances émergentes peuvent y prendre pleinement leur place et prospérer grâce à lui.

La résistance du système actuel signifie que nous devrions plutôt nous attaquer à ses excès et à ses carences non pas en partant de zéro mais en revenant aux principes fondateurs : en réinvestissant les éléments du système qui encouragent l'engagement, l'intégration et la modération et en les renforçant[10]. Plus ces structures seront ouvertes consensuelles et réglementées et plus les bénéfices seront largement distribués, plus elles seront capables de défendre les intérêts des puissances émergentes par le biais de l'intégration et de l'adaptation plutôt que par le conflit. Si les Européens et les Américains veulent préserver leur capacité à façonner un environnement dans lequel les puissances émergentes peuvent faire des choix stratégiques déterminants pour leur participation à la marche du monde, ils doivent travailler ensemble afin de renforcer les règles et les institutions qui soutiennent cet ordre, encourageant davantage les puissances contestatrices à s'intégrer qu'à s'opposer, faisant en sorte qu'il leur soit difficile d'être des opposants ou des concurrents. En acceptant de se conformer à des règles communes, nous encourageons les autres à s'engager à vivre selon nos normes, pas seulement dans le domaine de la finance mondiale, mais également dans des domaines tels que la sécurité alimentaire, la santé publique, la propriété intellectuelle ainsi que la protection de l'environnement et du travail. Nous mettons également en place des moyens de mesurer cette conformité.

Revenir aux principes fondateurs implique également de s'assurer que la gouvernance mondiale est aussi une bonne gouvernance. Les mécanismes et institutions mondiaux doivent être fondés sur l'Etat de

---

[10] Voir G. John Ikenberry, "The rise of China and the Future of the West" *Foreign Affairs*, Janvier/Février 2008 ; Daniel S. Hamilton et Joseph Quinlan, Germany and Globalization (Washington, D.C. : Center for Transatlantic Relations, 2009).

droit et sur des normes de transparence, de non-discrimination, de responsabilité, de représentation et de réactivité. Ces caractéristiques garantissent une meilleure efficacité, la minimisation de la corruption et la prise en compte des points de vue des minorités. Nous devrions appliquer ces principes à la réforme de chacune des principales institutions de gouvernance mondiale.

D'autres nations sont sans doute prêtes à adhérer à ces normes, pas seulement car elles souhaitent accéder à nos marchés mais aussi car elles sont de plus en plus conscientes qu'un système basé sur ces normes est essentiel pour qu'elles puissent tirer profit de la mondialisation. Et cela peut leur permettre de prendre part à la résolution de certains conflits, pour chercher à créer un développement économique équitable et pour promouvoir une utilisation durable des ressources nationales.

Alors que les sommets du G20 se succèdent pour répondre à la crise économique mondiale, une réforme générale de la gouvernance mondiale semble moins probable que des adaptations progressives associées à un renforcement des mécanismes de gouvernance informelle, sur le modèle de la coopération , encore informelle, entre les banques centrales à l'automne 2008. De tels mécanismes informels pourraient reposer sur un renforcement du Forum de stabilité financière et sur des initiatives telles qu'un collège de superviseurs. Le G20 pourrait supplanter le G8 comme vecteur de ces efforts, ce qui se révèlerait une innovation utile. Cependant, si Paris et Washington s'accordent sur le format du G20, les gouvernements français et américain pourraient simultanément envisager un retour aux consultations originelles qui avaient conduit à la création du G8, à savoir des contacts et rencontres informels et personnels entre les responsables des grands pays occidentaux, à savoir les États-Unis, la France, le Royaume-Uni, l'Allemagne et peut-être d'autres pays. Si ces pays ne sont pas suffisants, à eux seuls, pour orienter la gouvernance économique mondiale, ils restent néanmoins nécessaires.

La relance des négociations commerciales multilatérales du programme de Doha pour le développement constitue un défi annexe. En juillet 2008, les négociations sur les grandes lignes permettant d'achever le cycle de Doha ont échoué en raison de la complexité des négociations, de la faiblesse du contenu du potentiel accord ainsi que du climat politique et du calendrier. Le secrétaire général de l'OMC, Pascal

Lamy, estimait que l'incapacité à parvenir à un accord coûtait potentiellement au monde 130 milliards $ en tarifs douaniers. Cependant, dans ce contexte de récession mondiale, les perspectives de progrès rapides sont faibles.

Résumé

Pris globalement, ces quatre défis forment un agenda bien chargé mais impressionnant pour la coopération entre Paris et Washington. Au cours de sa mise en œuvre, il sera impératif, pour les responsables des deux côtés de l'Atlantique, de résister aux tentations protectionnistes, d'éviter les idées superficielles de découplage et de dérives transatlantiques et de rappeler ce qui rend la relation transatlantique originale : lorsque les deux rives de l'Atlantique sont d'accord, nous restons au cœur de toute coalition mondiale efficace ; lorsqu'elles sont en désaccord, aucune coalition mondiale ne peut être efficace. Notre partenariat reste indispensable. Mais aujourd'hui, il est insuffisant pour répondre à toute une série de défis auxquels aucune nation ne peut faire face seule, de manière efficace. Alors que nous sommes confrontés à une crise financière et à une récession mondiale, notre défi consiste à adapter nos économies nationales, notre partenariat transatlantique et nos mécanismes de gouvernance mondiale, de sorte que chacun soit plus intégré, plus efficace et plus réactif face aux défis du siècle à venir.

Deuxième partie :

points de vue stratégiques

Chapitre trois
Les défis stratégiques, 2009–2012

Bruno Tertrais

Résumé

Les relations franco-américaines dans le domaine stratégique sont aujourd'hui très bonnes, mais trois questions pourraient susciter des tensions entre Paris et Washington : une demande américaine de renforcement de la présence militaire de l'OTAN en Afghanistan ; un changement radical d'attitude envers l'Iran ; et l'engagement des États-Unis en faveur d'un « monde libre d'armes nucléaires ».

La relation euro-américaine sur les questions stratégiques : état des lieux

À la veille d'un renouvellement des équipes politiques à Washington, il existe une relation solide entre les deux rives de l'Atlantique sur les questions stratégiques. Près de vingt ans après la fin de la Guerre froide, les pays de l'OTAN partagent encore une perspective stratégique commune. L'existence de l'article 5 du traité de l'Atlantique nord n'a pas été remise en question, et il y a un accord général sur l'idée selon laquelle l'Alliance doit être capable de conduire des opérations de paix hors de la zone du traité. Les pays membres sont liés par le Concept stratégique adopté au sommet de Washington (1999), et par la Directive politique adoptée au sommet de Riga (2006). Après le 11 septembre 2001, l'OTAN a invoqué l'Article 5 pour la première fois de son histoire, et a initié des opérations communes visant à patrouiller dans le ciel des États-Unis et à surveiller l'espace maritime méditerranéen. La plupart des pays de l'Alliance ont immédiatement donné leur accord pour participer à l'opération *Enduring Freedom (Liberté immuable)*, y compris en mer.[1] L'OTAN a ensuite pris en charge la Force de stabili-

---

[1] La coalition alliée CTF-150 (Combined Task Force 150), qui patrouille autour de la Corne de l'Afrique, est l'opération la plus importante de la Marine allemande depuis la fin de la Seconde guerre mondiale.

sation en Afghanistan. La publication de la Stratégie européenne commune de sécurité (2003) a réconcilié la communauté transatlantique sur l'évaluation de la menace et la stratégie politique. Après un « creux » de quelques années dû à la crise irakienne, les populations européennes ont de nouveau une image favorable de l'OTAN.[2] Le terrorisme et la prolifération nucléaire sont reconnues comme étant les deux menaces de sécurité les plus immédiates par les pays membres, l'Iran étant considéré comme une menace potentielle particulièrement inquiétante. Enfin, tous les sondages montrent que le terrorisme international est systématiquement considéré comme la menace prioritaire par les opinions, des deux côtés de l'Atlantique.[3]

Qui aurait pensé, à l'époque de l'ouverture du Mur de Berlin, que vingt ans plus tard, les pays membres de l'Alliance partageraient encore une telle vision commune ? Cet état de fait est d'autant plus remarquable qu'un renouvellement presque complet des élites politiques et intellectuelles a eu lieu dans l'intervalle.

Le prochain président des États-Unis bénéficiera immédiatement d'un *a priori* positif dans les opinions européennes, pour la simple raison qu'il ne s'appellera pas George Bush. Mais il n'est pas évident que l'Alliance atlantique gardera sa cohésion face aux défis stratégiques qui s'annoncent.

Les défis stratégiques qui s'annoncent

La Russie et la Chine

Il existe un décalage de perceptions entre l'Europe et les États-Unis sur la Russie et sur la Chine. L'affaiblissement de la démocratie en Russie est vu avec inquiétude au sein de la population américaine (70%), davantage qu'en Europe (58%)[4]. Quant à la Chine, elle est considérée comme une menace potentielle par près de la moitié des Améri-

---

[2] *Transatlantic Trends 2008*, The German Marshall Fund of the United States, septembre 2008.

[3] Voir par exemple *Transatlantic Trends 2008*, The German Marshall Fund of the United States, septembre 2008 ; TNS Emnid poll for the Berterlsmann Stiftung, 22 octobre 2007 ; Harris Interactive Survey for France 24 and the International Herald Tribune, 28 mars 2008.

[4] *Transatlantic Trends 2008*, The German Marshall Fund of the United States, septembre 2008.

cains (48%), contre seulement 29% des Britanniques, proportion la plus élevée des grands pays européens[5]. Et 20% des Américains la voient même comme un « ennemi », proportion qui n'a pas d'équivalent en Europe, sauf en Turquie (25%).[6]

Si du fait de l'insistance américaine pour une entrée rapide de la Géorgie ou de l'Ukraine dans l'OTAN, les relations entre Washington et Moscou devaient se tendre davantage, des tensions transatlantiques pourraient en résulter. Malgré l'intervention en Géorgie, seuls les pays d'Europe centrale et orientale semblent prêts à suivre les États-Unis dans une ligne dure. Au sein des opinions publiques, seuls les Britanniques considèrent la Russie comme un ennemi potentiel, alors que ce n'est pas le cas dans la plupart des autres grands pays de l'OTAN.[7] La réaction à avoir face à une possible aggravation de la crise du Caucase, par exemple, pourrait être un vrai test de la solidarité de l'Alliance atlantique.

L'Afghanistan

Le président Obama est prêt à renforcer l'implication militaire des États-Unis (envoi de 21.000 hommes supplémentaires) et a demandé des efforts supplémentaires aux alliés européens pour l'effort commun en Afghanistan.

Mais la conduite des opérations de combat contre les Talibans continue de diviser profondément les opinions des pays membres de l'Alliance: 76% des Américains y sont favorables, contre seulement 43% des Européens.[8] Et dans certains pays de l'OTAN (Turquie, Pologne, Espagne, France, Allemagne), il existe une majorité pour un retrait des forces de l'Alliance.[9]

---

[5] Harris Interactive Survey pour France 24 et *The International Herald Tribune*, 28 mars 2008. La proportion en France est de 16%.

[6] 24-Nation Pew Global Attitudes Survey, The Pew Global Attitudes Project, 12 juin 2008.

[7] Harris Poll n° 19, 20 février 2008. Le Royaume-Uni est également le pays européen dans lequel l'on trouve la proportion la plus forte de sondés (31%) considérant la Russie comme une menace militaire potentielle (Harris Interactive Survey pour France 24 et *The International Herald Tribune*, 28 mars 2008).

[8] *Transatlantic Trends 2008*, The German Marshall Fund of the United States, septembre 2008.

[9] 24-Nation Pew Global Attitudes Survey, The Pew Global Attitudes Project, 12 juin 2008.

L'annonce de la fermeture du camp de Guantanamo — un symbole cher aux yeux de nombreux Européens — n'a pas suffi à persuader les parlements des pays alliés d'autoriser des déploiements supplémentaires en grand nombre pour une opération militaire encore souvent perçue, à tort, comme une aventure américaine.

La crise iranienne

La crise iranienne restera, dans les mois et les années qui viennent, l'un des problèmes stratégiques les plus importants et les plus sensibles pour la communauté transatlantique, tant du point de vue des gouvernements que de celui des opinions.

L'Iran est unanimement perçu comme le pays le plus menaçant par les opinions publiques des pays membres de l'OTAN.[10] La proportion de ceux qui sont opposés à l'acquisition par Téhéran de l'arme nucléaire varie entre 83% (Bulgarie) et 97% (Allemagne).[11] Un Iran nucléaire serait considéré comme une menace directe et sérieuse par de larges majorités, de 65% des Bulgares à 87% des Italiens.[12]

En tant que candidat, Barack Obama n'a pas souhaité exclure l'option d'une action militaire contre l'Iran, et tout porte à croire que cette hypothèse restera d'actualité, même si sa réalisation à court terme demeure assez improbable (sauf énorme provocation iranienne, ou escalade incontrôlée à la suite d'un incident dans le Golfe). En effet, le président élu demandera certainement un « passage en revue » de la politique iranienne, le temps d'examiner ses options. Par ailleurs, Washington pourrait attendre l'issue de l'élection présidentielle de juin 2009 pour réexaminer ses choix.

Si le président Obama evait décider d'une action militaire contre l'Iran, il provoquerait sans doute une grave crise transatlantique. Même s'il n'existe pas de majorité absolue aux États-Unis en faveur du maintien de l'option militaire contre l'Iran (47% soutiennent cette idée), les Européens y sont, eux, très majoritairement opposés (18% seulement souhaitent que cette option soit maintenue)[13]. Selon une

---

[10] Harris Interactive Survey for France 24 and the International Herald Tribune, 28 mars 2008.

[11] 47-Nation Pew Global Attitudes Survey, The Pew Global Attitudes Project, 27 juin 2007.

[12] 47-Nation Pew Global Attitudes Survey, The Pew Global Attitudes Project, 27 juin 2007.

[13] *Transatlantic Trends 2007*, The German Marshall Fund of the United States, septembre 2007.

autre étude, réalisée en octobre 2007, la « diplomatie seule » (sans sanctions) ne recueille l'assentiment que de 36% des Américains, contre, par exemple, plus de 50% des Espagnols, des Italiens et des Allemands ; et l'option militaire est soutenue par 21% des Américains contre 7 à 8% des Allemands, des Italiens, des Français et des Espagnols.[14]

À l'inverse, un président américain tenté par une politique d'ouverture sans condition envers Téhéran, en dépit des positions communes affichées dans le cadre du groupe des « Cinq plus Un » depuis 2005, pourrait faire face à l'hostilité des gouvernements européens les plus en pointe sur le sujet — comme c'est le cas pour la France. On se trouverait alors dans une étrange configuration politique, à bien des égards l'inverse, quoique sans doute en moins violent, de celle que nous avions connu à propos de l'Irak en 2002-2003. Il en serait sans doute de même au cas — très improbable — où, dans les quatre ans qui viennent, des évolutions politiques majeures allaient jusqu'à altérer la nature même du régime iranien, qui renoncerait notamment à tout soutien au terrorisme. En effet, dans un tel cas les États-Unis seraient beaucoup moins enclins à se préoccuper du programme nucléaire du pays, alors que pour les gouvernements européens, la question continuerait à se poser dans les mêmes termes. Car pour l'Amérique, c'est la nature même du régime politique iranien qui pose problème, alors que pour l'Europe, c'est d'abord et avant tout l'impact de la crise sur le régime de non-prolifération nucléaire dans son ensemble.[15]

Enfin, la simple poursuite de la ligne actuelle, qui consiste à exiger la suspension des activités nucléaires sensibles avant toute reprise des négociations formelles, ne recueillera pas nécessairement le consensus au sein de la communauté transatlantique. L'approbation de cette ligne a diminué un peu partout dans le monde entre 2006 and 2008.[16] En l'absence de provocation iranienne, les positions de Washington, Berlin, Londres et Paris pourraient se trouver de plus en plus isolées.

---

[14] Harris Interactive Survey pour France 24 and *The International Herald Tribune*, 9 novembre 2007.

[15] Sur ce thème, voir Bruno Tertrais, « A Fragile Consensus », *The National Interest*, printemps 2006.

[16] Globescan poll for the BBC World Service, February 2008.

La défense antimissile

Le déploiement d'un site d'intercepteurs destinés à la défense contre les missiles à longue portée est un autre sujet possible de contentieux.[17] Il n'y a pas de divergence fondamentale d'appréciation quant à la menace. Selon le Secrétaire général de l'OTAN Jaap de Hoop Scheffer, « *il existe sans conteste une perception commune de la menace entre Alliés. Les Alliés sont tous d'accord pour dire que les missiles balistiques constituent une menace* ».[18] De fait, la déclaration faite par les pays membres lors du Sommet de l'OTAN de Bucarest (2008) indique que « *la prolifération des missiles balistiques représente une menace croissante pour les forces, le territoire, et la population des pays de l'Alliance* ».[19] Certes, les Alliés ont officiellement donné leur bénédiction au projet américain : «*La défense antimissile s'inscrit dans le cadre d'une réponse plus large visant à contrer cette menace. Nous reconnaissons donc la contribution substantielle que le projet d'implantation en Europe de moyens de défense antimissile des États-Unis apporte à la protection des Alliés contre les missiles balistiques à longue portée*».[20] Mais les opinions y restent très réticentes. La plupart des Européens y sont opposés (notamment 71% des Allemands), alors qu'environ la moitié (49%) des Américains y sont favorables.[21] Le sujet a pris une dimension nouvelle depuis août 2008 en raison de la crise géorgienne. Le gouvernement polonais a confirmé sa disponibilité à accueillir le site d'intercepteurs, et la signature de l'accord avec les États-Unis, qui était prévue depuis plusieurs jours, n'a pas été remise en cause. La nouvelle administration américaine a confirmé son intention de principe de construire ce site, mais à condition que les défenses soient efficaces, et à un coût abordable. Par ailleurs, elle a précisé que le calendrier de ce déploiement devrait suivre de près celui de la menace; autrement dit, elle a adopté une approche qui se veut pragmatique, et non idéologique.

---

[17] Le site comprendrait jusqu'à 10 intercepteurs à deux étages GBI (*Ground-Based Interceptors*). Steven A. Hildreth & Carl Ek, *Long-Range Ballistic Missile Defense in Europe*, CRS Report for Congress, Congressional Research Service, 9 janvier 2008, p. 4.

[18] Jaap De Hoop Scheffer, Conférence de presse, 19 avril 2007.

[19] *Déclaration du Sommet de Bucarest, publiée par les Chefs d'État et de gouvernement participant aà la réunion du Conseil de l'Atlantique Nord tenue à Bucarest le 3 avril 2008*, Communiqué de presse (2008) 49.

[20] *Déclaration du Sommet de Bucarest, publiée par les Chefs d'État et de gouvernement participant aà la réunion du Conseil de l'Atlantique Nord tenue à Bucarest le 3 avril 2008*, Communiqué de presse (2008) 49.

[21] Harris Interactive Survey pour France 24 et The International Herald Tribune, 28 mars 2008.

L'avenir des armes nucléaires

Plusieurs facteurs vont faire des questions de politique nucléaire, dans les années qui viennent, un élément important du débat transatlantique.

La révision prochaine du Concept stratégique de l'OTAN, qui a été décidée lors du sommet de 2009, sera l'occasion de rouvrir la question de la présence nucléaire américaine en Europe. Or les pays membres de l'Alliance atlantique voudront réussir la prochaine conférence quinquennale d'examen du Traité de non prolifération des armes nucléaires (TNP), qui se tiendra au printemps 2010 — et ce d'autant plus que la précédente conférence d'examen en 2005, avait été un échec complet. Par ailleurs, il se trouve que, pour des raisons techniques (remplacement des avions porteurs en raison de leur vieillissement), les « pays hôtes » de la présence nucléaire américaine devront prendre des décisions dans les années 2010-2012 quant au maintien ou non de la capacité de leurs forces aériennes à emporter des armes nucléaires américaines.[22] Enfin, c'est vers 2012 que les premiers éléments d'un système de défense antimissile de l'OTAN devraient être déployés. Il ne fait guère de doute que la question « faut-il que l'OTAN soit protégée à la fois par des armes nucléaires et des défenses antimissiles ? » sera posée.

Le débat transatlantique qui s'annonce sur cette question sera complexe, et n'opposera pas l'Europe d'un côté aux États-Unis de l'autre.

Les États-Unis affirment désormais plus fortement leur pleine souscription à l'objectif d'un « monde libre d'armes nucléaires ». Une telle évolution est appréciée positivement par la grande majorité des gouvernements et des opinions des partenaires de l'Amérique au sein de l'OTAN — même si certains d'entre eux n'y sont guère favorables. De même, la ratification probable du Traité d'interdiction complète des essais nucléaires (TICE) serat-elle certainement applaudie par tous. Enfin, M. Obama dit souhaiter une poursuite de la réduction de l'arsenal nucléaire américain, et cette position n'a pas été affectée par le récent refroidissement des relations avec la Russie.

---

[22] Selon les sources ouvertes, cinq pays non-nucléaires accueillent aujourd'hui des armes nucléaires américaines : l'Allemagne, la Belgique, l'Italie, les Pays-Bas et la Turquie. Le Royaume-Uni accueille lui aussi, depuis longtemps, des armes nucléaires destinées aux bombardiers américains ; mais selon une source récente, ces armes auraient été retirées. Voir Hans Kristensen, « US Nuclear Weapons Withdrawn from the United Kingdom », FAS Strategic Security Blog, Federation of American Scientists, 26 juin 2008.

Mais des gestes plus forts de la part des États-Unis dans ce domaine pourraient ouvrir une véritable faille au sein de l'Alliance atlantique. Le retrait des armes américaines d'Europe ou l'adoption d'une politique de « non-emploi en premier » de l'arme nucléaire (concevable sous la présidence Obama, de nombreux experts proches de lui étant favorables à cette option) seraient en effet perçus négativement par les pays les plus proches de la Russie (Pologne, pays baltes), ainsi que par la Turquie.

Ankara, dont la relation stratégique avec les États-Unis est devenue plus complexe, s'interroge sur la valeur de la garantie de sécurité accordée par l'OTAN.[23] Les avancées du programme nucléaire iranien l'inquiètent. Les Turcs sont 57% à s'inquiéter du programme nucléaire de l'Iran, contre, par exemple, 21% des Français.[24] Si le « parapluie » américain devait sembler se rétracter aux yeux de la Turquie, l'hypothèse d'un programme nucléaire national turc ne serait certainement pas à exclure.[25]

Perspectives pour les quatre prochaines années

Comme on le voit, il serait déraisonnable de partir du principe que la prochaine mandature présidentielle américaine sera nécessairement une nouvelle lune de miel euro-américaine.

Il ne fait guère de doute que les premiers mois de la prochaine administration se prêteront tout particulièrement bien à une relance de la coopération stratégique euro-américaine. La fermeture très probable du camp de Guantanamo, l'annonce de la réduction, voire du départ du gros des forces de combat d'Irak, la poursuite des réductions nucléaires et la possible ratification du Traité d'interdiction complète des essais

---

[23] Pas moins de 70% des Turcs considèrent les États-Unis comme « un ennemi ». 24-Nation Pew Global Attitudes Survey, The Pew Global Attitudes Project, 12 juin 2008.

[24] 47-Nation Pew Global Attitudes Survey, The Pew Global Attitudes Project, 27 juin 2007.

[25] Actuellement, la Turquie entretient un important programme nucléaire civil, mais ne dispose pas des installations nécessaires à la fabrication de matière fissile. Elle aurait donc besoin, à cette fin, d'une installation d'enrichissement de l'uranium ou d'un réacteur plutonigène dédié. La production de matière fissile dans des installations de ce type impliquerait le retrait du TNP. Une option nucléaire nationale turque ne serait sans doute concevable que si trois conditions étaient remplies : une sévère crise de confiance entre Ankara et Washington, un effondrement du TNP, et enfin un pessimisme quant aux chances de la Turquie d'entrer dans l'Union européenne à échéance prévisible. Il semble en effet inconcevable que l'Union puisse accepter en son sein une nouvelle puissance nucléaire.

nucléaires — tous ces événements devraient faciliter la coopération transatlantique dans les années 2009-2010. D'autant plus que le sommet du 60ème anniversaire de l'OTAN (2009) a vu l'annonce du retour français dans l'organisation militaire intégrée de l'OTAN.

L'arrivée de M. Obama à la Maison-Blanche, en dépit du fait qu'il était clairement le candidat préféré des Européens, n'a pas résolu les tensions transatlantiques. La demande d'un soutien militaire plus grand en Afghanistan n'a pas rencontré l'assentiment de tous les pays européens. Il en est de même pour certains problèmes non évoqués plus haut, comme par exemple l'élargissement de l'OTAN à l'Ukraine et à la Géorgie, pour lequel la demande américaine est beaucoup plus forte que la demande européenne. Enfin, le maintien de l'option militaire contre l'Iran continuera à mettre mal à l'aise la très grande majorité des gouvernements et des opinions publiques en Europe.

De plus, les positions diplomatiques annoncées de Barack Obama sur l'Iran — vis-à-vis duquel il envisage un dialogue direct, avec seulement un minimum de conditions — pourraient gêner certains gouvernements européens.

Par ailleurs, si le Congrès est resté démocrate, il n'y a pas au Sénat de majorité suffisante pour ratifier à coup sûr certains des traités auxquels les Européens accordent une importance particulière (traité d'interdiction des essais, convention sur l'interdiction des mines antipersonnel, traité instituant la Cour pénale internationale, etc.)

Enfin, les Européens tendent parfois à oublier que certains des traits les plus discutés de la politique étrangère américaine sont assez consensuels et ne disparaîtront pas avec le départ de M. Bush et l'arrivée de M. Obama: c'est le cas par exemple de la disponibilité des États-Unis à l'action unilatérale si nécessaire, de la méfiance de Washington à l'égard des traités susceptibles de contraindre la liberté d'action des États-Unis et sa préférence systématique pour le droit national au détriment des normes internationales, du soutien à la politique israélienne, ou du lobbying en faveur de l'entrée rapide de la Turquie dans l'Union européenne.

Voilà pourquoi il importe d'appréhender cette nouvelle phase des relations stratégiques transatlantiques avec réalisme, et sans optimisme excessif.

La dimension franco-américaine

Dans ce contexte, la relation franco-américaine pourrait constituer un point d'ancrage pour les relations transatlantiques. Elle connaît en effet une phase extraordinairement coopérative sur les questions stratégiques. Ce n'est certes pas la première fois que les deux pays connaissent une telle « lune de miel », mais celle qui a commencé en mai 2007 apparaît particulièrement durable.

La France entend ainsi reprendre toute sa place au sein de « *la famille occidentale* », selon l'expression qu'affectionnent M. Sarkozy et ses conseillers. Cette décision est désormais justifiée par le fait que dans une époque de transition vers « *l'ère de la puissance relative* », il est nécessaire pour la France d'affirmer plus nettement ses valeurs et intérêts essentiels.[26]

Certes, la réintégration dans la structure militaire de l'OTAN fait débat dans les cercles politiques français, mais l'opposition n'a pas choisi d'en faire un cheval de bataille. Il est vrai que, contrairement à ce à quoi l'on pourrait s'attendre, l'Alliance atlantique reste assez populaire en France (55% des Français souhaitent son maintien… contre 54% des Américains).[27] Par ailleurs, le soutien plus clair et plus ouvert de l'administration Bush au développement de l'Europe de la défense, qui s'est manifesté depuis l'élection de M. Sarkozy — en « contrepartie » de la disponibilité française à rejoindre la structure intégrée de l'OTAN — satisfait bien sûr les diplomates français.

Le Moyen-Orient

C'est sans doute sur les questions relatives au Proche — et au Moyen-Orient que la convergence de vues et la coopération franco-américaine est la plus visible. Dès l'entrée en fonction de M. Sarkozy, ses déclarations d'amitié envers Israël, ainsi que le voyage du ministre des affaires étrangères Bernard Kouchner en Irak (août 2007), ont inauguré une nouvelle atmosphère dans les débats franco-américains sur ces questions.

---

[26] Nicolas Sarkozy, Discours de M. le Président de la République, 16ème conférence des ambassadeurs, 27 août 2008.

[27] Harris Interactive Survey pour France 24 et *The International Herald Tribune*, 28 mars 2008.

Si la décision française d'initier un dialogue avec la Syrie a au départ suscité des froncements de sourcils à Washington, les États-Unis ont eux-mêmes emboîté le pas en invitant Damas à participer à la conférence d'Annapolis (novembre 2007). Au résultat, les États-Unis et la France se sont engagés à co-parrainer une future négociation directe entre la Syrie et Israël. Par ailleurs, sur le Liban, les États-Unis et la France, qui travaillaient déjà étroitement ensemble depuis 2004, continuent de rechercher de concert les moyens de garantir l'indépendance du pays.[28]

Par ailleurs, comme on le sait, les services de renseignement des deux pays entretiennent une bonne relation de travail dans le domaine du contre-terrorisme (relation qui n'a guère été affectée par l'évolution en dents de scie de la relation bilatéraler au cours des années 2001-2008). La persistance de la menace djihadiste au Moyen-Orient et en Afrique du nord (la France étant particulièrement visée par « Al-Qaida au Maghreb islamique ») rendra la poursuite de cette coopération particulièrement opportune.

L'Iran

À propos de l'Iran, le terme « d'alignement » sur les États-Unis a parfois été employé pour qualifier la position française depuis 2007. Pourtant, les positions des deux administrations étaient déjà largement convergentes depuis deux ou trois ans. Mais le langage employé par la Présidence de la République est désormais aussi fort que celui de son homologue américain. Tous deux ont fait savoir à plusieurs reprises qu'il serait « inacceptable » que l'Iran se dote de l'arme nucléaire. MM. Sarkozy et Kouchner ont repris à leur compte le thème de « *l'alternative catastrophique* » (la bombe iranienne ou le bombardement de l'Iran) qui avait été évoqué pour la première fois par John McCain[29]. Certains choix possibles de M. Obama pourraient toutefois susciter des tensions entre Paris et Washington. Lorsqu'il était candidat, Barack Obama s'était en effet prononcé en faveur d'une diplomatie excluant « *les préconditions menant tout droit à l'échec* » (*self-defeating preconditions*).[30] Or la

---

[28] Voir Conférence de presse conjointe avec M. George W. Bush, Président des États-Unis d'Amérique, Palais de l'Élysée, 14 juin 2008.

[29] Nicolas Sarkozy, Discours de M. le Président de la République, 16ème conférence des ambassadeurs, 27 août 2008.

[30] Barack Obama, Intervention devant l'American-Israel Public Affairs Committee, 4 juin 2008.

France, tout comme ses partenaires européens, insiste sur le respect de la condition de suspension des activités sensibles de l'Iran avant toute reprise formelle d'un dialogue d'ensemble. Et M. Obama insiste par ailleurs, comme on l'a rappelé plus haut, sur le fait que l'option militaire doit demeurer un choix possible — option à laquelle on voit mal la France se ranger sans un mandat des Nations-Unies.

Le nucléaire

Les questions de politique nucléaire faisaient, sous l'administration Bush, l'objet d'un consensus assez fort entre les États-Unis et la France. Le conservatisme traditionnel de Paris dans ce domaine rencontrait en effet les préoccupations de l'administration américaine. Mais cette convergence pourrait être moins forte sous l'actuelle administration. Barack Obama soutient en effet clairement, dans le discours en tout cas, l'objectif d'un « monde libre d'armes nucléaires ». Cette insistance nouvelle sur le désarmement nucléaire, qui trouve son origine dans un mouvement intellectuel lancé par quatre personnalités américaines en janvier 2007, met Paris mal à l'aise[31]. En revanche, une éventuelle ratification par le Sénat des États-Unis du Traité d'interdiction complète des essais nucléaires serait applaudie par Paris. Barack Obama s'est engagé à promouvoir cette ratification et à créer à cet effet un consensus bipartisan ; la France encouragera le nouveau président américain à s'engager rapidement dans cette direction, notamment en prévision de la conférence d'examen du Traité de non-prolifération nucléaire qui se tiendra au printemps 2010.

Par ailleurs, la France sera certainement réceptive à des demandes américaines de soutien et de coopération dans le domaine de la « réduction de la menace nucléaire », annoncée comme une priorité absolue par la nouvelle administration afin de lutter contre le risque de terrorisme nucléaire. Elle dispose en effet d'une certaine expérience dans ce domaine (aide à l'ex-Union soviétique) et est un participant actif à l'initiative prise à cet effet par le G8 à Kananaskis en 2002.

---

[31] George P. Shultz, William J. Perry, Henry A. Kissinger, Sam Nunn, "A World Free of Nuclear Weapons", *The Wall Street Journal*, 4 janvier 2007.

La défense antimissiles

L'installation d'un site de défense antimissiles en Europe n'est pas populaire chez les Français (58% s'y opposent), mais la question ne fait guère les grands titres des journaux, et Paris a adopté une attitude de soutien mesuré à cette initiative.[32] Comme on l'a dit plus haut, Barack Obama n'est pas opposé à l'installation du site, mais refuse tout déploiement hâtif et souhaite que celui-ci n'ait lieu qu'à la condition que le système ait démontré son efficacité, et qu'il ne suscite pas de nouvelles divisions en Europe. Il est douteux que ce thème soit un sujet majeur de débat entre la France et les États-Unis à l'avenir, Paris ne préférant rester en deuxième ligne sur cette question — contrairement à ce qui avait été le cas dans les années 1999-2000, lorsque la France s'opposait au projet américain de *National Missile Defense*, par crainte d'une nouvelle course aux armements. Par ailleurs, les systèmes de défense antimissile seront probablement affectés par les probables coupes qui ne manqueront pas d'être faites dans le budget américain de la défense.

La Russie

Sur les relations avec la Russie, la France a adopté une attitude prudente qui devrait garantir l'absence de divergence majeure avec l'administration Obama. Toutefois, celle-ci pourrait vouloir faire pression sur ses alliés pour accélérer le processus d'adhésion de la Géorgie et de l'Ukraine à l'OTAN : la France n'y est actuellement pas favorable, même si elle ne rejette pas totalement, à ce stade, l'idée de proposer à ces deux pays d'adhérer au Plan d'action pour l'adhésion (MAP), première étape vers l'adhésion.

En revanche, la France n'aura aucun problème à adhérer à l'idée d'une pertinence nouvelle pour l'article 5 du Traité de Washington, chère aux nouveaux alliés qui se méfient de la résurgence russe. En effet, même en temps que membre non intégré de l'OTAN, elle a toujours insisté sur le fait que la défense collective était et devait rester la première mission de l'Alliance atlantique.

---

[32] Harris Interactive Survey pour France 24 et *The International Herald Tribune*, 28 mars 2008.

L'Afghanistan

Enfin, l'engagement allié en Afghanistan fait partie des rares questions qui pourraient susciter certaines tentions entre les deux pays. En effet, depuis le printemps 2008, avec la décision de renforcer la présence français en Afghanistan, annoncée au sommet de Bucarest, l'engagement français dans ce pays est devenu un thème de politique intérieure. (Lors du débat qui avait eu lieu à ce sujet à l'Assemblée nationale, le Parti socialiste avait déposé une motion de censure.) Ceci n'a pas altéré la nature de l'engagement français, le président Sarkozy se prévalant d'avoir convaincu ses alliés d'une révision de la stratégie transatlantique à l'occasion du Sommet de Bucarest. Mais le contexte politique a changé avec l'embuscade du 18 août qui a coûté la vie à 10 soldats. De plus, en raison d'une réforme constitutionnelle, le Parlement a désormais son mot à dire dans la prolongation des opérations militaires extérieures, ce qui rend celles-ci davantage tributaires du contexte politique intérieur.

Or les Français sont désormais très majoritairement opposés au maintien de l'engagement national en Afghanistan.[33] Et le Parlement lui-même est aujourd'hui divisé, tant au sein de la majorité que de l'opposition. Il ne fait aucun doute que la France restera engagée en Afghanistan. M. Sarkozy emploie à propos de l'engagement de son pays des termes que ne renieraient pas George Bush, et il a décidé de renforcer légèrement le contingent français, qui est passé à 2800 hommes à la fin 2008[34]. Par ailleurs, il a été décidé au printemps 2009 que des gendarmes français allaient être envoyés pour la formation de l'armée afghane, et que la France augmenterait son aide civile au pays. Il sera sans doute difficile à M. Sarkozy de faire plus sans susciter un trouble sérieux au sein même de sa majorité.

---

[33] 62% selon une enquête BVA/Orange/L'Express réalisée les 12 et 13 septembre 2008. Citée in Jean-Dominique Merchet, « L'Afghanistan débarque au Parlement », *Libération*, 22 septembre 2008.

[34] « *Quelle serait l'alternative ? Un retrait militaire serait suivi du retour des Talibans et d'Al-Qaïda, et sans doute de la déstabilisation du Pakistan voisin. Ce n'est pas concevable. Soyons clairs : la France, membre permanent du Conseil de sécurité, assumera ses responsabilités. Elle ne cèdera pas aux terroristes. Elle les combattra, partout où ils se trouvent, avec la conviction que le peuple afghan, appuyé par ses alliés, l'emportera sur la barbarie et pourra progressivement y faire face par lui-même* » (Discours de M. le Président de la République, 16ème conférence des ambassadeurs, mercredi 27 août 2008).

En résumé, si les relations franco-américaines dans le domaine stratégique sont aujourd'hui très bonnes, plusieurs questions pourraient susciter des tensions entre Paris et Washington dans les quatre prochaines années : les opérations de l'OTAN en Afghanistan ; la crise nucléaire iranienne ; et l'engagement ; et un engagement plus net des États-Unis en faveur d'un « monde libre d'armes nucléaires ».[35]

Paradoxalement, alors que le monde entier a fêté l'élection de M. Obama, la relation franco-américaine sur les questions stratégiques pourrait ainsi être un peu plus tendue dans les quatre prochaines années qu'elle ne l'a été dans les deux dernières. Et l'absence de bonnes relations personnelles entre les deux présidents ne contribuera guère à dissiper les tensions et éventuels malentendus. Rappelons à cet égard que les relations entre les deux pays sont suffisamment volatiles pour que les prévisions dans ce domaine soient sujettes à caution. Souvenons-nous, en effet, que ces relations avaient été très bonnes après l'élection de Jacques Chirac en 1995, mais avaient connu leur pire crise depuis longtemps avec le même président français sept ans plus tard.

---

[35] On pourrait y ajouter de probables tensions à propos des dossiers relatifs à l'industrie de la défense, le camp démocrate se montrant de plus en plus sensible aux sirènes du protectionnisme. Cette question n'est pas traitée ici dans la mesure où elle relève davantage du contentieux commercial que des problèmes stratégiques.

Chapitre quatre

Les relations de sécurité euro-atlantiques et la coopération franco-américaine

Leo Michel

Le monde étant moins divisé, les interconnexions ont pu s'y développer. Les évènements se sont enchaînés à une vitesse telle que nous n'avons pas pu les contrôler : crise économique mondiale, changements climatiques, persistance des dangers liés à de vieux conflits, nouvelles menaces et prolifération d'armes « catastrophiques ». Aucun de ces défis ne peut être résolu rapidement et facilement. Mais tous nous obligent à nous écouter mutuellement et à travailler ensemble, à nous concentrer sur nos intérêts communs et non sur nos différences ponctuelles, à réaffirmer nos valeurs communes qui sont plus fortes que tout ce qui peut nous séparer. Voici le travail que nous devons poursuivre. Voici le travail que je suis venu commencer en Europe.

Extrait du discours du Président Barack
Obama à Prague le 5 avril 2009[1]

Quatre mois après le début de la présidence d'Obama et suite à sa visite en Europe, les responsables et journalistes des deux rives de l'Atlantique ont loué sa façon de s'y prendre avec le Vieux Continent. Certains Américains et Européens se demandent néanmoins quand se terminera la « lune de miel ».

L'explication est facile à comprendre. Durant cette même période, de nombreux événements ont souligné les difficultés à formuler et maintenir de réelles réponses transatlantiques aux défis cités par le Président américain. Voici quelques exemples :

---

[1] Discours disponible à l'adresse : http://www.whitehouse.gov/the_press_office/Remarks-By-President-Barack-Obama-In-Prague-As-Delivered/.

- Après avoir montré ses capacités dans les domaines militaire, énergétique, politique et du renseignement dans ce que le Président Medvedev nomme « les régions d'intérêt privilégié », la Russie est toujours installée chez son voisin géorgien, ayant redessiné visiblement, et peut-être durablement, les frontières d'un partenaire des Etats-Unis et d'un candidat à l'adhésion à l'OTAN.

- En Afghanistan, les talibans, Al-Qaïda et d'autres forces insurgées témoignent d'ambitions croissantes et d'une meilleure coordination, poussant ainsi les Etats-Unis à augmenter leur présence militaire dans le cadre de leur nouvelle stratégie qui vise à « désorganiser, démanteler et vaincre Al-Qaïda et ses zones protégées au Pakistan »

- En même temps, la volonté affichée du gouvernement pakistanais de concéder un véritable contrôle de certaines parties de son territoire à des militants islamistes armés a récemment conduit la Secrétaire d'Etat Hillary Clinton à émettre une mise en garde selon laquelle le « Pakistan constitue une menace mortelle pour la sécurité et la sûreté des Américains et du monde ».

- Dans le reste de « l'arc de crise », l'Iran continue de résister aux efforts entrepris en vue de mettre fin à ses activités supposées liées aux armes nucléaires. L'Irak, en dépit du succès des élections provinciales et de l'amélioration des conditions de sécurité, reste sujette à la violence. De même, le processus de paix au Moyen-Orient semble gelé alors que des tensions sous-jacentes entre Israël, les Arabes et la bande de Gaza, contrôlée par le Hamas, menacent d'éclater sans préavis ou presque.

- Dans ce sombre contexte sécuritaire, qui omet, entre autres, les crises humanitaires au Darfour, en Somalie, au Zimbabwe et en République démocratique du Congo, les Etats-Unis et leurs partenaires du G20 doivent aussi faire face à la plus grave crise économique depuis la Grande Dépression. Washington et les capitales européennes sont ainsi obligées de mettre en place de vastes plans nationaux de relance et de coopérer pour réformer le système financier international.

L'interaction de ces défis s'apparente à des mouvements tectoniques. L'année dernière, Francis Fukayama, dont l'essai *La fin de l'Histoire ?*, publié en 1989, prônait que les idées libérales avaient fini par triompher à la fin de la Guerre froide, reconnaissait la réalité du monde « post-américain » de Fareed Zakaria, dans lequel « les Etats-Unis allaient décliner en raison de l'absence de limites à leur influence »[2]. De leur côté, les principaux stratèges français avaient déjà prévu, à long terme, une redistribution de la puissance et de l'influence mondiale, délaissant le terme problématique d'« hyper-puissance ». Le *Livre blanc français sur la Défense et la Sécurité nationale* publié en juin 2008 mettait en garde contre la sous-estimation du dynamisme américain et prévoyait trois grandes dominantes dans les 15 années à venir : une baisse relative de la capacité des Etats-Unis à façonner les événements mondiaux, liée en partie à l'influence grandissante de la Chine et à la plus grande confiance en elle de la Russie ; l'évolution de la focalisation des États-Unis, passant de l'Europe aux crises urgentes du Moyen-Orient et de l'Asie ; et, de façon toutefois moins certaine, un re-centrage vers les questions internes chez une partie de la population américaine.

Il reste à voir comment cette nouvelle Administration Obama parviendra à s'atteler à ces problèmes, à tenir compte de ces tendances, sans oublier d'éventuelles surprises ! On peut néanmoins affirmer sans se tromper que les Etats-Unis et la France seront obligés de travailler ensemble pour faire avancer leurs intérêts communs et/ou parallèles, tout en évitant d'écarter les priorités et/ou politiques divergentes qui apparaissent inévitablement. Voici quelques-unes des questions stratégiques clés auxquelles ils auront à faire face, notamment en matière de coopération sur la défense et la sécurité transatlantiques, ainsi que quelques suggestions de domaines dans lesquels ils pourraient travailler de façon bilatérale pour renforcer un partenariat euro-atlantique aux contours plus larges.

L'OTAN sous tension

L'OTAN, soutenue par les engagements militaires et politiques forts des Etats-Unis envers l'Alliance, est, depuis 1949, le premier garant de la défense européenne en cas d'attaque armée. Avec la fin de la Guerre froide, l'OTAN s'est vu confier de nouvelles missions : création de partenariats pour la défense et la sécurité avec les nouvelles démocraties d'Europe centrale et orientale, ce qui, pour beaucoup

---

[2] Francis Fukayama, "They Can Only Go So Far," *The Washington Post*, 24 août 2008 ; et Fareed Zakaria, "The Rise of the Rest," *Newsweek*, 12 mai 2008.

d'entre elles, fut le prélude à l'intégration dans l'Alliance ; proposition d'un dialogue et d'une coopération sur les problèmes politico-militaires à la Russie, l'Ukraine et les autres anciennes républiques soviétiques ; conduite d'opérations militaires complexes dans les Balkans et en Afghanistan. Durant ses 60 années d'existence, l'OTAN a aussi été le promoteur essentiel d'une collaboration intra-européenne et transatlantique en matière d'évaluation des menaces, de stratégie politico-militaire, de planification de défense, de normes d'équipements et d'interopérabilité et enfin de formation et de manœuvres.

La plupart des Européens souhaitent conserver, par le biais de l'OTAN, des liens politiques et militaires solides avec les Etats-Unis qui sont renforcés par ceux relatifs aux bases militaires, aux échanges d'information et autres relations bilatérales. Toutefois, « le moment unipolaire » de l'OTAN est dépassé, notamment en raison de deux tendances majeures. D'une part, à mesure que le souvenir de la Guerre froide s'estompe, les menaces pesant sur leur sécurité et les outils nécessaires pour y faire face ne sont plus considérés, par les Européens, comme essentiellement militaires. D'autre part, même si les sondages indiquent que les opinions européennes sont légèrement plus favorables aux Etats-Unis que pendant la guerre en Irak de 2003-2004, il apparaît que les Européens restent moins confiants qu'il y a dix ans sur la compatibilité des intérêts, de la stratégie et des politiques américaines avec les leurs[3]. Leur confiance dans la capacité militaire des Etats-Unis et dans leurs façons de traiter les extrémistes faits prisonniers, qui sont des points sensibles lors d'opérations militaires conjointes, a également été ébranlée.

Les Européens ne sont pas les seuls à remettre en question les hypothèses qui précèdent. Au cours de l'année passée, d'intenses discussions sur l'avenir de l'OTAN se sont développées au sein de l'influente communauté des « think-tanks » de Washington qui repose sur des experts non membres du gouvernement, y compris des diplomates et officiers militaires de premier rang à la retraite, mais qui fréquentent de près des fonctionnaires encore en service. Un tel réexamen de l'OTAN n'est ni inhabituel, ni nécessairement alarmant. De fait, cela fait des dizaines d'années que le dialogue transatlantique connaît certaines tensions.

---

[3] Voir par exemple "European Views of U.S. Leadership in World Affairs", dans "Transatlantic Trends 2008", une étude des attitudes européennes réalisée par le German Marshall Fund des Etats-Unis, disponible à l'adresse : http://www.transatlantictrends.org/trends/doc/2008_English_Key.pdf.

Rappelons par exemple les débats sur le réarmement de l'Allemagne et l'affaire de Suez dans les années 50, le retrait de la France des structures militaires de l'OTAN dans les années 60, les différentes approches face à la détente dans les années 1970, le déploiement de forces nucléaires intermédiaires dans les années 80 et les interventions de l'OTAN dans les guerres des Balkans dans les années 90. En fin de compte, l'Alliance s'est révélée forte et résistante parce que ses membres n'ont pas laissé leurs différences mettre en péril les intérêts et valeurs qu'ils partagent, que ce soi de façon superficielle ou en profondeur. De moins en moins d'experts américains pensent aujourd'hui que le passé peut servir de tremplin. Au contraire, ils sont de plus en plus préoccupés par l'éventuelle incapacité de l'Alliance de s'adapter suffisamment rapidement à l'évolution de l'environnement sécuritaire.

Le défi de l'Afghanistan

Beaucoup d'Américains sont d'avis que l'Afghanistan, pays pour lequel les alliés et partenaires européens contribuent à hauteur de 28 000 hommes environ sur les 59 000 soldats, dont près de 26 000 Américains, que compte la Force internationale d'assistance et de sécurité (FIAS)[4], sera déterminant pour la solidarité et la réussite de l'OTAN. Les responsables américains et européens s'accordent généralement pour dire que si l'Afghanistan devenait un pays en déliquescence, les réseaux terroristes s'y installeraient à nouveau, ce qui accroîtrait les menaces en Europe et aux Etats-Unis. Cependant, si les Américains continuent à soutenir fermement la mission en Afghanistan, le soutien des Européens en faveur de la FIAS diminue.

Les alliés et les partenaires européens ont promis d'accroître d'environ 5 000 soldats leurs contingents dans la FIAS, dans la dernière ligne droite précédant l'élection présidentielle en Afghanistan en août 2009 mais d'autres renforcements sont peu probables. De fait, certains alliés ont même prévu de réduire, voire de mettre fin, à leur rôle dans la FIAS au cours des deux prochaines années, notamment dans le Sud du pays où, contrairement aux attentes initiales, les missions de combat

---

[4] Source : Chiffres de l'OTAN en avril 2009. Le Canada (membre de l'OTAN) et l'Australie (non membre de l'OTAN) fournissent respectivement 2830 et 1090 hommes. Quelque 10 000 militaires américains supplémentaires servent en Afghanistan dans la task-force conjointe et combinée 101, dans le cadre de l'opération Liberté immuable (Enduring Freedom). Depuis la fin de 2008, toutes les forces américaines en Afghanistan relèvent du commandant de la FIAS, le général américain David McKiernan.

ont fréquemment éclipsé les missions de maintien de la paix et de reconstruction.

Les difficultés de l'OTAN à satisfaire les besoins des forces de la FIAS vont bien au-delà du besoin en hommes. Certains alliés continuent d'évoquer les « notifications d'avertissement (Caveats) » relatifs aux modalités et aux lieux d'utilisation de leurs forces par le commandant de la FIAS. La plupart des responsables politiques et militaires européens sont conscients des risques d'une OTAN à deux niveaux. Il est vrai que certains contributeurs importants à la FIAS se heurteraient à une forte opposition nationale si leurs gouvernements proposaient de déplacer leurs troupes des régions du Nord et de l'Ouest, relativement stables, vers des opérations plus risquées dans les régions du Sud et de l'Est. D'ailleurs, dans l'opinion publique de certains membres de l'Alliance, la réticence à voir leurs troupes de « maintien de la paix » attaquer les forces d'opposition est presque aussi forte que leur réaction en cas de victimes dans leurs propres contingents.

De plus, pour plusieurs des pays européens participant à la FIAS, les coûts à supporter deviennent de plus en plus lourds. Selon les règles applicables aux missions de l'OTAN, les nations doivent prendre à leur charge la majorité des dépenses liées à leur participation aux opérations, ce qui est particulièrement décourageant pour les alliés qui ont la volonté politique de maintenir ou d'accroître leurs contributions en hommes dans les missions les plus difficiles mais qui ne disposent pas de ressources budgétaires suffisantes pour le faire. Toutefois, certains alliés n'acceptent pas la suggestion visant à soutenir les opérations de l'OTAN par l'augmentation du financement commun ou à acquérir davantage de moyens collectifs. Certains semblent ne pas vouloir augmenter les capacités de peur d'avoir à les utiliser. D'autres encore, qui ont des budgets de défense limités et relativement stables, s'inquiètent certainement d'une augmentation du financement commun de l'OTAN qui se ferait au détriment de leur programme national.

L'Afghanistan suscite également des questions délicates sur le rôle de l'OTAN dans des missions de stabilisation de long terme. L'approche « globale » et « régionale » arrêtée au sommet de l'OTAN à Bucarest en 2008 et révisée au sommet de Strasbourg/Kehl en 2009 tend à associer l'assistance civile et militaire internationale au gouvernement afghan afin de recruter, entraîner et équiper des forces de sécurité compétentes, de développer l'économie, d'améliorer la gouvernance et le respect de l'Etat de droit et de s'attaquer au problème des stupéfiants. Toutefois, l'engagement militaire des Européens dans la reconstruction, la guerre contre la drogue et d'autres missions moins traditionnelles ne relève pas d'une approche commune. Et à Washington, beaucoup ont été déçus par la capacité et/ou la volonté des Européens à fournir des experts civils pour aider à la reconstruction de la capacité de développement et de gouvernance de l'Afghanistan, soit à travers des programmes nationaux, soit sous les auspices de l'Union européenne. De leur côté, certains responsables européens s'inquiètent en privé de l'intention des Etats-Unis de conduire l'OTAN à construire ses propres capacités civiles qu'elle pourrait utiliser parallèlement aux capacités militaires dans les opérations de stabilisation ; ces responsables craignent cette évolution car elle consisterait à dupliquer et à diminuer les efforts des Nations Unies, de l'Union européenne et des autres acteurs internationaux.

Les frustrations américaines dues à leurs alliés européens se multiplient depuis un moment déjà. En décembre dernier, sous couvert d'anonymat, un officier militaire américain exprimait le sentiment prédominant : « Il y a ceux (à Washington) qui diraient « Abandonnons l'OTAN une fois pour toutes ». Mais l'OTAN représente la réalité en Afghanistan et nous avons besoin que [les alliés] y réussissent »[5]. Les Etats-Unis disposent de moyens d'incitation importants pour essayer de renforcer l'engagement de l'Alliance en Afghanistan plutôt que de revenir à une approche de « coalition de volontaires », privilégiée par beaucoup dans l'administration Bush. En effet, sans sous-estimer les défis susmentionnés en Afghanistan, la capacité des Alliés à maintenir et même à accroître leur engagement dans la FIAS au cours de ces dernières années témoigne de la solidité des structures de l'Alliance en matière de consultation, de planification, de prise de décisions, de développement des capacités et de soutien mutuel dans les opérations difficiles.

Les questions sont néanmoins nombreuses. La décision des Etats-Unis d'accroître leurs forces en Afghanistan d'au moins 21 000 hommes durant l'année à venir va-t-elle permettre de stabiliser la sécurité ? Cette augmentation d'effectifs va-t-elle renforcer l'impression, en Europe, qu'il s'agit d'une « guerre américaine » et par là même renfor-

---

[5] "Officials work toward best Afghanistan strategy," *American Forces Press Service*, 12 décembre 2008.

cer les pressions, au sein de certains pays alliés, visant à diminuer leur participation militaire ? Et si l'engagement militaire des Européens dans la FIAS commence à s'éroder, maintiendront-ils leur promesse de contribuer davantage aux aspects non militaires de « l'approche globale », tels que la formation et l'encadrement de la police, le financement d'une importante armée nationale afghane, la recherche d'alternatives de développement durables pour remplacer la culture de pavot destiné à l'opium et enfin la création de capacités pour la mise en place de ministères civils et de gouvernements régionaux[6] ?

La détérioration rapide et récente de la situation au Pakistan pourrait renforcer les tensions au sein de l'Alliance. Suite au sommet de Strasbourg/Kehl, l'engagement de l'OTAN au Pakistan pourrait être accru par un renforcement de la coordination militaire, par une amélioration de l'engagement à haut niveau et par un meilleur accès des officiers pakistanais à des formations en Europe. Toutefois, à l'inverse des États-Unis, aucun des alliés européens ne semble prêt à envisager un engagement militaire au Pakistan, quel qu'il soit, en dépit des problèmes évidents posés à la FIAS par les caches des insurgés. En réalité, certains craignent qu'une pression militaire américaine accrue contre ces caches au Pakistan exacerbe davantage les tensions régionales. De plus, à quelques notables exceptions près, la plupart des Européens ne sont pas prêts à renforcer les liens politiques, économiques et de développement relativement limités qu'ils entretiennent avec le Pakistan. Si cette hésitation peut se comprendre, elle porte néanmoins en elle le risque que beaucoup d'Européens tiennent Washington pour responsable en cas d'effondrement du Pakistan.

Le facteur russe

L'engagement croissant de l'OTAN en Afghanistan a soulevé, dans plusieurs capitales européennes, des questions relatives à la stratégie d'ensemble de l'Alliance et à ses priorités. Plus particulièrement, l'attitude de la Russie en Géorgie et dans l'ancien espace soviétique, associée à des déclarations d'intention menaçantes telles la promesse de Medvedev de « protéger la vie et la dignité des citoyens (russes), où qu'ils se

---

[6] La stratégie d'une « approche globale » de l'OTAN pour l'Afghanistan est décrite dans la déclaration du Sommet de l'OTAN à Bucarest, accessible à l'adresse : http://www.summitbucharest.ro/fr/doc_201.html.

trouvent », a recentré l'attention sur le rôle de défense collective de l'OTAN.

L'amélioration des relations avec la Russie représentera un défi stratégique majeur pour les Etats-Unis et l'Europe[7]. Ceux qui, tel le secrétaire d'Etat à la Défense Robert Gates, croient que « l'incursion en Géorgie finira par être reconnue, au mieux, comme une victoire à la Pyrrhus ou comme une action stratégique trop ambitieuse et très coûteuse », pourraient avoir raison, à condition que l'Europe et les Etats-Unis puissent se mettre d'accord sur une politique à l'égard de la Russie qui soit « aussi durable et souple que ne l'était la politique d'endiguement pendant la Guerre froide »[8]. Pour l'instant, les Américains et les Européens n'ont toutefois pas la même appréciation des motivations et de la stratégie de la Russie, et il n'y a pas non plus d'accord au sein des Etats-Unis et de l'Europe. Certains considèrent largement les actions russes en Géorgie comme une action « unique », comme une démonstration de force opportuniste destinée à déstabiliser un voisin faible mais impulsif et à empêcher tout nouvel élargissement de l'OTAN. D'autres y voient une stratégie russe plus délibérée et plus globale pour décourager les investissements dans les gazoducs du Sud et intimider l'Ukraine et les autres voisins du « voisinage proche » de la Russie et progressivement semer la discorde à l'intérieur de l'Europe et le désaccord entre l'Europe et les Etats-Unis.

Il est certain que la Russie ne représente pas le type de menace existentielle posée par l'Union Soviétique et qu'aucun gouvernement allié ne défend ouvertement un retour aux modèles de la Guerre froide pour la défense du territoire. Mais beaucoup de responsables craignent que l'OTAN perde sa *raison d'être*, ainsi que le soutien vital du parlement et de la population en se focalisant sur des missions expéditionnaires qui semblent déconnectées des menaces plus immédiates contre les territoires nationaux. De fait, certains alliés, et notamment ceux qui sont les plus proches de la Russie, cela n'est pas surprenant, cherchent à avoir confirmation de la capacité de l'OTAN à tenir ses engagements de l'article 5 sur la défense collective. Plus précisément, ils veulent que l'Alliance fournisse une évaluation actualisée des menaces et un renforcement de la planification et des exercices des contingents de

---

[7] Voir aussi l'article de Celeste Wallander sur la Russie.
[8] Discours de Robert Gates à Oxford Analytica, Royaume-Uni, 19 septembre 2008 ; et Jim Hoagland, *Washington Post*, 17 août 2008.

l'OTAN visant à prévenir et si nécessaire à répondre à toute intimidation militaire potentielle par la Russie. D'autres alliés, plus éloignés de la Russie, se montrent moins inquiets pour leur sécurité face à d'éventuelles menaces militaires et pourraient considérer ces dispositions comme d'inutiles provocations. Dans ce dernier groupe, certains pays sont bien conscients de l'importance de leur dépendance à l'égard des approvisionnements énergétiques russes

Les Etats-Unis doivent être sensibles aux inquiétudes de ces deux groupes de pays mais ils sont aussi confrontés à d'autres préoccupations stratégiques telles que la garantie de la coopération russe sur les questions de non-prolifération, en Iran ou en Corée du nord par exemple, et lorsque cela est possible, pour combattre le terrorisme et les extrémismes. Ainsi, au regard des évolutions récentes au Pakistan et au Kirghizstan, la coopération avec la Russie est importante pour établir un réseau logistique flexible et fiable afin de soutenir les opérations en Afghanistan. De plus, Washington et Moscou vont bientôt entamer des négociations officielles afin de remplacer le traité de réduction des armes stratégiques de 1991, dit « START 1 » avant qu'il n'expire en décembre 2009. Trouver un juste équilibre entre la coopération avec la Russie quand cela est possible et une certaine résistance à sa mauvaise conduite quand c'est nécessaire relève sans aucun doute d'une saine stratégie. Mais cela ne garantit pas un accord au sein de l'Alliance sur les tactiques à appliquer aux diverses circonstances.

L'UE cherche à définir son rôle

Les menaces moins traditionnelles pesant sur la sécurité de l'Europe devenant plus nombreuses, l'OTAN va de plus en plus souvent devoir assurer la sécurité en coopération avec l'Europe. Presque 10 ans après son lancement officiel par quelques responsables européens, l'idée que la Politique européenne de sécurité et de défense (PESD) fasse « contrepoids » à l'influence américaine en Europe et au-delà a été largement discréditée. Néanmoins, si les gouvernements de l'UE ne sont souvent pas d'accord sur les priorités et ressources qu'ils sont disposés à accorder à la PESD, même les plus « atlantistes » d'entre eux ont fini par l'accepter comme un pilier légitime de l'influence mondiale de l'UE.

Désormais, la PESD est bien ancrée dans le cadre institutionnel et juridique de l'UE, avec des structures de prise de décisions civiles et militaires calquées sur celles de l'OTAN, mais avec des effectifs bien plus réduits. Elle repose sur la Stratégie européenne de sécurité, promulguée en 2003 et mise à jour en 2008, lors de la présidence française du Conseil de l'UE. Ce document définit une vision assez large des menaces, des objectifs politiques et des lignes directrices d'une action collective. Si l'on observe les opérations civiles et militaires menées dans le cadre de la PESD, plus de vingt à ce jour, qui se sont toutes déroulées dans le cadre de résolutions du Conseil de sécurité des Nations Unies approuvées par les Etats-Unis, le bilan est globalement positif, même si la plupart d'entre elles étaient de taille modeste, d'une durée limitée et peu risquées.

A l'intérieur de l'UE, le débat relatif à la PESD porte principalement sur le juste équilibre entre les moyens militaires et civils de gestion de crises et les modalités permettant d'améliorer les capacités militaires et civiles. Au départ, les actions de la PESD étaient principalement militaires, plutôt ambitieuses et largement influencées par « l'expérience » de l'incapacité de l'Europe à gérer elle-même le conflit des Balkans dans les années 1990. Dans « l'objectif global d'Helsinki » (Helsinki Headline Goal) en 1999, l'UE s'était par exemple engagée à développer, d'ici à 2003, la capacité de déployer, dans un délai de soixante jours, une force de 50 à 60 000 hommes sur des terrains de crises situés à des milliers de kilomètres de l'Europe et à l'y maintenir pendant au moins un an pour des missions humanitaires, de maintien de la paix et de séparation des parties en conflit.

Confrontée à une forte insuffisance en capacités, l'UE a revu ses ambitions en 2004, décidant la création de quinze « groupements tactiques » de bataillons renforcés (environ 1500 hommes). Deux de ces formations sont mobilisables pendant des périodes de six mois et devraient théoriquement pouvoir se déployer dans les dix jours qui suivent une décision de l'UE et rester en opération jusqu'à 120 jours. A ce jour, l'UE n'a pas déployé concrètement de groupement tactique mais selon certains responsables européens, l'Afrique serait particulièrement adaptée à leur déploiement.

Certains gouvernements de l'UE, la France en particulier, continuent à faire du développement d'éléments militaires « autonomes » au sein de la PESD une priorité. Ils favorisent la conduite régulière d'opérations militaires « autonomes » de plus en plus ambitieuses, c'est-à-dire des opérations sans l'assistance de l'OTAN par le biais des accords « Berlin Plus » de 2004, afin de démontrer concrètement la valeur de la PESD et de développer des habitudes de coopération intra-européennes. Au travers de programmes conjoints de recherche, de développement, de groupements et d'acquisitions menés par l'Agence européenne de défense (AED), ils cherchent également à encourager l'augmentation des dépenses de défense et le renforcement de la base industrielle de défense européenne.

Les limites de ces efforts sont néanmoins devenues plus visibles au cours de ces dernières années. Concernant les opérations militaires, la première mission maritime de la PESD, composée de navires et d'avions de patrouille destinés à protéger les bateaux au large des côtes somaliennes, est opérationnelle depuis décembre 2008. La force européenne s'inscrit dans un effort international de lutte contre la piraterie qui comprend des bateaux de l'OTAN et de partenaires tels que la Chine et l'Inde. La force de l'UE a capturé quelques pirates et sans doute dissuadé quelques attaques mais les responsables européens reconnaissent que la véritable solution réside dans la restauration de la sécurité et de la stabilité sur le sol somalien par les autorités gouvernementales elles-mêmes, ce qui serait une immense tâche que l'UE, à l'instar des autres organisations internationales, préférerait éviter. Dans d'autres régions d'Afrique, on peut considérer comme une réussite la mission d'un an qui s'est récemment terminée au Tchad et en République Centrafricaine et qui a respecté son mandat, certes limité mais les efforts déployés pour y parvenir, largement encouragés et soutenus par les Français, se sont avérés plus difficiles et plus coûteux que prévu. La lassitude d'action des Etats membres de l'UE explique sans doute largement pourquoi la présidence française de l'UE a refusé d'accéder, à l'automne 2008, à la demande du Secrétaire Général des Nations Unies d'envoyer une nouvelle force de l'UE en renfort des 17 000 « casques bleus » dans l'Est de la République démocratique du Congo. Alors que plusieurs Etats membres de l'UE, également membres de l'OTAN, ont des difficultés à maintenir ou à accroître de façon marginale leur contribution à la FIAS, ils seront probablement peu enclins à accepter de nouveaux engagements militaires au sein de l'UE.

De même, un rapport de juillet 2008[9] réalisé par l'ancien directeur général de l'Agence européenne de défense, Nick Witney, dresse un bilan décevant du développement des capacités de l'UE. Le résumé du rapport souligne ainsi : « Près de 20 ans après la fin de la Guerre Froide, la plupart des armées européennes sont davantage prêtes à réagir à une guerre totale sur l'ancienne frontière entre les deux Allemagne, qu'à maintenir la paix au Tchad ou à contribuer à la sécurité et au développement en Afghanistan. Les ressources de la défense européenne continuent à être consacrées à l'entretien de 10 000 chars, de 2 500 avions de combat et de près de 2 millions d'hommes et de femmes en uniforme, soit plus d'un demi million de plus que l'hyper-puissance américaine. Mais 70% des forces terrestres de l'Europe sont tout simplement incapables d'être opérationnelles en dehors du territoire national tandis que les avions de transport, les communications, les drones de surveillance et les hélicoptères (sans compter les policiers et les experts de l'administration civile) manquent de façon chronique. Cette incapacité à moderniser les moyens disponibles signifie qu'une bonne partie des 200 milliards € que l'Europe dépense chaque année pour la défense est purement et simplement gâchée ».

La persistance de budgets de défense peu élevés en Europe empêche d'investir massivement dans les programmes de l'Agence européenne de défense, notamment lorsque certains Etats membres les considèrent comme une duplication des efforts de l'OTAN ou comme biaisés afin d'avantager l'industrie de défense d'un autre Etat membre.

De plus en plus, de nombreux membres de l'UE considèrent leurs capacités civiles, et notamment l'encadrement de la police, les experts judiciaires, les maisons d'arrêt, les douanes et l'administration publique, comme des outils vitaux à déployer lors d'opérations de prévention ou de gestion de crises. Ces capacités peuvent être associées à une assistance financière et à une aide au développement de l'UE et, en théorie, à une composante militaire de la PESD[10]. Mais comme le suggère M. Witney, l'engagement, la formation et le déploiement de civils qualifiés

---

[9] Nick Witney, "Re-energizing Europe's Security and Defence Policy," European Council of Foreign Relations, 29 juillet 2008, disponible à l'adresse : www.ecfr.eu/content/entry/european_security_and_defence_policy.

[10] À ce jour, cependant, la plupart des opérations militaires de la PESD n'ont pas été accompagnées d'une importante composante civile de l'UE, en partie car ces opérations ont été relativement courtes.

à ces fins n'a pas été facile, notamment quand l'UE s'est retrouvée elle-même concurrencée par ses propres membres.

Les gouvernements européens vont rester attentifs à la protection de leurs prérogatives nationales dans la conduite des politiques étrangère, de défense et de sécurité. Comme le fait remarquer M. Witney, aucun Etat Membre « n'acceptera d'être obligé d'entrer en conflit ou de modifier les dépenses de son budget de défense par « Bruxelles », qu'il s'agisse d'une institution européenne ou de la majorité de ses partenaires »[11]. Cependant, la tendance de ces dix dernières années visant une plus grande coordination au sein de l'UE a peu de chances de s'inverser et pourrait même s'accélérer si l'UE arrive à surmonter le revers de la ratification du traité de Lisbonne qu'a occasionné l'échec du référendum en Irlande en juin 2008.

Vers une architecture de défense et de sécurité plus souple

D'un point de vue américain, les tensions évidentes au sein de l'OTAN et de l'UE, associées à la hausse des demandes d'action émanant du monde entier, renforcent l'argument d'une coopération plus étroite entre les deux organisations. Heureusement, la plupart des Européens ne contestent plus ce point. Les demandes de déploiement d'opérations adressées aux forces d'intervention limitées de l'UE associées aux prévisions réduites de dépenses en matière de défense, constituent, pour chacune des deux organisations, un frein important aux incitations à élargir les missions existantes ou à créer de nouvelles structures qui seraient potentiellement des doublons. Concernant la doctrine, la formation et l'interopérabilité des équipements, les commandants militaires européens sont conscients que des pratiques contradictoires au sein de l'OTAN et de l'UE conduiraient à augmenter le risque inhérent aux opérations militaires.

Quelques signes timides montrent que la coopération entre l'OTAN et l'UE fonctionnerait mieux en pratique qu'en théorie. Au Kosovo, la Force pour le Kosovo (KFOR) de l'OTAN, avec ses 14 000 hommes, travaille avec la mission Etat de droit (EULEX) de l'UE qui compte près de 1900 officiers de police, juges, avocats et douaniers de tous les pays. En vertu d'un accord sans précédent et prometteur d'octobre 2008, quelque 100 formateurs de police travaillent au sein d'EULEX.

---

[11] Ibid.

En Afghanistan, près de 200 formateurs de police européens (EUPOL) viennent compléter la coalition d'entraîneurs, bien plus nombreux, dirigée par les États-Unis et l'UE vient d'accepter de doubler les effectifs d'EUPOL. Une coopération pragmatique sur ces deux champs d'opération est cependant limitée par l'absence d'accords officiels entre les deux organisations et par leur dialogue limité aux niveaux supérieurs à Bruxelles.

Un certain nombre de mesures pourraient améliorer la situation, par exemple : des réunions plus fréquentes et mieux structurées entre le Conseil de l'Atlantique Nord de l'OTAN et le Comité politique et de sécurité de l'UE, pour permettre aux deux organisations de se consulter réellement sur les questions d'intérêt mutuel, au-delà de leur coopération en Bosnie ; un mécanisme de planification conjointe OTAN-UE centré sur un développement et une mise en œuvre plus systématique de « l'approche globale », par opposition aux accords ad hoc et improvisés observés en Afghanistan et au Kosovo ; une meilleure coopération opérationnelle en matière de développement des capacités. Il faut noter la réaction positive de Washington à la suggestion de la France, en 2008, de créer un groupe informel de haut niveau, qui comprendrait le Secrétaire Général de l'OTAN et le Haut Représentant de l'UE, les présidents des comités militaires respectifs, les principaux commandants d'opérations militaires de chaque organisation et un représentant de la Commission européenne, qui se réunirait au début des discussions et de la planification d'une nouvelle opération[12].

Bien que certains spécialistes européens de la sécurité aient proposé « une division du travail » formelle entre les deux organisations, elle est improbable dans un avenir proche. Les gouvernements de l'UE auraient du mal à se mettre d'accord sur un « plafond » fixe d'opérations militaires dans le cadre de la PESD, que ce soit en termes de types de mission, de composition et de capacités des forces, et de régions d'intervention, tout comme l'OTAN aurait du mal à fixer un « plancher » à son engagement. De même, aucune des deux organisa-

---

[12] Dans une déclaration publiée à l'issue du sommet de l'UE des 11-12 décembre 2008, le Conseil européen « réaffirme également l'objectif de renforcer le partenariat stratégique entre l'UE et l'OTAN afin de faire face aux besoins actuels, dans un esprit de renforcement mutuel et de respect de leur autonomie de décision. À cette fin, il appuie l'établissement d'un groupe informel à haut niveau UE-OTAN afin d'améliorer de façon pragmatique la coopération entre les deux organisations sur le terrain ». A ce jour, aucune action ne semble avoir été prise pour établir effectivement ce groupe.

tions ne subordonnera à l'autre son autonomie de décision, et il ne faut pas s'attendre à ce qu'elles le fassent, et aucune d'elles ne devrait chercher à s'immiscer systématiquement dans des missions conduites ou envisagées par l'autre partie.

Certaines différences supposées en termes de niveau d'ambition existent toutefois déjà dans chaque organisation. Ainsi, aucun des membres de l'UE n'est prêt à s'engager dans des opérations de combat à grande échelle sans les États-Unis, bien que seul le Royaume-Uni l'ait exprimé aussi explicitement. D'autre part, de nombreux Européens pensent que l'UE a un avantage comparatif grâce à l'éventail de moyens civils et militaires et de développement dont elle dispose pour la prévention et la gestion de crises dans certaines parties d'Afrique. Et ce n'est pas remis en question par Washington, comme en témoignent les déclarations faites par de hauts responsables américains au début de l'année 2008.

Les objectifs à long terme des relations OTAN-UE devraient être d'assurer la transparence, d'éviter les contradictions dans leurs approches respectives et aussi de développer de nouvelles capacités et d'apporter de la « valeur ajoutée » à la prévention des conflits et à la gestion des crises. En adaptant le concept militaire « d'interopérabilité », par exemple dans la doctrine, les niveaux d'équipement et la façon d'opérer, à la relation OTAN-UE, les deux organisations disposeraient de meilleurs outils de coopération lorsqu'une décision politique est prise en ce sens, renforçant l'opportunité et la réussite de leur effort commun[13].

En même temps, la coopération en matière de sécurité euro-atlantique ne peut être limitée à la relation OTAN-UE. La mondialisation a brouillé les lignes de démarcation entre la sécurité « extérieure » et « intérieure » (ou « nationale »). Les principales sources de préoccupation des Européens relèvent des compétences de structures de l'UE qui n'ont que peu ou pas de lien avec les instruments de la PESD, comme par exemple l'immigration illégale, l'extrémisme « endogène », les crimes transnationaux, la protection des infrastructures sensibles et la sécurité environnementale. Alors que ce type de problèmes peut avoir de sérieux impacts sur les relations transatlantiques, beaucoup ont des

---

[13] Voir, par exemple, la déclaration du Représentant permanent des États-Unis à l'OTAN, l'Ambassadeur Victoria Nuland, à Paris en février 2008, accessible à l'adresse : http://nato.usmission.gov/Article.asp?ID=21A35613-E9D6-431D-9FD5-36FDD1389EB0.

rapports directs limités, voire nuls, avec les compétences centrales de l'OTAN. On ne s'étonnera donc pas que de nombreux analystes européens et américains soient favorables à un renforcement de la relation entre les Etats-Unis et l'Union européenne.

Il existe déjà une relation bilatérale forte, qui ne cesse de se renforcer, entre les Etats-Unis et l'UE, dans les domaines du maintien de l'ordre, de la lutte contre le terrorisme et les stupéfiants, de la sécurité des transports et de la non-prolifération. D'autres domaines de coopération doivent se développer, concernant la mise en place d'une aide humanitaire par exemple. L'Union européenne étant de plus en plus souvent le théâtre des discussions stratégiques et de la prise de décision sur les questions de sécurité qui n'impliquent pas d'engagements militaires, comme par exemple la question des ambitions nucléaires de l'Iran, les Etats-Unis vont vouloir s'assurer que leur point de vue est bien pris en compte avant que les politiques européennes ne soient figées. La question politique régulièrement posée à Washington peut alors être délicate : où tracer la limite entre la discussion des questions stratégiques au sein de l'OTAN, où les Etats-Unis disposent d'un siège à la table des négociations, et avec l'UE, dont les Etats-Unis sont un interlocuteur et non un membre à part entière ?

Une autre question délicate concerne les suggestions faites par certains responsables et analystes européens selon lesquelles, compte tenu des blocages politiques existant dans les relations OTAN-UE, les Etats-Unis et l'UE devraient élargir leurs liens bilatéraux aux questions de défense. Il existe néanmoins des limites inhérentes aux relations bilatérales entre les États-Unis et l'UE concernant les questions de défense. L'un des facteurs est la non-adéquation évidente des appartenances : 21 des 27 membres de l'Union européenne sont certes aussi des alliés de l'OTAN mais les Etats-Unis ne vont pas mettre en péril leurs relations militaires et politiques avec les alliés non-membres de l'UE (Canada, Turquie, Norvège et Islande) en évitant les comités de l'OTAN pour consulter, planifier et lancer des opérations avec les autres alliés, membres de l'UE. Un second facteur, bien que moins évident, est tout aussi important : la force et l'efficacité de l'OTAN tiennent en grande partie à ses structures civiles et militaires multinationales (et à plusieurs niveaux) dans lesquelles les Américains, les Canadiens et les Européens se retrouvent côte à côte pour discuter, planifier, décider et mettre en œuvre de nombreuses tâches politiques et militaires. Une relation bilatérale Etats-Unis-UE ne comporterait pas ces structures, et il est difficile de voir comment celles-ci pourraient être compatibles avec l'importance de prise de décisions et de capacités « autonomes » soulignée par l'UE. Il n'y a d'ailleurs aucune raison valable pour les dupliquer puisqu'elles existent déjà dans l'OTAN. Un troisième facteur relève de la raison d'être même de la PESD : si l'Union européenne envisage sérieusement la création de nouvelles capacités pouvant être utilisées « de façon autonome », on ne voit pas bien pourquoi encourager une dépendance de l'UE à l'égard des moyens et des capacités des Etats-Unis afin d'accomplir les opérations de l'UE. Il ne faut pas pour autant fermer la porte à une coopération modeste et au cas par cas, par exemple entre le commandement des Etats-Unis en Afrique et les Européens qui apportent en Afrique une aide réelle et précieuse, mais ceci ne justifierait pas de consacrer tous les moyens militaires américains à une coopération régulière avec l'UE, comme c'est le cas pour l'OTAN.

Suggestions pour un programme de coopération franco-américaine

Washington et Paris ont tout intérêt à renforcer les liens transatlantiques en matière de sécurité et de défense qui concernent l'OTAN, la relation OTAN-UE et la coopération bilatérale.

Actuellement, sur le terrain des opérations, les militaires français et américains coopèrent, principalement en Afghanistan et au Kosovo, et il ne fait pas de doute qu'ils coopéreront à l'avenir dans des missions, des théâtres d'opération et des structures de nature diverse à l'intérieur et à l'extérieur de l'Europe. Pour ce faire, ils doivent pouvoir communiquer, échanger des informations, se former ensemble, se proposer un soutien mutuel et, quand nécessaire, combattre côte à côte. Une vaste coopération entre les Etats-Unis et la France existe aussi dans de nombreux domaines non militaires qui ont leur importance pour la sécurité nationale des deux pays, tels que les services de renseignement, la lutte contre le terrorisme et les réponses d'urgence aux catastrophes civiles[14].

De plus, les politiques de la France relatives à la défense et à la sécurité nationale ainsi que ses capacités influencent, directement ou non,

[14] Voir, par exemple, Dana Priest, "Help from France Key in Covert Operations," *The Washington Post*, 3 juillet 2005.

celles d'autres alliés ou partenaires de premier plan. Des différences d'ordre politique ou tactique apparaissent régulièrement entre Washington et Paris à l'OTAN, dans les relations OTAN-UE et sur les théâtres d'opération, comme c'est parfois le cas avec d'autres pays d'Europe. Toutefois, les intérêts des Etats-Unis sont globalement mieux servis par une structure de défense et de sécurité nationale française plus compétente, plus réactive et plus coopérative qui encourage ses compatriotes européens, en pratique comme en théorie, à accroître leurs capacités militaires et à les mettre à la disposition des missions de l'OTAN et de l'UE. Ce serait exagéré de suggérer que pour avoir un partenaire européen plus compétent, les États-Unis doivent passer par Paris, en dépit de l'influence française dans l'UE. Cependant, il ne faudrait pas sous-estimer les avantages, pour les questions de défense, d'une plus grande convergence des approches américaine et française.

Ainsi, en Afghanistan, l'accroissement de la participation française dans les opérations de combat depuis mi-2008 aide à renforcer la solidarité de l'Alliance dans une opération qui se poursuivra sans doute pendant plusieurs années. Dans ce contexte, il est important de noter la déclaration du général Jean-Louis Georgelin, chef d'état-major des armées françaises lors d'un entretien en octobre 2008 : « Ce que je regrette, c'est que dans une coalition internationale, les Nations placent ce que l'on appelle des caveats, c'est-à-dire des restrictions à l'emploi de la force, ce qui obère, d'une manière lourde, la liberté d'action du commandant de la FIAS. Supposez que vous ayez besoin d'une action temporaire extrêmement forte dans le Sud de l'Afghanistan, et que vous estimiez que la région Nord soit plus calme, le commandant de la force n'a pas la latitude de faire basculer les forces du Nord au profit des forces du Sud, puisqu'il y a un caveat. Il n'a donc pas une liberté d'action totale, les caveats sont un peu le poison des organisations internationales»[15].

Il ne fait aucun doute que les chefs militaires américains partagent l'avis du général Georgelin qui est d'autant plus intéressant en raison de l'exemple cité et du fait que le partenaire le plus proche de la France, l'Allemagne, dirige la majorité des forces dans le Nord.

---

[15] Voir, par exemple, Dana Priest, "Help from France Key in Covert Operations," *The Washington Post*, 3 juillet 2005.

Concernant l'OTAN, les Etats-Unis ont salué pour plusieurs raisons le renforcement de la participation française annoncé par le président Sarkozy lors du Sommet de Strasbourg-Kehl. L'arrivée de nouveaux officiers et sous-officiers français de talent dans la structure militaire intégrée apportera de nouvelles compétences de commandement et de planification afin d'améliorer la performance de l'OTAN dans ses opérations, qui s'avèrent de plus en plus exigeantes et complexes. Alors que les responsables français n'ont pas exprimé publiquement leur vision d'une nouvelle structure de commandement avec de nouveaux quartiers généraux, ils apparaissent favorables au réalignement et à la réduction des effectifs militaires de l'OTAN, ouvrant ainsi la voie à une coopération étroite avec les Etats-Unis et les autres alliés désireux d'améliorer l'efficacité et de redistribuer équitablement les responsabilités et les charges. Sur le plan civil, en sa qualité de membre du comité des plans de défense, la France peut contribuer à améliorer la cohérence du processus de planification des forces de planification qui permet à l'OTAN d'identifier ses besoins militaires afin d'atteindre le niveau général d'ambition établi par ses responsables politiques.

Contrairement à l'opinion exprimée par certains commentateurs et responsables politiques français avant la décision du président Sarkozy, il ne s'agit pas uniquement d'évolutions symboliques ou de « concessions » faites aux Etats-Unis. Chaque mesure prise par la France pour améliorer l'efficacité et la cohésion de l'OTAN finira, tôt ou tard, par profiter à la PESD. Cela vaut pour le développement des capacités, l'interopérabilité (de la doctrine, de la formation et des équipements) et les résultats dans les opérations actuelles. Si l'on garde en mémoire la forte imbrication des appartenances à l'OTAN et à l'UE et le fait que chacun des membres dispose de ses propres forces et de son propre budget de défense, l'OTAN n'est pas seulement un moyen pour la France de coopérer avec les Etats-Unis : c'est aussi un mécanisme vital pour la coopération intra-européenne. Lorsque le président Sarkozy a dévoilé *Le Livre blanc sur la défense et la sécurité nationale*, il a eu raison de réprimander ses compatriotes « [l'OTAN] est bien sûr l'alliance entre les Européens et les États-Unis. Mais c'est aussi, on ne le dit pas assez, un traité d'alliance entre les nations européennes elles-mêmes »[16].

---

[16] Discours du président de la République sur la défense et la sécurité nationale, 17 juin 2008, disponible à l'adresse : http://www.elysee.fr/documents/index.php?mode=cview&press_id=1513&cat_id=7&lang=fr.

La décision de la France de « prendre toute sa place » au sein de l'alliance devrait contribuer à élargir, au 21ème siècle, le dialogue stratégique avec les Etats-Unis aux questions de dissuasion nucléaire, de rapport à la non-prolifération et de défense anti-missile. Dans son article, Bruno Tertrais se demande si l'administration Obama souhaite mettre l'accent sur l'objectif « d'un monde libre d'armes nucléaires », indiquant que cela pourrait se heurter au « conservatisme traditionnel » de la France sur les questions nucléaires. A première vue, ses préoccupations pourraient sembler justifiées par le discours à Prague du président américain qui déclarait : « les Etats-Unis vont prendre des mesures concrètes en faveur d'un monde sans armes nucléaire. Pour mettre fin à la pensée de la Guerre froide, nous allons réduire le rôle des armes nucléaires dans notre stratégie de sécurité nationale et encourager les autres pays à en faire de même ». Mais il est important ici de se rappeler la phrase suivante énoncée par le président : « Ne vous y trompez pas : aussi longtemps que ces armes existeront, les Etats-Unis maintiendront un arsenal sûr, sécurisé et efficace afin de dissuader tout adversaire et de garantir la défense de nos alliés, y compris la République tchèque»[17].

De mon point de vue, les remarques du Secrétaire d'Etat à la Défense Robert Gates, le seul membre du cabinet de Bush invité par Obama à rester à son poste, constituent un bon indicateur de l'approche de la nouvelle Administration. Comme il le disait en octobre 2008 : « Il ne faut pas ignorer les efforts faits par les Etats voyous tels que la Corée du Nord et l'Iran pour développer et déployer les armes nucléaires, ni les programmes de modernisation stratégique de la Russie et de la Chine. Tant que les autres Etats ont ou cherchent à avoir des armes nucléaires, et qu'ils peuvent potentiellement nous menacer ainsi que nos alliés et nos amis, nous devons disposer d'une capacité de dissuasion montrant clairement que tout défi lancé aux Etats-Unis dans le domaine nucléaire, ou avec d'autres armes de destruction massive, pourrait entraîner une réponse massive et effroyable... Qu'on le veuille ou non, la puissance des armes nucléaires et leur impact stratégique est comme un génie qu'on ne peut pas remettre dans la bouteille, du moins pendant très longtemps. Si notre objectif de long terme vise à abolir

---

[17] op. cit., Discours à Prague.

définitivement les armes nucléaires, étant donné le monde dans lequel nous vivons, nous devons rester réalistes à cet égard»[18].

Il est certain qu'il s'agit là d'un sujet sensible mais les Etats-Unis et la France, tout comme le Royaume-Uni, voudront éviter d'être progressivement isolés, ou presque, au sein de la communauté transatlantique du fait de leur besoin de maintenir des forces nucléaires crédibles et sûres. Si les responsables français venaient à conclure que le soutien politique des Européens à la dissuasion nucléaire était mis à rude épreuve, ils pourraient être amenés à reconsidérer les avantages à rejoindre une structure de l'OTAN dans laquelle les questions nucléaires pourraient être discutées. Cela impliquerait de renommer et de restructurer l'actuel Groupe des plans nucléaires (l'un des comités de l'OTAN que la France n'a pas encore rejoint) afin d'inscrire dans ses compétences les politiques de lutte contre la prolifération et de défense anti-missile, domaines qui intéressent fortement la France en dépit de quelques différences avec les Etats-Unis. Ainsi, la France pourrait contribuer à maintenir un consensus européen sur la nécessité d'une composante nucléaire dans la stratégie plus large de dissuasion et de défense de l'OTAN.

En principe, cela pourrait se faire sans avoir à franchir l'une des lignes rouges du Livre blanc en ce qui concerne le respect de « l'indépendance » et de « l'autonomie » nucléaire de la France. Dans cette optique, la politique nucléaire britannique pourrait être un modèle pertinent pour la France car elle souligne que « la prise de décision et l'utilisation du système [nucléaire] continuent à relever entièrement de la souveraineté du Royaume-Uni [et] seul le premier ministre peut autoriser l'utilisation de la force de dissuasion nucléaire britannique, même si les missiles sont lancés dans le cadre d'une réponse de l'OTAN »[19].

La question russe est un autre domaine dans lequel un dialogue stratégique entre les Etats-Unis et la France pourrait jouer un rôle

---

[18] Discours à la Carnegie Endowment for International Peace, 28 octobre 2008. Accessible à l'adresse : http://www.defenselink.mil/speeches/speech.aspx?speechid=1305.

[19] Ministère de la Défense, "The Future of the United Kingdom's Nuclear Deterrent: Defence White Paper 2006" (L'avenir de la dissuasion nucléaire du Royaume-Uni: Livre blanc sur la défense 2006), disponible à l'adresse : www.mod.uk/DefenceInternet/AboutDefence/CorporatePublications/PolicyStrategyandPlanning/HeFutureOfTheUnitedKingdomsNuclearDeterrentDefenceWhitePaper2006cm6994.htm.

positif en développant un consensus euro-atlantique plus fort. Ici, l'attitude de Washington à l'égard du rôle de la présidence française du Conseil de l'UE dans le conflit russo-géorgien peut s'avérer instructive. En dépit de quelques différences tactiques entre Paris et Washington, cette dernière a en effet accepté de s'écarter, sans pour autant se retirer complètement, lorsque le président Sarkozy a négocié un cessez-le-feu entre les parties et mobilisé le soutien de l'UE par une mission civile de surveillance en Géorgie. Certes, il s'agissait d'un accord imparfait mais si ces efforts avaient été conduits par les États-Unis, les résultats auraient sans doute été encore plus problématiques. Dans le même temps, l'envoi rapide d'une aide humanitaire et de reconstruction civile américaine en Géorgie tout comme les visites à Tbilissi de hauts responsables américains suite à la conclusion du cessez-le-feu du président Sarkozy ont permis aux Etats-Unis de rester présents, en affichant une solidarité générale et non une concurrence avec les efforts de l'UE. Il ne s'agit peut-être pas d'un modèle de coopération transatlantique parfait pour l'avenir, mais il pourrait bien s'agir d'un pas dans la bonne direction.

Dans tous ces efforts, le ton des relations Etats-Unis/France sera d'une importance vitale. De nombreux Américains font régulièrement référence au « leadership » américain au sein de l'Alliance, pensant que ce concept reflète fidèlement des faits objectifs, et notamment les disparités réelles en termes de capacités militaires entre les Etats-Unis et nos alliés. En revanche, pour beaucoup en France, et sans aucun doute aussi ailleurs en Europe, la notion de « leadership américain » est parfois considérée comme une notion désuète de la Guerre froide, ou pire comme l'expression, par une hyper-puissance imparfaite, d'une domination qui énerve. Il est intéressant de se demander si les Etats-Unis pourraient mieux atteindre leurs objectifs de long terme en faisant moins référence à leur rôle de « leadership » et en faisant davantage ce qu'ils ont souvent si bien fait, mais pas toujours, à savoir consulter, écouter et agir résolument, toujours dans un esprit de véritable partenariat, comme un catalyseur, un constructeur et un défenseur ultime d'une communauté transatlantique démocratique et prospère. Ainsi, les Américains seront obligés, de temps en temps, de laisser davantage de place à nos alliés européens et de leur accorder une plus grande confiance. Le président Obama et ses principaux conseillers en sécurité nationale semblent prêts à agir ainsi, comme en témoigne leurs déclarations en Europe.

Dans le même temps, les dirigeants français devront être réalistes concernant leurs capacités nationales et leur vision de la défense européenne. Dans le cadre de l'Alliance, de l'UE et des relations bilatérales avec les États-Unis, les Français devront aussi continuer à chercher des solutions pragmatiques et « gagnant-gagnant » même si, politiquement, elles ne sont pas les plus visibles. A long terme, une approche qui reflète réellement la perception du président Sarkozy selon laquelle l'OTAN est une « une alliance de nations européennes elles-mêmes » va renforcer les partenariats et le poids de la France au sein de l'Europe, ainsi que ses relations avec les Etats-Unis.

Troisième partie :

points de vue régionaux

Chapitre cinq

Les priorités américaines d'une stratégie transatlantique pour la Russie

Celeste A. Wallander

Le président Barack Obama doit faire face en 2009 à de fortes attentes et à d'importantes préoccupations concernant les relations entre les États-Unis et la Russie. Les relations entre les deux pays n'ont jamais été aussi mauvaises depuis la fin de la Guerre froide, et sont peut-être même plus mauvaises encore que pendant les dernières années de la Guerre froide, lorsque l'Union soviétique (dirigée par Gorbatchev) et les États-Unis (sous l'ère Reagan puis sous l'ère Bush I) étaient parvenus à négocier toute une série d'accords approfondis et de vaste portée concernant la sécurité/défense ou encore les domaines politique, économique et social/culturel. La maîtrise des armements diminue et pourrait même disparaître : les traités existants sur les armes stratégiques sont sur le point d'expirer, la Russie menace de se retirer du Traité sur les forces nucléaires à portée intermédiaire, elle a suspendu son adhésion au Traité sur les forces conventionnelles en Europe et il existe un risque, faible mais néanmoins dangereux, que les États-Unis et la Russie se lancent dans une nouvelle course aux armements sur les systèmes antimissiles balistiques, réarmement qui avait si bien été évité pendant la Guerre froide et qui en avait été l'un des principaux succès en matière de sécurité.

Concernant la politique de sécurité, les responsables russes ont clairement montré qu'ils considèrent l'OTAN, l'un des principaux engagements des États-Unis en matière de sécurité globale, comme incompatible avec les intérêts nationaux de la Russie en Eurasie, et même comme une menace. Ils considèrent la politique américaine comme une politique d'encerclement destinée à contenir, affaiblir et peut-être même démanteler la Fédération de Russie. Pour leur part, les spécialistes et les responsables politiques américains sont de plus en plus nombreux à penser que les objectifs de sécurité de la Russie consistent à neutraliser ses voisins de l'ancien empire russe/soviétique, voire peut-être à les subordonner. L'utilisation par la Russie d'instruments politiques, économiques, énergétiques et cybernétiques pour corrompre l'indépendance et la souveraineté de ses voisins n'avait suscité que de légères inquiétudes en Occident qui se sont fortement aggravées lorsque la Russie s'est montrée prête à utiliser la force en août 2008, en envahissant et en occupant son voisin, la Géorgie. Peut-être ne s'agit-il que de fausses perceptions et d'un manque d'assurance, mais les raisons de penser que la Russie et les États-Unis sont enfermés dans des conceptions incompatibles de la sécurité en Eurasie sont de plus en plus nombreuses : les Américains voient la sécurité en termes d'intégration euro-atlantique et globale tandis que la vision russe est fondée sur une zone « d'intérêts privilégiés » dans laquelle les voisins ne sont pas autorisés à choisir les relations politique, économique, sécuritaire, etc. qu'ils peuvent entretenir avec les autres pays.

Sur le plan économique, la situation est un peu moins grave, mais uniquement car les relations économiques entre les États-Unis et la Russie sont peu développées, ce qui limite les conflits d'intérêts directs. Les États-Unis n'ont toujours pas supprimé l'application de l'amendement Jackson-Vanik à la Russie, même si les raisons justifiant cette restriction commerciale (restrictions soviétiques à l'égard des émigrants juifs) sont désormais obsolètes, ce qui conduit à l'absurdité, pour le pouvoir exécutif américain, de devoir chaque année renouveler une dérogation à cette restriction. La Russie n'est toujours par membre de l'Organisation mondiale du commerce (OMC). Les responsables russes (et l'opinion publique) acceptent mal ces deux restrictions considérées, non sans raison, comme des sanctions politiques inutiles de la part d'un pays qui prône des théories économiques et d'affaires dissociées du politique.

Cette triste situation n'est pas due au conflit entre la Russie et la Géorgie : la guerre et la querelle actuelle sur sa résolution témoignent de la gravité du problème et illustrent le danger de continuer à prendre le défi de la Russie au sérieux. Rendre cette relation pragmatique et coopérative pourrait être dangereux pour l'avenir de la sécurité de l'Europe car la détérioration des relations États-Unis/Russie a également compliqué les politiques européennes à l'égard de la Russie. Une véritable politique américaine à l'égard de la Russie doit comporter une dimension transatlantique et les relations UE-Russie ne seront véritablement plausibles que si les États-Unis et la Russie coopèrent pour résoudre les problèmes politiques, économiques et de sécurité.

La Russie qui nous fait face

La Russie n'est pas une démocratie : les élections n'y sont pas libres et régulières, le pluralisme, avec des politiques concurrentes ou alternatives, n'est pas de mise durant les campagnes électorales, tandis que le dépouillement et le déroulement des scrutins n'est pas surveillé par des observateurs internationaux ou nationaux crédibles ou indépendants. Les raisons pour lesquelles les responsables russes ne souhaitent pas autoriser d'élections libres et régulières sont loin d'être évidentes : avec des taux d'approbation de l'ordre de 70-80%, il est fort probable que Vladimir Poutine (et le parti politique qu'il dirige désormais, Russie Unie) l'emporterait, même s'il s'agissait d'élections légitimes. Les responsables russes en savent peut-être plus que nous mais quoiqu'il en soit, le processus électoral en Russie ne laisse pas beaucoup de doute quant aux résultats...

L'absence de médias professionnels indépendants capables de rendre compte des actions et des fautes du gouvernement rend par essence impossible, pour les citoyens russes, de tenir le gouvernement pour responsable des politiques et des résultats obtenus. L'atmosphère d'intimidation est telle que même des journalistes indépendants ont tendance à s'autocensurer, même si leur journal n'est pas directement contrôlé ou possédé par l'État. Les rédacteurs en chef et les reporters savent que certaines affaires ou certains thèmes ne doivent pas être abordés, sauf à en subir les conséquences. Si tous les reportages indépendants n'ont pas pour autant disparu, ils sont néanmoins sévèrement limités.

Les limites de la contestation ne s'arrêtent pas aux adversaires politiques et aux médias. Les milieux d'affaires et la société civile sont autorisés tant qu'ils ne défient pas les autorités politiques et ne leur demandent rien. Début 2005, les manifestations des retraités contre la monétisation de leurs allocations sociales ont été remarquées, précisément car elles étaient inhabituelles. Les intérêts privés sont présents dans la sphère politique russe : non pas en tant qu'acteurs indépendants s'adressant aux responsables politiques qui les représentent ou réclament leur soutien, mais à l'inverse en tant qu'intérêts ou individus dont le succès dans les affaires dépend de leur acceptation de règles et de demandes formulées par les responsables politiques. Ceci conduit certains à qualifier la Russie d'Etat corporatiste[1].

Toutefois, si la Russie n'est pas une démocratie (ni même le pluralisme naissant des années 1990), ce n'est pas non plus le système politique totalitaire de la grande ère soviétique, ni l'autoritarisme répressif du système soviétique déclinant des années 1970 et 1980. La Russie est un système autoritaire reposant sur la corruption et la menace sélective plutôt que sur l'idéologie ou sur un contrôle politique généralisé. Le gouvernement n'est pas responsable devant ses citoyens/la société et il gouverne en partageant le pouvoir, les privilèges et la richesse avec une élite restreinte. Il s'agit d'un système politique fondamentalement fragile, et non d'un État fort. Sa légitimité repose sur les résultats, au sens premier du terme : tant que les citoyens russes ont un sens basique de la stabilité et de l'amélioration de la prospérité, ils tolèrent leurs responsables et la corruption.

Le danger des ennemis étrangers constitue l'autre pilier de la légitimité du système. Le gouvernement de Poutine (et maintenant de Poutine-Medvedev) justifie les mesures prises pour limiter la responsabilité devant les citoyens et les libertés politiques en prétextant que les ennemis externes cherchent à menacer la Russie depuis l'étranger et à l'affaiblir de l'intérieur. Pour justifier le contrôle étroit des ONG par exemple, le gouvernement russe a évoqué un financement externe et des agents étrangers cherchant à provoquer le système politique russe. Pour justifier sa loi sur les secteurs stratégiques, qui restreint la propriété privée de certains secteurs essentiels de l'économie russe, le gouvernement de Poutine a conseillé d'éviter que les richesses de la Russie ne soient possédées ou contrôlées par des étrangers qui se targueraient de ce titre de propriété pour affaiblir le pays. Les responsables politiques russes cherchent à participer à l'économie internationale et aux structures politiques internationales pour accéder à la prospérité et à l'influence politique que peuvent se permettre le monde globalisé, mais une véritable intégration risquerait d'affaiblir le rôle de l'État russe dans les affaires en faisant entrer en jeu de nombreux acteurs non assujettis à la puissance politique russe et fonctionnant selon les pratiques occidentales. Pour justifier le rôle leader de l'État sur le plan interne,

---

[1] Leon Aron, "21st Century Sultanate," *The American* (online), 14 November 2008 (http://www.american.com/archive/2008/november-december-magazine/21st-century-sultanate).

les responsables russes mettent en garde contre l'hostilité du monde extérieur[2].

L'évolution vers un État autoritaire corporatiste repose sur une économie prometteuse mais vulnérable. En terme de potentiel, l'économie russe a été l'une des plus performantes du monde au cours de la dernière décennie. Son taux de croissance annuel s'est élevé entre 6 et 8%, et le PIB par tête a quadruplé. Les Russes ont voyagé de plus en plus, ont pu acheter leur maison et leur voiture et vivre la vie moderne d'un Européen moyen. Jusqu'à l'automne 2008, la Russie détenait 600 milliards $ de réserves de devises, connaissait un excédent de sa balance courante, des excédents budgétaires d'au moins 5% pendant plusieurs années et disposait d'un des marchés boursiers les plus performants de toutes les économies émergentes.

Cependant, l'économie russe est fondamentalement dépendante de la production énergétique qu'elle exporte en quantité massive. Les chiffres de la Banque mondiale ont montré une croissance réelle des autres secteurs de l'économie russe au cours des dernières années, notamment dans les secteurs de la construction et de la consommation, mais les fonds qui alimentaient cette croissance provenaient essentiellement des revenus issus du secteur énergétique. Les importantes réserves de la Russie ont contribué à maîtriser les effets de la crise financière internationale qui ont néanmoins été importants et ont conduit au déclin économique en 2009. Le gouvernement russe a déjà dépensé plus de 190 milliards $ de ses réserves pour fournir des liquidités à ses banques en difficulté et pour défendre la valeur du rouble. Le marché boursier a perdu les deux tiers de sa valeur depuis le mois d'août ; Gazprom a perdu 25% de la valeur la plus élevée qu'il avait atteinte en 2008. La Banque mondiale a revu à la baisse, à 4,5%, ses estimations de la croissance russe en 2009 et prévoit une nouvelle fuite des capitaux car les investisseurs recherchent des marchés plus sûrs. Le chômage augmente car la majorité des industries assurant la croissance, et notamment le secteur de la construction, ont connu un arrêt quasi-total dû à des problèmes de liquidité et à la baisse de la consommation[3].

---

[2] Celeste A. Wallander, "Russian Transimperialism and its Implications" in *Global Powers in the 21ⁱˢᵗ Century: Strategies and Relations*, edited by Alexander T.J. Lennon and Amanda Kozlowski, (Cambridge MA: The MIT Press, 2008), pp. 217-235.

[3] Banque mondiale, "18ème rapport économique sur la Russie" (Moscou: Bureau de la Banque mondiale en Russie, Mars 2009).

Bien sûr, la Russie est loin d'être le seul pays à être confronté aux sérieuses conséquences de la crise financière mondiale, voire de la récession mondiale. Toutefois, en raison de sa dépendance aux exportations de ses ressources et aux investissements étrangers (c'est-à-dire la dette) au cours des dernières années, de l'échec de sa diversification de l'économie et de l'important retard dû à des investissements inadaptés dans les infrastructures, la Russie est plus vulnérable que de nombreuses autres grandes économies face la période économique difficile des une ou deux années à venir.

Selon la Banque mondiale, cela devrait inciter d'autant plus le gouvernement russe à envisager sérieusement la diversification, à encourager les investissements étrangers, à adhérer rapidement à l'OMC et à adopter d'autres politiques de libéralisation qui formeront la base de la croissance future. Les dirigeants russes pourraient finir par tenir compte de ces conseils mais jusqu'à présent, le Premier ministre Poutine et le Président Medvedev ont cherché à tenir la communauté internationale en général, et les États-Unis en particulier, pour responsables de la crise[4]. On ne sait pas encore si les dirigeants russes décideront s'ils ont davantage besoin des États-Unis et de l'Europe pour affronter les prochaines années, qui seront difficiles sur le plan économique ou s'ils essaieront d'isoler le pays des effets de la crise financière mondiale et d'augmenter l'intervention de l'État.

La Russie sera moins riche et son économie interne ralentira, ce qui pourrait amener les citoyens russes à s'interroger sur leur soutien aux dirigeants actuels. Si une récession mondiale conduit à une situation difficile au plan interne, le gouvernement perdra en popularité et disposera de moins de ressources pour plaider sa cause. Il est frappant que les responsables russes aient insisté pour éviter une dévaluation du rouble (il s'agissait du principal thème abordé par Dimitri Medvedev dans son discours devant le Conseil des relations étrangères à Washington, D.C. en novembre 2008, durant le sommet du G20) et que la Banque centrale russe ait dépensé près d'un tiers des réserves du pays pour défendre sa valeur. Les Russes gardent un souvenir douloureux du krach du Rouble, de sa dévaluation et de la situation de défaut de paiement en août 1998 qui avaient rendu Eltsine si impopulaire. Si la

---

[4] Voir "Putin promises economic strength; blames crisis on U.S.," *International Herald Tribune*, 20 November 2008 (http://www.iht.com/articles/ap/2008/11/20/business/EU-Russia-Financial-Crisis.php).

légitimité du gouvernement de Poutine-Medvedev est liée à la valeur du rouble, elle peut aussi connaître une dévaluation.

La situation économique globale coïncide avec une période cruciale pour l'avenir de la Russie comme principal producteur énergétique d'Eurasie. La Banque mondiale estime que les investissements étrangers dans le secteur énergétique russe ont déjà diminué lorsque l'État russe a renforcé son contrôle sur ce secteur et lorsque la Russie a adopté la loi limitant les investissements étrangers dans les secteurs stratégiques russes. Avec la baisse actuelle de la croissance de la production pétrolière et l'incapacité russe à respecter ses engagements contractuels en matière d'approvisionnement en gaz naturel sans avoir à acheter du gaz d'Asie centrale et à le réacheminer, la situation de la Russie comme principal fournisseur de pétrole et de gaz naturel aux Européens est à la croisée des chemins. Soit les investisseurs russes devront eux-mêmes commencer à développer sérieusement de nouveaux champs, soit les investisseurs étrangers devront être autorisés à faire les investissements massifs et complexes nécessaires au développement de nouveaux champs gaziers et pétroliers. Une économie russe affaiblie et plus vulnérable pourrait motiver les dirigeants Poutine et Medvedev à ne plus penser uniquement au court terme et à renforcer la capacité de l'Europe de négocier plus efficacement avec un secteur énergétique russe moins capable de dicter ses conditions.

Ils pourraient aussi faire de l'Asie un véritable concurrent concernant les futurs investissements dans le développement du secteur énergétique en Russie. Fin octobre 2008, la Russie et la Chine ont signé un accord selon lequel la Chine prêterait 20-25 milliards $ aux compagnies pétrolières russes pour les aider à rembourser leurs dettes auprès des banques et investisseurs occidentaux. En échange, l'entreprise russe Transneft construirait un oléoduc vers la Chine, accord que le gouvernement russe avait jusqu'à présent refusé, en garantissant à la Chine, en guise de remboursement du prêt, son approvisionnement en pétrole russe provenant des champs d'extrême Orient. Les spécialistes en énergie estiment que la Russie privilégie les relations énergétiques avec l'Europe car elles sont fondées sur des coûts relativement bas et des rendements élevés du fait de l'existence d'infrastructures d'oléoducs/gazoducs et de la relative facilité de négociations avec chacun des États membres de l'Union européenne et des entreprises. En revanche, pour produire de l'énergie pour la Chine, la Russie devra investir massivement dans de nouveaux pipelines et dans le développement de nouveaux champs, et négocier avec un seul interlocuteur qui a réussi à ne pas payer le prix fort pour le gaz naturel. Cela explique partiellement pourquoi la Chine a fini par négocier directement avec l'Asie centrale et devrait prochainement achever un oléoduc venant du Kazakhstan et signer un accord sur un gazoduc parallèle qui pourrait également continuer jusqu'au Turkménistan. La perspective de perdre son monopole sur le gaz d'Asie centrale pourrait obliger la Russie à restructurer sa politique énergétique, qui plus est si l'Europe se montre prête à repenser sa relation énergétique stratégique avec la Russie, à la lueur aussi de l'évolution des dynamiques géopolitiques et des nouvelles contraintes sur l'économie russe.

En 2009, la politique étrangère russe, reposant sur ces éléments internes, se caractérisait par un sentiment manifeste de puissance et de privilèges combiné à du ressentiment et à un sentiment d'insécurité multidimensionnelle. Parallèlement, la Russie a envoyé des bombardiers stratégiques et une force navale au Venezuela, tout en indiquant que le déploiement de dix intercepteurs de missiles en Pologne constituait une menace existentielle pour les 2000 (ou plus) armes nucléaires stratégiques de la Russie. La politique étrangère russe est totalement différente de celle des deux autres puissances mondiales émergentes. La Chine et l'Inde ont mis en œuvre des politiques étrangères et des relations bilatérales prenant pleinement en compte l'objectif prioritaire de développement interne et de croissance. La Chine cherche à rassurer les grandes puissances, et notamment les États-Unis, en adoptant une stratégie de participation dans les institutions internationales et en évitant la confrontation. De la même manière, lorsque l'Inde connaissait une croissance extraordinaire, sa politique étrangère consistait à éviter le défi et la vantardise ainsi que la confrontation et le défi et à trouver des domaines dans lesquels elle pouvait se développer[5].

Par contraste, la politique étrangère russe a cherché à défier la puissance américaine et le système des institutions internationales fondé sur un ordre juridique et inscrit dans l'ordre post Seconde guerre mondiale et le processus européen d'Helsinki qui reste l'un des résultats les plus durables de la détente. Les États-Unis ont élu un nouveau président dont le succès et le leadership reposent largement sur son message indiquant que la guerre en Irak était une erreur et qu'il remettrait les

---

[5] Fareed Zakaria, *The Post-American World*, (New York: W.W. Norton, 2008), chapitres 4 et 5.

États-Unis sur la voie d'un leadership responsable exerçant sa puissance par le biais des institutions et en coopération avec des amis et des alliés. De leur côté, les dirigeants russes défient le monde en refusant de reconnaître qu'ils ont violé le droit international en envahissant la Géorgie, en reconnaissant unilatéralement l'Abkhazie et l'Ossétie du Sud et en ne parvenant pas à respecter les engagements de cessez-le-feu pris auprès de l'Union européenne (représentée par la France) en août et septembre 2008. Les responsables russes ne semblent pas avoir tiré les leçons de l'expérience américaine : l'exercice unilatéral de la puissance militaire et le mépris pour un leadership et une responsabilité raisonnables avaient sapé la capacité des États-Unis à parvenir à leurs objectifs de sécurité.Il ne sera donc pas simple de traiter avec la Russie. Le président Medvedev a salué le 5 novembre la victoire électorale du président élu Obama dans un discours menaçant de déployer des missiles de faible portée en Europe (c'est-à-dire à Kaliningrad), ce qui n'est pas véritablement un discours montrant la volonté de la Russie d'ouvrir un nouveau chapitre dans les relations États-Unis/Russie. Il est donc d'autant plus urgent de se mettre immédiatement au travail en 2009 et de disposer d'une stratégie transatlantique sérieuse et forte pour commencer à construire les bases d'une résolution efficace des problèmes et du développement de la confiance.

Les intérêts et le potentiel d'un véritable partenariat transatlantique avec la Russie

La liste des intérêts américains en Russie est relativement simple, et étonnamment constante au fil du temps :

La sécurité des armes, matériels et technologies militaires de la Russie ;

- La participation constructive de la Russie à la géopolitique en Eurasie, y compris en limitant les déploiements et les ventes d'armes conventionnelles ;

- La stabilité et la viabilité de l'approvisionnement énergétique russe ;

- La participation constructive de la Russie sur les marchés économiques et financiers mondiaux ;

- L'évolution des politiques intérieures russes vers un système plus stable, global et viable[6].

Si l'ordre des priorités peut varier par rapport à l'Europe, il convient de noter que rien, sur cette liste, ne contredit les intérêts européens en Russie. Au cours des huit dernières années, les relations transatlantiques se sont détériorées à de nombreux égards et les conflits les plus dommageables et les plus problématiques ont été suscités par des désaccords sérieux sur la Russie. Cependant, les problèmes n'étaient pas liés à ces intérêts fondamentaux mais aux choix des dirigeants et à leurs désaccords sur la stratégie et les priorités.

Toutefois, outre ces désaccords relatifs aux politiques, les États-Unis et l'Union européenne (et les Européens entre eux) ont douté de l'engagement de la Russie en faveur des intérêts communs et de l'intégration européenne. Il était plus facile d'avoir une politique transatlantique constructive lorsque la Russie s'engageait plus clairement en faveur de l'intégration. Durant les années 1990, les responsables russes semblaient favorables à la promesse d'une réforme démocratique, à des marchés libres et à l'intégration occidentale. En effet, comme l'a montré Stephen Sestanovich dans une étude poussée des premières années de présidence de Poutine, le potentiel de coopération entre les Russes et les Américains était très important et les succès et accords nombreux. Le gouvernement de Poutine ne considérait pas l'OTAN comme une force hostile et avait réussi à renforcer son rôle dans les délibérations conjointes pour résoudre les problèmes de sécurité que la Russie et l'OTAN considéraient comme un intérêt commun. Malgré les désaccords avec l'Administration Bush après son abrogation du Traité sur les missiles antibalistiques, la Russie et les États-Unis ont conclu en 2002 un nouveau traité sur les armes stratégiques, ce qui a contribué à une évolution constructive des relations russo-européennes[7].

Les États-Unis et la Russie comptent de nombreux intérêts mutuels et la Russie dispose du potentiel pour devenir un acteur constructif du système international. Mais les choix de la Russie en 2008 remettent en

---

[6] Adapté de l'excellente analyse d'Eugene Rumer, "Mind the Gap: Russian Ambitions vs. Russian Reality," in *Strategic Asia: Challenges and Choices*, edited by Ashley J. Tellis, Mercy Kuo, and Andrew Marble (Washington, D.C. : The National Bureau of Asian Research, 2008), pp. 167-196, at p. 190.

[7] Stephen Sestanovich, "What has Moscow Done? Rebuilding U.S.-Russian Relations," *Foreign Affairs*, vol. 87, numéro 6 (Novembre/Décembre 2008), pp. 12-28.

cause le potentiel de sécurité et de prospérité fondé sur la coopération et l'État de droit international. Dans ces circonstances, où allons-nous ? Une nouvelle stratégie américaine visant à poursuivre les intérêts sécuritaires, politiques et économiques avec la Russie devrait reposer sur quatre éléments clés :

1. définir les conditions de la sécurité en Eurasie (le plus essentiel étant de réaffirmer l'indépendance et la souveraineté de tous les États post-soviétiques) ;

2. ancrer la Russie en Europe en étroite coordination avec les alliés européens ;

3. développer une approche transatlantique commune sur les politiques énergétiques en Eurasie ;

4. lancer de véritables négociations de contrôle des armes sur les plans bilatéral et multilatéral.

Ces objectifs doivent être atteints conformément à nos valeurs, à une époque où les priorités de valeurs/d'intérêts constituent une question délicate dans les relations transatlantiques. L'intégration de la Russie et des autres pays de l'ex-Union soviétique dans une communauté de nations pacifiques, prospères et fondées sur l'Etat de droit reste un intérêt stratégique américain. La Russie conserve le potentiel d'émerger comme un important partenaire et comme un contributeur pour la résolution de certains des défis régionaux et mondiaux les plus urgents. Les États-Unis ont fortement intérêt à signer avec la Russie un accord sur le commerce du nucléaire et à voir la Russie devenir membre de l'OMC et de l'OCDE. Mais pour bénéficier des avantages liés à cette appartenance, la Russie doit accepter l'intégralité des conditions générales et des responsabilités. Une coopération plus étroite entre l'OTAN et une Russie démocratique, y compris son adhésion, devrait rester un objectif stratégique de long terme.

Les États-Unis ne devraient pas exclure la possibilité de la Russie de choisir de se réengager dans la communauté internationale de manière responsable et crédible. Les progrès réalisés sur la voie d'accords qui pourraient être signés au sommet États-Unis/Russie en juillet 2009 laissent penser que cette approche stratégique pragmatique est prometteuse. C'est à la Russie de faire son choix mais c'est de la responsabilité des États-Unis de continuer à le rendre possible. Même si le défi est bien plus important qu'il ne semblait l'être il y a vingt ans, la bonne stratégie consiste à se réengager en faveur d'une véritable intégration, sérieuse, de la Russie. Et seule une approche transatlantique peut concrétiser une telle approche.

La France, l'Union européenne et les États-Unis face à la Russie

Maxime Lefebvre

Résumé

Depuis la fin de la guerre froide, la Russie et l'Occident n'ont pas réussi à construire un partenariat solide. A une phase de coopération relative dans les années 1990 a succédé une phase de confrontation croissante, dont la crise géorgienne a constitué un moment paroxystique.

Il faut tirer les leçons du conflit de Géorgie, et reconstruire une unité transatlantique sur la Russie, à la fois par une remise à plat dans la nouvelle Administration américaine, et par un dépassement des divergences intra-européennes.

Trois réflexions majeures peuvent nous aider à avancer: la valorisation d'une stratégie de coopération et non de confrontation, la consolidation de l'architecture européenne de sécurité, l'association de la Russie à la gestion des enjeux globaux.

Une leçon à méditer : l'incapacité de l'Occident et de la Russie à construire un partenariat solide depuis la fin de la Guerre froide

L'échec des offres occidentales à une Russie affaiblie

Entre novembre 1989 (chute du mur de Berlin) et décembre 1991 (éclatement de l'URSS), tout l'Empire soviétique s'écroule. La politique des Occidentaux combine alors l'optimisme et la prudence. Ils se persuadent, un peu facilement, que la démocratie va succéder au communisme dans un « nouvel ordre mondial » en gestation. Mais, par réalisme, ils s'efforcent en priorité de gérer les risques d'instabilité, en visant le retrait des troupes russes des anciennes démocraties populaires (achevé en 1994), la dénucléarisation des républiques non russes de l'URSS (1992-1996), et des accords de désarmement nucléaire et conventionnel (traité sur les forces conventionnelles en Europe en 1990, révisé en 1992 ; traités START I et START II en 1991 et 1993) qui laissent augurer un nouvel ordre de sécurité en Europe.

La Russie cependant ne se résigne pas facilement au rétrécissement de ses frontières étatiques et stratégiques. Elle doit abandonner dans des États désormais étrangers (États Baltes, Ukraine, Kazakhstan…) un grand nombre de russophones (environ 20 millions de « pieds rouges »). Cette situation n'aboutit pas, comme en Yougoslavie, à des affrontements militaires sanglants. Mais la Russie maintient des emprises stratégiques au-delà de ses frontières. Elle s'impose, dans les années 1992-1994, comme médiatrice dans les conflits qui éclatent en Moldavie (Transnistrie), en Géorgie (Abkhazie et Ossétie du Sud), ou entre l'Arménie et l'Azerbaïdjan (Haut Karabakh). Elle conserve une présence militaire à Sébastopol, en partageant la flotte de la mer Noire avec l'Ukraine, et elle favorise un statut d'autonomie pour la Crimée, que Khrouchtchev avait rattachée à l'Ukraine en 1954 (à l'occasion du 300ᵉ anniversaire de l'union entre la Russie et l'Ukraine), mais qui est peuplée surtout de russophones. La Russie tente aussi de s'imposer comme la force organisatrice de l'espace post-soviétique, dans ce qu'elle appelle son « étranger proche » (création de la Communauté des États indépendants en décembre 1991 et de l'Organisation du traité de sécurité collective en 1992 ; projet d'une union douanière avec la Biélorussie et le Kazakhstan en 1995).

Les années qui suivent voient en Europe l'affrontement de deux courants contraires et de force inégale. D'un côté, l'Union européenne (1993) puis l'OTAN (1994) se lancent dans une politique d'élargissement visant à consolider la stabilisation démocratique à l'Est de l'Europe. D'un autre côté, la Russie maintient une influence privilégiée dans l'ancienne URSS, mais sans réussir à mettre en place un modèle d'intégration efficace. Les Occidentaux, sans se laisser détourner de leurs objectifs, essaient de mettre en place une relation de coopération et de confiance avec Moscou, malgré l'indignation causée par la première guerre de Tchétchénie (1994-1996). La participation de la Russie au « groupe de contact » sur les Balkans renforce les pressions de la communauté internationale sur les Serbes durant la guerre de Bosnie, ce qui conduit ces derniers à accepter la paix de Dayton en 1995. Et la décision d'élargissement de l'OTAN à la Pologne, à la Hongrie et à la République tchèque en 1997 s'accompagne de la conclusion d'un « Acte fondateur » OTAN-Russie, qui vise à rassurer Moscou et à l'associer à la politique de l'OTAN[1]. Des troupes russes participent d'ailleurs à la force de paix de l'OTAN en Bosnie. Et la confiance est renforcée par des déclarations mutuelles sur le déciblage des missiles nucléaires.

Une première crise survient cependant avec l'affaire du Kosovo. La Russie, de plus en plus affaiblie par la transition post-communiste (comme en témoigne la grande crise financière de 1998), prend le parti de Belgrade mais ne peut influer sur le cours des événements, au-delà de sa capacité d'empêchement au Conseil de sécurité de l'ONU. Les Occidentaux, de leur côté, convaincus qu'ils n'arrêteront que par la force un nouveau nettoyage ethnique de la part de Milosevic, utilisent l'OTAN pour faire la guerre à la Serbie, en dépit de l'absence d'autorisation de l'ONU. La Russie se résigne pourtant à rentrer dans le jeu pour mettre un terme au conflit, dans le cadre du G8 et du Conseil de sécurité (résolution 1244), en passant une forme de compromis : le Kosovo est arraché à l'autorité de Belgrade et mis sous protection de l'ONU et de l'OTAN, mais l'intégrité territoriale de la Yougoslavie (Serbie — Monténégro) est réaffirmée (juin 1999). L'éclatement de la Seconde guerre de Tchétchénie (qui durera de 1999 à 2005) alourdit malgré tout le climat entre Moscou et les Occidentaux.

Cette crise de 1999 est surmontée durant les premières années de l'Administration de G. W. Bush. Celui-ci prétend avoir « lu l'âme de Poutine dans ses yeux » et s'allie avec la Russie dans la guerre contre le terrorisme. Moscou soutient l'intervention militaire américaine en Afghanistan et ne s'offusque pas de voir l'Amérique installer des bases militaires dans les pays d'Asie centrale, anciens territoires soviétiques. Une Charte OTAN-Russie est conclue en 2002, alors que l'OTAN décide de s'élargir à 7 nouveaux États anciennement communistes (dont les trois pays baltes, qui furent annexés à l'URSS et comprennent d'importantes minorités russes). Mais si les Occidentaux offrent à la Russie une relation de partenariat et de coopération très poussée, ils ne vont pas jusqu'à lui offrir une perspective d'adhésion qui lui donnerait un droit de veto. La confiance a ses limites.

---

[1] Cette même année 1997 entre en vigueur l' « accord de partenariat et de coopération » signé entre l'UE et la Russie en 1994, qui vient à échéance au bout d'une période de dix ans, mais se renouvelle automatiquement d'année en année.

Les années 2003-2008 : une confrontation croissante

Si l'adhésion à l'OTAN est vue, par les Occidentaux et par les États est-européens qui y aspirent, comme un moyen de renforcer la stabilité et la démocratie en Europe, il est perçu par la Russie comme une opération hostile visant à l'isoler et à rétrécir sa sphère d'influence. Après l'élargissement de 2002, entré en vigueur en 2004, l'OTAN compte une longue frontière commune avec la Russie et les pays de l'ex-URSS. L'élargissement de l'OTAN précède et accompagne l'élargissement de l'Union européenne : celle-ci passe en effet, en mai 2004, de 15 à 25 États membres (puis à 27 en 2007).

Ce « bond vers l'Est » des institutions occidentales « euro-atlantiques » rétrécit l'espace tampon avec la Russie, désormais réduit à la Biélorussie, à l'Ukraine, à la Moldavie, et aux trois pays du Caucase. Ces six pays sont couverts par la « politique de voisinage » lancée par l'Union européenne depuis 2003, qui leur offre non l'adhésion mais un rapprochement maximal avec l'Union européenne. Or c'est justement dans cet espace tampon que se produisent les « révolutions de couleur » qui installent, en Géorgie (« révolution des roses », 2003) puis en Ukraine (« révolution orange », 2004), des régimes pro-occidentaux méfiants vis-à-vis de la Russie.

Ces évolutions sont ressenties avec hostilité par Moscou. Peut-être contribuent-elles au raidissement autoritaire et nationaliste qui s'opère là-bas : le Président Poutine, réélu confortablement en 2004, restaure l'autorité de l'État russe (la « verticale du pouvoir »), s'appuie sur les « services spéciaux » (l'ex-KGB, dont il est lui-même issu) et sur les structures de force pour gouverner, réprime brutalement la révolte tchétchène et les attentats terroristes (Moscou en 2002, Beslan en 2004), nationalise les richesses pétrolières en expropriant les oligarques, limite la liberté de la presse et des ONG, et prend des accents de plus en plus nationalistes et critiques vis-à-vis de l'Occident. Ce retour à l'ordre est en même temps populaire dans le pays car il met fin à la période anarchique des années Eltsine, et s'accompagne d'un véritable redressement économique, il est vrai favorisé par la montée des prix de l'énergie exportée plus que par une véritable diversification de l'économie.

La tension entre « l'Occident » (pris comme un tout) et la Russie ne se développe pas d'un coup. En 2002-2003, lorsque l'Administration Bush en plein crise d'unilatéralisme prétend faire la guerre à l'Irak, la France et l'Allemagne sont gouvernées par des dirigeants qui ont à la fois de la sympathie pour la Russie poutinienne et de la méfiance pour les nouveaux dirigeants américains. Les trois pays font cause commune contre Washington pour tenter de l'empêcher d'attaquer l'Irak. Et comme la France est celle qui s'y oppose le plus frontalement, c'est à elle que Condoleeza Rice, encore Conseillère nationale pour la sécurité du Président Bush, réserve sa vindicte après la victoire contre l'Irak (son mot d'ordre est alors de « pardonner l'Allemagne, ignorer la Russie, punir la France »). La force de l'axe Paris-Berlin-Moscou est telle que l'Union européenne lance en 2003, sur une proposition franco-allemande, la négociation des « quatre espaces » de coopération UE-Russie (économie ; sécurité intérieure ; sécurité extérieure ; culture, éducation et recherche), qui s'achève en 2005 par la mise au point de quatre feuilles de route (sous la forme de catalogues de coopérations concrètes). Ce partenariat UE-Russie, parallèle à la coopération OTAN-Russie, contribue peut-être à rassurer la Russie sur l'élargissement des institutions occidentales vers l'Est.

La situation change cependant à partir de 2005. Le deuxième mandat de G. W. Bush s'ouvre sur une relance du partenariat transatlantique sous le signe de la croisade pour la liberté. Washington s'appuie sur les ressentiments anti-russes de la « nouvelle Europe » (qui l'a soutenu sans faillir dans la crise irakienne) pour rétablir le schéma d'un partenariat transatlantique uni contre un ennemi commun, voire une menace commune. Le soutien à l'Ukraine et encore plus à la Géorgie devient un credo pour les tenants de cette ligne washingtonienne, qu'on trouve aussi en Europe occidentale, y compris parfois en France, voire en Allemagne. Même la politique énergétique n'échappe pas à ce schéma : Washington pousse les projets de diversification énergétique qui permettraient de protéger le talon d'Achille de l'Europe (sa dépendance énergétique par rapport à la Russie), en lui faisant accéder directement aux ressources en hydrocarbures de la Caspienne (via les pipelines traversant le Caucase, prolongés notamment par le gazoduc Nabucco traversant les Balkans).

Il serait malgré tout caricatural de considérer que toute la « nouvelle Europe » s'est laissée prendre à cette politique. La Suède y a participé de plus en plus activement, tout en n'ayant jamais été dans l'OTAN ni dans l'orbite russe. La Pologne a joué le rôle de fer de lance, en mettant seule son veto, entre la fin 2006 et le printemps 2008, au lancement de la négociation d'un nouvel accord cadre entre l'Union européenne et la Russie destiné à succéder à l'accord de partenariat et de coopération.

La Pologne et la République tchèque sont d'ailleurs des pays tellement proches de Washington qu'ils n'ont pas hésité à braver Moscou en accueillant sur leur sol des éléments du bouclier anti-missiles américain. La Lituanie s'est montrée des plus actives pour durcir la politique de l'Union européenne face à la Russie et renforcer son engagement aux côtés de la Géorgie. L'Estonie et la Lettonie ont également une sensibilité à vif dans la relation avec Moscou. Mais à l'inverse, des pays comme la Hongrie, la Slovaquie, la Bulgarie ou la Slovénie ont adopté une stratégie beaucoup plus modérée, faisant passer au premier plan le renouvellement de leurs contrats d'approvisionnement gazier.

Ces différences s'expliquent sans doute par une gradation des sentiments de vulnérabilité: les Tchèques, les Polonais et les Baltes ont subi beaucoup plus fortement à la fois l'impérialisme soviétique d'hier et l'impérialisme nazi d'avant-hier. Leurs frontières sont d'ailleurs moins sûres historiquement (territoires tchèques et polonais autrefois peuplés d'Allemands ; forte présence de minorités russophones dans les pays Baltes aujourd'hui). Il n'est pas étonnant, par conséquent, qu'ils éprouvent davantage le besoin de s'appuyer sur le garant de l'ordre international et européen que sont les Etats-Unis.

La crise géorgienne : un tournant

Le conflit en Géorgie est moins la manifestation conquérante du nouvel impérialisme russe, que la réaction courroucée et brutale d'une puissance qui a été trop poussée dans ses retranchements. Il est vrai que la Russie n'a rien fait pour changer le statu quo en Géorgie, qui lui assurait deux gages dans le Caucase et en particulier sur son petit voisin géorgien. Mais il est vrai aussi que l'agressivité russe a été réveillée par la « révolution des roses » et la « révolution orange » (qui ne sont pas sans évoquer, *mutatis mutandis*, la « révolution cubaine » de 1959 dans la sphère d'influence américaine), et encore davantage par la volonté de plus en plus affirmée des dirigeants géorgiens et occidentaux (en particulier des États-Unis et de leurs meilleurs alliés de la « nouvelle Europe ») de forcer la réintégration de l'Abkhazie et de l'Ossétie du Sud à la Géorgie. La reconnaissance de l'indépendance du Kosovo, qui avait pourtant été clairement et publiquement considérée par Moscou comme un précédent possible pour le règlement d'autres conflits gelés dans l'ex-Union soviétique, a évidemment joué un rôle, de même que la promesse de l'OTAN, en avril 2008, d'intégrer à terme la Géorgie. On pourra longuement discuter entre historiens sur le point de savoir dans quelle mesure la Géorgie a déclenché son entreprise de reconquête de l'Ossétie du Sud en réaction à la posture de plus en plus menaçante de la Russie, et dans quelle mesure c'est la Russie qui a réagi à une posture de plus en plus belliqueuse de la Géorgie. Les faits ne sont en tout cas pas contestés : l'offensive russe contre la Géorgie est survenue au lendemain de l'offensive militaire géorgienne sur l'Ossétie du Sud.

Il importe à présent de tirer toutes les leçons du conflit géorgien.

Première leçon : sur la politique de la Russie elle-même. Elle a montré qu'elle continue de raisonner en État nationaliste, en sphères d'influence, en jeux géopolitiques à somme nulle. La Russie n'est pas allée jusqu'à renverser le régime du Président Saakachvili, mais elle a refusé d'abandonner le contrôle de l'Ossétie du Sud et l'Abkhazie. Et tout en voulant conserver et consolider ses positions, elle se montre peu capable de proposer une relation d'intégration régionale et de coopération avec l'Union européenne qui permettrait de dépasser les conflits avec ses voisins. Sa proposition de rééditer l'Acte final d'Helsinki (qui avait posé les règles d'une coexistence pacifique en Europe en 1975) paraît d'ailleurs viser davantage à consolider ses positions stratégiques qu'à ouvrir la voie à une véritable coopération paneuropéenne bénéfique pour tous. Ce comportement pose un défi fondamental aux Occidentaux : sont-ils capables d'influencer cette perception et cette conduite de la Russie, et comment ?

Seconde leçon : sur la politique des Occidentaux. L'Administration Bush s'est pour le moins montrée imprudente en encourageant (ou en ne décourageant pas) le président Saakachvili dans ses postures offensives : son incapacité à venir au secours de son allié lorsque celui-ci s'est fait envahir par l'armée russe a révélé que le roi était nu. L'Union européenne, quant à elle, a fait prévaloir son penchant pour la diplomatie, la stabilité, le *soft power* : elle a pu arrêter le conflit par sa médiation, mais n'a pas évité une consolidation des positions russes sur le terrain, puisque la totalité de l'Ossétie du Sud et de l'Abkhazie ont désormais échappé à la souveraineté géorgienne. L'OTAN, enfin, voit sa crédibilité entamée, car la promesse d'adhésion faite à la Géorgie (ainsi qu'à l'Ukraine) a plutôt eu pour effet d'attiser l'agressivité russe que de renforcer la sécurité de la Géorgie.

Troisième leçon: sur la place que doivent occuper les questions du « voisinage commun » dans notre relation avec la Russie. Le conflit du mois d'août 2008 a créé un fait accompli qui sera difficile à renverser, alors que la Russie a désormais reconnu l'indépendance des deux nouveaux « États » : on peut anticiper, au mieux, une situation à la chypriote qui sera gelée pour longtemps ; au pire, la multiplication d'incidents sur le terrain, dans lesquels les observateurs européens risquent de se retrouver impliqués, et qui pourrait conduire à une reprise des hostilités. Les options sont limitées et il s'agit de décider, tant pour les États-Unis que pour les Européens, laquelle est la plus souhaitable. Mais d'autres conflits potentiels peuvent dégénérer dans l'espace post-soviétique : par exemple en Transnistrie, que la Russie ne laissera pas se réunifier avec la Moldavie sans arracher au pays un statut fédéral et de neutralité, et en Ukraine, où habitent d'importantes minorités russophones (un cinquième de la population totale). Le conflit géorgien doit nous rappeler que, compte tenu des positions russes dans la région, tout scénario d'escalade risque d'aboutir à une conflagration tragique et contre-productive.

La relation avec la Russie : quels intérêts en jeu pour le partenariat transatlantique ?

Il faut analyser les choses à la fois du point de vue américain et du point de vue de l'Union européenne et des États membres.

Du point de vue américain

Il s'agit de se demander quelle place occupera la Russie dans l'agenda global de l'Administration Obama.

Depuis la fin de la Guerre froide, le monde n'est plus dominé par la relation entre les deux Grands. Les États-Unis ont encore longtemps maintenu un partenariat privilégié avec la Russie, notamment dans le domaine de la parité nucléaire stratégique et des accords de désarmement, mais cette relation n'est allée qu'en s'atténuant, alors que la puissance américaine s'affirmait de plus en plus et que d'autres pôles émergeaient (Europe, Chine, Inde, etc.).

Mais même si les États-Unis ne sont plus enclins à voir dans la relation américano-russe un partenariat global essentiel à la stabilité du monde, ils ont quand même besoin de Moscou dans de nombreux dossiers : la gestion de son arsenal nucléaire qui reste considérable ; la lutte contre la prolifération ; et tous les enjeux globaux pour lesquels une coopération entre les grandes puissances reste indispensable (maintien de la paix à l'ONU, gestion des approvisionnements énergétiques, préservation de l'environnement et lutte contre le réchauffement climatique, etc.). L'Administration Obama a justement commencé son dialogue avec la Russie en mettant l'accent sur les sujets d'intérêt commun (le désarmement et la non-prolifération, l'Iran, l'Afghanistan), plutôt que sur ceux qui fâchent (la Géorgie, la défense anti-missiles, ou les droits de l'homme).

En même temps, Washington va sans doute garder sur la durée les « fondamentaux » de sa politique à l'égard de la Russie, qui sont à peu près les mêmes que ceux qui guidaient sa politique hier à l'égard de l'URSS : en particulier une forte méfiance à l'égard de cette puissance trop peu démocratique qui domine « l'Eurasie », et une volonté d'endiguer sa possible expansion (*containment*), tout en consolidant la stabilité et la sécurité euro-atlantiques via l'OTAN

Du point de vue européen

Les choses sont beaucoup plus compliquées car les dernières années ont montré la difficulté à définir une politique unie à l'égard de la Russie (cf. le veto mis par la Pologne puis la Lituanie au démarrage de la négociation d'un nouvel accord de partenariat UE-Russie).

Schématiquement on pourrait considérer qu'il y a en fait deux politiques russes dans l'Union européenne. La politique de ce qui constitue *grosso modo* la « vieille Europe » (France, Allemagne, Italie, Espagne, Benelux, Grèce, Chypre, Finlande, etc.) met en avant les intérêts économiques et le souci de stabilité ; alors que la politique de la « nouvelle Europe » (en y incluant le Royaume-Uni et la Suède, mais pas forcément tous les nouveaux États membres, comme on l'a vu plus haut) est prompte à voir dans la Russie une menace qu'il faut prévenir par une attitude ferme. Cette opposition recoupe un peu, mais imparfaitement, l'opposition géopolitique traditionnelle entre les pays maritimes et continentaux. Elle reflète surtout le positionnement des États membres par rapport à la politique américaine et à sa stratégie du *containment* : le Royaume-Uni est traditionnellement attaché à un partenariat transatlantique fort ; la « nouvelle Europe » a été le fer de lance de la croisade démocratique de l'Administration Bush (elle fait partie, tout comme la Turquie, la RFA, le Japon, la Corée du Sud au temps de la Guerre froide, du *rimland*, « l'anneau terrestre » sur lequel s'appuie la puissance maritime américaine pour contenir la Russie) ; quant à la Suède, elle a un positionnement dur face à la Russie qui est tout à fait singulier, puisque ce pays n'est pas membre de l'OTAN, mais qui peut s'expliquer par l'histoire (le vieil antagonisme suédo-russe), par l'attachement aux droits de l'Homme et à l'environnement, voire par un sentiment de supériorité morale, à quoi s'ajoute un facteur politique plus conjoncturel.[2]

Ces classifications sont imparfaites et évolutives. La politique russe fait débat à l'intérieur des différents pays : en Allemagne, par exemple, la gauche est plus pro-russe (comme on l'a vu sous le chancelier Schröder) et la CDU plus atlantiste ; en Pologne, le départ d'un des frères Kaczysnki s'est traduit par un assouplissement de la politique russe de Varsovie. Il n'empêche que les continuités sont frappantes, de la gauche à la droite italienne, ou de Chirac à Sarkozy, qui se veut en rupture avec son prédécesseur mais s'est empressé de nouer une relation privilégiée avec Moscou. La volonté de bonnes relations avec Moscou n'interdit pas d'ailleurs un attachement sincère à un partenariat transatlantique efficace et solide : c'est là aussi une constante de la politique italienne, c'est plus net de la part de la droite espagnole et allemande que de la gauche, alors qu'en France ces préférences dépassent souvent les clivages politiques (il y a un continuum de De Gaulle à Chirac en passant par Mitterrand sur les États-Unis et la Russie, et une certaine inflexion atlantiste de la part de Sarkozy, comme l'a montré le retour dans la structure militaire de l'OTAN).

Quoi qu'il en soit, l'Administration Bush a été tellement polarisante[3] qu'elle ne pouvait qu'attiser ces positionnements. Que fera l'Administration Obama ? Elle jouit d'un préjugé très favorable en Europe, et ses premières initiatives (visant à appuyer sur le bouton « reset », selon le mot employé par le vice-président américain Joe Biden à la conférence annuelle sur la sécurité de Munich, la *Wehrkunde*) offrent l'opportunité

---

[2] La droite suédoise, et notamment son ministre des affaires étrangères Carl Bildt, est nettement plus atlantiste que la social-démocratie qui a traditionnellement dominé le pays. Celle-ci pourrait revenir au pouvoir aux élections législatives de 2010.

[3] « Qui n'est pas avec nous est contre nous », déclarait le Président Bush quelques temps après les attentats du 11 septembre 2001.

de reconstruire une politique nouvelle et plus efficace à l'égard de la Russie, qui permettra peut-être de transcender les divergences passées.

Comment construire un agenda transatlantique renouvelé sur la Russie?

Trois questions fondamentales doivent être posées.

Changera-t-on la Russie par la confrontation ou par la coopération ?

Bien sûr, on peut considérer que la Russie s'est elle-même éloignée des canons démocratiques : c'est ce que prétendent les tenants de la ligne dure, en dédouanant l'Occident de toute responsabilité dans le raidissement autoritaire et nationaliste en Russie.

Il est fondamental de partir d'une analyse juste et fine, plutôt qu'idéologique, des réalités. La Russie d'aujourd'hui, même si elle prétend peser sur l'intégrité territoriale et l'indépendance de ses voisins immédiats, n'est pas l'URSS de 1945-1948. Elle n'a probablement ni la volonté, ni les moyens, de relancer un projet impérial. Sa situation économique est fragile (retards technologiques, corruption, dépendance aux exportations de produits primaires et à quelques secteurs économiques isolés, tels que l'armement ou le spatial). Sa situation démographique l'est encore plus (elle perd entre 0,5 et 1 millions d'habitants par an, même si Poutine a réussi à relancer un peu la natalité). Bien sûr, si elle devenait plus menaçante, la question d'une stratégie de dissuasion se poserait sous un jour nouveau. Ce scénario ne peut être totalement exclu. Mais il ne faut pas le présupposer et l'encourager dans une sorte de prophétie auto-réalisatrice. La leçon du conflit géorgien doit être méditée à cet égard: à vouloir bouger les lignes par la force, on joue les apprentis sorciers.

Quant à la démocratie et aux droits de l'Homme, c'est une question difficile et qui le restera, comme le vieux débat sur la place de la morale dans la politique internationale. La Russie n'est pas le seul pays problématique à cet égard. Mais à la vision d'un pays despotique qui ne pourra jamais fonctionner autrement, on peut opposer une vision plus optimiste (trop naïve ?) d'une transition autoritaire qui était peut-être nécessaire, pour reprendre en main une situation d'anarchie politique et économique, mais qui peut déboucher demain sur un véritable processus de modernisation économique, sociale et politique. Les jeunes Russes d'aujourd'hui n'ont-ils pas envie de voyager et de s'ouvrir, comme les Occidentaux de leur génération ? La libéralisation du régime de visas est d'ailleurs l'un des rares sujets sur lesquels les autorités russes se montrent véritablement quémandeuses à l'égard de l'Union européenne.

Le choix entre la confrontation et la coopération doit être bien pesé. Avec la Russie, une dose de rapport de forces est inévitable, et le dialogue de la part de l'Union européenne et des États-Unis ne doit pas être interprété comme un signe de faiblesse dans la défense de nos intérêts et de nos valeurs. Mais la confrontation est une stratégie risquée, qui alimente en retour l'autoritarisme et le nationalisme, alors que le dialogue, l'ouverture et la coopération offrent la perspective d'une modernisation progressive de l'économie, de la société et des élites russes. Certains disent que nous aurons la Russie que nous mériterons ; en tout cas il pourrait être bénéfique de ne pas s'enfermer dans une vision manichéenne du partenaire / adversaire, et de tenter de se mettre à sa place, de le comprendre, d'approfondir un dialogue, tout difficile qu'il soit. Les États-Unis et l'Union européenne pourraient essayer d'en définir ensemble les termes, à condition de revenir à une approche réaliste et raisonnée. Et l'Union européenne pourrait commencer par s'inspirer de la démarche américaine en identifiant des sujets d'intérêt commun avec la Russie (par exemple l'énergie, ou la coopération transfrontalière, ou la coopération en matière de recherche) pour rétablir une relation de confiance et de coopération.

Comment reconstruire la sécurité en Europe ?

L'architecture européenne de sécurité repose aujourd'hui principalement sur deux piliers.

L'OSCE est le legs de la conférence d'Helsinki (1973-1975). Elle offre potentiellement la légitimité d'un cadre pan-européen de sécurité, mais son efficacité est aujourd'hui très limitée. Elle fait surtout de l'observation électorale, ce qui occasionne des tensions entre les démocraties occidentales et les pays plus éloignés des canons démocratiques (Russie, Biélorussie, Asie centrale…). Elle joue encore un rôle dans les questions de respect des minorités nationales. Son régime de maîtrise

des armements est en crise, du fait des contentieux sur le stationne-
ment de troupes russes dans les « conflits gelés », de la querelle des
boucliers anti-missiles, et de la suspension par la Russie du traité FCE.

L'OTAN a joué un rôle croissant en occupant largement l'espace
laissé vide par la disparition du Pacte de Varsovie, et en se transformant en organisation chargée de maintenir la paix (d'abord dans les
Balkans, et depuis 2003 en Afghanistan, c'est-à-dire en dehors de son
champ géographique traditionnel). L'OTAN n'a pas jugé que la Russie
était un partenaire suffisamment fiable pour mériter une perspective
d'adhésion, qui lui donnerait un droit de veto paralysant. Mais il ne faut
pas s'étonner, *a contrario*, que la Russie perçoive l'OTAN comme une
organisation qui lui est au mieux étrangère, au pire hostile.

Quant à l'Union européenne, elle a développé elle aussi une fonction de plus en plus affirmée de maintien de la paix à travers sa « politique européenne de sécurité et de défense » (PESD), dans les Balkans
et en Afrique, mais aussi ailleurs (Indonésie, Irak, Palestine). Cependant l'autonomie de l'UE par rapport à l'OTAN est limitée, car la
défense territoriale de l'Europe repose en premier lieu sur l'OTAN
(article 5 du traité de Washington), et la puissance de la structure militaire de l'OTAN est telle que toute opération d'envergure de l'Union
européenne doit s'appuyer sur elle.

La situation d'ensemble en Europe est instable, encore un peu dans
les Balkans, mais plus encore dans l'espace post-soviétique. Il y a en fait
deux scénarios possibles d'évolution. Le scénario de la confrontation
pourrait voir le renforcement de l'OTAN dans sa fonction de défense
territoriale contre la peur que suscite encore la Russie, ce qui se tradui-
rait par la relance d'une course aux armements en Europe, par une
dépendance croissante de l'UE par rapport à l'OTAN et aux États-
Unis sous l'angle de la sécurité, voire par une guerre froide ou même
par des affrontements armés aux confins de la zone d'influence russe
(Caucase, Moldavie, Ukraine).

L'autre scénario (stabilisateur) consisterait à restaurer une relation
de confiance et de coopération avec la Russie. Il devrait passer par une
pause dans la politique d'élargissement de l'OTAN à la Géorgie et à
l'Ukraine, par la relance des discussions sur le désarmement en Europe
(y compris les discussions russo-américaines sur le désarmement
nucléaire et les systèmes anti-missiles), et par un rôle accru de l'Union

européenne. Celle-ci, en renforçant ses relations avec ses voisins orientaux mais aussi avec la Russie, peut jouer un rôle majeur dans l'amélioration du climat de confiance. L'UE est pourvoyeuse de sécurité collective dans une logique de *soft power* (maintien de la paix) tandis que l'OTAN est davantage pourvoyeuse de *hard security* (défense territoriale, interventions armées lourdes). L'établissement d'un véritable partenariat entre l'UE et la Russie dans le domaine de la PESD, de même que le rétablissement d'une coopération OTAN-Russie dans le maintien de la paix, nous éloigneraient d'une guerre froide en Europe, et nous rapprocheraient d'une gestion coopérative de la sécurité, non seulement en Europe dans le cadre d'une OSCE revitalisée, mais aussi dans le monde dans le cadre de l'ONU. Cela pourrait s'accompagner du règlement, négocié avec la Russie, de certains conflits gelés comme ceux de Transnistrie ou du Haut Karabakh.

Le second scénario est possible, mais il suppose une volonté suffisante de la part de quelques pays moteurs en Europe (en premier lieu la France et l'Allemagne, mais aussi le Royaume-Uni) ainsi qu'une bonne disposition de la part de Washington. Quant à la Russie, il faut faire le pari qu'elle ne souhaite pas fondamentalement un scénario de confrontation auquel elle a beaucoup à perdre, et il faut lui parler et être à l'écoute de ses intérêts de sécurité. La proposition Medvedev d'un traité sur la sécurité européenne peut offrir à cet égard l'opportunité d'un chemin plus coopératif, comme le montre le dialogue qui s'est engagé dans le cadre de l'OSCE.

Comment créer un partenariat avec la Russie sur les enjeux globaux ?

C'est une question qui est liée, tout simplement, à l'avenir du multilatéralisme. Pour les Européens, le choix est clair et c'est un choix de nature : si l'Union européenne reconnaît sa dette aux États-Unis avec lesquels elle partage un fonds de valeurs communes, occidentales, démocratiques, ainsi qu'une solidarité de destin, elle est elle-même d'essence multilatérale et elle sera d'autant plus forte que le multilatéralisme sera plus fort au niveau mondial. Ce choix s'est exprimé on ne peut plus clairement dans la stratégie européenne de sécurité de 2003, à un moment où les États-Unis étaient gagnés par le « moment néoconservateur », et a été réaffirmélors de la révision de la stratégie de sécurité à la fin 2008. Pour les États-Unis, les choses sont moins nettes :

leur puissance leur donne le choix ; leur attachement au système multilatéral ne va pas jusqu'à se priver des moyens d'action que peut leur donner l'utilisation unilatérale de leur puissance. Mais on a des raisons d'espérer qu'une Administration Obama se montrera plus universaliste, plus multilatéraliste, que l'Administration précédente.

Cela doit passer par une redécouverte de la place des enjeux globaux : le désarmement et la lutte contre la prolifération, la refondation d'un système mondial de sécurité collective (cf. le dossier de l'élargissement du Conseil de sécurité de l'ONU), la consolidation d'une base universelle de défense des droits de l'Homme et de lutte contre la pauvreté, une meilleure régulation de la mondialisation dans tous ses aspects (économie, finance, marchés de matières premières, crime organisé, environnement). Dans tous ces domaines, la Russie est un partenaire incontournable. Elle est, avec les États-Unis, l'Union européenne, la Chine, l'Inde et le Japon, un des grands pôles du monde. Son statut de géant énergétique (un quart des réserves mondiales de gaz, mais aussi pétrole et nucléaire) en fait un partenaire indispensable pour sécuriser les approvisionnements à l'échelle européenne et mondiale. Il faut s'efforcer de l'inclure dans des règles communes, ne pas chercher à l'exclure du G8, et commencer par régler son adhésion à l'Organisation mondiale du commerce, qui n'a que trop tardé. Sa particicipation aux réunions du G20 sur la crise mondiale est un premier pas dans la bonne direction.

Une stratégie d'intégration de la Russie dans l'économie globale serait triplement bénéficiaire : pour lutter contre ces défis communs ; pour rétablir un climat de confiance et de coopération ; et pour ouvrir et moderniser l'économie et la société russes.

Les Européens et la nouvelle Administration américaine sont, pas moins que la Russie elle-même, devant un choix fondamental. Nous pouvons contribuer à un raidissement accru. Mais nous pouvons aussi modifier ensemble le cours des choses. Car la politique, c'est le réalisme des rapports de force mais aussi la liberté du choix. Au fond d'eux-mêmes, la majorité des Européens préféreraient la coopération à l'escalade. Les Etats-Unis ont su faire ce choix à certaines périodes de la guerre froide, et les orientations prises par l'Administration Obama montrent qu'ils en sont à nouveau capables. Il y a donc matière aujourd'hui à redéfinir une stratégie d'engagement lucide autant que résolue vis-à-vis de la Russie.

Les priorités stratégiques en Méditerranée et au Moyen-Orient

Ian Lesser

Depuis des décennies, les crises et les situations explosives au Moyen-Orient et en Méditerranée ont tenu une place centrale dans la politique étrangère américaine et ont épuisé l'énergie politique des diverses Administrations. Les évolutions à la périphérie méridionale de l'Europe sont également devenues un élément central des relations transatlantiques. Avec la nouvelle Administration à Washington, il est peu probable que les défis de cette région perdent de leur intérêt. La crise à Gaza souligne cette réalité. Mais la capacité d'engagement américaine et la dynamique de partenariat qui va du Maroc jusqu'au Golfe et même au-delà pourraient fortement évoluer au cours des prochaines années. Le nouvel agenda régional sera certainement marqué par une interaction croissante entre Paris et Washington avec de nouvelles incitations pour renforcer la coordination politique. La stratégie « méditerranéenne », qui constitue un intérêt français de longue date mais qui est relativement peu développée dans la politique étrangère américaine, devrait elle aussi faire l'objet d'une plus grande coopération.

Un Moyen-Orient en expansion

Traditionnellement, la politique américaine à l'égard du Moyen-Orient se concentre sur un nombre limité de questions centrales, notamment le conflit israélo-palestinien et la stabilité et sécurité énergétique dans le Golfe. L'Afrique du Nord et le Levant ne sont pas pour autant absents de l'équation mais ils ont rarement eu l'importance que leur accordait la politique européenne. Ou alors ils n'étaient perçus qu'à travers le processus de paix au Moyen-Orient, comme cela a sans aucun doute été le cas pour le Liban. Les relations étroites entre les Etats-Unis et le Maroc ont très souvent été dictées par l'attitude modérée de Rabat et sa volonté de servir d'intermédiaire dans les relations des pays arabes avec Israël. Pendant la dernière décennie, plusieurs facteurs ont contribué à élargir la portée de la politique au Moyen-Orient et le concept américain de région compris comme « espace stratégique ». Les événements du 11 septembre ont fortement renforcé la tendance déjà existante visant à accentuer le caractère transrégional des défis qui ont un impact sur la donne sécuritaire dans une zone bien plus large, même si le conflit israélo-palestinien en constitue le centre de gravité. Les crises de gouvernance et de légitimité politique, la montée des politiques islamiques, le terrorisme et la violence politique et des tensions interétatiques non résolues ont encouragé les stratèges américains à appréhender cette région comme un arc de crise s'étendant de « Marrakech au Bangladesh » Il est désormais coutumier de se référer à un « grand » Moyen-Orient, notion profondément ancrée dans l'Initiative de partenariat pour le Moyen-Orient de l'Administration Bush. L'Administration Obama suivra certainement une ligne moins dure en matière de démocratisation et de réforme, optant plutôt pour un agenda plus traditionnel centré sur les droits de l'Homme, mais cette approche géopolitique expansive du Moyen-Orient perdurera sans doute, même si le vocabulaire change.

Cette évolution de la représentation mentale de la région pourrait encourager une convergence des perspectives françaises et américaines, même si cela était impossible ces huit dernières années.

L'Europe n'a jamais limité sa politique au Moyen-Orient au Levant et au Golfe. Pour la France et particulièrement pour les pays d'Europe méridionale, l'Afrique du Nord et la Méditerranée ont toujours été des pivots essentiels de l'environnement stratégique, l'avenir de ces régions s'inscrivant dans la stratégie de sécurité et de prospérité européenne. Il s'agit du voisinage immédiat de l'Union européenne et donc d'une zone où le désengagement est impossible. Par contraste, dans le grand Moyen-Orient, les Etats-Unis auront la possibilité de réduire leur présence politique et sécuritaire. À l'exception non négligeable du processus de paix au Moyen-Orient et du défi iranien, le très haut degré d'engagement américain actuel ne peut être considéré comme acquis pour la prochaine décennie. La concurrence avec les exigences stratégiques en Asie et la rigueur économique pourraient engendrer une situation dans laquelle la présence américaine serait trop faible au goût des Européens. Ce n'est pas le scénario le plus probable, mais face à la conjoncture, il est préférable de le prendre en compte.

Redynamiser le processus de paix

Comme le démontre la crise à Gaza, le conflit israélo-palestinien est désormais au centre des inquiétudes transatlantiques en matière de sécurité, comme cela n'avait plus été le cas depuis l'apogée du terrorisme palestinien en Europe dans les années 1970 et 1980. Il ne fait aucun doute qu'un accord global comportant une solution à deux Etats restera pour Washington la récompense diplomatique suprême. À leur entrée en fonction, les Administrations américaines successives étaient bien décidées à relancer le processus de paix israélo-palestinien. Dans les faits, elles hésitaient à prendre le risque de ternir leur réputation par une action diplomatique au Moyen-Orient avant que les conditions ne semblent réunies ou avant que les évènements sur place ne les forcent à agir. Lorsque les Etats-Unis étaient activement impliqués, ils préféraient manifestement garder le contrôle du processus, minimisant le rôle des autres acteurs qu'ils soient régionaux ou européens. On pourrait soutenir que les responsables américains ont un peu abandonné l'idée de confiner l'Europe à un rôle limité, particulièrement sur le plan financier, mais des réserves persistent, même au sein des cercles les plus progressistes.

On se demande encore si Washington, à l'approche d'un accord global, sera prêt à faire appel au multilatéralisme incarné par le Quartet ou la réunion d'Annapolis. L'Administration Obama hérite d'un processus de paix diplomatique au cours duquel, à quelques rares exceptions près, les Etats-Unis étaient peu disposés à céder l'initiative et à faire pression sur les parties au-delà des limites traditionnelles. Même si la nouvelle Administration est encline à rompre avec les traditions et à s'engager rapidement dans la diplomatie israélo-palestinienne, la crise sécuritaire et humanitaire actuelle à Gaza ne laissant peut-être pas d'autre choix, les parties ne sont certainement pas en mesure de parvenir rapidement à un accord. La stratégie transatlantique devrait donc se concentrer sur la maîtrise durable des conséquences de l'absence de paix, en encourageant la détente régionale (avec la Syrie par exemple), même si les principaux problèmes ne sont pas résolus. La capacité grandissante d'acteurs plus lointains comme l'Iran ou même le Pakistan à jouer un rôle et à menacer directement ou indirectement la sécurité d'Israël aura des implications croissantes sur la notion de « fin de conflit ». En ce sens, Paris et Washington seront confrontés à l'énigme d'un processus de paix qui s'est développé avec la définition du Moyen-Orient en tant que zone stratégique.

Retrait d'Irak

Bien plus que le 11 septembre, l'Irak constitue un tournant dans les relations transatlantiques et particulièrement les relations franco-américaines. La guerre d'Irak continue d'être une source de désaccords politiques entre Washington et pratiquement tous ses partenaires internationaux. Plus significatif encore, les différences sur l'Irak ont alimenté un débat bien plus sérieux et bien plus persistant sur la nature de la puissance américaine au sein des opinions publiques et des responsables en Europe. Bien sûr, ce débat existait déjà avant 2003. Mais la guerre d'Irak a cristallisé la critique sur la puissance et le leadership américains dans des dimensions nouvelles et fortes. Dans le même temps, l'expérience irakienne a incité les Américains à réfléchir sur le style de leur politique étrangère et sur leurs priorités. Au sein de la communauté chargée de la politique étrangère à Washington, l'invasion de l'Irak est vue depuis longtemps comme un prodigieux échec des services de renseignement et une erreur de jugement majeure, un mauvais calcul aux lourdes conséquences stratégiques. Le retrait d'Irak est désormais la priorité des priorités. Limiter à défaut de réparer les conséquences de l'aventure irakienne ne sera pas chose facile et ce sera complètement impossible sans le concours actif des acteurs régionaux et des alliés principaux.

Si l'Administration Obama respecte l'agenda annoncé et si la pression irakienne pour accélérer le retrait américain augmente, Bagdad devra très rapidement montrer sa capacité à fournir les conditions minimales de sécurité dans le pays. A plus long terme, la capacité de l'Irak à demeurer un État unitaire ne peut être tenue pour acquise. Le Kurdistan nord-irakien est déjà sur le point d'émerger comme une entité indépendante, même si le reste du pays demeure unifié et chaotique. Dans ces conditions, la Turquie devra relever de très difficiles défis d'adaptation. La gestion de l'Irak post-occupation ainsi que la lutte contre une plus grande déstabilisation de la région nécessiteront une diplomatie régionale plus sérieuse — dans le style de celle du rapport « Baker/ Hamilton », jamais sérieusement mise en œuvre. Les organisations internationales devraient également jouer un plus grand rôle en Irak. Ces deux initiatives seraient grandement renforcées s'il existait une approche transatlantique concertée et un véritable mandat des Nations Unies.

Engagement militaire ou endiguement en Iran ?

La situation pourrait désormais se prêter à un renforcement de la convergence entre la France et les Etats-Unis sur le dossier iranien. L'Administration américaine a clairement exprimé sa volonté d'étudier un dialogue stratégique avec l'Iran, de sorte qu'une détente des relations irano-américaines n'est plus à exclure dans les années à venir. En Europe, les inquiétudes sur les conséquences de l'acquisition de la bombe nucléaire par l'Iran sont grandissantes en raison notamment de sa vulnérabilité face la portée des missiles balistiques iraniens transméditerranéens. Cela dit, Washington demeurera sans doute très sensible à l'éventualité d'un Iran nucléarisé (les progrès réalisés sur ce terrain constitueront un véritable test pour tout dialogue avec Téhéran) et l'éventualité d'une attaque militaire contre les infrastructures nucléaires iraniennes est toujours d'actualité. La France, tout comme les Etats-Unis (et Israël) seraient exposés aux conséquences immédiates et de long terme d'un tel acte.

Il est également envisageable que Téhéran fasse le choix de prolonger cette situation de quasi puissance nucléaire, en retardant le développement d'une capacité déployable jusqu'à ce que les conditions soient plus propices, minimisant les conséquences défavorables sur le plan diplomatique et sécuritaire, dans le Golfe et ailleurs. Un scénario de ce type, qui prévoit une certaine intransigeance dans le développement nucléaire mais n'est pas loin de provoquer une intervention occidentale, obligerait la France, les Etats-Unis et les autres à penser en termes de stratégie durable d'endiguement. Elle pourrait s'étendre à de nouvelles assurances multilatérales en matière de sécurité dans le Golfe ou en Israël et tirerait grandement profit de l'évolution du processus de paix au Moyen-Orient. Téhéran s'efforcerait sans doute de saper le processus à Gaza, au Liban et ailleurs.

Les enjeux européens visant à endiguer les ambitions nucléaires iraniennes sont certainement aussi forts, voire plus directs que ceux de Washington. Si les Etats-Unis ont un intérêt systémique à empêcher l'émergence d'une nouvelle puissance nucléaire, l'Europe, France incluse, serait stratégiquement bien plus exposée à un Iran nucléarisé. La portée des missiles balistiques fait partie de l'équation. Mais l'Europe devra également prendre en compte les éventuels effets en cascade d'un Iran nucléarisé voire sur le point de l'être. Une augmentation des incitations à la prolifération au Moyen-Orient pourrait modifier l'équilibre militaire dans une zone très vaste, allant de la mer Egée à l'Asie centrale. La stratégie russe, déjà très dépendante de la force nucléaire, pourrait accentuer son effort dans cette direction au moment où l'OTAN sera en train d'évaluer et de refondre sa doctrine et sa stratégie. Un Iran nucléarisé ou en voie de nucléarisation aura plusieurs conséquences négatives pour l'environnement stratégique du voisinage oriental et méridional de l'Union européenne. Si la question du contrôle des armements est réinscrite dans l'agenda transatlantique, le nouveau débat portera très certainement, de manière bien plus approfondie, sur les dynamiques moyen-orientales. Le Pakistan, l'un des confins de l'arrière-pays méditerranéen, sera également l'une des données de l'équation. Cet État nucléaire fortement instable et au bord de l'effondrement économique pourrait rapidement devenir un exemple majeur de gestion de crise englobant la problématique nucléaire. À la différence de l'Iran, le Pakistan présente bien plus d'intérêts convergents pour chaque rive de l'Atlantique. La dynamique politique précaire et l'arsenal nucléaire existant (à quel point est-il sécurisé ?) sont autant de raisons pour envisager l'éventualité, dans des conditions chaotiques, d'une opération militaire au Pakistan d'une coalition incluant les Etats-Unis, la France et d'autres pays, dans le but de sécuriser les infrastructures nucléaires pakistanaises. Non pas une action moyen-orientale ou méditerranéenne au sens strict, mais plutôt une action qui aurait des répercussions politiques et sécuritaires importantes dans les régions limitrophes.

La dimension méditerranéenne

Les Etats-Unis sont une puissance méditerranéenne depuis plus de deux cents ans. Mais malgré l'ancienneté de leur présence, la politique américaine à l'égard de la Méditerranée demeure diffuse et fragmentée. La conscience méditerranéenne américaine est faible comparée à la France, l'Italie et partout en Europe méridionale. L'Union européenne dispose d'une véritable stratégie méditerranéenne, même si elle est insuffisante à plusieurs égards. De nouvelles stratégies, y compris l'Union pour la Méditerranée, d'inspiration française, reflètent l'importance de la Méditerranée et des pays riverains en tant que véritable zone stratégique. A l'inverse, les Etats-Unis continuent de diviser la région, tant sur le plan intellectuel que bureaucratique, en fonction de régions aux frontières rigides : l'Europe d'un côté, le Moyen-Orient et l'Afrique du Nord de l'autre. Les sous-régions stratégiques et les problématiques qui y sont liées, telles que les Balkans, la mer Egée, le conflit israélo-palestinien et la Turquie, sont rarement placés dans un cadre méditerranéen explicite. Cette asymétrie entre la vision française et la vision américaine devrait perdurer, même lorsque l'avenir de l'Afrique du Nord et les problématiques thématiques en Méditerranée joueront un rôle plus important dans la coopération transatlantique.

Dans cette région, les intérêts américains sont variés : les responsables politiques appréhendent la Méditerranée comme un élément de la sécurité européenne (vision qui prévalait pendant la Guerre froide), comme un élément stratégique pour l'accès à des zones telles que le Golfe (rôle du canal de Suez et de la base aérienne d'Incirlik) et comme un élément crucial pour la gestion de crise (Sahara occidental, Chypre ou Liban). L'engagement politique américain repose encore largement sur des relations bilatérales étroites, comme celles entretenues avec le Maroc et Israël, plutôt que sur une politique méditerranéenne *per se*. Le caractère transrégional de commandements militaires américains tels que le commandement des Etats-Unis pour l'Europe (EUCOM), qui couvrait l'Europe et l'Afrique a constitué une notable exception. AFRICOM, qui reste situé en Allemagne, est désormais un commandement indépendant qui couvre aussi le Maghreb. La sixième flotte couvrait également toute la Méditerranée.

À l'avenir, plusieurs problématiques devraient guider les actions transatlantiques en Méditerranée et pourraient contribuer à renforcer la coopération franco-américaine. Tout d'abord, l'Afrique du Nord est devenue plus centrale au regard des préoccupations stratégiques européennes et américaines. Le Maghreb est étroitement lié à l'Europe en raison de son statut de territoire de départ et de passage pour l'immigration, de ses perspectives politiques et économiques incertaines et des liens avec le terrorisme et la violence politique qui touchent les intérêts européens. La relance du processus de Barcelone, y compris l'Union pour la Méditerranée, sera partie intégrante de la nouvelle approche européenne concernant un voisinage plus large, où les Etats-Unis auront un rôle important. En dépit du scepticisme à l'égard de'Union pour la Méditerranée, on peut noter que l'initiative a suscité une attention inhabituelle à Washington, où elle constitue désormais un sujet de débat très prisé. Cela reflète peut-être une attention croissante des Etats-Unis pour la Méditerranée et l'Afrique du Nord, mais la dimension française ne peut être écartée alors que les deux pays souhaitent reconstruire les liens franco-américains.

Washington et Paris (et Rome) seront les principaux acteurs des relations politiques et économiques avec l'Afrique du Nord, qui devront notamment relever le défi de la réintégration de l'Algérie et de la Libye, après respectivement une décennie d'instabilité et de violence et des décennies d'isolement diplomatique et de sanctions internationales. Aucune de ces tâches ne sera facile. L'Algérie fait face à une crise de gouvernance et de développement latente et à une résurgence du terrorisme et de la criminalité. Le nationalisme algérien non reconstruit et la conscience de la souveraineté continueront à compliquer les relations des Européens, des Américains et des Russes avec Alger. La Libye reprend pratiquement à zéro ses relations avec les Etats-Unis et même avec l'Europe, les relations pourraient prendre des formes tout à fait nouvelles et différentes. La réintégration de ces pays en tant qu'acteurs régionaux sera primordiale pour renforcer les efforts visant à améliorer la coopération Sud/Sud, considérée comme une priorité des deux côtés de l'Atlantique.

Deuxièmement, les réseaux terroristes originaires d'Afrique du Nord devraient être de véritables sources de préoccupation pour les stratèges américains et français dans les années à venir. Ce sera une source de risques majeure pour l'Europe et un élément à prendre en compte dans la recherche de stabilité dans le Sud de la Méditerranée. De nombreux combattants maghrébins et égyptiens sont apparus en Irak et pourraient désormais gagner l'Afghanistan. Ils pourraient constituer un élément fixe de l'équation sécuritaire au Moyen-Orient et en Asie du Sud-Est et leur retour en Afrique du Nord ou en Europe pourrait contrarier les services de renseignements et de sécurité dans les années à venir.

Troisièmement la sécurité énergétique constituera un autre enjeu des intérêts transatlantiques en Méditerranée, avec des caractéristiques très différentes dans le Golfe et en Asie centrale. La prolifération de nouveaux gazoducs et oléoducs et de nouvelles lignes électriques va conduire à l'émergence d'un marché de l'énergie méditerranéen pouvant contrebalancer la dépendance européenne au gaz russe. L'Algérie et la Libye sont à cet égard des acteurs clés, mais le Maroc, la Tunisie et la Turquie jouent le rôle principal en matière de transport d'énergie. A l'évidence, la France et l'Europe du Sud sont plus directement concernés que les Etats-Unis dans l'équation de la sécurité énergétique en

Méditerranée. Mais tant que le marché du gaz naturel continue de se développer, la participation américaine devrait augmenter. Aujourd'hui le débat américain sur l'énergie porte essentiellement sur les questions pétrolières, essentiellement dans le Golfe. A l'inverse, le débat européen concerne essentiellement le gaz. Cette asymétrie de points de vue pourrait façonner les discussions transatlantiques sur la stratégie de sécurité énergétique dans les années à venir.

Quatrièmement, la Méditerranée constitue déjà un environnement multipolaire et pourrait le devenir encore plus avec le retour de la Russie comme acteur commercial, politique et sécuritaire. Il est probablement trop tôt pour juger l'étendue et l'importance du modeste retour de la Russie dans la région en tant que puissance navale et partenaire militaire de l'Algérie, de la Libye et de la Syrie, mais une relation stratégique plus tendue entre Moscou et l'Occident pourrait accroître la concurrence autour de la Méditerranée. Parallèlement, la Chine, l'Inde et les États du Golfe acquièrent des intérêts économiques dans les pays riverains de la Méditerranée et dans leur voisinage, concurrençant parfois directement l'Europe et les Etats-Unis. La crise économique mondiales pourrait ralentir voire interrompre cette tendance, mais la perspective d'ensemble tend vers une diversification des relations entre les acteurs intra- et extrarégionaux. À l'avenir, les relations de l'Europe et des Etats-Unis avec les partenaires du Sud de la Méditerranée pourraient s'inscrire dans une atmosphère concurrentielle plus forte.

Cinquièmement, du point de vue américain, l'évolution des relations stratégiques avec la France aura une influence déterminante sur la politique américaine en Méditerranée. À la différence des régions plus lointaines, le bassin méditerranéen est une zone où l'engagement et les capacités américaines et françaises sont relativement équilibrés et les intérêts *devraient* y être largement convergents. La coopération militaire dans la région est bien développée, depuis longtemps. Alors que la France a rejoint le commandement militaire intégré de l'OTAN, cette coopération pourrait s'intensifier et être plus visible. Il y a 10 ans certains responsables politiques américains auraient été mal à l'aise à l'évocation de cette idée. Aujourd'hui le concept serait le bienvenu dans nombre de centres de commandement et pourrait redynamiser les objectifs et les moyens à la périphérie européenne.

Le rôle de la Turquie dans les relations transatlantiques

Enfin, la Turquie devrait aussi faire l'objet du nouveau débat franco-américain sur les priorités stratégiques, et ce pas uniquement en raison de l'activisme croissant d'Ankara et de sa capacité de projection de puissance au Levant et dans le Golfe. Washington continuera sans doute, pour des raisons stratégiques, à soutenir la candidature turque à l'entrée dans l'Union européenne, bien que la capacité des Etats-Unis à défendre cet argument et à influencer les décideurs européens soit en déclin. La qualité des relations transatlantiques sera effectivement un facteur important, mais des questions structurelles et techniques auront aussi leur importance, celles-ci étant progressivement devenues plus prépondérantes dans les relations entre la Turquie et l'Union européenne. Comme en témoigne la réponse immédiate et critique du président Sarkozy aux déclarations du président Obama sur la candidature de la Turquie en avril et en juin 2009, la question turque demeure une source potentielle de frictions transatlantiques. Au départ, les Etats-Unis ne s'intéressent pas à l'adhésion en soi de la Turquie à l'Union européenne, mais plutôt à la poursuite de la convergence turque vers les règles européennes dans divers domaines, de la gouvernance à la sécurité. À cet égard, les intérêts français et américains en Turquie sont parfaitement compatibles.

Sur les questions sectorielles majeures comme l'énergie ou la défense, le périmètre d'une coopération purement bilatérale avec Ankara se réduit tandis que dans la plupart des instances internationales, l'approche transatlantique convient à chaque partie. La Turquie cherchant de nouveaux partenaires et des garanties de sécurité en raison de l'instabilité à ses frontières avec le Moyen-Orient, y compris concernant l'avenir de l'Irak, la multiplicité des partenaires sera d'actualité. La décision du Président Obama de se rendre en visite officielle en Turquie au tout début de son mandat a été un signe fort, essentiellement parce qu'il a choisi de l'effectuer lors d'un voyage en Europe et non au Moyen-Orient.

Quelques priorités stratégiques

La définition élargie du Moyen-Orient en tant qu'espace stratégique incluant la dimension méditerranéenne rend possible le renforcement du partenariat franco-américain. Ce tournant dans le style de la politique étrangère américaine et cette approche plus large des intérêts français et européens à la périphérie du continent créeront les conditions nécessaires à une coopération plus étroite. Sur les deux rives de l'Atlantique, la rigueur économique et les pressions visant à renationaliser les politiques étrangère et de sécurité pourraient aller à l'encontre de cet objectif, comme le ferait une crise imprévue en Asie ou ailleurs. Une liste restreinte des priorités stratégiques communes devrait comprendre :

- La stabilité à Gaza et la relance du processus de paix par la nouvelle Administration américaine s'accompagnant de moins de réserves quant à l'engagement européen, moins de rigidité intellectuelle sur la personnalité des intermédiaires dans ce processus (le modèle des accords d'Oslo) et des garanties de sécurité multilatérale si besoin.

- Une approche diplomatique régionale commune en faveur du retrait américain d'Irak, incluant des stratégies pour se protéger contre le chaos et l'effondrement de l'Etat unitaire.

- Un plan pour relever le défi d'un Iran nucléarisé, incluant certainement une stratégie durable d'endiguement si l'Iran choisit de rester à la limite du statut de puissance nucléaire.

- Le développement d'une approche franco-américaine plus visible pour la sécurité et le développement en Méditerranée, à la fois à l'intérieur et à l'extérieur du cadre de l'OTAN. Encourager une meilleure intégration Sud/Sud devrait être l'un des thèmes clef d'une politique plus concertée à l'égard de l'Afrique du Nord.

La prépondérance de ces questions dans les calculs stratégiques effectués de chaque côté de l'Atlantique et la proximité géographique de l'Europe feront de la politique méditerranéenne et moyen-orientale un test clef, à court terme, quant à l'attachement à la relance de la relation transatlantique.

Chapitre huit

Pour un dialogue franco-américain dépassionné en Méditerranée

Jean-Pierre Filiu

Résumé

Le Président Obama a renouvelé l'engagement de Washington envers une solution durable du conflit du Proche-Orient, passant par l'établissement d'un Etat palestinien aux côtés d'Israël. La France encourage cette volonté américaine de relance d'un authentique processus de paix, tout en proposant sa contribution à la reprise de pourparlers directs entre Israël et la Syrie. Confrontés à un défi d'une telle ampleur, Washington et Paris doivent aussi faire face à la diffusion en Méditerranée des réseaux du jihad global. De manière générale, les Etats-Unis doivent mieux prendre en compte la légitimité des interventions françaises au Moyen-Orient, tandis que les préventions françaises à l'égard de la politique américaine au Maghreb gagneraient à être dépassées. Les échanges d'expertise universitaire, mais aussi la coopération parlementaire, peuvent ouvrir de nouveaux espaces de dialogue à cet égard.

Pour la France de même que pour les Etats-Unis, la Méditerranée et le Moyen-Orient représentent un terrain d'affirmation d'une certaine idée d'eux-mêmes comme de leur vision du monde. Cette projection privilégiée de puissance mobilise des ressources prioritaires à Washington et à Paris, elle ne saurait donc être réduite à la somme des intérêts multiformes de la France ou des Etats-Unis dans la région, car ses enjeux sont tout autant symboliques que politiques et économiques. En outre, Washington est régulièrement tenté au Moyen-Orient par un unilatéralisme faisant fi du droit international et de l'ONU, tandis que les présidents français successifs ont pu sembler par le passé vouloir s'affranchir des références et de la discipline européennes.

Au-delà d'Annapolis et de Paris

Cette dimension fondamentalement politique confère une importance majeure aux initiatives présidentielles, ainsi qu'à leur perception par l'opinion nationale et internationale. Nicolas Sarkozy a choisi le soir même de son élection, le 7 mai 2007, pour lancer son projet d'Union méditerranéenne, tandis que le conflit israélo-arabe fut un des sujets les plus débattus de la campagne présidentielle américaine. C'est pourquoi la comparaison entre les deux grandes conférences réunies en 2007-08 par les chefs d'Etat américain et français est éclairante. Pour George W. Bush, il s'agissait d'achever son second mandat par une contribution décisive au processus de paix israélo-arabe, suspendu depuis 2001. Pour le président français, une nouvelle dynamique politique devait se déployer dans l'espace méditerranéen:

— la conférence pour la paix au Proche-Orient, convoquée par le président George W. Bush à Annapolis le 27 novembre 2007, a concerné 49 Etats et institutions internationales. Les invités d'honneur étaient le Premier ministre Ehud Olmert et le président Mahmoud Abbas, tandis que l'Arabie saoudite n'était représentée que par son ministre des Affaires étrangères et la Syrie par le numéro deux de sa diplomatie. La Maison blanche a souhaité ainsi ouvrir un nouveau cycle de négociations israélo-palestiniennes, dans la perspective de l'établissement d'un Etat palestinien indépendant et viable avant la fin de 2008. La déclaration adoptée à Annapolis est pourtant restée très vague sur les éléments d'un statut final et Washington a refusé d'adopter un rôle de médiateur actif entre les parties israélienne et palestinienne, appelées à négocier directement. La communauté internationale s'est engagée à hauteur de 7,4 milliards de dollars sur trois ans, lors de la conférence des donateurs pour l'Etat palestinien, réunie à Paris le 17 décembre 2007. Mais les pourparlers israélo-palestiniens se sont enlisés et aucune percée significative n'a été enregistrée après Annapolis.

— le sommet de lancement de l'Union pour la Méditerranée (UPM), accueilli à Paris sous la coprésidence de Nicolas Sarkozy et d'Hosni Moubarak, le 13 juillet 2008, a effectivement rassemblé 43 partenaires, les 27 membres de l'Union européenne et leurs 16 associés du pourtour méditerranéen. Seule la Libye a boycotté cette initiative, à laquelle les pays de la rive Sud, à l'exception notable du Maroc, ont généralement répondu par une participation au plus haut niveau. Les secrétaires généraux de l'ONU, de la Ligue arabe, de l'Union Africaine, de l'Union du

Maghreb Arabe et de l'Organisation de la Conférence Islamique étaient présents, ainsi que le Qatar, au titre de la présidence du Conseil de Coopération du Golfe. Le sommet tripartite franco-israélo-palestinien et l'annonce de l'établissement de relations diplomatiques entre Damas et Beyrouth ont rehaussé le profil de cette réunion. Mais l'UPM, dont le projet initial a été déjà remanié pour prendre en compte l'acquis du processus euro-méditerranéen de Barcelone, reste largement à construire.

Les toutes dernières semaines de l'administration Bush ont été marquées par une offensive d'une violence sans précédent de l'armée israélienne contre la bande de Gaza, qui n'a pas sensiblement affaibli le mouvement islamiste Hamas, à la domination toujours incontestée dans ce territoire palestinien. Cette « guerre des 22 jours », menée du 27 décembre 2008 au 17 janvier 2009, n'a pas non plus épargné un désaveu électoral à Tzipi Livni, successeur d'Ehud Olmert à la tête du parti Kadima. Les législatives israéliennes du 10 février 2009 ont en effet débouché, après de laborieuses négociations, sur la constitution d'un gouvernement dirigé par Benyamin Netanyahou, pour le Likoud, avec Ehud Barak (travailliste) à la Défense, et Avigdor Lieberman (Israel Beitenou) aux Affaires étrangères, qui remet explicitement en cause les principes d'Annapolis. L'impasse politique et l'escalade militaire ont donc conforté les options radicales, rendant à la fois plus nécessaire et plus complexe une intervention internationale pour surmonter un tel blocage.

Barack Obama a, peu après son investiture, exprimé son engagement en faveur de l'établissement d'un Etat palestinien aux côtés d'Israël. Hillary Clinton a souligné la détermination présidentielle au Proche-Orient et la désignation d'un émissaire spécial de la Maison blanche, George Mitchell, a confirmé cette mobilisation au sommet de l'Etat américain. La collaboration franco-américaine a été remarquable lors de la conférence de Charm al-Cheikh, réunie le 2 mars 2009, sous la coprésidence d'Hosni Moubarak et de Nicolas Sarkozy. Les participants se sont alors engagés à verser 4,5 milliards de dollars pour la reconstruction du territoire de Gaza, dévasté par l'offensive israélienne. Mais la violence de la « guerre des 22 jours » a aussi laissé de profondes séquelles diplomatiques et la dynamique de l'Union pour la méditerranée (UPM) demeure suspendue, à l'initiative de la partie arabe.

Le défi pour les Etats-Unis comme pour la France est de relancer les processus initiés à Annapolis et à Paris, de profiter du formidable potentiel de mobilisation de la communauté internationale à cet égard (et ce, malgré la palpable « fatigue des donateurs ») et de promouvoir une sortie par le haut d'un contexte régional aussi défavorable.

Des intérêts partagés

Les Etats-Unis et la France partagent le même intérêt profond et stratégique et à ce que la Méditerranée et le Moyen-Orient connaissent:

- la stabilité, que seul peut garantir le règlement durable du conflit israélo-arabe dans toutes ses dimensions. Washington et Paris, tous deux irrévocablement attachés à la sécurité d'Israël, sont désormais convaincus que celle-ci dépend de l'établissement, aux côtés de l'Etat juif, d'un Etat palestinien indépendant et viable. Au Maghreb, c'est la question du Sahara occidental qui est la clef d'une authentique détente régionale.

- le développement de la rive sud de la Méditerranée, car cette mer est traversée par certains des écarts de revenus les plus élevés du monde, ce qui encourage la pression migratoire, mais aussi des mouvements de contestation plus ou moins populaires. Ce sont des dizaines de millions d'emplois qui doivent être créés au Sud pour y absorber le potentiel de main d'oeuvre.

- la démocratisation de régimes marqués par une troublante permanence (le doyen des chefs d'Etat de la région, le colonel Qaddafi, est au pouvoir depuis 1969), alors que la classe moyenne, de plus en plus étoffée, et la jeunesse, de plus en plus diplômée, peinent à traduire leurs aspirations dans le champ politique.

La nouvelle administration américaine doit gérer le lourd passif de la présidence Bush. L'image des Etats-Unis s'est fortement dégradée dans le monde arabe, où ils sont accusés, suivant les circonstances, de mener une politique d'agression, de pratiquer les deux poids/deux mesures en faveur d'Israël, ou de récuser les rares avancées démocratiques, lorsqu'elles favorisent ceux qu'ils perçoivent comme des opposants à leur politique. Un potentiel de haine à l'égard de l'ensemble des pays occidentaux se crée, lourd de conséquences et porteur du choc des civilisations que l'on veut éviter. Ce potentiel a été sensiblement aggravé par la gestion médiatique de la « guerre des 22 jours » à Gaza: l'interdiction opposée par Israël à la presse étrangère a effectivement amorti l'impact de l'offensive dans les opinions occidentales, mais la diffusion massive par les télévisions arabes des images tournées à Gaza, durant les pires moments des bombardements, a suscité une véritable vague de fond d'horreur et d'indignation.

Barack Obama a heureusement repris l'initiative dès sa prise de fonctions. Son intervention sur la chaîne satellitaire « Al-Arabiyya », ses déclarations sur l'Etat palestinien ou son séjour officiel en Turquie ont permis d'endiguer la montée spectaculaire de l'anti-américanisme. L'abandon de fait de la « guerre globale contre la terreur », l'annonce de la fermeture de Guantanamo et le refus de tolérer la torture ont été salués avec beaucoup d'espoir. Mais la tâche est immense pour Washington et ses partenaires. La France, du fait de son crédit historique et politique dans le monde arabe, sera un allié déterminant dans l'indispensable entreprise de rétablissement de l'image de l'Occident en général, et des Etats-Unis en particulier.

Le grand dessein néo-conservateur d'un "Grand Moyen-Orient", où la démocratisation par la force des régimes arabes devait faire l'économie d'un traitement de la question palestinienne ("La route de Jérusalem passe par Bagdad"), a sombré sans retour. Paris, du fait de sa capacité de proposition et d'initiative, peut accompagner Washington dans le retour au principe de base du processus de paix israélo-arabe, celui de l'échange de la terre contre la paix. Un conflit territorial est par définition susceptible d'être résolu, à la différence d'un conflit portant sur l'essence et sur l'identité. Et les Etats-Unis auront besoin de tous les renforts lorsqu'ils relèveront enfin le défi de l'occupation et de la colonisation de la Cisjordanie.

Mais le legs le plus calamiteux de l'administration Bush est la transformation de l'Irak en pôle d'attraction et de mobilisation d'une nouvelle génération de jihadistes transnationaux. Après les "Afghans" de la décennie 1980 et les "Tchétchènes" de la décennie suivante, ce siècle s'ouvre avec la diffusion dans toute la Méditerranée de réseaux "irakiens", depuis Fath al-Islam au Liban à la transformation en Algérie du Groupe Salafiste pour la Prédication et le Combat (GSPC) en Al-Qaida au Maghreb Islamique (AQMI). La France est explicitement visée par cette menace d'un type inédit, qui la désigne comme suppôt de la "croisade" américaine.

De manière générale, la France ne souhaite ni l'isolement des Etats-Unis dans la région, ni le revers de leur politique : elle a démontré que ses mises en garde sur l'engrenage irakien étaient aussi pertinentes du point de vue des intérêts nationaux américains et elle combat les tentations isolationnistes au profit d'un engagement américain, structurant et raisonné. Mais Paris est parfaitement en droit de demander à Washington de pouvoir peser sur les décisions qui, au Moyen-Orient, affectent son environnement de sécurité.

L'enjeu syro-libanais

Paris dispose dans la région du réseau le plus implanté à côté de celui des Etats-Unis et sa diplomatie est, après l'américaine, la plus active et la plus constante dans la zone. La présence culturelle et commerciale de la France est certes concurrencée, mais elle demeure primordiale. Des centaines de milliers de Français vivent et travaillent dans la zone. La France y conduit avec presque tous les pays d'ambitieuses opérations de coopération et cette politique régionale, participant à son image internationale, lui vaut crédibilité et soutien.

Le Liban constitue de longue date un terrain de coopération actif entre la France et les Etats-Unis. Sans remonter aux temps de la Force Multinationale à Beyrouth en 1982-84, on peut rappeler que Paris et Washington ont parrainé de 1996 à 2000 un arrangement indirect entre Israël et le Hezbollah, qui proscrivait les cibles civiles et qui a neutralisé l'escalade de plusieurs crises. A partir de 2004, les Etats-Unis et la France ont oeuvré de concert pour obtenir la fin de l'occupation syrienne du Liban. C'est avec l'appui de Washington que la Force Intérimaire des Nations Unies au Liban (FINUL) est montée en puissance en août 2006, avec un important investissement français à la frontière avec Israël. Et l'expérience française de dialogue avec la Syrie est pleine d'enseignements pour l'administration Obama, qui peut difficilement pratiquer l'exclusive à l'encontre de Damas, tout en tendant la main à Téhéran. Cette équation syrienne est d'autant plus cruciale pour Paris et Washington que la crise de Gaza a torpillé les pourparlers indirects entre Israël et la Syrie, sous l'égide de la Turquie.

Le président Sarkozy a voulu ouvrir une nouvelle ère de coopération franco-américaine, entre autres au Moyen-Orient, dans une démarche qui n'est pas sans rappeler la détermination de François Mitterrand, en 1981, à lever les réserves de Paris envers le processus de Camp David. La France s'est mobilisée sans compter pour assurer le succès de la dynamique d'Annapolis et elle a accueilli dès le mois suivant une conférence internationale de bailleurs de fonds pour l'Etat palestinien, dont elle assure le suivi attentif. Enfin, la diplomatie française est disponible pour assurer, aux côtés des Etats-Unis et le moment venu, le co-parrainage de négociations directes entre Israël et la Syrie.

Clichés et arrière-pensées

Malgré l'intensité du dialogue quotidien entre Paris et Washington dans la région, les dirigeants américains restent nombreux à considérer que c'est surtout la capacité de nuisance de la France qu'il convient de neutraliser, tandis que le cliché d'Etats-Unis méprisants et déstabilisants prévaut encore souvent sur les bords de la Seine. Parmi les préjugés tenaces qui continuent de parasiter une authentique vision commune, deux séries de trois stéréotypes peuvent être mis en avant de part et d'autre de l'Atlantique.

Vu de Washington, l'action de la France est caricaturée comme étant profondément conservatrice, le soutien aux régimes en place, quel que soit leur caractère dictatorial, tenant lieu de boussole pour défendre les situations acquises et les rentes historiques. Cette caricature est aggravée d'une projection du communautarisme anglo-saxon sur la réalité sociopolitique française. C'est ainsi que la présence en France de la principale population musulmane d'Europe (environ 5 millions de personnes, soit quelque 8% de la population française) a été mise en avant pour "expliquer" les orientations de la diplomatie française, par exemple face au conflit irakien. Dans le même ordre d'idées, c'est l'importante présence arménienne en France qui sert de justification mécanique aux réserves de Paris envers l'ouverture de l'Union européenne à la Turquie.

Vu de Paris, les Etats-Unis sont parfois décrits comme engagés dans une politique systématique d'exclusion et d'élimination de toute puissance concurrente, même amie, et cet hégémonisme agressif au Moyen-Orient se doublerait depuis peu d'une campagne anti-française en Afrique du Nord, plus encore en Algérie qu'au Maroc. La volonté supposée de saper les positions historiques de la France au Maghreb s'accompagnerait d'encouragements plus ou moins discrets en direction des islamistes arabes. Enfin, la Turquie est réduite à un "cheval de Troie" de l'influence américaine, dont l'insertion dans l'UE parachèverait l'alignement européen entamé par l'élargissement aux nouveaux membres est-européens.

Quatre grands défis communs

La France et les Etats-Unis font face, dans la région, à quatre grands défis et les réponses qu'ils choisissent d'y apporter gagneraient à être, au moins en partie, coordonnées ou concertées:

- la route vers l'établissement d'un Etat palestinien doit impérativement être rouverte, avec des perspectives claires dans le temps et l'espace. Il convient de ne plus poser le registre humanitaire comme une fin en soi, et donc d'inscrire l'assistance à la population dans une démarche politique de long terme. La formation de la jeunesse palestinienne doit dès lors redevenir une priorité claire comme investissement d'avenir. Et le soutien à l'Autorité palestinienne ou aux écoles de l'ONU, suffisant pour l'enseignement primaire et secondaire, ne répond plus aux besoins d'universités largement privées. Il y a là un enjeu fondamental pour une génération de cadres qui ont consciemment refusé l'option de l'expatriation.

- la stabilité de la frontière nord d'Israël et de la frontière sud du Liban est subordonnée à un règlement du conflit israélo-syrien, et donc à un processus de négociations sur le Golan. Le contentieux sur l'enclave dite des "fermes de Chebaa", libanaise selon Beyrouth, syrienne selon Israël (qui en maintient l'occupation comme prolongement du Golan), lie le volet libanais et le volet syrien du conflit avec Israël. La France a envisagé la mise de cette enclave sous tutelle de l'ONU, dont les forces garantissent déjà le cessez-le-feu au Sud-Liban comme sur le Golan. Ce pourrait être le premier pas vers un règlement global, où la France comme les Etats-Unis auraient toute leur part à prendre.

- le naufrage du "Grand Moyen-Orient" a laissé de durables séquelles et créé contre ses promoteurs de vives rancoeurs, que seule la promotion d'une nouvelle perspective partagée peut permettre de surmonter. Tel peut être pour les Etats-Unis un des intérêts majeurs de l'Union pour la Méditerranée, à la fois du fait de sa perspective inclusive et de la rigoureuse égalité entre les partenaires du Nord comme du Sud.

• la diffusion en Méditerranée des réseaux du jihad global, surtout sous la forme d'Al-Qaida au Maghreb Islamique (AQMI), représente un enjeu de sécurité majeur. Mais deux écueils doivent être évités: celui du "tout-sécuritaire", voire du "tout-répressif", qui est parfois contre-productif lorsque la cible visée est trop large, et qui occulte souvent le travail en amont (sur les jihadistes potentiels) et le travail en aval (sur les terroristes repentis); celui de l'ingérence occidentale, facteur de ressentiment nationaliste. Il convient de ne pas oublier que, en Méditerranée comme ailleurs, ce sont les sociétés civiles musulmanes qui sont en première ligne face à Al-Qaida et qui paient le prix le plus lourd à sa terreur.

Sept pistes de dialogue

A défaut de relance formelle de la coopération américano-française dans la région, un nouvel esprit pourrait prévaloir et se fonder sur l'appréciation réciproque des intérêts et des expertises: Washington doit considérer légitimes les interventions de Paris au Moyen-Orient et prendre en compte les avis argumentés de ses spécialistes, tandis que la France a à respecter de la même façon les initiatives et les analyses des Etats-Unis au Maghreb. Au-delà de ce climat général plus favorable, sept pistes de dialogue plus opérationnel peuvent être tracées:

• les parlementaires américains et français ne se pratiquent et ne se connaissent pas assez sur ces sujets à haute visibilité en politique intérieure et les canaux bilatéraux entre les administrations des deux pays gagneraient à être accompagnés par une diplomatie parlementaire plus active, et donc à encourager le développement des échanges entre le Congrès, l'Assemblée nationale et le Sénat.

• la France a développé une expertise universitaire incontestable au Moyen-Orient, qui pourrait être mieux diffusée aux Etats-Unis par le biais de traductions et d'invitations, tandis que les spécialistes américains du Maghreb mériteraient de voir leurs travaux mieux connus en France, avec possibilité de projets conjoints avec les laboratoires concernés ou avec les centres de recherche français en Afrique du Nord.

• les Etats-Unis et la France doivent réfléchir ensemble aux moyens de régler définitivement le conflit sahraoui, dont la persistance compromet tous les efforts de construction maghrébine ou de coopération à l'échelle de l'Afrique du Nord. L'Espagne peut utilement être associée à cette réflexion conjointe, voire à une démarche concertée sur ce sujet.

• Al-Qaida au Maghreb Islamique (AQMI) constitue un thème privilégié de coopération anti-terroriste franco-américaine, à la fois du fait de la menace représentée par la seule "franchise" de Ben Laden en position offensive, mais aussi de part l'interaction entre le théâtre irakien, catalyseur de la mutation du Groupe Salafiste pour la Prédication et le Combat (GSPC) en AQMI, et les espaces traditionnels d'intervention du GSPC.

• la France et les Etats-Unis doivent travailler ensemble à la viabilité à long terme du futur Etat palestinien, qui repose sur la qualité de la formation de ses cadres, et donc sur la solidité des institutions académiques en Cisjordanie et à Gaza. Paris et Washington peuvent de concert amener une meilleure intégration des universités palestiniennes dans l'engagement international en faveur de l'Etat palestinien.

• la France peut faciliter la prise en compte par les Etats-Unis au Moyen-Orient de l'ONU comme cadre de référence juridique et d'éventuelle intervention. Dans le prolongement du déploiement des "casques bleus" à la frontière israélo-libanaise, une mise sous tutelle de l'ONU du territoire contesté des "fermes de Chebaa" peut être étudiée, à titre d'expérience à faire valoir sur le volet syrien, voire palestinien du processus de paix.

• la France a déjà promu une vision originale, volontariste et dynamique, de la Méditerranée au sein de l'UPM, et elle peut intéresser les Etats-Unis à l'ambitieux dessein d'un espace Eurogolfe de coopération, dont la Méditerranée constituerait le centre, et où les formidables ressources du Golfe pourraient promouvoir le développement et les échanges.

La relance des relations franco-américaines, impulsée par le président Sarkozy, a incontestablement impressionné les décideurs américains, dans l'Administration comme au Congrès. Quant au président Obama, il jouit d'une cote de popularité exceptionnelle dans l'opinion comme chez les responsables français, ce qui ne peut que conforter les bonnes dispositions de part et d'autre de l'Atlantique. Mais la tendance lourde reste trop souvent à Washington d'écarter les propositions françaises sur la région, sans prendre le temps de les évaluer, ni de les discuter. La nouvelle administration, encouragée par Paris à s'engager résolument au Moyen-Orient, pourra surmonter ces réflexes bureaucratiques. Quant à la contribution française, son caractère constructif n'est pas mis en question, mais il gagne en force et en visibilité chaque fois qu'il s'inscrit dans une dynamique européenne. Le temps des emportements semble heureusement révolu et le dialogue franco-américain peut dès lors gagner en substance en Méditerranée.

Chapitre neuf
Dynamiques africaines

Nathalie Delapalme

Résumé

Au début du nouveau siècle, alors que la généralisation de la récession, la fragilisation effarante des systèmes financiers, l'enlisement préoccupant des conflits irakien et afghan ébranlent les grandes démocraties développées occidentales, l'accélération des dynamiques africaines impose à la fois une relecture approfondie de la situation et des perspectives du continent africain et la redéfinition de nos modes de relations à son égard.

Plusieurs évolutions fondamentales caractérisent désormais l'Afrique: la poursuite d'une forte poussée démographique, à rebours du reste de la planète, l'installation d'une croissance moyenne très supérieure à celle des économies développées, la conclusion de plusieurs conflits historiques que la plupart des observateurs considéraient définitivement enlisés. Surtout, ce grand continent mitoyen de l'Europe concentre sur son territoire tous les principaux enjeux du monde globalisé, qu'ils touchent à la poursuite d'une croissance durable et équitable ou à la garantie d'une sécurité globale. Car il héberge le spectre le plus large des grands risques contemporains — terrorisme, épidémies émergentes, catastrophes environnementales, migrations massives incontrôlées, trafics de drogues et d'armes, prises d'otages et piraterie maritime. Mais il recèle aussi un potentiel vital pour la poursuite de la croissance des économies développées, qu'il s'agisse des ressources naturelles ou du formidable marché potentiel lié aux perspectives démographiques.

L'afflux récent de nombreux nouveaux partenaires sur le continent africain atteste de l'ampleur des enjeux. La concurrence qui s'y exerce désormais devient forte. Le temps d'un monopole occidental sur les équilibres politiques et les perspectives économiques de l'Afrique est révolu.

L'enjeu pour l'Europe, voisin immédiat et vieillissant de la remuante Afrique, peut sembler plus aigu que pour les Etats-Unis, plus distants géographiquement. De fait, avec l'adoption en décembre 2007 à Lisbonne de la Stratégie conjointe UE — Afrique, l'Europe s'organise désormais pour construire des partenariats concrets portant sur des sujets d'intérêt mutuel, comme les migrations, l'énergie ou le changement climatique. Mais l'interpénétration des enjeux et des risques dans un monde globalisé atténue cette apparente différence. Surtout, l'élection de Barack Obama modifie sensiblement l'impact du message américain sur nos interlocuteurs africains et accroît dès lors la responsabilité américaine, au moment où, dans ce contexte de concurrence inédite, les partenaires traditionnels européens paraissent handicapés par leur passé colonial.

Dans ce cadre profondément bouleversé, il est essentiel pour les partenaires occidentaux — Etats-Unis et Europe — du continent africain de bien mesurer les enjeux d'une part, et l'évolution de la « concurrence » de l'autre, afin de définir une stratégie nouvelle qui valorise à la fois leurs intérêts, leurs avantages comparatifs et leur potentiel de complémentarités.

Trop souvent, le continent africain apparaît encore comme le parent sombre, presque maudit, de la famille planétaire, voué à la pauvreté sans avenir, aux guerres civiles sans issue, aux épidémies sans rémission. De fait, l'approche des pays développés à son égard, qu'il s'agisse des responsables politiques ou surtout des opinions publiques, repose encore trop souvent sur une logique définie par la compassion, l'obligation morale, ou la fidélité à une histoire momentanément partagée. Alors même que la généralisation de la récession, la fragilisation effarante des systèmes financiers, l'enlisement préoccupant de la crise en Afghanistan, en Irak ou au Moyen-Orient, ébranlent les grands pays développés occidentaux, l'accélération des dynamiques africaines, illustration emblématique des grandes évolutions géostratégiques du monde contemporain — démographiques notamment, impose à la fois une relecture approfondie de la situation et des perspectives de ce grand continent et la redéfinition des modes de relations des partenaires occidentaux à son égard.

Vers l'apaisement des conflits africains ?

Les dix dernières années ont été marquées par la fin presque inespérée de plusieurs conflits lourds, interminables- plusieurs dizaines d'années — et apparemment sans issue : Angola, ex-Zaïre, Burundi, Sierra-Leone, Liberia, Sud-Soudan. Certes, la situation reste fragile en République démocratique du Congo. Certes, de nouveaux fronts se sont ouverts. À la lisière de la frontière entre le continent africain et le Moyen-Orient, le dramatique conflit du Darfour est une crise majeure. Il fait peser un risque d'implosion sur le Soudan et peut remettre en cause la conclusion de l'accord sur le Sud-Soudan. Il menace tout autant d'un côté son voisin ougandais et, au-delà, une région des Grands Lacs à peine apaisée, et, de l'autre, la bande sahélienne qui se fragilise d'Est en ouest de façon croissante, de la Mauritanie à l'Erythrée, en passant par le Niger, la Centrafrique et le Tchad. Immédiatement sous la péninsule arabique, la Corne de l'Afrique, en particulier la Somalie, reste un foyer majeur d'instabilité. D'anciens « champions » longtemps choyés par les pays occidentaux, comme la Côte d'Ivoire ou le Kenya, sont désormais handicapés par une profonde crise politique, aux lourdes conséquences économiques.

Mais la tendance est là, qui traduit deux évolutions essentielles. La première, c'est la prise de conscience, par les protagonistes locaux, que les intérêts économiques de la paix peuvent désormais dépasser ceux de la guerre. Dès lors, l'incitation pratique à terminer un conflit, qui fit tant défaut lors du dernier quart de siècle, semble commencer à prévaloir.

La deuxième, qui découle en partie de la précédente, c'est l'implication déterminante des acteurs régionaux, sur la base d'une analyse cynique de leurs intérêts bien compris, bien davantage que sous la pression des déclarations faits dans les enceintes onusiennes. L'endogénéisation, l'africanisation des processus de règlement des conflits est désormais un élément-clé de réussite, la condition incontournable de leur aboutissement. Si la crise ivoirienne s'achemine lentement vers son issue, c'est moins grâce à la détermination de la communauté occidentale — qui a même pu contribuer parfois à la durcir — qu'à cause de l'implication devenue constructive du Burkina-Faso, dès lors que celui-ci, mesurant que la communauté internationale ne le débarrasserait pas de son voisin, a bien voulu considérer qu'il valait mieux pour lui faire avec que contre. De la même façon, la solution de la crise du Darfour repose d'abord et essentiellement sur la reconnaissance mutuelle de leur intérêt politique par les présidents Omar Béchir et Idriss Deby, et sur l'attitude constructive de leurs différents voisins ou parrains régionaux, notamment l'Érythrée, l'Éthiopie, l'Egypte et la Libye. La encore, les prises de position des partenaires occidentaux ont parfois compliqué l'issue, dès lors que ceux-ci semblaient choisir un camp plus que défendre une solution.

Dynamiques africaines

L'installation de la croissance économique sur le continent africain constitue une autre évolution fondamentale qui marque le passage au $21^{\text{ème}}$ siècle. Pendant maintenant plus de dix ans, de 1995 à 2007, la croissance économique moyenne africaine a été supérieure à 5%, soit le triple de la croissance moyenne de la zone euro sur la même période (de l'ordre de 1,4%). Le grand isolement du continent africain, oublié des grands circuits financiers mondiaux, atténue désormais en partie la contagion de la crise financière qui secoue les économies développées, et pourrait bien constituer un avantage comparatif inédit, après avoir longtemps paru son principal handicap. De fait, alors que les perspectives du FMI[1] pour 2008 et 2009, très fortement révisées à la baisse par la crise, tablent désormais sur un ralentissement généralisé de la croissance mondiale, ce décrochage va persister, avec l'entrée en récession de la zone euro et des Etats-Unis, tandis que la croissance africaine ne devrait que légèrement s'affaisser : +1,5% en 2009 puis +4% en 2010 pour l'Afrique subsaharienne, contre -4,2%, puis 0,4% pour la zone euro, et -2,8 %, puis 0% pour les Etats-Unis.

Emergence des classes moyennes

Certes, on part de très bas. Certes, le nombre total de pauvres continue de s'accroître, dès lors que la croissance démographique demeure supérieure à la croissance économique. Mais la tendance est là. Surtout, la croissance du revenu moyen africain, entamée depuis le milieu des années 90, s'accélère et s'élargit. En 2007, 39 pays africains ont enregistré une croissance de leur PIB par habitant, contre 27 en 2000[2].En dix ans, de 1997 à 2007, 23 pays ont enregistré une croissance moyenne de

---

[1] FMI — Perspectives de l'économie mondiale et Perspectives économiques régionales : Afrique subsaharienne — avril 2009.

[2] FMI — Perspectives économiques régionales — Afrique subsaharienne — octobre 2008.

5% à plus de 50% du PIB réel par habitant, supérieure à 25% pour 12 d'entre eux.[3] Même si elle se traduit d'abord par le renforcement parfois flagrant des inégalités de niveau de vie, cette évolution inédite est aussi porteuse d'une conséquence essentielle : l'émergence d'une classe moyenne désormais évaluée, avec des divergences, au tiers environ des 900 millions d'Africains. Cette donnée majeure, déjà visible dans la plupart des capitales africaines, pèsera nécessairement sur l'évolution économique mais aussi sur les équilibres politiques des pays africains, comme elle l'a fait dans les pays asiatiques.

Le grand écart démographique

Plus fondamental que le décrochage des dynamiques de croissance, l'extraordinaire élan démographique du continent africain va profondément modifier les équilibres économiques et politiques, à la fois au sein du continent et vis-à-vis de ses partenaires. D'ici 2050, une génération à peine, la population africaine devrait plus que doubler, passant de 906 millions en 2000 à 1937 millions, soit de 14% à 21% du total mondial. L'Europe, pendant ce temps, régressera de 488 millions à 472 millions (7,5% à 5,2% du total). Les États-Unis, grâce à la poursuite assumée d'une forte immigration, devraient passer de 297 à 409 millions.[4]

D'ores et déjà, les 2/3 de la population africaine ont moins de 25 ans, dans une proportion presque inversée avec le continent européen. Fondamentalement surtout, désormais, nos partenaires africains considèrent leur poids démographique moins comme un frein à leur développement économique que comme un élément essentiel pour conforter leur poids politique dans un jeu mondialisé. Enfin, le « *Yes we can* » qui vient de porter un président noir à la tête des États-Unis nourrit manifestement, comme l'ont montré les réactions de la presse et de la rue africaines, un formidable élan, notamment chez les jeunes générations.

---

[3] 25% à 50% : Burkina-faso, Ethiopie, Gambie, Ghana, Madagascar, Mali, Sao-Tomé, Tanzanie ; croissance supérieure à 50% : Tchad, Mozambique, Nigeria, Sierra-Leone.

[4] Nation unies — Département des affaires économiques et sociales — Perspectives de la population mondiale —dernière révision 2006.

Fragilité des interlocuteurs traditionnels et conflits de génération

Ces évolutions lourdes s'accompagnent d'une modification sensible des équilibres internes du continent. Celle-ci se traduit d'abord par l'apparition de risques de fragilisation chez les « grands » États du continent, partenaires longtemps privilégiés des pays développés occidentaux — Afrique du Sud, Nigeria, Égypte, Sénégal, Côte d'Ivoire, Kenya, Ethiopie, notamment — soit parce que l'excellence de leur image à l'international s'est construite au détriment de leur consolidation intérieure, soit parce qu'ils sont ou seront, à brève échéance, comme d'autres d'ailleurs à ce titre, — Algérie, Gabon, Guinée équatoriale, Cameroun, Libye notamment — confrontés à des successions difficiles. Les puissances montantes du continent, comme déjà le Ghana, la Tanzanie, ou le Mozambique, sont désormais plutôt des pays de taille moyenne, qui privilégient la diversification de leurs relations, bien au-delà des seuls membres occidentaux du Conseil de sécurité ou du G8.

De fait, cette fragilisation reflète d'abord l'impact, inédit sur un continent traditionnellement respectueux de l'âge et de l'ancienneté, inévitable avec l'accélération du rajeunissement démographique et le poids nouveau des médias et de l'internet, d'un phénomène de conflit de générations, qui se traduira par une exigence accrue pour un véritable changement de génération (de dynastie… ?) de la plupart des responsables politiques africains.

Déplacement du centre de gravité africain vers le monde arabe et asiatique

Ce rééquilibrage se traduit aussi par un déplacement sensible du centre de gravité du continent africain vers son flanc est — immédiat avec les pays du Golfe, plus lointain avec la Chine et l'Inde, alors que semblent se distendre, avec les pays européens anciens colonisateurs, les liens forgés par l'histoire, plus que par la mitoyenneté géographique. Significativement, alors que le nombre total de passagers transportés par avion a stagné dès 2007, les liaisons aériennes entre le continent africain et le Moyen-Orient ont continué de progresser de près de 7% et de près de 10% avec l'Asie.[5]

---

[5] IATA — International Air Transport Association.

La Chine est désormais, devant la France et après les États-Unis, le deuxième partenaire commercial de l'Afrique,[6] dont elle importe le tiers de ses besoins pétroliers actuels[7]. En 1960, l'Europe représentait les deux tiers (66%) des exportations africaines. En 2006, elle n'en représente plus que 40%. Dans le même temps, la part de l'Asie est passée de 6% à 16%.

Mais l'Afrique n'est pas seulement pour la Chine un réservoir stratégique de ressources énergétiques, minières, forestières et même agricoles.[8] C'est aussi un débouché essentiel pour sa population active, un marché conséquent pour ses entreprises, un terrain nouveau de présence militaire,[9] un périmètre de partenariat privilégié pour son système financier, bref fondamentalement un enjeu politique majeur dans la redistribution des cartes du jeu international. L'itinéraire choisi par le président Hu Jintao pour sa sixième visite sur le continent noir, à la mi-février 2009, est significatif : Mali, Sénégal, Tanzanie, Maurice, Arabie saoudite : trois pays francophones, aucun enjeu pétrolier, une étape essentielle dans le Golfe… C'est bien d'un nouveau « partenariat stratégique » dont il s'agit.[10]

Moins explicite et moins connue, la stratégie indienne poursuit les mêmes objectifs de sécurisation des ressources énergétiques et minières, de renforcement des débouchés, et de représentativité dans les instances internationales. Enfin, les relations avec les pays pétroliers musulmans, monarchies du Golfe, mais aussi Iran ou Malaisie, se renforcent de façon marquée dans le domaine commercial et financier, comme dans celui de la coopération militaire. Les fonds souverains arabes se concentrent en particulier sur la maîtrise des infrastructures

---

[6] En 2005 : 32,1 Mds$ pour la Chine, 60,6Mds$ pour les Etats-Unis et 56,4 Mds$ pour l'Union européenne.

[7] OMC — Organisation mondiale du commerce.

[8] En Tanzanie, le groupe Chongqing Seed a acquis 300 hectares de terres et investi 143 millions de dollars pour y cultiver du riz. La Chine a prévu de créer une quinzaine de zones du même type sur le continent africain. Hu Jintao vise la mise en place de trois zones économiques spécialisées en Afrique: la première en Zambie pour les métaux (cuivre, uranium, diamants), la deuxième en Tanzanie pour les transports autour du port de Dar es Salaam, la troisième à Maurice dédiée au commerce et aux services financiers.

[9] Avec 1 628 soldats, policiers, ou observateurs militaires sur le terrain, la Chine est désormais de loin le premier contributeur de Casques bleus en Afrique, une priorité pour elle puisqu'elle y positionne 75% de ses personnels déployés(contre 40% pour la France…).

[10] « *We will seek China-Africa pragmatic relationship and promote the fuller development of our new strategic partnership* » — Hu Jintao — Dar Es Salaam — 16 février 2009.

de débouchés. Ainsi, déjà présent dans les ports de Djibouti, Dakar, Le Cap, *Dubaï Ports World*[11] s'intéresse désormais aux Comores et à Alger.[12]

Géostratégie

Cette évolution majeure n'est pas circonscrite aux intérêts économiques et commerciaux. Elle s'inscrit dans une stratégie politique de long terme, qui inclut, exactement comme chez les puissances occidentales au siècle précédent, le décompte des positions dans les enceintes multilatérales. La Chine draine désormais davantage de voix africaines au Conseil de sécurité que la France. Sur la Côte d'Ivoire, sur le Zimbabwe, sur le Soudan, elle a clairement contré les positions occidentales dans les débats du Conseil. De façon croissante, dans les enceintes collectives africaines, notamment à l'Union africaine, sur les grands sujets transversaux — changement climatique, migrations internationales, maîtrise de l'urbanisation, perspectives d'emploi, approvisionnement en eau — comme dans le règlement des crises du continent, le partenariat arabe prend le pas sur le partenariat occidental. Le Qatar participe activement depuis l'origine aux sommets et réunions de l'Union africaine. De fait, il est devenu pour le Conseil de sécurité ou l'Union européenne un intermédiaire incontournable sur les nombreux dossiers africains qui les préoccupent, qu'il s'agisse du Darfour ou de la Mauritanie. Dans le règlement difficile de la crise du Darfour, l'Union africaine privilégie désormais la liaison avec la Ligue arabe et l'OCI.

Dans ce cadre profondément bouleversé, il est donc essentiel pour les partenaires occidentaux du continent africain de bien mesurer les enjeux d'une part, et l'évolution de la « concurrence » de l'autre, pour définir une stratégie nouvelle qui valorise à la fois leurs intérêts, leurs avantages comparatifs et leur potentiel de complémentarités.

Dans le contexte mondialisé du siècle qui commence, la fracture n'est plus entre pays du nord riches et pays du sud pauvres. Elle est désormais celle qui s'élargit entre pays vieillissants, essentiellement préoccupés par leur sécurité et la stabilité de leur situation acquise, et pays jeunes, obsédés par leurs perspectives et animés par une volonté parfois violente de changement. Le vrai risque est dès lors celui qui

---

[11] Filiale de Dubaï World, société holding propriété du gouvernement émirati.

[12] La Tanzanie, qui débouche sur l'Océan indien, pourrait héberger à terme une base ou des facilités pour la marine chinoise.

consisterait à alimenter, ou simplement entretenir, la contradiction entre la sécurité des premiers et les aspirations des seconds. Bien au contraire, la sécurité des pays développés, et leur capacité à maintenir une croissance durablement forte, dépendent, de façon étroite et immédiate, du développement et de la stabilisation du continent africain.

Dans ce cadre, l'enjeu pour l'Europe, voisin immédiat et vieillissant de la remuante Afrique, peut sembler plus aigu que pour les États-Unis, à la fois plus distants géographiquement et plus proches démographiquement. Mais l'interpénétration des enjeux et des risques dans un contexte désormais globalisé atténue cette apparente différence.

Afrique-Occident : des risques partagés

De fait, nouveau théâtre géostratégique, le continent africain concentre sur son territoire tout l'éventail des risques du monde contemporain. Risque sécuritaire, d'abord. Plus de dix ans avant le 11 septembre 2001, c'est d'abord sur le sol africain qu'ont eu lieu les premiers attentats terroristes — DC10 d'UTA au-dessus du désert du Ténéré, en 1989, puis Dar-es-Salaam en Tanzanie et Nairobi au Kenya en 1998. Aujourd'hui encore, sur un continent qui réunit à la fois les facteurs et les instruments de la menace avec un niveau aléatoire de contrôle et de sécurité, le risque demeure élevé d'une nouvelle atteinte à des intérêts ou à des symboles occidentaux. La transformation récente du GSPC (Groupe Salafiste pour la Prédication et le Combat) initialement centré exclusivement sur l'Algérie, en AQMI (Al Qaïda Maghreb Islamique), l'élargissement de son terrain privilégié d'activités à l'ensemble de la bande sahélienne, et le durcissement de ses modes opératoires en attestent. Au-delà de la seule menace terroriste, le déport massif des grands circuits de trafics de drogues chassés du sous-continent sud-américain vers le continent africain, est préoccupant, de même que le développement de la piraterie maritime et des trafics financiers, les risques inédits qui menacent la sécurité informatique et l'arrivée constante d'armements déclassés en provenance des anciens théâtres de l'Est.

Risque sanitaire aussi, dans un contexte de progression exponentielle des voyages, sur un continent qui présente la proportion la plus élevée au monde de maladies transmissibles — sida, certes, mais aussi recrudescence de la tuberculose, de la rougeole et des méningites, et qui héberge toutes les épidémies émergentes — SRAS, grippe aviaire ou porcine, chikungunya.

Risque environnemental enfin, qu'illustrent déjà l'avancée des zones désertiques, l'enlisement progressif des grands fleuves conjointement à l'inondation de leurs deltas, l'engorgement incontrôlé des zones urbaines, la déforestation, l'extension des risques phytosanitaires dans un continent à prédominance agricole. Sur le continent africain, première victime du changement climatique, tout en étant pourtant le moins « pollueur », l'apparition prévisible d'un afflux de réfugiés climatiques, tant redoutée par le nouveau patron du Haut Commissariat aux réfugiés, Antonio Guterres, risque de peser sur les perspectives de développement et de raviver les facteurs de conflits.

Un potentiel considérable

Mais s'il héberge des risques majeurs, le continent africain recèle aussi un potentiel considérable. Il ne détient pas seulement 12% de la production mondiale de pétrole et 10% des réserves aujourd'hui connues — en-dehors des zones encore inexplorées. Il possède aussi, souvent en monopole, parfois en partage avec l'Australie ou la Russie, la plupart des métaux et minerais essentiels à la poursuite de la croissance industrielle et au développement des nouvelles technologies : près de 90% des réserves prouvées de platine, chrome et coltan, 60% des réserves de manganèse, 30% des réserves d'or et de phosphates, de cobalt, d'uranium et de bauxite, 25% des réserves de titane. Alors que la pression de la demande, notamment asiatique, s'inscrira nécessairement dans la durée, ce potentiel reste encore largement sous-exploité, en raison de l'insuffisance des infrastructures de production et de commercialisation ainsi que des crises qui ont secoué et secouent encore certains grands producteurs potentiels, gelant toutes perspectives en dehors des trafics liés aux conflits. De fait, ainsi qu'on l'a vu, l'apaisement des conflits en Angola, en République démocratique du Congo (RDC), et au Sud-Soudan a ouvert des perspectives considérables — qui ne sont pas étrangères à l'accélération du règlement de ces crises —, et attiré de nombreux « nouveaux amis ».

Surtout, la très forte croissance démographique qui marquera encore longtemps le continent désormais le plus jeune de la planète comporte certes un indéniable risque économique, social et politique à court terme pour les pays concernés d'abord et leur environnement régional immédiat, et un risque migratoire réel qui préoccupe leurs voisins européens. Mais elle représente aussi un formidable marché potentiel en termes de biens de consommation ou de grandes infrastructures. Pour des économies occidentales menacées par la récession induite par la crise financière, alors même que le vieillissement démographique altère déjà les perspectives de demande, l'enjeu devient vital à brève échéance.

Une concurrence inédite

L'afflux récent de nouveaux partenaires sur le continent africain atteste de l'ampleur de cet enjeu. La concurrence qui s'y exerce désormais devient forte. Le temps d'un monopole occidental sur les équilibres politiques et les perspectives économiques de l'Afrique est révolu.

Pendant que l'Europe peinait près de dix ans pour organiser après le premier sommet du Caire en 2000, la deuxième édition fin 2007 à Lisbonne du sommet entre l'Union européenne et l'Afrique, en raison du blocage britannique sur le Zimbabwe, les grands partenaires émergents du continent ont multiplié les rencontres : premier sommet Afrique-Chine et premier sommet Afrique-Amérique latine en 2006, deuxième sommet IBSA[13] en 2007, quatrième TICAD[14] au Japon et premier sommet Afrique-Inde en 2008. La présence marquée d'Hugo Chavez et Mahmoud Ahmadinejad, invités d'honneur au sommet de l'Union africaine de juillet 2006, a constitué un signal essentiel. De fait, à l'instar de la Chine et de l'Inde, le Venezuela, mais aussi le Brésil, comme l'Iran déjà du temps de Khomeiny, mettent en place en Afrique une véritable stratégie économique et politique. Depuis 2000, le montant des échanges commerciaux entre le Brésil et le continent africain a été multiplié par quatre, le président Lula a effectué sept voyages sur le continent et y a ouvert douze nouvelles ambassades. Comme l'Inde, le Brésil développe sa coopération dans des domaines de compétence très pointus : agriculture tropicale, médicaments génériques, bio- carburants. La Russie elle-même, nouvelle venue sur le continent, témoigne d'un intérêt croissant pour l'Afrique, dans une stratégie de maîtrise des approvisionnements énergétiques, mais surtout d'équi-

---

[13] *India — Brazil — South Africa.*
[14] *Tokyo International Conference on Development.*

libre des puissances. La Turquie enfin, régulièrement invitée d'honneur aux sommets de l'Union africaine, renforce ses liens avec le continent et souligne volontiers sa capacité à être « à la croisée des mondes ».

L'émergence des acteurs non-étatiques

Au-delà des relations classiques d'État à État, le paysage est également modifié par l'apparition d'un maillage étroit entre partenaires non-étatiques et par le développement des opérateurs et instruments de partenariat non-publics. Les diasporas libanaise, ismaélienne, indienne et chinoise jouent un rôle croissant en Afrique, complémentaire à celui des diasporas africaines installées à l'extérieur du continent. Grands bailleurs émergents, les fondations — comme la fondation Gates, qui dépense chaque année pour la santé en Afrique davantage que l'OMS, ou la fondation Aga Khan, présente depuis longtemps dans le secteur des infrastructures sur le flanc est du continent et qui intervient désormais dans les pays de la bande sahélienne — et surtout les fonds souverains[15], deviennent des acteurs majeurs, dont les marges de manœuvre financières sont sans commune mesure avec les disponibilités budgétaires des bailleurs étatiques occidentaux. La Banque Mondiale travaille désormais au montage d'un partenariat qui pourrait porter sur 1% des disponibilités actuelles estimées des fonds souverains, soit une enveloppe de 30 milliards de dollars, c'est-à-dire presque l'équivalent du montant total des investissements directs étrangers (IDE) en Afrique en 2007 (....et l'équivalent des bonus distribués en 2007 par les banques occidentales). Les banques islamiques, avec l'appui des pays du Golfe et de l'Iran, deviennent des partenaires importants, voire privilégiés, des banques et des investisseurs locaux, tout en jouant un rôle croissant pour héberger les capitaux africains expatriés, récemment évalués par le Parlement britannique à plus de 700 milliards de dollars.

Priorités françaises

Avocat privilégié depuis l'origine du traitement de la dette africaine et de la mise en place de financements innovants pour le développe-

---

[15] Aujourd'hui estimés à 3 000 Mds $, dont *Abu Dhabi Investment Authority*: 875 Mds $, *Kuwait Investment Authority* : 213 Mds $, *State Administration of Foreign Exchange*(Chine) : 311Mds $.

ment dans les grandes enceintes internationales, la France souligne depuis longtemps le lien incontournable entre développement et résolution des conflits. Ces dernières années, elle s'est engagée résolument dans la résolution des crises africaines, y compris sur le terrain militaire, en Ituri avec l'opération Artémis en 2003 comme en Côte d'Ivoire avec l'opération Licorne dès 2002. Avec le dispositif RECAMP, elle a contribué de façon essentielle à la formation des forces africaines au maintien de la paix sur leur propre continent. Elle a œuvré pour la mise en place de la Facilité de paix européenne, qui permet depuis 2004 de financer les opérations de maintien de la paix menées par l'Union africaine, à partir des ressources non affectées du FED (Fonds européen de développement).

L'accent est mis désormais sur le renforcement des instances régionales africaines — économiques, politiques, et militaires — et sur le partenariat entre l'Union européenne et l'Union africaine, enceintes privilégiées pour traiter les grandes problématiques communes : migrations, changement climatique, sécurité énergétique, notamment. Enfin l'appui au secteur privé comme vecteur essentiel de la croissance économique, seule à même de garantir le développement, est un élément déterminant de la politique mise en œuvre par le président Nicolas Sarkozy.[16]

Faire évoluer les opinions

Dans un contexte de préoccupation domestique croissante en matière économique et sociale, ces évolutions soulèvent généralement incompréhensions ou critiques auprès d'une opinion publique lassée qui, alternativement, considère que l'engagement pour la « stabilité » en Afrique revient à préserver coûteusement des régimes corrompus, ou que l'accent porté sur l'« appropriation africaine » et la mise en valeur d'« intérêts mutuels » sacrifie notre devoir de solidarité et masque le retrait de notre aide. Ces réticences sont évidemment confortées par le rejet inédit, souvent rageur, parfois violent, de l'ancien colonisateur par les jeunes générations des pays francophones, rejet démultiplié par le développement des médias et le recours généralisé au net.

---

[16] Discours au Cap (Afrique du sud) — 28 février 2008.

Plus que jamais pourtant, l'enjeu partagé du développement et de la stabilisation du plus grand continent de la planète doit être mesuré et traité. L'arrivée de Barack Ismail Obama permet à cet égard des perspectives nouvelles considérables. Moins sur la perception des dossiers africains par la nouvelle administration: Barack Obama est un Américain, qui défendra en priorité les intérêts de son pays que, de façon essentielle, sur la perception des États-Unis par les Africains : le fait que la majorité du peuple américain ait pu choisir de porter un noir à la tête des États-Unis modifie très profondément la donne et conférera aux positions américaines une écoute et un impact sans précédent.

Sécurité et développement : le lien clé

Dans ce cadre, plusieurs pistes d'action, conjointes ou complémentaires, peuvent être évoquées pour nourrir un nouveau partenariat transatlantique sur les dossiers africains.

La première porte sur la nécessaire accélération de la résolution des conflits et sur la relation incontournable entre sortie de crise et développement. Mis en évidence par les travaux de Paul Collier[17], le lien entre paix et développement doit être conforté et surtout lu dans les deux sens. Car pas de développement sans paix et sécurité certes, mais pas non plus de sécurité durable sans développement, ni surtout de sortie de crise possible sans perspectives économiques concrètes pour les protagonistes. De fait, l'intervention des partenaires occidentaux dans la résolution des crises africaines gagnerait à se déplacer du terrain de la médiation politique, devenu improductif, voire contreproductif, dans un contexte de durcissement des revendications à la souveraineté politique, et de montée en puissance des médiations régionales, vers un terrain plus économique, visant à faire en sorte que les dividendes de la paix apparaissent clairement plus prometteurs et plus durables que les intérêts de la guerre. Le cadre récemment mis en place avec la Commission de consolidation de la paix des Nations-Unies pourrait être conforté par une liaison plus forte avec les grandes institutions financières internationales, les organismes et agences d'aide, et les banques régionales de développement.

En outre, si les États occidentaux souhaitent réellement privilégier l'intervention sur le terrain des forces africaines, l'appui financier à

---

[17] Paul Collier, *Breaking the Conflict Trap*, 2003 et *The Bottom Billion*, 2007.

l'Union africaine et la formation des brigades régionales devront impérativement être complétés par la mise à disposition effective de moyens de communication, de surveillance et de transport, notamment hélicoptères, qui font cruellement défaut sur les théâtres africains — le cas du Darfour est emblématique à cet égard.

En tout état de cause, une attention plus étroite doit être portée à la zone grise qui continue de menacer le passage de l'étape prolongée du maintien coûteux de la paix — plus de 5 milliards de dollars sont consacrés chaque année aux seules OMP (Opérations de maintien de la paix) sur le continent africain, généralement enlisées bien plus de dix ans, — et de l'urgence humanitaire à celle d'un développement plus autonome.

La réforme de l'aide publique

La deuxième piste porte sur la nécessaire évolution de l'aide publique au développement. Dans un contexte de régression générale des capacités d'aide publique des grands donateurs du CAD (Comité d'aide au développement) de l'OCDE, au moment où parallèlement le Plan Paulson envisage de consacrer, sous diverses formes, 700 milliards de dollars au seul sauvetage des banques occidentales, soit dix fois le montant auquel les pays du G8 s'étaient engagés en 2005 à Gleneagles à porter leur aide annuelle à l'Afrique d'ici à 2010, un effort particulier, au minimum de pédagogie, devra être fait sur ce sujet. Le retard flagrant sur la réalisation des Objectifs du Millénaire pour le Développement (OMD)[18], dont un premier bilan est attendu dès 2010, pèse déjà sur les relations avec les pays en développement, dans un contexte ou le discours sur la gouvernance risque de devenir inaudible, et fortement contesté, au regard des errances financières massives enregistrées chez les pays développés.

La coordination et la complémentarité des bailleurs deviennent un objectif prioritaire, réclamé par les pays bénéficiaires eux-mêmes[19]. Les principes de « bonne conduite » établis par la Déclaration de Paris de mars 2007[20] méritent d'être élargis aux pays non-membres du CAD de l'OCDE. Y associer aussi, autant que faire se peut, les bailleurs émer-

---

[18] Rapport du groupe de réflexion sur le retard pris dans la réalisation des ODM — Banque mondiale — 2008.

[19] On compte aujourd'hui dans le paysage de l'aide, pour les seuls donateurs institutionnels, 280 donateurs bilatéraux, 242 programmes multilatéraux, 24 banques de développement, 40 agences onusiennes.

[20] Cf OCDE -CAD : *2006 Survey on monitoring the Paris Declaration.*

gents que sont désormais les grandes fondations et les fonds souverains est essentiel. Ces principes doivent également être étendus à la problématique de la dette, face aux risques réels d'un ré-endettement massif et non régulé auprès de créanciers extérieurs au Club de Paris- au premier rang desquels la Chine, alors même que le service de la dette continue de dépasser le budget consacré à la santé dans 52 pays africains sur 54 et le budget consacré à l'éducation dans 19 d'entre eux. Au regard de l'effort massif qui a été consacré jusqu'ici consacré par les membres du Club de Paris, en particulier la France, au traitement des dettes africaines, il y a là un enjeu considérable.

À la complémentarité entre bailleurs doit enfin correspondre la complémentarité entre bailleurs et bénéficiaires. Cette démarche répond à la logique de partenariat revendiquée de part et d'autre. Elle permettra aussi de mieux partager les responsabilités face à des résultats jugés insuffisants. En particulier, dans ce cadre, la gouvernance passera du statut de condition d'octroi de l'aide à celui de facteur essentiel de son efficacité. C'est l'insuffisance de gouvernance qui explique l'inefficacité de l'aide, bien davantage que l'insuffisance des montants octroyés. Et l'insuffisance de gouvernance doit moins susciter la baisse de l'aide que sa réaffectation.

De fait, l'accent devra être mis sur l'identification des résultats dans les pays bénéficiaires plus que sur le montant des moyens octroyés comme seul « témoin » de l'engagement des donateurs, sur la capacité d'absorption des partenaires, sur la complémentarité de l'aide extérieure avec les budgets nationaux, sur la nécessaire hiérarchisation des secteurs d'intervention, et enfin sur l'importance de la croissance économique comme moteur du développement, en complément de l'aide.

Les conditions d'une croissance équitable et durable

Essentiel, cet accent mis sur la croissance implique qu'une attention plus soutenue soit portée au développement du secteur privé et aux facteurs qui le favorisent : maîtrise cruciale de l'approvisionnement énergétique, développement des grandes infrastructures de communication — réseau routier et aéroports régionaux mais aussi accès aux nouvelles technologies et à internet large bande —, mise en place de structures bancaires solides de nature à canaliser à la fois l'épargne des migrants, les capitaux des diasporas et les capitaux expatriés, et surtout intégration des pays africains dans les grands circuits commerciaux mondiaux. L'aboutissement des négociations du cycle de Doha est à cet égard une priorité. Mais pour se traduire par l'augmentation concrète des résultats à l'exportation du continent africain, elle devra impérativement être complétée par l'amélioration des infrastructures de production, de transformation et de commercialisation.[21]

Une attention prioritaire devra enfin être portée à la sécurité alimentaire et au développement agricole du continent africain, dont le potentiel pourtant considérable, déjà handicapé par les retards de productivité et les contraintes diverses des marchés européen et américain, est désormais lourdement menacé par les conséquences du changement climatique. De fait, la nécessité de préserver les équilibres écologiques et environnementaux devra être intégrée dès l'amont dans la définition des stratégies de croissance. La quasi-disparition de la part de l'aide publique au développement consacrée à l'agriculture — de 16,9% en 1982 à 3,5% en 2004 doit être inversée, avec un effort particulier en direction des infrastructures rurales, des intrants, des régimes fonciers et de l'information sur les marchés et leurs normes.

L'inéluctable réforme de l'architecture de la gouvernance mondiale

Tout ceci implique un effort pédagogique préalable auprès des opinions publiques, pour sortir des stéréotypes sur une Afrique vouée à la crise, qui n'appellerait en retour qu'opérations militaires de maintien de la paix, observations électorales, et actions humanitaires.

Une réflexion conjointe devra enfin être menée sur l'approche adéquate de plusieurs notions emblématiques — démocratie, gouvernance, droits de l'Homme, justice internationale. En effet, sur ces sujets qui restent prioritaires pour nos opinions publiques, l'approche occidentale se confronte désormais à la posture des grands partenaires émergents du continent africain, et en particulier de la Chine, attentifs à préserver la souveraineté politique de ceux qu'ils prennent soin de traiter comme leurs homologues, ce qui leur confère un réel avantage comparatif dans un contexte de concurrence inédite.

---

[21] Cf CNUCED : le développement économique en Afrique 2008 — Résultats à l'exportation après la libéralisation du commerce — Quelques tendances et perspectives.

Au-delà, cette réflexion partagée devra porter sur les contours et la configuration institutionnelle adéquate d'une « communauté internationale » qui ne peut plus raisonnablement se limiter à ceux qui ont été dessinés au lendemain de 1945, sauf à se voir, *horresco referrens*, désormais qualifiée par certains d'« ordre cannibale ».[22] Les discussions tenues à Washington à l'automne dernier attestent de l'ampleur et de l'enjeu du chantier primordial de la reconstruction de l'architecture de la gouvernance mondiale. L'élection de Muammar Gaddafi à la tête de l'Union africaine laisse prévoir une forte revitalisation du projet des Etats-Unis d'Afrique. Au total, dans un cadre nécessairement remanié, les grands dossiers africains — stabilisation des conflits et des zones grises, capacités d'insertion dans le commerce mondial, sécurité alimentaire, emploi local, renforcement des capacités de gouvernance, notamment. — pourront être les sujets privilégiés d'une coopération transatlantique renforcée.

---

[22] Jean Ziegler.

Chapitre Dix

La politique africaine à l'ère de la coopération franco-américaine

Gwendolyn Mikell

Vue d'ensemble

Alors que l'Administration Obama vient de prendre ses fonctions, les Etats-Unis et la France ont une nouvelle occasion de redéfinir les orientations qu'ils doivent prendre à partir de 2008-2009 concernant l'Afrique. Ils devraient agir en ayant une meilleure connaissance de la complexité des réalités locales et mondiales auxquelles l'Afrique et la communauté mondiale dans son ensemble sont actuellement confrontées. Mes années de recherche sur l'Afrique m'incitent à considérer la formulation des politiques et l'intérêt national comme un défi perpétuel obligeant à surveiller le contexte social et la manière dont les Africains et les Américains perçoivent les changements dans leur vie. Ces derniers temps, l'agenda américain à l'égard de l'Afrique a été essentiellement guidé par des préoccupations liées à l'unilatéralisme, à la lutte contre le terrorisme et à la sécurité/défense. Toutefois, la nouvelle Secrétaire d'Etat, Hillary Clinton, a insisté sur le fait que la politique américaine devait associer les principes et le pragmatisme : « les trois piliers de la politique étrangère américaine sont la défense, la diplomatie et le développement, et deux de ces piliers relèvent du Département d'Etat et de l'Agence américaine pour le développement international (USAID) »[1]. Espérons que cela signifie qu'en dépit de la situation économique mondiale difficile, le Département d'Etat et l'Administration Obama vont examiner les défis politiques et les possibilités multilatérales dans des contextes sociaux plus intégrés disposant d'institutions plus vastes et dans des structures multilatérales plus larges que dans le passé.

---

[1] Hillary Rodhan Clinton, "Nomination Hearing to be Secretary of State", 13 janvier 2009. Voir aussi, Mark Silva, "Hillary Clinton: Its Going to Be Hard", *Chicago Tribune: The Swamp*, 22 février 2009.

Mon but ici est d'examiner les perspectives d'une coopération anglo-francophone en faisant ressortir les différences par rapport au passé, en explorant les dynamiques des acteurs stratégiques, en soulignant les défis de la sécurité/du maintien de la paix et de la gouvernance auxquels l'Afrique doit faire face, et en évoquant les opportunités, pour l'Afrique, offertes par les nouvelles communautés de la diaspora. Malgré les conflits en cours, de nombreux Etats africains ont dépassé les guerres civiles et les rebellions des années 1990, forts de nouvelles connaissances sur la façon de désamorcer un conflit militaire et de lutter contre des maladies comme le VIH/sida. Les crises des années 1990 ont vu l'épanouissement d'organisations issues de la société civile prêtes à critiquer le processus de construction de la nation. L'Occident a joué un rôle essentiel en soutenant cette évolution de la société civile, mais le travail est loin d'être fini. Le problème des réseaux terroristes qui pourraient exploiter les vulnérabilités des jeunes Etats africains forcent ces derniers à composer avec de nouvelles contraintes dans l'élaboration de leurs politiques. Heureusement, la plupart des Etats africains, y compris ceux à majorité musulmane, ont des cultures politico-religieuses modérées et n'ont pas adhéré à la démarche terroriste. Désormais, en termes de développement, nous avons besoin d'approches qui renforcent cette position modérée, et non qui la saborderaient. Ces approches contribueraient à encourager les Etats africains et l'Union africaine (UA) à s'engager dans la bonne direction et à exiger que les Etats-Unis, la France et l'Union européenne travaillent ensemble de manière sensible et efficace pour soutenir la voie africaine.

L'Administration Bush s'est intéressée à l'Afrique essentiellement de façon unilatérale, se concentrant sur les questions militaires et de sécurité, le commerce et la lutte contre le VIH/sida. Elle était consciente de l'histoire militaire et des relations commerciales de la France avec l'Afrique francophone, mais voyait dans ces relations un facteur potentiellement limitatif de l'influence américaine sur le continent, et avait cherché à les neutraliser par le biais de relations bilatérales en termes d'échanges commerciaux, de développement et de sécurité. L'approche de l'Administration Obama est encore embryonnaire, mais affirme soutenir le « renforcement des institutions démocratiques, la prévention des conflits, la promotion de la croissance économique, et la création d'un partenariat avec l'Afrique pour lutter contre les menaces mondiales »[2]. Alors qu'en substance elle ressemble aux précédentes, cette approche pourrait différer dans le style et offrir aux Etats-Unis l'opportunité de travailler plus étroitement avec la France et les autres pays de l'UE. Cela impliquera une rupture avec les anciens comportements afin que les initiatives multilatérales soient plus en phase avec les besoins de l'Afrique et l'évolution sur le terrain.

L'ancienne politique américaine

Initialement, les Etats-Unis n'avaient pas de politique cohérente en Afrique, s'appuyant plutôt sur les stratégies de la Guerre froide et les sphères d'influence européennes en Afrique. Historiquement, seuls le Liberia et l'Afrique du Sud ont entretenu des relations avec les Etats-Unis, mais à partir des années 1960, les Etats-Unis se sont liés au régime fort du Congo/Zaïre sous le président Mobutu Sese Seko et ont entretenu des relations stratégiques fluctuantes avec l'Ethiopie et la Somalie[3]. A la fin de la Guerre froide, les Etats-Unis ont préféré s'appuyer sur les Nations Unies pour contrer l'expansion des conflits violents en Afrique, en dépit de ses différences avec l'ONU en termes de budget et de participation financière. Après l'échec des interventions américaines en Somalie en 1992, les Etats-Unis se sont inquiétés de « l'élargissement des missions » et sont devenus plus réticents à s'engager en Afrique sur les questions sécuritaires, politiques et de développement. L'Administration du Président Bill Clinton a créé une nouvelle diplomatie économique pour l'Afrique par le biais des ministères du commerce et des transports dans les années 1990. Les réticences antérieures à s'engager sur les questions politiques et militaires ont continué à hanter la politique américaine et, lors du génocide rwandais en 1994, l'échec des Etats-Unis à agir a sérieusement endommagé les relations afro-américaines. Les Américains se sont contentés de compter sur les Nations Unies comme acteur majeur ainsi que sur les Fran-

---

[2] Tami Hultman, "Africa: Carson Outines Obama Administration's Policy Priorities," *allAfrica.Com*, 29 avril 2009.

[3] Marguerite Michaels, "Retreat from Africa," *Foreign Affairs*, 1992/3. Elliott P. Skinner, *African Americans and U.S. Foreign Policy Toward Africa, 1850 – 1924: In Defense of Black Nationality*. Washington, D.C. : Howard University, 1993.

çais, les Belges et la mission des Nations Unies au Rwanda, bien qu'ils se soient révélés incapable d'endiguer le conflit[4].

En 1994, les Américains se sont concentrés sur l'Afrique du Sud qui venait de sortir de l'apartheid et organisait des élections démocratiques. Par le biais des conférences binationales pour l'Afrique du Sud, le Vice-Président Al Gore a supervisé une série d'échanges et de discussions entre le Foreign Service Institute américain (Institut américain du service extérieur), les ministères américains du Commerce, de l'Agriculture, des Transports et de l'Education et leurs équivalents sud-africains. Sous le régime du général Sani Abacha au Nigeria, les Etats-Unis ont retiré la plupart des ressources diplomatiques et financé délibérément des organisations pro-démocratiques de la société civile qui sont devenues les porte-paroles du rétablissement de la démocratie. Lorsque le régime Abacha a pris fin, le processus d'adaptation de l'aide au développement aux besoins spécifiques du nouveau gouvernement ainsi que l'association des politiques d'assistance et de sécurité à travers une relation bilatérale (comme en Afrique du Sud) ont été reproduits en 1999 lors de la prise de fonctions du président Obasanjo. Le processus de restauration de la démocratie après les élections au Nigeria a été plus compliqué pour les Etats-Unis : il impliquait de restaurer les ressources diplomatiques, de naviguer entre les tensions entre chrétiens et musulmans dans le pays, de renforcer la capacité du Nigeria à jouer un rôle central dans la résolution des conflits par l'ECOMOG (Groupe de la CEDEAO chargé du contrôle et de la mise en œuvre du cessez-le-feu), à cibler les financements sur les groupes de femmes de la société civile et à lutter contre le VIH/sida comme s'il s'agissait d'une question civile et militaire. Toutefois, le renforcement des relations entre le Nigeria et les Etats-Unis ne s'est pas encore traduit par une amélioration du développement démocratique de ce pays[5].

---

[4] Victoria K. Hult and Moira K. Shanahan, "African Capacity-Building for Peace Operations: UN Collaboration with the African Union and ECOWAS", http: //www.stimson. org/fopo/pdf/Africa_Capacity-building.pdf.

[5] Gwendolyn Mikell, "Players, Policies, and Prospects: Nigeria/US Relations," in Adekeye Adebayo and Abdul Raufu Mustapha (Ed), *Gulliver's Troubles: Nigeria's Foreign Policy After the Cold War*, Scottsville SA: University of KwaZulu-Natal Press, 2008, pp. 281-313. Voir aussi, Gwendolyn Mikell and Princeton Lyman, "Critical Bilateral Relations in Africa: Nigeria and South Africa," Chapter 6 in J. Stephen Morrison and Jennifer Cook (ed), *Africa Policy in the Clinton Years: Critical Choices for the Bush Administration*, Washington, D.C. : CSIS Significant Issues Series, 2001.

Les relations américaines et françaises avec l'Afrique se sont concentrées sur la compétitivité économique des Etats-Unis et de la France, ce qui pouvait sembler cohérent dans les années 1990, mais les résultats ont souvent été mitigés pour l'Afrique. Les Etats-Unis et la France comptaient sur le Nigeria et l'Angola pour les exportations de pétrole brut peu sulfuré et soutenaient les relations des entreprises avec ces deux pays. En Angola, les Etats-Unis ont soutenu Jonas Savimbi, le chef de guerre rebelle contre le gouvernement socialiste pendant trente ans ; c'est seulement après la mort de Savimbi en 2002 qu'ils ont renforcé les relations avec le gouvernement angolais et soutenu la transition démocratique[6]. Quant à la France, elle a soutenu les séparatistes de la province de Cabinda en Angola après l'indépendance du pays puis soutenu les ventes d'armes françaises au Président dos Santos pour combattre les rebelles, dans les années 1990. De même, le géant pétrolier français Total possède les plus grandes concessions au Soudan et la France dispose d'intérêts importants dans le projet de pipeline Tchad-Cameroun, ce qui la conduit à soutenir la stabilité gouvernementale, malgré les conflits actuels dans ces pays. Alors que les entreprises américaines ont des intérêts pétroliers importants au Soudan, les Etats-Unis ont mis l'accent sur la lutte contre les violations des droits de l'Homme dans ce pays, en réponse aux pressions de ses groupes religieux et de la société civile.

La pression de l'opinion publique américaine a influencé les politiques de l'Afrique émergente et cela pourrait aussi être le cas en France. Les bases de la Loi sur la croissance et les opportunités en Afrique (African Growth and Opportunity Act ; AGOA) ont été posées au cours de la période de transition 1998-2002 alors que la société civile américaine réclamait une législation cohérente visant à lever les restrictions tarifaires sur les importations africaines aux Etats-Unis et plus largement sur le commerce africain. Le président Bush a triplé l'aide publique au développement (APD) pour l'Afrique et signé une version actualisée de l'AGOA, la transformant ainsi en loi, lors de ses premiers mois à la présidence en 2001. En outre, les Américains ont été touchés par les crises humanitaires et sanitaires en Afrique.

Ce n'est pas pour ses initiatives en matière de sécurité que le Président Bush a obtenu plus de 85% d'approbation auprès des Africains,

---

[6] Fred Bridgland, "Ghost of Savimbi haunts Angola," 22 février 2003, *NEWS.scotland.com*. "Angolagate: les principaux acteurs de l'affaire", *Le Figaro*, 28 mars 2007.

mais pour son enthousiasme à voyager dans divers pays africains afin d'évaluer le commerce et le développement ainsi que les projets humanitaires, pour sa volonté de parler avec le peuple africain des processus démocratiques, pour avoir « dansé » comme il l'a fait au Liberia et au Ghana, et pour son engagement passionné contre le VIH/sida et autres maladies présentes en Afrique. Il affirme fièrement avoir plus que doublé l'aide au développement en Afrique par rapport à son niveau de 2004 et avoir travaillé à des partenariats avec les dirigeants africains pour surmonter la pauvreté en développant leurs économies. La signature de la Loi sur la croissance et les opportunités en Afrique (AGOA-2001), l'Initiative pour l'Education en Afrique (2002), les subventions du Millenium Challenge Corporation, un organisme gouvernemental travaillant avec certains pays en voie de développement, totalisant 3 milliards de dollars destinées aux pays africains démocratiques et en voie de libéralisation (2003) et le Plan d'aide d'urgence du Président pour la lutte contre le sida (President's Emergency Plan for AIDS Relief ; PEPFAR-2003) comptent parmi les initiatives politiques du Président. Le PEPFAR a été controversé aux Etats-Unis en raison de son approche « ABC » (abstinence, fidélité et utilisation de préservatifs) et de sa dépendance aux groupes religieux qui soutenaient ces initiatives. Le slogan républicain « Dites juste non » avait été adopté par le plan d'aide PEPFAR. Pourtant, les critiques doivent féliciter Bush, même à contrecœur, pour l'impact des médicaments antirétroviraux et des conseils qui sont en train de changer le visage du VIH/sida dans de nombreuses régions africaines[7]. Ces succès et ces échecs montrent de nouvelles possibilités de collaborations entre les Etats-Unis, la France et l'Union européenne, en particulier si elles ne portent pas uniquement sur les médicaments mais cherchent à mettre en place de véritables systèmes de santé et des modules d'éducation à la santé, essentiels à une politique de santé publique efficace.

Parmi les initiatives de Bush on compte aussi l'Initiative présidentielle contre la Malaria (2005), l'Initiative d'allègement de la dette multilatérale (2005), cinq nouveaux fonds d'investissement soutenus par la Société de promotion des investissements du secteur privé (Overseas Private Investment Corporation ; OPIC), l'Initiative en faveur de la compétitivité globale africaine (African Global Competitiveness Ini-

---

[7] Giles Bolton, "How is America's Extra Aid Being Spent?" in *Africa Doesn't Matter: How the West has failed the Poorest Continent and What We can do about It* (NY: Arcade Publishers, 2008), p. 279.

tiative ; AGCI-2006), et la formation de plus de 39 000 gardiens de la paix africains dans 20 pays différents (en particulier dans la CEDEAO), outre la coopération avec des partenaires locaux pour traiter les problèmes de sécurité et les perspectives de paix en Afrique. Les Etats-Unis sont le plus grand donateur au Haut commissariat aux réfugiés (HCR), dont plus de 40% du budget a été attribué à l'Afrique en 2007. C'est aussi « le plus grand contributeur au Fonds mondial de lutte contre le sida, la tuberculose et le paludisme, promettant plus de 3,5 milliards de dollars et déboursant plus de 2,5 milliards de dollars depuis 2001 »[8]. En recevant une distinction d'Africare pour sa politique africaine, en particulier pour ses initiatives en faveur de la santé en Afrique, le Président Bush avait fièrement noté : « Dans toute l'Afrique, les gens parlent désormais d'un « effet Lazare » : des communautés laissées pour mortes sont ramenés à la vie »[9].

La politique de l'Administration Bush consistant à trouver « des solutions africaines aux problèmes africains » et à s'appuyer sur les puissances régionales pour répondre aux demandes relatives à la sécurité a été plus critiquée en Afrique. Les Etats-Unis ont été progressivement poussés à soutenir plus fermement les mesures multilatérales de maintien de la paix de l'Organisation des Nations Unies. Les stratégies de sécurité américaines de 2002 et 2006 du Président Bush qui privilégiaient les mesures préventives de lutte contre le terrorisme et cherchaient à « élargir le cercle de développement par l'ouverture des sociétés et par la mise en place d'infrastructures démocratiques »[10] ont été très controversées au départ. Pourtant, les initiatives pour l'Afrique du Président Bush ont pris de plus en plus en compte l'importance géostratégique de ce continent et ont dans l'ensemble été considérées comme un succès. En Afrique de l'Ouest, les Etats-Unis ont progressivement soutenu le rôle du Nigeria dans la mission de maintien de la paix de la CEDEAO au Liberia et en Sierra Leone. Toutefois, les stratégies de sécurité ont eu moins de succès ailleurs sur le continent.

L'Administration Obama se voit pressée d'élargir le plan d'aide d'urgence à la lutte contre le sida (PEPFAR) en y incluant plus largement

---

[8] Ibid.

[9] Le PEPFAR a financé le traitement d'1,7 million d'Africains ; son budget a été augmenté de $48 milliards en 2007 par le Congrès. Voir Brian Kennedy, "Top U.S. Charity Lauds Bush Africa Policy," *AllAfrica.Com*, 17 novembre 2008, Washington, D.C.

[10] *The National Security Strategy of the United States of America*, George W. Bush, The White House, 16 mars 2006.

des systèmes de santé et en supprimant le traitement préférentiel des groupes religieux pour le financement des projets. De même, l'Administration Obama devrait poursuivre et approfondir le soutien américain aux questions sécuritaires en Afrique. Le nouveau commandement américain pour l'Afrique (AFRICOM) proposé en 2007 et mis en place en octobre 2008 en est certainement le meilleur symbole. Certaines des questions de sécurité et des critiques seront développées plus loin.

Les pays incontournables et la stratégie américaine en Afrique centrale, en Afrique de l'Est et dans la Corne de l'Afrique

Les intérêts et besoins politiques, tout comme les intérêts nationaux, divergent selon les époques. Les attaques terroristes du 11 septembre 2001 aux Etats-Unis, prises dans le contexte des attentats contre les ambassades américaines de Nairobi au Kenya et de Dar es-Salaam en Tanzanie en 1998, ont renforcé les préoccupations américaines en termes de sécurité et d'engagement du président George W. Bush en faveur de la diplomatie préventive. A partir de 2002, le Président Bush a commencé à établir un nouvel type de relations avec l'Afrique : initialement fondées sur le modèle traditionnel des administrations républicaines et mettant donc l'accent sur la sécurité et le commerce, elles ont progressivement été conçues de manière à empêcher que les pays africains ne soient exploités par les militants islamistes et les réseaux terroristes mondiaux. Avec la multiplication des engagements mondiaux et africains pour mettre fin aux guerres civiles et pour permettre la résolution des conflits, le degré d'intégration des dynamiques économiques et conflictuelles a été mieux perçu. Pourtant, la prise de conscience et la sensibilité dans les approches stratégiques occidentales doivent être améliorées.

Tout d'abord, il est nécessaire d'effectuer des analyses approfondies régionales et spécifiques à chaque pays qui soient bien adaptées aux conditions de terrain dans la Corne de l'Afrique. Cette région reste une préoccupation majeure, d'autant que l'anxiété au sujet des réseaux transnationaux opérant en Somalie a nourri le plaidoyer américain en faveur de « l'assèchement des marais » et alimenté la collaboration entre Ethiopiens et Américains et que les tensions africaines se sont accrues dans la région[11]. Le Parlement français a également débattu de la politique à adopter dans la Corne de l'Afrique et en particulier dans le cadre de son dialogue avec les représentants de la région, mais il n'est parvenu à aucune conclusion satisfaisante[12]. Plus récemment, le phénomène de la piraterie au large des côtes somaliennes a renforcé l'idée que la politique dans ce domaine ne peut pas être uniquement une question unilatérale mais doit être le résultat de discussions entre les Américains, les pays francophones et les Nations Unies sur la manière de lutter contre la pauvreté, qui peut nourrir la piraterie au large de la Corne de l'Afrique[13].

A l'évidence, l'administration Obama doit davantage se consacrer à la résolution de questions telles que la piraterie en Somalie, la guerre civile au Soudan et la reconstruction post-conflit en République démocratique du Congo (RDC). Dans le cas de la piraterie en Somalie, le récent sauvetage du capitaine et de l'équipage américains pris en otage par des pirates au large des côtes démontre l'ingéniosité de la marine et des militaires américains face à la criminalité maritime. Néanmoins, nos approches doivent être plus systématisées et limiter les pertes humaines si nous ne voulons pas voir d'escalade de la violence le long des côtes somaliennes. Simpkins a très justement souligné la faiblesse des processus internationaux de maintien de la paix dans cette région et a insisté sur le fait que, malgré les problèmes historiques avec la Somalie, ce pays doit devenir une priorité de la politique américaine à l'égard de l'Afrique. En outre, il a expressément appelé à travailler avec l'Autorité intergouvernementale sur le développement (Intergovernmental Authority on Development ; IGAD) afin de stopper les flux d'armes légères et les potentielles cellules terroristes[14].

Il est évident que le droit international sur la piraterie est de peu de secours : personne ne veut ramener les pirates aux Etats-Unis ou en Europe pour les juger, ce qui engagerait d'énormes difficultés juri-

---

[11] Princeton Lyman and J. Stephen Morrison, "The Terrorist Threat in Africa," *Foreign Affairs*, January/February 2004. Voir aussi "Draining the Swamp: The Financial Dimension," Council on Foreign Relations, The American Response to Terrorism series, 25 mars 2002 ; et "Why Ethiopian and American Interests Conflict on Somalia: Commentary," *Ogaden Online Editorial Board*, 15 janvier 2002.

[12] "France Renews Ties with the Horn of Africa," *Ethiomedia*, 6 février 2004.

[13] "Pirates force the world to see sad plight of Somalia," *Irishtimes.com*, 29 octobre 2008.

[14] Gregory B. Simpkins, "Raising the Level of Engagement between America and Africa: A Leon H. Sullivan Foundation White Paper, Washington, D.C., Avril 2009.

diques et financières, tant sur le plan national qu'international. C'est pourquoi, nous ne devons pas uniquement définir des approches maritimes internationales et des accords multilatéraux, nous devons aussi mieux comprendre les conditions locales conduisant à la piraterie et rechercher des solutions locales impliquant l'utilisation du capital social et culturel de la Somalie et de l'Afrique. La piraterie dans le golfe d'Aden est facile : il s'agit d'une stratégie économique née de la colère des habitants de la côte face au non-respect, par les colonisateurs puis les pays du monde entier, des eaux territoriales et des frontières somaliennes, infractions qui restent impunies. Les pirates fonctionnent par extension des réseaux terrestres fondés sur la descendance/la parenté, l'amitié et le clientélisme pour fournir nourriture, emplois et autres ressources indispensables aux personnes vivant dans un Etat inexistant en proie à une crise galopante. Etant donné qu'ils fonctionnent dans l'ombre des vieux réseaux politiques, je crois que la solution est à trouver sur t erre.

L'idée qu'un leadership africain soit essentiel à la résolution du problème de la piraterie doit être prise au sérieux par les Etats-Unis et la France. Certains ont insinué que la piraterie somalienne ne prendrait pas fin tant que l'on n'aura pas fait appel aux dirigeants locaux issus des régions originaires des pirates ; certains précédents montrent que les dirigeants islamiques locaux peuvent aider à résoudre les conflits et à mettre fin aux assassinats dans la région[15]. Je suggère que cette solution implique au départ l'utilisation du capital social somalien mais aussi d'autres pays africains. Il est temps d'élaborer une stratégie de développement pour la Somalie, qui offre des incitations professionnelles qui excluent la piraterie comme stratégie économique. Les approches institutionnelles africaines doivent être élargies pour y inclure d'autres structures judiciaires régionales africaines afin de faire face à la piraterie. Il est donc essentiel de travailler avec l'IGAD mais ce n'est probablement pas suffisant. La question est de savoir si la solution des problèmes somaliens doit inclure la création d'un tribunal pour la Corne de l'Afrique ou la création d'une nouvelle institution s'occupant des questions économiques et de sécurité.

En substance, des « solutions africaines », sans soutien ni partenariat occidental, ne sont pas la bonne réponse. Le soutien du G8 doit

---

[15] Abdi Samatar, "The Road Ahead: Violence and Reconciliation in Somalia, Council on Foreign Relations, podcast, *http://www.cfr.org/publication/13209/road_ahead.html.*

être construit de façon réfléchie et en collaboration avec l'Afrique. Bien que la création du Tribunal pénal international pour le Rwanda ait été innovante et essentielle, elle a néanmoins court-circuité les autres approches de résolution des conflits en Afrique et déclenché des tensions franco-britanniques. Rétrospectivement, nous voyons aussi les problèmes imprévus créés dans les communautés côtières swahilies par la poursuite des suspects des attentats au Kenya et en Tanzanie. Les procédures judiciaires engagées contre des suspects d'Al-Qaïda nous enseignent que les questions judiciaires doivent être traitées selon les normes locales africaines et mondiales afin de résister à l'examen[16]. Notre approche sécuritaire doit tenir compte des impacts locaux et engager des partenariats locaux. Il est essentiel que les Etats-Unis, la France et l'Union européenne trouvent un terrain d'entente dans la lutte pour la sécurité dans la Corne de l'Afrique et en Afrique de l'Est, d'autant que la possibilité d'invoquer l'autorité de l'ONU reste limitée.

Les crises mondiales touchant à la sécurité ont accru l'importance de l'Afrique pour les Etats-Unis car environ 22% des importations de pétrole brut peu sulfuré aux Etats-Unis proviennent de cette zone[17]. Désormais, les populations musulmanes des zones productrices de pétrole sont sensibles à la manière dont nous traitons les questions de sécurité dans les pays musulmans[18]. On peut citer par exemple les questions du renforcement et de la rationalisation des institutions militaires en Afrique, de la résolution des conflits, de l'amélioration de la diplomatie publique, de la sensibilisation au monde islamique africain, ainsi que le soutien renforcée que les institutions de défense américaines pourraient apporter aux relations civilo-militaires en Afrique. Ces initiatives, combinées à la stratégie de sécurité nationale des Etats-Unis de 2002[19] visant à défendre et préserver la paix, promouvoir la démo-

---

[16] Susan F. Hirsch, *In the Moment of Greatest Calamity: Terrorism, Grief, and a Victim's Quest for Justice*, Princeton University Press, 2006. Voir aussi, "What if Torturers Go to Trial and Win?" *Yglesias*, 28 avril 2009, http://yglesias.thinkprogress.org/archives/2009/04/what-if-torturers-go-to-trial-and-win.php.

[17] "African Crude Exports to the US Jump," *Energy Tribune*, 18 avril 2007. Voir aussi David Shin, "China, Africa, and Oil," Center for Strategic and International Studies, Washington, D.C., 2006.

[18] Ibrahim Addo Karawa, "Exploring Mutual Perceptions: Dialogue between U.S. and Northern Nigerian Opinion Leaders," 27-28 janvier 2003. Voir aussi Gwendolyn Mikell, "America's Response to Terrorism: Fundamentalist Movements in Africa," Council on Foreign Relations, Washington, D.C., 5 décembre 2001.

[19] President George W. Bush, "National Security Strategy of the United States," *New York Times*, 20 septembre 2002.

cratie, prévenir les agressions des réseaux terroristes et enfin suspendre le financement du terrorisme, ont eu des impacts significatifs en Afrique. L'Administration Obama doit maintenant agir.

Le conflit au Darfour (Soudan) pose aujourd'hui des problèmes qui exigent l'utilisation du capital social et culturel africain pour renforcer les capacités de maintien de la paix et de résolution des conflits. Les dysfonctionnements évidents de la force hybride ONU/Union africaine (MINUAD) s'expliquent par de nombreuses raisons. Outre l'insuffisance des ressources financières et institutionnelles nécessaires à l'Union africaine pour fournir suffisamment de troupes de maintien de la paix à la MINUAD, les Etats membres du Conseil de sécurité font preuve d'une volonté politique insuffisante pour financer, pourvoir en personnel et mettre en place une mission fournissant la protection nécessaire pour les réfugiés du Darfour. On observe par ailleurs une certaine suspicion quant à la volonté américaine de recourir à la Cour pénale internationale (CPI) pour contrôler un pays musulman tandis que certains conflits apparaissent au sein de l'Union africaine sur la sagesse politique de l'ONU à détenir le Président al-Bachir et des responsables soudanais pour qu'ils rendent compte des atrocités commises.

La question est de savoir quelles sont les limites de la France dans l'utilisation de son autorité morale pour aider à résoudre les crises régionales au Soudan. L'intervention militaire destinée à renforcer le président tchadien Idriss Déby à l'automne 2008 a démontré l'importance de la France dans les affaires régionales mais a relancé la question de l'intérêt national français[20]. Le mandat d'arrêt de la CPI contre le Président Omar al-Bachir, légitimement arrivé au pouvoir, est sans précédent, ce qui a irrité les dirigeants nord africains ainsi que les dirigeants de l'Union africaine. Alors que les dirigeants de l'Union africaine nient ou négligent les atrocités commises au Darfour, ils semblent craindre des interventions au Soudan qui contesteraient la souveraineté de l'Etat, prévoyant que l'Union africaine serait divisée si ces interventions étaient tolérées. Cette division pourrait réellement exister, étant donné le rôle joué par le président libyen Mouammar Khadafi et d'autres chefs d'Etat qui tirent profit de l'aide financière à destination de pays africains pour contrôler les dynamiques au sein de l'Union africaine. Il en résulte le soutien de l'Union africaine au Prési-

---

[20] Mark Tran, "France Threatens Military Action against Chad Rebels," *The Guardian*, Tuesday, 5 février 2008, http://www.guardian.co.uk/world/2008/feb/05/france.sudan

dent al-Bachir, ce qui le protège de la menace mondiale et lui permet de préserver son contrôle sur la politique soudanaise.

Ce bourbier pose d'énormes problèmes aux Etats-Unis, à l'ONU et à l'Union africaine et la solution ne peut pas facilement venir des Africains eux-mêmes. Le président Obama a déjà nommé un envoyé spécial pour le Soudan, le Général Gracian, et on peut espérer quelques progrès. Toutefois, il est peut-être temps pour les Américains de discuter avec les membres du G8 de l'efficacité des stratégies sur le Soudan. Une approche au G8 implique le recours à une instance extérieure à l'Organisation des Nations Unies qui compterait les Chinois et les autres membres permanents du Conseil de sécurité. La Chine est en effet la clé d'une solution au Soudan. Le Secrétaire général de l'ONU Ban Ki-moon a déjà engagé une partie de son autorité morale pour appeler la Chine à coopérer au Soudan, mais les résultats risquent d'être limités. L'ancien Secrétaire général Kofi Annan n'avait pas hésité à assister aux réunions des sommets de l'Union africaine, ou à utiliser son autorité pour contribuer à l'évolution du discours et du comportement de l'Union africaine sur les questions de résolution des conflits, de gouvernance, etc. Il est peut-être temps pour la nouvelle Administration de commencer à travailler avec l'Union européenne, le Canada, les Scandinaves et les Nations Unies pour encourager la tenue de nouvelles rencontres en Afrique au cours desquelles ces questions pourraient être examinées. Ensemble, ils pourraient proposer une conférence spéciale du G8 sur le Soudan qui se tiendrait en marge du prochain sommet de l'Union africaine.

La création du nouveau commandement AFRICOM modifie les discours sur la sécurité. En 2007, l'Afrique et de nombreux groupes américains étaient sceptiques face à la création, par l'Administration Bush, du commandement des Etats-Unis pour l'Afrique, mais également face à ce qu'ils percevaient comme une « politique étrangère militarisée ». A cette époque, le projet AFRICOM prévoyait des mesures en faveur du développement considérées comme inadaptées et plus appropriées au service américain d'aide au développement USAID. Toutefois, depuis, des réponses ont été apportées à bon nombre de ces critiques. Les Américains ont réagi plus positivement après la création d'AFRICOM en octobre 2008. Parallèlement, l'Union africaine acceptait de coopérer plus étroitement avec l'AFRICOM, qui avait décidé de construire sa base à Stuttgart en Allemagne plutôt que sur le continent

africain[21], du moins au départ. Les Etats-Unis et autres pays occidentaux peuvent en tirer des leçons qui seront davantage approfondies
ultérieurement : les approches post-Guerre froide fondées sur la sécurité ne prennent généralement pas suffisamment en compte le fait que
les défis terroristes sont souvent les résultats prévisibles de l'échec des
politiques de développement qui offre peu d'alternatives aux populations pauvres.

La concurrence entre les Etats-Unis et la France, qui avait tendance
à dominer les relations dans les années 1990, est aujourd'hui plus faible
mais anime toujours les relations en matière de sécurité avec les pays
africains. Tout comme celle des Etats-Unis, mais de manière moins
visible en raison du poids du Congrès et du bipartisme, la politique
étrangère de la France est passée par différentes phases. Pendant un
siècle, la France a entretenu de fortes relations économiques et militaires avec les pays d'Afrique subsaharienne tels que le Sénégal, le Mali,
le Niger, le Nigeria, le Burkina Faso, la Côte d'Ivoire, le Tchad, la
République centrafricaine, le Gabon, le Zaïre/RDC, le Rwanda et le
Burundi.

Avec plus de 250 000 ressortissants français résidant en Afrique et
des liens économiques établis grâce aux échanges et aux investissements dans les gisements de minerais et de pétrole africains, l'importance de la France dans ses anciennes colonies s'est renforcée[22]. Durant
la dernière décennie, les dynamiques mondiales ont encouragé les
Africains des régions francophones à être pragmatiques, à traverser les
frontières pour trouver du travail, à profiter de l'éducation et des
opportunités d'emploi et à participer aux mouvements sociaux favorables à une évolution en dehors de l'orbite française. Le découplage du
franc CFA et du franc français en 1994 a entraîné certaines ruptures,
mais ce sont les relations militaires difficiles au Rwanda en 1994 et au
Zaïre/RDC en 1997 qui ont renforcé l'enchevêtrement des relations
entre les pays francophones et anglophones en Afrique. Depuis l'an
2000, la France semble prête à renoncer aux engagements militaires
bilatéraux au profit d'une coopération multilatérale en matière de paix

---

[21] "African Union Rejects America's AFRICOM Military Base," *Ligali*, 19 février 2008.
"AFRICOM: Assessing the African Perspective," Council on Foreign Relations, Wash-
ington, D.C., 1er octobre 2008. Voir aussi Gwendolyn Mikell, "U.S. Academics and the
Security Sector: Issues and Concerns," Plenary Paper for the AFRICOM Symposium,
The Africa Center for Strategic Studies, National Conference Center, 10 juin 2008.

[22] Andrew Hansen, "The French Military in Africa," *Backgrounder*, 8 février 2008.

et d'aide humanitaire, mais les Français restaient engagés dans les interventions militaires au Tchad en 2007-2008, en RCA en 2006, et en Côte d'Ivoire en 2005-2006[23]. L'intensité des dynamiques de mondialisation ont peut-être accéléré la recherche, par la France, d'un nouveau type de relations avec les pays africains. Hansen cite le sénateur André Dulait qui affirmait en 2006 : « Le continent africain est notre voisin et nous ressentons les conséquences des secousses qui l'affectent »[24]. Bon nombre de citoyens et de responsables français ont commencé à repenser leurs priorités stratégiques et militaires en Afrique en fonction des intérêts qu'ils détenaient depuis longtemps en Asie, ou de ceux qu'ils viennent d'acquérir en Amérique du Sud.

L'année 2009 apporte une réelle opportunité de changement à la fois pour les Etats-Unis et la France car la transition d'après Guerre froide est désormais terminée en Afrique et une nouvelle phase de dialogue à l'échelle continentale et mondiale a débuté. Les pays de l'Union européenne réussiront-ils à regarder au-delà de leurs frontières ou à s'entendre pour faire la différence ? Les Etats-Unis et la France travailleront-ils ensemble dans le cadre du G8 et du Conseil de sécurité de l'ONU pour présenter une approche africaine commune ? Partout dans le monde, la vision du « terrorisme mondial » est plus nuancée qu'il y a sept ans. De nombreux immigrés africains, devenus citoyens américains ou français, votent et désirent voir les candidats qu'ils ont choisi faire émerger une politique pragmatique et nuancée. Dans cette nouvelle phase, les pays africains contrôlent mieux leur propre destinée, essayant de créer des mécanismes régionaux et continentaux pour faire face aux nombreuses crises auxquelles ils doivent faire face. La manière dont les pays occidentaux collaboreront avec l'Afrique pour relever ces défis aura une incidence sur les perspectives mondiales.

Les acteurs stratégiques émergents en Afrique

Le développement de l'Union africaine, et notamment de ses structures institutionnelles, économiques, politico-juridiques et de sécurité, constitue le premier facteur stratégique ; il est donc essentiel pour l'avenir du continent. Le terrain a changé et les anciennes divisions

---

[23] Ibid. Voir aussi, David Gauthier-Villars, "Continental Shift: Colonial Era Ties to Africa Face a Reckoning in France," *Wall Street Journal*, 16 mai 2007.

[24] Compte-rendu de la séance du 5 octobre 2006 au Sénat : http://www.senat.fr/seances/s200610/s20061005/s20061005001.html.

coloniales nées de la Conférence de Berlin disparaissent mais l'Afrique n'est pas encore parvenue à prendre pleinement conscience de ses nouveaux intérêts stratégiques collectifs. Les Américains n'ont plus le sentiment que l'Afrique appartient aux Européens ; désormais, ils ne savent plus trop quand et où ils doivent intervenir, ni comment ils doivent répondre aux demandes d'assistance de l'Afrique sans pour autant augmenter les tensions internationales. Au cours des deux dernières décennies, principalement guidés par des intérêts économiques et sécuritaires, les Etats-Unis et la France ont rivalisé pour renforcer leur influence dans l'ensemble du continent africain. Concernant les questions économiques et de sécurité, il n'existe pas encore de véritable collaboration entre les grandes puissances, peut-être à cause de la concurrence historique, des tensions au sein de l'Assemblée générale des Nations Unies ou des divergences de priorités, malgré le dialogue et les engagements sur l'Afrique à l'ordre du jour du G8. Certains ont fait valoir que la concurrence franco-américaine afin de renforcer les échanges économiques et d'obtenir des accords de protection a eu des répercussions régionales négatives, en particulier sur la Communauté de développement d'Afrique australe (SADC). Le commerce avec l'Afrique du Sud constitue le gros lot, garantissant aux produits français et américains des débouchés sur un immense marché national et régional. Toutefois, l'impact sur les autres pays, plus petits, de la Communauté de développement d'Afrique australe pourrait être dévastateur, selon de nombreux spécialistes de l'Afrique australe[25].

Le Nouveau Partenariat pour le développement de l'Afrique (NEPAD) reflète la détermination de l'Afrique à coordonner le développement régional et continental. Les Etats-Unis, la France et l'Union européenne ont encore à élaborer une réponse politique cohérente aux programmes de développement du NEPAD et le ralentissement économique mondial ne facilite pas la tâche. Les pays occidentaux ont eu tendance à poursuivre leurs propres intérêts nationaux/stratégiques, négligeant les initiatives multilatérales. D'énormes problèmes économiques doivent encore être débattus, en particulier sur les moyens de se focaliser sur l'agriculture durable, qui doit être au cœur de la lutte

---

[25] Margaret C. Lee, "The 21st Century Scramble for Africa," *Journal of Contemporary African Studies*, Vol. 24, No. 3, septembre 2006, pp. 303-330 (Publié aussi dans *Africa in Global Power Play: Debates, Challenges and Potential Reforms*, Behekinkosi Moyo, ed., London: Adonis & Abbey Publishers, Ltd (2007). Voir aussi "European Union-South Africa Free Trade Agreement: In Whose Interest?" *Journal of Contemporary African Studies*, Vol. 20, No. 1, 2002, pp. 81-106.

contre la pauvreté dans les années à venir. Ni la Loi sur la croissance et les opportunités en Afrique (AGOA), ni aucune autre initiative n'a suffisamment pris en compte l'importance d'encourager la production agricole et l'agro-industrie locales qui permettent de soutenir les communautés locales. Ces initiatives n'ont pas été considérées comme des stratégies de lutte contre la pauvreté car elles équilibrent les dynamiques du marché mondial. Elles n'ont pas non plus pris conscience de l'importance du genre dans le développement rural, bien que le rôle des femmes soit essentiel pour un développement économique régional et national durable en Afrique. Si les Etats-Unis souhaitent soutenir la réalisation des objectifs du Millenium Challenge Corporation d'ici 2015, il est important que les initiatives de cet organisme intègrent d'importantes mesures en faveur de la lutte contre la pauvreté et de l'égalité des sexes.

L'Union africaine débat actuellement de l'éventuelle réunion des Etats africains dans des « Etats-Unis d'Afrique » ; à l'avenir, la collaboration sera essentielle. Les trois positions différentes prises par les Etats africains dans le grand débat sur le panafricanisme, lors du 9ème Sommet de l'Union africaine, ont été emblématiques de la difficulté des défis auxquels est confrontée l'Afrique[26] : comment unir des Etats qui sont différents en termes de stades de développement et de capacités institutionnelles et constitutionnelles, qui n'appartiennent pas aux mêmes partenariats et réseaux internationaux et dont le potentiel et les résultats économiques actuels divergent ? Les Africains sont de plus convaincus que les divisions issues des colonisations francophones, anglophones et lusophones ne sont plus pertinentes et qu'ils doivent trouver les politiques nationales et étrangères qui répondent à leurs besoins, quelles que soient leurs origines ainsi que les partenaires avec lesquels ils doivent s'allier. Ces nouvelles possibilités impliquent une meilleure coopération des Etats-Unis, de la France et de l'Union européenne, qui doivent par ailleurs être plus créatifs dans leur conception d'une intégration plus productive et plus efficace des initiatives locales et de leurs politiques économique, sécuritaire et de développement en général.

---

[26] Les trois positions sont l'instantanéité (l'unité maintenant), le gradualisme (d'abord l'intégration régionale) et l'opposition (uniquement la souveraineté nationale). Voir T. Murithi, "Institutionalizing pan-Africanism: Transforming African Union values and principles into practice. ISS Paper, No. 143, 2007. Voir aussi James Butty, "Analyst suspects Khadafi phobia in Summit Outcome," Ngwane http://www.gngwane.com/2007/07/analyst-suspect.html.

L'arrivée de la Chine sur la scène mondiale change les dynamiques stratégiques. Tout d'abord, elle modifie l'équilibre économique en offrant à certains Etats africains de nouvelles possibilités et approches ainsi qu'une nouvelle concurrence pour les ressources africaines. La première Conférence internationale de Tokyo sur le développement de l'Afrique (TICAD) avait suggéré que le Japon serait le partenaire asiatique digne d'intérêt[27], mais la situation a énormément changé en 2000 avec l'évolution de l'économie mondiale et lorsque le Japon a concentré ses relations en Asie, au nom du commerce mondial et de l'aide internationale. Cette émergence de l'Asie a créé un certain traumatisme et de l'anxiété dans bon nombre de pays occidentaux, étant donné les possibilités de développement des intérêts américains, chinois et français. Il n'a pas encore été possible de négocier avec la Chine sur l'impact de ses échanges commerciaux et de ses prêts concessionnels sur la pauvreté et la croissance dans les pays d'Afrique, mais cette possibilité ne doit pas être exclue dans le contexte économique mondial difficile que nous traversons. Les importations et exportations chinoises doivent-elles servir à accroître la dépendance de l'Afrique, sans contribuer à la mise en place de stratégies de croissance à long terme ? Les échanges commerciaux avec la Chine bénéficient-ils de manière disproportionnée de l'allégement de la dette africaine en absorbant du capital qui pourrait servir au développement ou en occupant l'espace de développement ?

Ces préoccupations ont été soulevées par des chercheurs qui s'intéressent tout particulièrement à l'augmentation de la pénétration chinoise en Afrique en termes de « relations commerciales, d'investissements dans le secteur pétrolier, de projets d'infrastructures, d'avantages diplomatiques et de participation à des missions de maintien de la paix »[28]. Que la situation soit décrite comme une « diplomatie du pétrole » ou une « nouvelle course pour l'Afrique »[29], beaucoup affirment : « La majorité des études de cas montrent que les économies des Etats africains deviennent rapidement trop dépendantes des exporta-

---

[27] TICAD : http://www.ticad.net/french/home.shtml.

[28] Ray Gilpin, "China in Africa: An Analysis of Recent Developments," *The Africa Center for Strategic Studies*, octobre 2006.

[29] Margaret C. Lee, "Uganda and China: Unleashing the Power of the Dragon," in Margaret C. Lee, Henning Melber, Sanusha Naidu, and Ian Taylor, China in Africa, Nordic Africa Institute, Current African Issues 35, Uppsala, Sweden: Nordic Africa Institute, 2007, pp. 26-40.

tions vers la Chine, tout en ignorant la nécessité de concevoir des politiques industrielles nationales solides et cohérentes »[30].

Le lien entre le pétrole et les armes tient une place centrale dans leur analyse, en particulier lorsque le désintérêt de la Chine pour les droits de l'Homme dans les pays avec lesquels elle entretient des relations commerciales a un impact négatif sur la gouvernance démocratique. Dans le cas du Soudan et du Zimbabwe, la Chine a d'abord protesté, indiquant qu'elle n'avait pas mélangé la politique et les affaires[31]. Ensuite, elle s'est défendue en invoquant le principe de non-ingérence de la Chine dans les affaires intérieures d'un autre pays, en dépit de l'effervescence créée par ses livraisons d'armes au Zimbabwe et au Soudan[32]. Initialement, le Conseil de sécurité de l'ONU a été incapable de mettre suffisamment de pression sur la Chine pour qu'elle contribue à persuader le président soudanais Bashir d'accepter des troupes des Nations Unies et de l'Union africaine. La prolongation de la crise du Darfour témoigne de cette absence de volonté politique pour résoudre la crise. Néanmoins, la Chine a commencé à évoluer sur la question du Darfour et nous devons mieux comprendre comment Bashir a été convaincu d'accepter la force hybride de la MINUAD, en 2008.[33]

Les nouveaux acteurs stratégiques rendent les équations politique et économique plus complexes. De nombreuses leçons peuvent être tirées des crises au Soudan, notamment sur la complexité des délibérations au sein de l'Union africaine, sur les alliances entre la Libye, le Soudan et d'autres pays arabes lors des négociations sur le Soudan aux Nations Unies, et sur les difficultés de l'Afrique subsaharienne à mettre en doute la « fraternité » africaine en mettant la pression sur Bashir au Darfour. Par ailleurs, la Chine pourrait être en passe de devenir un partenaire mieux intégré dans les alliances mondiales ; et des pressions coordonnées des pays occidentaux pourraient peut-être commencer à

---

[30] Kweku Ampiah and Sanusha Naidu (Ed), *Crouching Tiger, Hidden Dragon? Africa and China*, Scottsville SA: University of KwaZulu-Natal Press, 2008, pp. 11-12.

[31] China/Sudan Fact Sheet, http://www.savedarfur.org/newsroom/policypapers/china_and_sudan _fact_sheet/.

[32] Lloyd Sachikonye, "Crouching Tiger, Hidden Agenda? Zimbabwe-China Relations" in Ampiah and Naidu (Ed), *Crouching Tiger, Hidden Dragon? Africa and China*, Scottsville SA: University of KwaZulu-Natal Press, 2008. Hilary Anderssen, "China is Fueling War in Darfur," *BBC News*, 13 juillet 2008. Voir aussi "South African Union Refuses to Unload Chinese Arms Headed for Zimbabwe," *Reuters*, 18 avril 2008.

[33] "China Presses Sudan Over Darfur," Reuters, *New York Times*, Asia-Pacific, 12 juin 2008.

altérer le lien entre le commerce et les armes mis en place par les Chinois et contesté par le reste du monde. Les Etats-Unis, la France et l'Union européenne doivent trouver les moyens d'accroître la collaboration avec la Chine sur la question du Zimbabwe[34] et de mieux intégrer la Chine dans les dialogues sur la sécurité et la gouvernance. Cela permettrait d'améliorer la coordination dans le cadre de la résolution multilatérale des conflits et d'accroître les ressources morales disponibles pour soutenir des initiatives démocratiques africaines.

L'Inde est également un nouvel acteur mondial en Afrique, mais si ce n'est pas vraiment le cas en réalité. Les Indiens sont présents en Afrique de l'Est depuis cent ans mais l'existence de relations étatiques est récente. Le sommet du Forum Afrique-Inde qui s'est tenu à Delhi en avril 2008 a montré que les liens entre ces deux régions se renforceraient au cours des prochaines décennies. Par ses relations avec les pays du Marché commun d'Afrique orientale et australe (COMESA) (Kenya, Tanzanie, Afrique australe), l'Inde recherche de nouveaux marchés pour ses produits comme les machines, les équipements de transport, les produits dérivés du pétrole et du bois, les textiles, les métaux et les produits agricoles, technologiques et pharmaceutiques[35]. En outre, l'Inde dispose d'un programme de coopération agricole et technique avec les pays africains portant sur plus d'un milliard de dollars et spécialisé sur l'enseignement et la médecine à distance[36]. Les préoccupations indiennes et africaines sur le commerce dans l'océan Indien, les relations maritimes et les évolutions écologiques pourraient rejoindre les intérêts occidentaux et être contradictoires ou en adéquation avec ceux d'Asie. Les Etats-Unis pourraient être en mesure de jouer les médiateurs dans les relations entre la Chine, l'Inde, le Moyen-Orient et l'Afrique, jouant ainsi un rôle plus important que les Européens mais les partenariats mondiaux pourraient être plus porteurs.

---

[34] Adekeye Adebajo, "An Axis of Evil? China, the United States, and France in Africa," Ampiah and Naidu (Ed), *Crouching Tiger, Hidden Dragon? Africa and China*, Scottsville SA: University of KwaZulu-Natal Press, 2008.

[35] "India — Boosting Trade with Africa," *Africa Business Pages*, http://www.africa-business. com/features/india_africa2.html.

[36] "India to offer Duty Free Access to Products from Africa," *Africa Business Pages*

Les transitions en termes de sécurité et de gouvernance en Afrique de l'Ouest et en Afrique australe

Si la politique étrangère doit régulièrement s'adapter aux réalités du terrain, les relations de la France et des Etats-Unis avec l'Afrique, en termes de sécurité et de gouvernance, devraient être moins militarisées et plus axées sur la sécurité humaine[37] pendant la présidence d'Obama et les présidences française et tchèque du Conseil de l'Union européenne. A quelques exceptions près, au cours de la dernière décennie, l'Afrique de l'Ouest est sortie des crises de l'immédiat après Guerre froide et a démontré l'excellente coopération régionale de la CEDEAO dans la résolution des conflits, la reconstruction nationale des institutions d'Etat après les guerres civiles et la collaboration régionale sur les projets pétroliers et gaziers avec le soutien des institutions financières internationales. Ces succès n'ont toutefois pas masqué les problèmes rencontrés par les Etats africains dans la recherche des ressources nécessaires pour relever les défis militaires/de sécurité posés par la guerre civile et l'action des rebelles, pour faire face aux difficultés de la « construction d'une nation » équilibrée à la fin des conflits, pour protéger et donner du pouvoir aux femmes, pour reconstruire l'économie agricole et le commerce afin de réduire la pauvreté et garantir la sécurité alimentaire et enfin pour s'attaquer au problème du VIH/sida à tous les niveaux.

Souvenons-nous que dans les domaines du maintien et de la consolidation de la paix et de la résolution des conflits avec leurs voisins d'Afrique de l'Ouest, le Liberia et la Sierra Leone étaient souvent bien intentionnés et ont soutenu avec enthousiasme le dialogue, les négociations et les accords relatifs à la paix. Toutefois, les dirigeants africains (Côte d'Ivoire, Ghana, Nigeria, Sénégal, CEDEAO et OUA) n'ont généralement pas eu suffisamment de forces tactiques et politiques ainsi que de ressources économiques pour gérer seuls le processus de paix et il s'est révélé inadapté de s'appuyer sur la puissance hégémonique régionale (Nigeria). L'accent doit toujours être mis sur l'appropriation, par l'Afrique, des processus de paix. Pourtant, les expériences

---

[37] Kofi A. Annan, *Dans une liberté plus grande. Développement, Sécurité et Respect des droits de l'Homme pour tous.* Nations Unies, mars 2005. Voir aussi, *Human Security in Africa*, Office of the Special Adviser on Africa (OSAA), Nations Unies, Dec. 2005, http://www.un.org/africa/osaa/reports/ Human%20Security%20in%20Africa%20FINAL.pdf. Voir aussi : African Human Security Initiative 2: *Enhancing the Delivery of Security in Africa: Complementing the African Peer Review Mechanism*, London: DFID, http://www.african review.org/.

ouest africaines obligent à nous interroger sur la nature des engagements bilatéraux et multilatéraux (ONU) qui sont essentiels au véritable fonctionnement des missions de paix en Afrique. Nous proposons donc ici deux exemples assortis de suggestions : l'un sur les processus de paix et l'autre sur la collaboration en termes de relations civilo-militaires en Afrique.

Il convient de s'intéresser à l'objectif de création de forces d'intervention de l'Union africaine qui pourraient être rapidement mobilisables sur les lieux d'émergence d'une crise. En effet, si l'Union africaine a la volonté de régler les conflits africains, elle n'en a pas les moyens financiers et logistiques. Désormais, les Africains se demandent pourquoi la création de l'AFRICOM fin 2008 n'a pas été accompagnée par un soutien à la force d'intervention de l'Union africaine. Tout au long des années 1990, les Américains ont hésité à envoyer des soldats sur le terrain pour contribuer à la cessation des combats. Beaucoup doutaient que l'ONU soit en mesure de gérer le financement et l'exécution des missions de paix et ils n'ont pas fait de lobbying auprès du Congrès ou du Département d'Etat pour obtenir des fonds supplémentaires et un soutien pour ces missions. La durée des conflits s'est donc allongée et les habitants du Liberia et de la Sierra Leone ont payé un lourd tribut en vies humaines et en capital social.

Cependant, si la volonté politique existe, tous les pays occidentaux disposent de capacités et de forces variées qui peuvent être associées aux forces africaines. Au Darfour par exemple, certains peuvent fournir des chars, d'autres des troupes, d'autres encore peuvent assurer la formation des troupes et d'autres enfin peuvent fournir des fonds pour financer l'opération. La leçon à tirer est que les Etats-Unis, la France, les Pays-Bas, l'Allemagne, le Canada et le Royaume-Uni, entre autres, doivent fournir un soutien coordonné et engagé aux Etats africains pour la reconversion de leurs troupes et la reconstruction de leurs capacités. Nous devons trouver des moyens novateurs pour soutenir l'Union africaine et les initiatives régionales dans les missions de paix. Nous devons par ailleurs être des partisans enthousiastes du soutien multinational au sein de l'Assemblée générale de l'ONU.

Dans les conflits au Liberia et en Sierra Leone, le Nigeria a porté le poids le plus lourd, en fournissant le plus grand nombre de troupes et en s'acquittant de la charge financière liée aux soldats et au matériel[38]. Après l'élection du président Obasanjo en 1999, les Nigérians n'avaient ni la volonté, ni la capacité de poursuivre sans le soutien de l'Occident à ce processus, et le Nigeria s'est retiré en mai 2000 de l'ECOMOG et de la MONUSIL en Sierra Leone. Comme la MONUL au Liberia, la MONUSIL en Sierra Leone était une mission de taille trop restreinte, non armée, avec seulement un mandat relevant du chapitre VI de la charte des Nations Unies, la rendant incapable de stopper le retour des forces rebelles à Freetown en janvier 1999. Olonisakin dit que malgré les fonds accordés, dans cet ordre d'importance, par le Canada, les Pays-Bas, le Royaume-Uni et les Etats-Unis, pour la nouvelle mission de la MINUSIL, ces fonds ont été insuffisants dans un premier temps[39]. La MINUSIL ne pouvait pas fonctionner sans les troupes ou l'influence du Nigeria ou sans l'autorisation de recours à la force conférée par le chapitre VI et elle ne pouvait pas non plus repousser les rebelles hors de Freetown sans l'aide des troupes bilatérales IMATT (équipe militaire internationale consultative en matière d'instruction) fournies par le Royaume-Uni. La MINUSIL seule n'aurait pas pu conduire les négociations qui avaient conduit à l'accord d'Abuja facilité par les Nigérians. Elle n'aurait pas pu non plus conquérir le « cœur » des Sierra-Léonais sans les initiatives humanitaires greffées à la mission MINUSIL initiale en 2000.

Ce n'est qu' en l'an 2000 qu'un changement majeur a pu être observé, sous la nouvelle direction du Britannique Sir Jeremy Greenstock et avec l'engagement de Richard Holbrooke, le nouveau Représentant permanent des Etats-Unis auprès des Nations Unies. Les efforts de M. Holbrooke ont conduit à un changement d'attitude du Congrès américain sur le financement des missions de maintien de la paix de l'ONU (ONU-DOMP) en Afrique. Ils ont par ailleurs contribué à renforcer le soutien à la mission de paix en Sierra Leone au sein du Conseil de sécurité des Nations Unies et à augmenter les troupes de la MINUSIL jusqu'à 17 500 hommes répartis dans tout le pays. La MINUSIL est devenue un modèle d'efficacité pour les forces de main-

---

[38] Margaret A. Vogt , ed., *The Liberian Crisis and ECOMOG: A Bold Attempt at Regional Peace Keeping*, Lagos: Gabumo Publishing Co, 1992. Voir George Klay Kieh, *Ending the Liberian Civil War: Implications for United States Policy Toward West Africa*, Washington, D.C. : TransAfrica Forum, 1996.

[39] Funmi Olonisakin, *Peacekeeping in Sierra Leone: The Story of UNAMSIL*, NY: International Peace Academy, 2008.

tien de la paix, bien que sa réputation ait également souffert des accusations d'exploitation des femmes et des enfants par les troupes de l'ONU.

Il faut noter aussi l'initiative du Conseil de sécurité visant à créer un Tribunal spécial pour la Sierra Leone, appuyé par les Nations Unies mais n'ayant pas l'autorisation requise par le chapitre VII, pour juger les affaires de crimes de guerre et de crimes contre l'humanité, deux ans exactement avant que la Sierra Leone n'établisse une commission Vérité et Réconciliation (TRC-2002) prévue par l'Accord de Lomé de 1999. De nombreux habitants de la Sierra-Leone ont signalé avec colère que le Tribunal spécial était une création du Conseil de sécurité et de l'Assemblée Générale des Nations Unis, fortement influencés par les Etats-Unis et qu'il enfreignait la Constitution de la Sierra Leone[40], alors que la commission Vérité et Réconciliation était née des négociations et des accords entre la Sierra Leone et l'Afrique. Le conflit résultait aussi du fait que le Tribunal spécial pouvait prononcer des mises en accusation et des condamnations, dont certaines sanctionnaient plus sévèrement des personnes moins haut placées dans la hiérarchie, menaçaient de déclencher un nouveau conflit dans le pays et étaient contradictoires avec la conception de la justice et des sanctions par les Africains (comme dans le transfert de Charles Taylor du Nigeria au Tribunal spécial, puis à la Haye). Si les actions brutales de Taylor ont été rarement pardonnées, le processus conduisant à son extradition n'en a pas moins été controversé.

L'exemple ci-dessus montre qu'un soutien national en faveur des processus de paix et de justice en Afrique peut avoir un immense impact sur le terrain, mais nous devons nous assurer qu'il est globalement positif. Ce n'est que lorsque Holbrooke a réussi à engager les Américains sur les problématiques de paix aux Nations Unis que de véritables avancées ont pu être constatées. La question est de savoir si un tel soutien, aussi bien accueilli et potentiellement efficace qu'il puisse être, peut aussi s'adapter aux institutions africaines et aux processus de paix et de justice dont la plupart ont été promus à l'initiative des femmes. Les femmes africaines ont travaillé dur pour amener le Conseil de sécurité des Nations Unies à voter, en 2000, la résolution 1325, qui appelle à

---

[40] Abdul Karim Bangura, Sami Gandi-Gorgla, and Abdul Razak Rahim, "An Appeal to Discontinue Funding the Special Court for Sierra Leone," et "An Open Letter to Sierra Leone's Parliamentarians," The Sierra Leone Working Group, 2004.

l'intégration des femmes dans les stratégies et les mécanismes de résolution des conflits. Cependant, elles soulignent, mais pas seulement elles, qu'il n'existe pas encore de système de contrôle pour veiller à l'intégration de leurs initiatives ou à la protection de leurs droits lors de conflits[41]. Alors que nous envisageons de renforcer la coopération dans les années à venir, nous devrions utilement nous informer sur ce que les Africains eux-mêmes ont à l'esprit, sur l'état d'avancement des institutions et accords qu'ils souhaitent mettre en œuvre, sur la réalisation de l'objectif d'égalité et d'équilibre des genres (« gender ») dans ces initiatives et sur la manière dont l'activisme bilatéral ou multilatéral pourrait accroître l'efficacité des approches consensuelles.

Où en est l'état de préparation militaire visant à prévenir un conflit terroriste tout en veillant à maintenir en Afrique de bonnes relations civilo-militaires, respectueuses de la démocratie ? Malgré le scepticisme initial des Africains face à la proposition américaine de 1996 de créer une Force de réaction aux crises africaines[42], l'Initiative africaine de réaction aux crises (ACRI) de 1997 a cherché à former les militaires africains pour qu'ils agissent efficacement dans les opérations de maintien de la paix ou d'assistance humanitaire sur le continent ... en réponse aux requêtes de l'ONU, de l'Union africaine ou de la CEDEAO[43]. Que ce soit par le biais de l'ACRI ou de son successeur, l'ACOTA (Africa Contingency Operations Training Assistance ; Aide la formation des opérations d'intervention en Afrique), les Etats-Unis ont fortement contribué au maintien de la paix entre 1997 et 2004 en Sierra Leone et en République centrafricaine, même si beaucoup plus de moyens auraient été nécessaires.

Les tensions liées au terrorisme mondial et à la guerre en Irak ont laissé des séquelles que les Etats-Unis et la France devront surmonter au cours des prochaines années. Ne nombreuses personnes ont eu le sentiment que l'AFRICOM cherchait à satisfaire les intérêts straté-

---

[41] Gwendolyn Mikell, Jeanne Maddox Toungara, and Vivian Lowery Derryck, *Empowerment of Women in Africa: Gender Equality and Women's Leadership*, British Embassy and DFID Policy Paper, Avril 2008 ; et *Empowerment of Women in Africa: Impact of the Changing Global Outlook*, Conference at the National Geographic, 8 mai 2009. Voir aussi Gwendolyn Mikell, *African Feminism: The Politics of Survival in Sub-Saharan Africa*, Philadelphia: University of Pennsylvania Press, 1997.

[42] Newsmaker: Warren Christopher, *Lehrer News Hour*, 15 octobre 1996.

[43] "African Crisis Response Initiative; African Contingency Operations Training and Assistance," *Global Security.Org*, Military. http://www.globalsecurity.org/military/agency/dod/acri.htm.

giques américains, c'est-à-dire à empêcher l'exploitation des Etats faibles par des terroristes islamistes. Peu de personnes ont compris les objectifs de cette initiative et même les responsables militaires américains n'avaient pas bien réfléchi à la mission de l'AFRICOM, à ses responsabilités, à l'emplacement de son quartier général, aux relations avec les militaires africains et avec les sociétés civiles africaine et américaine[44]. L'Union africaine avait rejeté l'idée de l'implantation d'une base AFRICOM dans n'importe quel pays du continent africain. La Présidente du Liberia Ellen Johnson-Sirleaf et le président éthiopien Lucha étaient les deux seuls chefs d'Etat à demander à accueillir la base de l'AFRICOM. Dans leur grande majorité, les responsables africains n'ont pas considéré l'AFRICOM comme l'équivalent des autres commandements régionaux américains tels qu'ils existent dans d'autres parties du monde. Outre les fonctions de combats, les dirigeants de l'AFRICOM ont insisté sur le fait que le commandement travaillerait avec l'agence américaine d'aide au développement (USAID) pour répondre initialement aux besoins humanitaires et de développement exprimés par les Africains. Plus récemment, les représentants de l'Union africaine ont témoigné d'une ouverture au dialogue sur l'AFRICOM[45], en particulier car sa base provisoire à Stuttgart laissera suffisamment de temps pour développer des relations de collaboration avec les Africains.

Les Etats-Unis n'étaient pas les seuls à faire l'objet de tels soupçons. Beaucoup d'Africains avaient considéré les accords de Linas-Marcoussis, signés à l'issue de la table ronde convoquée par la France en janvier 2003, comme une menace pour la souveraineté constitutionnelle de la Côte d'Ivoire, avant que l'ONU n'intervienne[46]. Dans ce processus, les Etats-Unis et la France avaient appris une leçon importante : la nécessité de s'engager dans des campagnes de relations publiques, dans l'éducation civique et dans l'échange d'idées systématique et approfondi sur

---

[44] Gwendolyn Mikell, "Academics and the Security Sector: Issues and Concerns," Presentation at the ACSS/AFRICOM Seminar, Dulles VA, 12 juin 2008.

[45] Ambassadeur Amina Salum Ali, Dialogue sur l'AFRICOM, Council on Foreign Relations, octobre 2008.

[46] J. Peter Pham, "Forgotten Interests: Why Cote d'Ivoire Matters," *World Defense Review*, 3 août 2006. Voir aussi J. Peter Pham, AFRICOM: Ready to Roll, 2 octobre 2008, site web: http://www.familysecuritymatters.org/, http://www.familysecuritymatters.org/publications/id.1340/pub_detail.asp. Voir aussi "AFRICOM: The Poisonous Fruit of the Mercy Industrial Complex," *The Zaleza Post*, 15 novembre 2007.

les initiatives politiques, avec de nombreux groupes de la société civile et les électeurs, avant, pendant et après la mise en œuvre de la politique.

De nombreux conflits ont porté tant sur les problèmes de gouvernance, politique et/ou financière, que sur la résolution des conflits. Dans le conflit en RDC, la faiblesse de l'Etat congolais a servi de base aux attaques contre le Rwanda ; en représailles, il a subi des incursions sur son territoire, de la part de ses voisins qui cherchaient également à exploiter les nombreuses ressources congolaises. Peu importent les justifications des Etats voisins pour expliquer leurs incursions sur le territoire de la RDC, il apparaît que ces conflits ont profité aux entreprises d'extraction de ressources présentes dans le pays. Dans ce climat politique, la responsabilité des Etats fait l'objet de peu de pressions. Il est peut-être temps pour les Etats-Unis de se joindre à la communauté internationale et de trouver une stratégie pour discuter d'un cadre régional pour la paix et le développement en RDC et pour commencer à s'interroger sur le lien entre développement et conflit. De nouveaux « principes de Sullivan» sont nécessaires, des principes relatifs aux liens actuels entre l'Etat et les affaires dans les Etats faibles qui ne peuvent ou ne veulent pas contrôler les frontières ou la violence, comme en RDC et dans les communautés côtières du delta du Niger.

Des questions importantes liées à la gouvernance émergent : quelles sont les marges de manœuvre pour la formation de relations civilo-militaires en Afrique qui associeraient largement ces deux composantes dans un dialogue établissant un lien explicite entre les questions de gouvernance et de préparation militaire ? La réflexion sur la professionnalisation de l'armée en Afrique doit porter aussi sur les questions de surveillance civile de l'armée[47]. Il est important de noter que les Etats-Unis et la France ont développé leurs propres mécanismes institutionnels pour traiter avec les institutions militaires en Afrique, en particulier en termes d'éducation et de formation. Malgré la fin de nombreux conflits et l'engagement de plusieurs pays sur la voie démocratique, l'héritage du régime militaire demeure souvent sous la forme d'institutions étatiques plus faibles que les institutions militaires et de la persistance d'une culture militarisée et sexiste.

---

[47] Claude E. Welch, No *Farewell to Arms? Military Disengagement from Politics in Africa and Latin America*, Boulder CO: Westview Press, 1987; et *Military Role and Rule: Perspectives on Civil-Military Relations*, North Scituate MA: Duxbury Press, 1974.

L'éducation et la formation sur le rôle du développement de la sécurité humaine et de la société civile devraient constituer une priorité.
Depuis 1999, l'African Center for Strategic Studies (Centre africain
d'études stratégiques ; ACSS), de la National Defense University (Université nationale de la défense) a proposé des séminaires de formation
avancée aux responsables militaires et de sécurité et organisé des dialogues avec les membres d'organisations de la société civile dans les pays
en voie de transition démocratique. Entre 2000 et 2006, l'ACSS a fonc-
tionné avec un mélange d'employés militaires et civils, américains et
africains, anglophones et francophones. Toutefois, lorsque l'ACSS est
davantage passée sous le leadership et la surveillance des militaires, il est
devenu plus en phase avec les préoccupations de sécurité nationale des
Etats-Unis. Ainsi, la lutte contre le soutien idéologique au terrorisme est
placée au premier plan, suivie par l'harmonisation des opinions sur les
défis de sécurité et enfin par la promotion de partenariats institutionnels pour relever les défis de défense et de sécurité auxquels est confrontée l'Afrique. Désormais, il est nécessaire de chercher un équilibre
entre le développement de la sécurité humaine et de la société civile et
la promotion de la formation civilo-militaire[48]. Compte tenu des dialogues civils sur les questions de sécurité humaine qui existent dans les
zones anglophones et francophones, ils pourraient constituer une
arène utile pour la collaboration entre les Français et les Américains.

Depuis 2000, les questions de gouvernance portent aussi sur les tensions ethniques et religieuses intra-étatiques qui ont explosé dans la
période d'après Guerre froide et de mondialisation. A leur paroxysme,
ces tensions ont conduit à des crises génocidaires de type Rwanda et
Burundi. Mais dans leur majorité, elles se sont manifestées sous forme
de conflits ethniques ou religieux (Côte d'Ivoire, Soudan, Tchad), de
questions constitutionnelles relatives aux limites du concept d'ethnie
(Nigéria, Ghana) et à ce que j'ai appelé « les entrepreneurs ethniques »
qui cherchent à saisir le pouvoir et déstabiliser les démocraties fragiles
ou naissantes (Liberia, Sierra Leone)[49]. Lorsque les conflits se calment,
les pays africains expriment un besoin d'institutions et de processus
qui serviraient de signaux d'alerte en cas d'imminence de conflits ou
qui pourraient empêcher les conflits ; les ressources nécessaires pour

---

[48] African Defense Attaché Seminar, Africa Center for Strategic Studies, 17-25 novembre
2008 www.africacenter.org.

[49] Gwendolyn Mikell, "Ethnic Particularism and New State Legitimacy in West Africa,"
Tulsa Journal of Comparative and International Law, Vol. 23, No. 1, 1997.

gérer ces réformes sont cependant souvent difficiles à trouver. Une institution ghanéenne sert d'exemple à cette mission d'anticipation : la Commission pour les droits de l'Homme et la justice administrative (CHRAJ ; Commission on Human Rights and Administrative Justice) vise à améliorer la bonne gouvernance, la démocratie, le respect des droits de l'Homme et la transparence, et tente de résoudre les conflits avant qu'ils n'explosent[50]. La CHRJA partage son expérience de la résolution des conflits avec d'autres pays de la CEDEAO. Quant aux parlementaires africains pour la paix, ils ont développé des stratégies sur les modalités de mobilisation des électeurs pour résoudre les conflits.

Un second aspect de la gouvernance porte sur la reconstruction des institutions étatiques parlementaires, juridiques, policières, etc., de sorte qu'elles puissent s'équilibrer avec la puissance historique des institutions militaires en Afrique. Des institutions étatiques fortes permettent au gouvernement de protéger les droits de la propriété, des femmes et des populations vulnérables, et de légiférer contre l'appropriation et l'abus des ressources nationales. De nombreuses ressources américaines ont servi à soutenir la démocratie et le renforcement des institutions en Afrique, par le biais du National Democratic Institute (Institut démocratique national) et de l'International Republican Institute (Institut républicain international) qui travaillent avec le Parlement, le système judiciaire, les forces de police et des ONG. Une collaboration entre les Américains et les Français pourrait s'établir dans ce domaine, notamment sur les modalités d'octroi des ressources essentielles et de leur soutien de façon à améliorer également la propriété et l'initiative locales. Une division rationnelle du travail doit dépasser les anciennes divisions anglophones, francophones ou lusophones, mettre l'accent sur les initiatives multilatérales et reconnaître les rôles importants que pourraient jouer de nouveaux acteurs stratégiques tels que la Chine et l'Inde dans la collaboration régionale.

Un troisième aspect de la gouvernance est lié à l'importance des transitions électorales et des stratégies de sortie des dirigeants et des présidents africains. Les Etats d'Afrique subsaharienne sont encore jeunes et ne disposent donc pas de la force institutionnelle, constitutionnelle et procédurale des pays occidentaux, plus âgés. La limitation

---

[50] "Ghana: CHRAJ calls for Tolerance as Election Day Approaches," *Accra Mail*, 19 novembre 2008. Voir aussi le site internet de la Commission du Ghana pour les droits de l'Homme et la justice administrative : http://www.chrajghana.org/

à deux mandats présidentiels est souvent remise en cause, le président en fonction cherchant à modifier la constitution pour rester en fonction plus longtemps. Ceci est prévisible compte tenu du nombre limité de possibilités de leadership pour les dirigeants à la retraite et de prise de la conscience limitée, par l'opinion, des dangers d'un mandat à vie. Les responsables africains décernant le prix Mo Ibrahim, qui récompense la bonne gouvernance en Afrique, marquent une étape supplémentaire dans la prise au sérieux du soutien à la gouvernance. Ce prix succède à la « Presidential Archives and residential fellowship initiative » (Initiative sur les archives présidentielles et les bourses de résidents) de l'Université de Boston (2002) qui reconnaît et récompense les dirigeants africains ayant mis en place des exemples de bonne gouvernance. Ainsi, l'ancien président du Sénat nigérian Ken Nnamani a contribué au mouvement visant à l'abolition de la possibilité d'un 3ème mandat au Nigéria et fourni un exemple africain de soutien à la bonne gouvernance et aux stratégies de sortie[51]. Le message de ces initiatives est cohérent : la bonne gouvernance constitue la voie d'avenir[52] ; et ces initiatives doivent être renforcées dans la collaboration entre francophones et anglophones.

Des preuves récentes montrent que les anciennes démocraties stables d'Afrique qui ont fait de grands progrès au cours de la dernière décennie sont encore vulnérables face à des scissions internes et à des bouleversements politiques, comme au Nigeria, en Afrique du Sud ou au Kenya par exemple. Seule l'audace de la société civile nigériane et la force de la communauté internationale ont empêché un embrasement du conflit. La transition électorale au Kenya menaçait de devenir violente et avait déjà généré des affrontements ethniques causant le déplacement interne des populations et l'afflux de réfugiés dans les pays voisins. Seule la demande de l'Union africaine associée au fort engagement de l'ancien Secrétaire général Kofi Annan et des autres partenaires occidentaux avait permis la négociation d'un règlement du conflit émergent. Même le Ghana, qui avait vu se succéder quatre élections démocratiques relativement réussies depuis 1992, a menacé de tomber dans les méandres des privilèges présidentiels et de parti quand la pos-

---

[51] Ken Nnamani and Sam Amadi, *Nnamani's Third Way: Selected Speeches on Legislative Leadership and Democratic Transformation in Nigeria*, Princeton NJ: Sungai Books, 2007.

[52] Celia Drugger, "Botswana's Former President Wins Prize for Good Governance," *Herald Tribune*, 21 octobre 2008 ; "Joaquim Chissano Wins the Largest Prize in the World," *Southern Africa Trust*, 22 octobre 2007.

sibilité d'un transfert du pouvoir à un nouveau parti est apparue. Seuls un dialogue systématique avec les organisations publiques et de la société civile au Ghana, la pression et le soutien de partenaires occidentaux et un contrôle systématique ont apparemment permis la tenue de l'élection.

Le soutien aux transitions démocratiques, même dans des pays africains relativement stables comme l'Afrique du Sud, doit être l'une des priorités de l'agenda d'un partenariat franco-américain. A la surprise de beaucoup, la rancœur qui a éclaté en 2008 entre le Président Mbeki et le Premier Ministre Zuma au sein du Congrès national africain d'Afrique du Sud, a montré qu'il restait encore beaucoup à faire pour s'assurer que ce pays reste sur la bonne voie. Après le succès des élections de 2009, le défi des Etats-Unis, de la France, du Royaume-Uni et de l'Union européenne consiste à offrir un soutien et un renfort moral permettant de faire face aux tensions intérieures mais aussi aux questions régionales. L'Afrique du Sud doit restaurer la confiance régionale liée à son rôle au sein de la SADC et fournir la marge de manœuvre nécessaire à la reconstruction du Zimbabwe. Mugabe partage désormais le pouvoir au sein d'un gouvernement unitaire tandis que le pays reconstruit son économie et stabilise son système parlementaire avant de réformer ses structures constitutionnelles et juridiques et de s'attaquer à la question des terres, ce qui pourrait permettre de relancer l'agriculture. Le Zimbabwe a un grand besoin de consensus et de stratégies occidentales ciblées et recherchées, afin de diminuer l'accroissement des tensions favorisées par Mugabe à propos des intentions occidentales.

Certes, il existe dans la Corne de l'Afrique des Etats faibles, ethniquement divisés ou en cours de consolidation (en particulier la Somalie) qui cherchent des approches démocratiques adaptées à leur passé ethnique. Ces « espaces sans gouvernance » posent un problème délicat à l'Occident. Les Etats-Unis ont consacré d'importantes ressources pour soutenir l'initiative de la Corne de l'Afrique, dont les résultats sont modestes[53], sans doute car les Américains n'étaient guidés que par l'idée de la sécurité/de l'antiterrorisme et car l'Islam radical constituait leur principale préoccupation. Il leur man-

---

[53] J. Swan, "U.S Policy in the Horn of Africa," U.S. Department of State, 4 août 2007 ; et James Butty with Terrence Lyons, "Avoiding Conflict in the Horn of Africa," *VOA News*, 22 décembre 2006.

quait des informations sur la conception de la gouvernance par les habitants de cette région et sur l'approche idéale que ces habitants en avaient. Ni les Américains, ni les Français n'ont réussi à travailler avec ces Etats. C'est peut-être en combinant les approches des deux pays que l'on pourra trouver des solutions. Je pense qu'il est temps d'établir un Agenda du G8 pour la Corne de l'Afrique, qui pourrait commencer par une conférence invitant les représentants régionaux et ceux de l'Union africaine à avancer leurs suggestions concernant les initiatives de gouvernance et de développement envisageables dans cette zone.

Les liens avec la diaspora

Les diasporas africaines en France et aux Etats-Unis sont des sources de connaissances sur l'Afrique ; elles cherchent généralement à s'engager sur les questions de politique africaine[54]. Les Etats-Unis accueillent notamment des Afro-Américains, des Ethiopiens, des Ghanéens, des Nigérians, des Sierra-Léonais, des Sud-Africains et des Soudanais alors qu'en France, il s'agit plutôt d'Algériens, de Congolais, de Sénégalais, d'Ivoiriens, de Marocains et d'Antillais. Au cours de la présidence d'Obama, les Etats-Unis pourraient fortement modifier leur politique africaine si le Département d'Etat américain et la Maison Blanche modifiaient leur façon de traiter les questions africaines. Trois mois après l'arrivée de la nouvelle Administration, le Département d'Etat s'est davantage intéressé à l'Europe, à l'Asie et au Moyen-Orient tandis que la Maison Blanche n'a pas essayé de mobiliser les connaissances américaines sur l'Afrique en vue d'initier une politique africaine cohérente. Toutefois, de nombreux électeurs et groupes de la société civile qui ont soutenu la campagne du Président s'attendent à ce qu'il fasse des questions africaines une priorité.

En attendant de voir quelles seront les priorités présidentielles, il peut être intéressant de réfléchir à l'analyse de Skinner sur l'utilisation de pouvoirs symboliques par les Afro-américains pour obliger les responsables politiques américains récalcitrants à tisser des liens avec l'Afrique, à la fin du 19ème siècle[55]. Il faut espérer que la puissance organisationnelle de masse qui a permis l'élection d'Obama incitera les responsables

---

[54] Voir Mel Foote, Gregory Simpkins, Gwendolyn Mikell, *African American Unity Caucus Plenary*, *Africa: Suggestions to the Obama Admin*, 16 avril 2009.

[55] Elliott P. Skinner, *African Americans and U.S. Policy Toward Africa, 1850-1924: In Defense of Black Nationality*, Washington, D.C. : Howard University Press, 1992, pp. 1-19.

du Congrès et du Département d'Etat à avoir une réflexion plus longue et plus approfondie avant d'élaborer de nouvelles politiques pour l'Afrique. L'Administration Obama pourrait s'appuyer sur ce qui a été réalisé par les précédentes administrations en matière de résultats économiques et de résolution des conflits[56] ; elle pourrait se recentrer sur les politiques de Bush en faveur de la réduction de la pauvreté et mettre le Congrès au défi de tenir ses promesses en matière d'aide extérieure à l'Afrique[57]. Espérons que l'Administration américaine se souviendra du conseil du Président de Tanzanie, Kikwete, au Président Obama : « être un aussi bon ami de l'Afrique que ne l'a été le Président Bush »[58].

Etant donné la pression symbolique et formelle croissante des nouveaux acteurs politiques, on peut penser que les Américains et les Français iront dans le même sens dans la résolution des problèmes africains. Les politiques de l'Administration Obama sont appelées à se montrer plus sensibles aux conditions sur le terrain en Afrique, à mieux utiliser les ressources diplomatiques dans les pays d'Afrique, à recourir à une diplomatie dans les situations difficiles telles le Darfour, le Zimbabwe et la République démocratique du Congo, et aussi à répondre davantage aux pressions du public. Mais en sera-t-il de même en France et dans l'ensemble de l'Union européenne au cours des prochaines années ? Trouver un équilibre entre la politique extérieure officielle, la diplomatie publique et le soutien informel à l'Afrique constituera un défi, certes intéressant mais ambitieux, pour les relations franco-américaines au cours de ces prochaines années.

RECOMMANDATIONS

Il est évident que des discussions approfondies entre les Etats-Unis et la France sur les aspects de la politique africaine mentionnés précédemment sont nécessaires. Suite aux arguments avancés dans cet article, il est possible d'identifier plusieurs grands thèmes de coopération et de collaboration :

---

[56] "Obama Presidency Would Bring New Dimension to Africa Policy; Africa Specialist Howard Wolpe discusses future of U.S.-Africa relations," http://www.america.gov/st/elections08-english/2008/October/20081022083943WCyeroCO.2450067.html.

[57] Giles Bolton, "Make Them Pay: What They Promised and By When," in *Africa Doesn't Matter: How the West has failed the Poorest Continent and What We can do about It*, NY: Arcade Publishers, 2008:156-7.

[58] "Bush Confronts Africa Policy Critics," AFP, 17 février 2008, http://rawstory.com/http://rawstory.com/ news/afp/Bush_confronts_Africa_policy_critic_02172008.html.

1. En dépit du déclin économique au niveau mondial, les Etats-Unis doivent continuer à développer leur politique africaine à travers la loi AGOA, le Millenium Challenge Corporation, le plan d'aide d'urgence PEPFAR ou via d'autres initiatives.

   - Quels sont les points forts de la France en termes de développement qui pourraient être intégrés à la collaboration franco-américaine sur le développement en Afrique ?

   - Comment la collaboration franco-américaine peut-elle renforcer l'impact sur le terrain des initiatives multilatérales comme celle du Fonds mondial de lutte contre le SIDA, la tuberculose et le paludisme ?

   - Comment les Etats-Unis et la France peuvent-ils renforcer leurs ressources diplomatiques en Afrique ?

2. Quelles sont les nouvelles initiatives possibles pour le développement de la Corne de l'Afrique ?

   - Comment les Américains et les Français peuvent-ils coopérer pour couper les liens entre ressources et conflits en Afrique ?

   - Comment la concurrence commerciale franco-américaine affecte-t-elle le développement, la cohésion et la résolution de problèmes au niveau régional ?

   - Comment renforcer l'engagement et le dialogue avec la Chine sur les liens entre commerce, ressources et conflits ?

3. Quelles différences empêchent les Etats-Unis et la France de collaborer davantage sur les questions de sécurité et de paix en Afrique ?

   - Quel mécanisme rendrait les Etats-Unis et la France plus coopératifs au sein du Conseil de sécurité des Nations Unies concernant une mission multilatérale de paix en Afrique ?

   - Quelles divisions du travail pourraient rendre cette collaboration plus efficace ?

- Quels mécanismes intéressants pourraient exister pour renforcer la collaboration franco-américaine en termes de formation militaire, de relations civilo-militaires et plus largement sur les questions de sécurité humaine ?

- Comment informer les Occidentaux sur l'importance des questions militaires et des commandements militaires ? Comment rendre l'armée plus réactive aux préoccupations de l'opinion concernant les questions militaires africaines ?

4. En période de post-conflit, comment les structures judiciaires peuvent-elles être plus finement adaptées pour répondre aux défis et utiliser le capital social existant en Afrique dans la résolution des conflits ?

- Quelles initiatives communes peuvent-elles être prises afin d'endiguer la violence contre les femmes dans les zones post-conflit ?

- Quelles nouvelles initiatives pourraient être soutenues par la France et les Etats-Unis pour enrayer la piraterie en recourant également aux structures de l'Union africaine et au capital social africain ?

- En utilisant les exemples du Rwanda, de la Sierra Leone et du Darfour, comment les Etats-Unis, la France et l'Union européenne peuvent-ils contribuer à rendre les tribunaux et les Tribunaux spéciaux plus réactifs à l'appropriation locale, plus sensibles à la question du genre (« gender ») et à les faire naître d'initiatives locales ?

5. Sur les questions de gouvernance, comment soutenir davantage les institutions démocratiques et les réussites du leadership en Afrique ?

- Quels mécanismes visant à entretenir la gouvernance démocratique pourraient être intéressants pour le Congrès et les parlements des Etats membres de l'Union européenne ? Pour les Chinois ? Pour les Indiens ?

- Comment soutenir davantage la formation et le développement des partis politiques en Afrique ?

- Comment les Etats-Unis, la France et l'Union européenne peuvent-ils coopérer sur cette question ?

6. Quelles sont les préoccupations des communautés de la diaspora aux Etats-Unis et en France qui pourraient fournir des indices sur les questions et les voies porteuses en termes de collaboration politique ?

- Quelles stratégies permettraient d'engager les diasporas africaines dans le dialogue politique ?

About the Authors
(*À propos des auteurs*)

Nathalie Delapalme is presently Inspecteur général des finances. She has been an advisor on African affairs and development issues to different French Ministers of Foreign Affairs and Undersecretaries for Cooperation and Development between 1995-1997 and 2002-2007. She is a member of the board of the Mo Ibrahim Foundation, and of Agrisud, and member of the editorial committee of *Commentaire*.

Nathalie Delapalme est diplômée de l'IEP (Institut d'études politiques) de Paris, et titulaire d'un DEA (diplôme d'études approfondies) en économie. Elle a notamment étudié les questions liées aux migrations et à l'économie du développement. Conseiller des services du Sénat, elle a effectué une partie de sa carrière à la Commission des finances, du budget et des comptes publics du Sénat, ou elle a notamment suivi les secteurs de l'aide au développement, des Affaires étrangères et de la Défense. Elle a été le conseiller pour l'Afrique de plusieurs ministres des Affaires étrangères et en charge de la coopération (de 1995 à 1997, puis de 2002 à 2007, Dominique de Villepin, Michel Barnier, Philippe Douste-Blazy, Pierre-André Wiltzer et Xavier Darcos). Elle est actuellement Inspecteur général des Finances. Elle est par ailleurs membre du conseil de rédaction de la revue *Commentaire*, du conseil d'administration de la fondation Mo Ibrahim, d'Agrisud, et de la fondation Elle. Elle a publié, dans les *Notes de la Fondation Robert Schuman*, avec Élise Colette, « *Union européenne/Afrique : un partenariat stratégique* » (décembre 2007).

Jean-Pierre Filiu is Associate Professor at the Paris Institute of Political Studies (Sciences Po), Middle East Chair, where he teaches in French, English and Arabic. He was visiting professor at Georgetown University during the 2008 fall semester. He has published several books at Fayard, in Paris, including *Mitterrand and Palestine* (2005) and *The Boundaries of Jihad* (2006). His *Apocalypse in Islam* (2008) was awarded the main prize by the French History Convention and it will soon be translated by the University of California Press. The title of his next book, expected in October 2009, will be *The Nine Lives of Al-Qaeda (Why Obama can Win)*.

Jean-Pierre Filiu est professeur associé à l'Institut d'études politiques de Paris (Sciences Po), où il enseigne en français, en anglais et en arabe au sein de la Chaire Moyen-Orient Méditerranée. Il revient d'un semestre comme professeur invité à Georgetown, dans le cadre du Centre d'études européennes de cette université. Il a notamment publié chez Fayard *Mitterrand et la Palestine* (2005) et *Les frontières du jihad* (2006). Son *Apocalypse dans l'Islam* (Fayard, 2008) a obtenu le prix Augustin-Thierry des derniers Rendez-vous de l'histoire de Blois. Ce livre sera prochainement traduit aux États-Unis.

Michel Foucher is a geographer and diplomat. Since 2007, he has been Professor of Geopolitics at the Ecole Normale Supérieure, Paris. He is a member of the Council of Foreign Affairs (advisory board to the Foreign Minister). His previous positions include special adviser to the French Foreign Minister, Hubert Védrine (1997-2002), head of the Policy Planning Staff (1999-2002), French Ambassador to Latvia (2002-2006), and Ambassador at large on EU affairs (2006-2007). He has been a member of the Scientific Council of the Robert Schuman Foundation since 2006 and is a member of the Scientific Committee on Defense (Task force on prospective, 2009). His latest publications include: *L'Europe et l'avenir du monde* (Odile Jacob, Paris, 2009), *L'Obsession des frontières* (Perrin, Paris, 2007), and *Rapport Schuman sur l'état de l'Union* (Lignes de repères, Paris, 2009).

Michel Foucher est Géographe et diplomate, il est professeur de géopolitique à l'École normale supérieure (Ulm) depuis 2007. Il est membre du Conseil des Affaires étrangères. Il a été conseiller spécial du ministre des Affaires étrangères Hubert Védrine (1997-2002), directeur du Centre d'analyse et de prospectives (1999-2002), ambassadeur de France en Lettonie (2002-2006) et ambassadeur en mission sur les affaires européennes (2006-2007). Il est aussi membre du comité scientifique de la Fondation Robert Schuman et membre du comité scientifique de la défense (Equipe Prospective, 2009). Il a publié *L'Europe et l'avenir du monde* (Odile Jacob, 2009), *L'obsession des frontières* (Perrin, 2007) et *Rapport Schuman sur l'état de l'Union* (Lignes de repères, 2009).

Daniel Hamilton is the Richard von Weizsäcker Professor and Director of the Center for Transatlantic Relations at the School of Advanced International Studies (SAIS), Johns Hopkins University; and Executive Director of the American Consortium on EU Studies (ACES). He is the host of *The Washington Post/Newsweek* online discussion forum *Next*

Europe. He has held a variety of senior positions in the U.S. Department of State, including Deputy Assistant Secretary for European Affairs; U.S. Special Coordinator for Southeast European Stabilization; and Associate Director of the Policy Planning Staff. He has authored and edited many articles and books, including *Alliance Reborn: An Atlantic Compact for the 21st Century* (2009); *The Transatlantic Economy 2009* (with Joseph P. Quinlan, 2009) and *France and Globalization* (with Joseph P. Quinlan, 2008).

Daniel Hamilton est professeur Richard von Weizsäcker et directeur du Centre d'études transatlantiques de la School of Advanced International Studies (SAIS) de l'Université Johns Hopkins; il est également directeur exécutif de l'American Consortium on EU Studies (ACES). Il est l'animateur du forum de discussion en ligne *Next Europe* de *The Washington Post/Newsweek*. Il a occupé divers postes importants au ministère américain des Affaires étrangères, notamment comme Sous-secrétaire d'Etat américain adjoint chargé des affaires européennes, coordinateur spécial américain pour la stabilisation dans l'Europe du Sud-Est, et directeur associé du Bureau de la planification politique. Il a écrit et dirigé de nombreux ouvrages, notamment *Alliance Reborn: An Atlantic Compact for the 21st Century* (2009); *The Transatlantic Economy 2009* (avec Joseph P. Quinlan, 2009) et *France and Globalization* (avec Joseph P. Quinlan, 2008).

Jean-François Jamet is an economist. A graduate from Ecole Normale Supérieure (Paris School of Economics), Harvard University and Sciences-Po, he is a Corps des mines engineer. A specialist of the European economy, he was a Consultant to the World Bank in 2007-2008. He is the author of several papers published by the Robert Schuman Foundation and the Aspen Institute, as well as academic articles and contributions to books on the European Union. He is currently teaching the political economy of the European Union at Sciences-Po in Paris.

Jean-François Jamet est économiste, consultant auprès de la Banque mondiale. Ancien élève de l'École normale supérieure et de l'Université Harvard, diplômé de Sciences-Po et de l'École d'économie de Paris, il est haut fonctionnaire (Corps des Mines). Spécialiste de l'économie européenne, il est l'auteur de nombreux Policy Papers (Question d'Europe) publiés par la Fondation Robert Schuman et l'Institut Aspen, d'articles académiques et de contributions à des ouvrages sur l'Union européenne. Il enseigne l'économie politique de l'Union européenne à Sciences-Po.

Maxime Lefebvre joined the French Ministry of Foreign Affairs in 1994. He was successively adviser in former French Foreign Minister Hubert Védrine's private office, responsible for strategic issues and countries of the former Yugoslavia and of the former USSR (1997-2000), Counselor at the French Embassy in Berlin (2000-2002), and seconded to the IFRI (Institut français des relations internationales), responsible for European issues (2002-2004). Since January 2005, he has been Counselor at the French Mission to the European Union, responsible for Eastern Europe, Caucasus and Central Asia. He is also professor of international relations in the Institute for Political Studies in Paris. He has published several articles and works, including *Le jeu du droit et de la puissance. Précis de relations internationales* (The Game of Law and Power, Handbook of international relations, PUF, 3rd edition, 2007) and *La politique étrangère américaine* (U.S. Foreign Policy, PUF, 2004).

Maxime Lefebvre est diplomate et professeur en questions internationales à l'Institut d'études politiques de Paris. Il est ancien élève de l'ENA, diplômé d'HEC et de Sciences Po Paris, et titulaire d'une maîtrise d'histoire. Il a commencé sa carrière au ministère des Affaires étrangères en 1994, a été conseiller technique au cabinet de Hubert Védrine, en charge des questions stratégiques, des Balkans et des pays de l'ex-URSS (1997-2000), conseiller à l'ambassade de France à Berlin (2000-2002), puis chargé des affaires européennes à l'Institut français des relations internationales (2002-2004). Il est depuis janvier 2005 conseiller « Europe orientale et Asie centrale » à la représentation permanente de la France auprès de l'Union européenne. Maxime Lefebvre a notamment publié *Le jeu du droit et de la puissance. Précis de relations internationales* (PUF Major, 3e édition, 2007), *La politique étrangère américaine* (PUF « Que sais-je ? », 2e éd., 2008), *La diplomatie. Les dessous des relations entre les États* (en collaboration avec Yves Doutriaux, éditions Autrement, 2008). Il a également publié de nombreux articles sur les questions européennes et coordonné une étude « Quel budget européen à l'horizon 2013 ? Moyens et politiques d'une Union élargie » (IFRI/CEES, 2004).

Ian Lesser is Senior Transatlantic Fellow at the German Marshall Fund of the United States in Washington, where he focuses on Mediterranean affairs, Turkey, and international security issues. Prior to joining GMF, Lesser was a Public Policy Scholar at the Woodrow Wilson International Center for Scholars where he led a project on the future of U.S.-Turkish relations. From 2002-2005, he was Vice President and Director of Studies at the Pacific Council on International Policy (the western partner of the Council on Foreign Relations). He came to the Pacific Council from RAND, where he spent over a decade as a senior analyst and research manager specializing in strategic studies. From 1994-1995, he was a member of the Secretary's Policy Planning Staff at the U.S. Department of State, responsible for Turkey, Southern Europe, North Africa, and the multilateral track of the Middle East peace process.

Ian Lesser est Senior Transatlantic Fellow au German Marshall Fund of the United States à Washington, où il travaille essentiellement sur les affaires méditerranéennes, la Turquie et les questions de sécurité internationale. Avant de rejoindre le GMFUS, I. Lesser a été Public Policy Scholar au Woodrow Wilson International Center for Scholars où il menait un projet sur l'avenir des relations américano-turques. De 2002 à 2005, il a été vice-président et directeur des études du Pacific Council on International Policy (le partenaire occidental du Council on Foreign Relations) après avoir travaillé pendant dix ans à la RAND comme analyste senior et directeur de recherche spécialisé dans les études stratégiques. En 1994-1995, il a été membre du Bureau de la planification politique du Département d'Etat américain, en charge de la Turquie, de l'Europe du Sud, de l'Afrique du Nord et des négociations multilatérales du processus de paix au Moyen-Orient.

Leo Michel is a Senior Research Fellow at the Institute for National Strategic Studies (INSS), National Defense University. He joined INSS in 2002 after 17 years in the Office of the Secretary of Defense; his positions included Director for NATO Policy, Director for Non-Nuclear Arms Control, and Secretary of Defense Representative to the U.S.-Russia Bilateral Consultative Commission. He previously served in the U.S. intelligence community, as a legislative aide to a member of Congress, and as a U.S. Navy officer. Michel holds an MA from Johns Hopkins School for Advanced International Studies (1975) and a BA from Princeton University (1969).

Leo Michel est Senior Research Fellow à l'Institute for National Strategic Studies (INSS) de la National Defense University. Il a rejoint l'INSS en 2002 après 17 années passées au cabinet du Secrétariat d'Etat américain à la Défense où il a notamment occupé les fonctions de directeur de la politique OTAN, directeur du contrôle des armes non-nucléaires et représentant du secrétaire d'Etat à la Défense dans la commission consultative bilatérale Etats-Unis/Russie. Auparavant, il avait travaillé dans la communauté américaine du renseignement, comme assistant parlementaire et comme officier dans la Marine américaine. Il est diplômé de Johns Hopkins School for Advanced International Studies (MA ; 1975) et de l'université Princeton (BA ; 1969).

Gwendolyn Mikell is Professor of Anthropology and Foreign Service at Georgetown University, and the former Director of the African Studies Program at the Edmund A. Walsh School of Foreign Service at Georgetown. She was Senior Fellow in African Studies at the Council on Foreign Relations from 2000-2003, President of the African Studies Association (1996-7), and held fellowships in the U.S., Africa, and Asia. Her research, writing, and fieldwork focus on political and economic transitions in Africa, gender and peace-building during African transitions, Africa and the UN, and electoral and religious issues in Ghana and Nigeria. Currently she is completing a book manuscript on the Kofi Annan Legacy for Africa, and a manuscript on African women and peace.

Gwendolyn Mikell est professeur d'anthropologie et de diplomatie à l'université Georgetown et ancienne directrice du programme d'études africaines à la Edmund A. Walsh School of Foreign Service à Georgetown. Elle a été Senior Fellow en études africaines au Council on Foreign Relations en 2000-2003, présidente de l'Association des études africaines (1996-7) et a enseigné aux États-Unis, en Afrique et en Asie. Ses recherches, ses articles et ses travaux portent sur les transitions politiques et économiques en Afrique, les questions de genre et de consolidation de la paix durant les transitions en Afrique, les relations entre l'Afrique et les Nations Unies et les questions électorales et religieuses au Ghana et au Nigeria. Elle achève actuellement deux ouvrages sur l'héritage de Kofi Annan en Afrique et sur les femmes africaines et la paix.

Bruno Tertrais is a Senior Research Fellow at the Fondation pour la recherche stratégique (FRS), and an Associate Researcher at the Centre de recherches et d'études internationales (CERI). He is a member of the Institute for Strategic Studies, a contributing editor of *Survival,* and a member of the editorial board of *The Washington Quarterly*. From 2007-2008, he was a member of the Commission on the French White Paper on Defense and National Security, and a member of the Commission on the White Paper on the Foreign and European Policy of France. He was previously Special Assistant to the Director of Strategic Affairs, Ministry of Defense (1993-2001); Visiting Fellow, RAND Corporation (1995-1996); Director of the Civilian Affairs Committee, NATO Assembly (1990-1992); and Research Assistant, NATO Assembly (1989). His publications include: *L'Asie nucléaire* (IFRI, 2001); *La guerre sans fin* (Seuil, 2004) ; *Dictionnaire des enjeux internationaux* (Autrement, 2006); *Iran, la prochaine guerre* (Le Cherche-Midi, 2007); *L'arme nucléaire* (PUF, collection «Que Sais-Je?», 2008); *Atlas militaire et stratégique* (Autrement, 2008). He earned his doctorate from the Institut d'études politiques de Paris in 1994.

Bruno Tertrais est maître de recherche à la Fondation pour la Recherche Stratégique (FRS), chercheur associé au Centre d'études et de recherches internationales (CERI). Il est membre de l'*International Institute for Strategic Studies* et du *Gerson Lehman Group Policy Council of Advisors*, et membre du comité de rédaction des revues *Survival*, *The Washington Quarterly*, et *Le Meilleur des Mondes*. En 2007-2008, il était membre de la Commission du Livre blanc sur la défense et la sécurité nationale, et membre de la Commission du Livre blanc sur la politique étrangère et européenne de la France. Il a auparavant été Directeur de la commission des affaires civiles à l'Assemblée de l'OTAN (1990-1993), Chargé de mission auprès du directeur des affaires stratégiques du Ministère de la défense (1993-2001), et *Visiting Fellow* à la *RAND Corporation* (1995-1996). Diplômé de l'Institut d'études politiques de Paris (1984) et titulaire d'une maîtrise en droit public (1985), Bruno Tertrais est docteur en science politique (1994), et titulaire d'une habilitation à diriger des recherches (1994). Il est l'auteur de : *L'Asie nucléaire* (IFRI, 2001) ; *La guerre sans fin* (Seuil, 2004) ; *Dictionnaire des enjeux internationaux* (Autrement, 2006) ; *Iran, la prochaine guerre* (Le Cherche-Midi, 2007) ; *L'arme nucléaire* (PUF, collection « Que Sais-Je ? », 2008) ; *Atlas militaire et stratégique* (Autrement, 2008).

Celeste A. Wallander is Associate Professor at American University. She has served as a visiting professor at Georgetown University, Director and Senior Fellow of the Russia and Eurasia Program at the Center for Strategic and International Studies, Senior Fellow at the Council on Foreign Relations, and Associate Professor at Harvard University. She is the founder of the Program on New Approaches to Russian Security. She is the author of over 70 publications, addressing U.S.-Russian security relations, Russian foreign and security policy, the geopolitics of energy in Eurasia, and international security institutions. She received her Ph.D., M.Phil. and M.A. degrees in political science from Yale University, and her B.A. (summa cum laude) in political science from Northwestern University.

Celeste A. Wallander est maître de conférences à l'American University. Elle a été professeur associée à l'université Georgetown, directrice et Senior Fellow du programme Russie et Eurasie au Center for Strategic and International Studies, Senior Fellow au Council on Foreign Relations et maître de conférence à l'université Harvard. Elle a fondé le Programme sur les nouvelles approches sécuritaires face à la Russie. Elle est l'auteur de plus de 70 publications portant sur les relations États-Unis/Russie en termes de sécurité, la politique étrangère et de sécurité de la Russie, la géopolitique de l'énergie en Eurasie et les institutions internationales de sécurité. Elle est diplômée en sciences politiques (Ph.D., M.Phil. et M.A.) de l'université Yale et de l'université Northwestern (B.A. ; summa cum laude).